Integrating College Study Skills

Reasoning in Reading, Listening, and Writing

Textbooks of Related Interest

...also by Peter Elias Sotiriou

Composing Through Reading, Second Edition (1994).

Steps to Reading Proficiency, Fourth Edition, Anne Dye Phillips and Peter Elias Sotiriou (1996).

...also from Wadsworth

Read and Succeed, Caroline Banks, Mary-Jane McCarthy, Middlesex Community College, and Joan Rasool, Westfield State College (1993).

Reading and Learning Across the Disciplines, Second Edition, Mary-Jane McCarthy, Middlesex Community College, Joan Rasool, Westfield State College, and Caroline Banks (1996).

Critical Thinking: Reading and Writing in a Diverse World, Second Edition, Joan Rasool, Westfield State College, Caroline Banks, and Mary-Jane McCarthy, Middlesex Community College (1996).

The Power to Learn: Helping Yourself to College Success, William Campbell, University of Wisconsin, River Falls (1993).

The Adult Learner's Guide to College Success, Revised Edition, Laurence N. Smith, Eastern Michigan University, and Timothy L. Walter, The University of Michigan (1995).

Your College Experience: Strategies for Success, Second Edition, John N. Gardner and A. Jerome Jewler, both of the University of South Carolina (1996).

Your College Experience: Strategies for Success, Concise Second Edition, John N. Gardner and A. Jerome Jewler, both of the University of South Carolina (1996).

Right from the Start: Managing Your College Career, Second Edition, Robert Holkeboer, Eastern Michigan University (1996).

The Language of Learning, Second Edition, JoAnn Carter-Wells and Jane Hopper, both of California State University, Fullerton (1994).

Mastering Mathematics: How to Be a Great Math Student, Second Edition, Richard Manning Smith, Bryant College (1994).

Orientation to College Learning, Dianna L. Van Blerkom (1995).

Integrating

College Study Skills

Reasoning

in Reading, Listening, and Writing

Fourth Edition

Peter Elias Sotiriou

Los Angeles City College

Wadsworth Publishing Company

I(T)P™ *An International Thomson Publishing Company*

Belmont • Albany • Bonn • Boston • Cincinnati • Detroit • London • Madrid •
Melbourne • Mexico City • New York • Paris • San Francisco • Singapore • Tokyo •
Toronto • Washington

English Editor: Angela Gantner Wrahtz
Assistant Editor: Rebecca Deans Rowe
Editorial Assistant: Royden Tonomura
Production: Greg Hubit Bookworks
Print Buyer: Barbara Britton
Permissions Editor: Bob Kauser
Copy Editor: Susan Phillips Hoffman
Cover Designer: John Odam
Cover Photograph: Craig McClain
Compositor: Thompson Type
Printer: Malloy Lithographing, Inc.

Printed in the United States of America
1 2 3 4 5 6 7 8 9 10—01 00 99 98 97 96 95

For more information, contact Wadsworth Publishing Company:

Wadsworth Publishing Company
10 Davis Drive
Belmont, California 94002, USA

International Thomson Publishing Europe
Berkshire House 168-173
High Holborn
London, WC1V 7AA, England

Thomas Nelson Australia
102 Dodds Street
South Melbourne 3205
Victoria, Australia

Nelson Canada
1120 Birchmount Road
Scarborough, Ontario
Canada M1K 5G4

International Thomson Editores
Campos Eliseos 385, Piso 7
Col. Polanco
11560 México D.F. México

International Thomson Publishing GmbH
Königswinterer Strasse 418
53227 Bonn, Germany

International Thomson Publishing Asia
221 Henderson Road
#05-10 Henderson Building
Singapore 0315

International Thomson Publishing Japan
Hirakawacho Kyowa Building, 3F
2-2-1 Hirakawacho
Chiyoda-ku, Tokyo 102, Japan

Library of Congress Cataloging-in-Publication Data
Sotiriou, Peter Elias,
      Integrating college study skills : reasoning in reading,
    listening, and writing / Peter Elias Sotiriou. — 4th ed.
          p.   cm.
      Includes index.
      ISBN 0-534-25686-4
      1. Study skills.   I. Title.
LB2395.S597   1996
378.1'702812—dc20   95-23160

Contents in Brief

Contents

Chapter 6   *Identifying Organizational Patterns*   101

Chapter 7   *Summarizing and Paraphrasing*   135

Part Four   *Study Skills Systems and Test-Taking Practices*   269

Chapter 13   *The SQ3R Study System*   271

Chapter 14   *Memory Aids*   291

Chapter 15   *Suggestions for Taking Objective Tests*   301

Preface

In this fourth edition of *Integrating College Study Skills*, I have listened attentively to my reviewers' astute and thoughtful comments, and my revisions are responses to their suggestions. I have made many changes in Part One, especially in Chapter 2. Now titled "Your Learning Inventory," Chapter 2 offers new sections on motivation, learning styles, and stress management. The exercises in this chapter, in Chapter 1 on "Getting to Know Your College," and in Chapter 3 on "Using the Library" also include more collaborative assignments, which call for groups of four or five students to complete a particular study skills activity. In addition, the library chapter has been moved to Chapter 3 from its former position as Chapter 12; it now contains a section on completing the research paper and addresses in more detail the uses of the computer as a college research tool. All of these changes have been made to enhance the value of Part One to both the beginning and returning college student.

The reviewers unanimously requested exercises that are based on longer textbook selections; so at the end of the chapters in Part Two— Basic Reading, Listening, and Writing Skills—I have included textbook excerpts that are more than twice as long as those they replace. Reviewers also suggested an additional full-length textbook chapter, so you will find a complete chapter on biology at the end of Part Five as well as the full-length sociology chapter that appeared in the third edition. Moreover, in response to praise for the thematic focus of many of the chapters, I have addressed three new college topics: Business in Chapter 5, Anthropology in Chapter 7, and Early Childhood Development in Chapter 12. In this fourth edition, then, seven chapters now have a thematic focus— Chapters 4–8 and Chapters 11 and 12. I have also replaced or revised dated exercises and material.

I have reorganized Part Three so that Chapter 11 discusses the traditional and commonly used note-taking techniques, while Chapter 12 offers additional material on how to visually represent lecture and study notes.

Yet I have retained much that has made the first three editions of *Integrating College Study Skills* so successful. The book is still based on the sound pedagogical premise that reading, listening, and writing are interconnected activities, informing and transforming each other. The exercises are still consistently sequential, building upon previous exercises and chapter material. All the exercises continue to be on topics college students initially study, and the expanded thematic focus gives students the opportunity to investigate more topics in greater depth. Finally, as in the previous editions, students who complete the exercises in this fourth edition will be mirroring in various ways the kinds of activities they will complete in their college courses. *Integrating College Study Skills* continues to be one of the more challenging study skills textbooks on the college market today.

I hope that this fourth edition responds to the varied and changing demands of both teachers and students for a textbook that, in one semester, successfully prepares students for the academic challenges of college work. In its fourth edition and its eleventh year of publication, *Integrating College Study Skills* encourages both teacher and student to view careful reading, listening, and writing as worthwhile college goals.

Acknowledgments

Many thanks go to Lisa Timbrell and Rebecca Deans Rowe, assistant editors, who smoothly moved this textbook through its preproduction stages; to Greg Hubit, who efficiently carried this fourth edition through its various production deadlines; to Calvin Anderson, librarian emeritus at Los Angeles City College, who provided useful suggestions and a careful reading of Chapter 3; and, as always, to my patient wife Vasi and understanding sons Elia and Dimitri, who gave me the many solitary hours required to complete this fourth edition.

I am also thankful for the comments made by my reviewers: Edith Alderson, Joliet Junior College; Janice Beran, McLennan Community College; Jan Bradley, Southwest Missouri State University; Kathy Clark, Linn-Benton Community College; Catherine Cavalaio, Marygrove College; Virda K. Lester, Tuskegee University; Kelli Jayn Nichols, University of Washington; Sharon Robertson, University of Tennessee, Martin; and Diane Scott, Mesa College.

How To Use This Book

There are several compelling reasons for enrolling in a study skills course. You may want to upgrade your textbook reading skills, you may want to improve your note-taking skills to capture the key points your instructors make, or you may want to improve your test-taking skills. If you complete the exercises in this textbook, you will become a more successful college student—one who is able to read, take notes, and complete exams more efficiently.

How This Book Is Organized

Before you begin to do the exercises in this textbook, you need to know how it is put together. The first part is called "Skills for Beginning Your College Career." Here, you will learn about the basic survival skills that college students need to know: how to use your college's counseling services, your particular learning style, when and what to study, how much time to devote to your studies, how to cope with stress in college, and other equally important skills. This first part will point you in the right direction.

The next part of the textbook is the longest, dealing with the essential reading, listening, and writing skills you will need to succeed in college. In this part, "Basic Reading, Listening, and Writing Skills," you will learn several key reasoning skills. You will be shown how to locate the main idea, how to identify and use details, and how to summarize and paraphrase. You will also learn how to read and listen for inferences and how to read graphs, charts, and tables. Throughout this part, you will see how these skills apply to reading, listening, and writing. This is a unique feature of *Integrating College Study Skills*. As the title suggests, you will learn to integrate each study skill into the three activities of reading, listening, and writing. In this part you will also be introduced to material from college subjects. In Chapters 4–8 and in Chapters 11 and 12, the exercises for each chapter focus on one college subject.

In Part Three, "Taking Lecture and Study Notes," you will be drawing on the skills learned in the previous part to improve your note-taking skills. You will learn how to condense information and use abbreviations. You will also be introduced to the numeral–letter, laddering, and Cornell note-taking systems, which will help you organize and remember your lecture and study notes, and to ladder and mapping—visual note-taking devices that are especially helpful when you are studying for exams and you want to organize your materials efficiently.

In Part Four, "Study Skills Systems and Test-Taking Practices," you will be given guidelines for taking various kinds of tests—objective, essay, and math or science. Most important, in this part you will learn about the SQ3R study system, a successful method for learning and remembering what you read from textbooks.

Finally, in Part Five, "Applying SQ3R to Textbook Material," you will apply SQ3R and all the previous study practices you have learned to reading and understanding two textbook excerpts and two complete textbook chapters.

How to Use This Text

Integrating College Study Skills follows a similar format throughout. Each chapter is divided into two parts—an introduction to specific study skills and then exercises that allow you to apply those skills. Follow these steps as you work through each chapter:

1. Read the introductory section carefully. The information in this section will give you the necessary skills to complete the exercises.

2. Before you begin an exercise, read the directions carefully. Know what you have to do before you begin.

3. Record your answers in the box accompanying most exercises.

4. After you complete the exercise, check your answers. You will find the answers to most odd-numbered exercises at the end of the text. Your instructor will provide the answers to the even-numbered exercises. You will also need to consult your instructor for the correct answers to all exercises involving paragraph writing and to many short-answer questions. Finally, your instructor will provide all of the answers for the examinations that follow the study readings in Part Five.

5. Follow the directions for scoring each exercise. Compare your score with the percentage score printed in boldface type. This percentage is the acceptable score, one that shows reasonable mastery of the material. If you score below the acceptable percentage, check your errors to see what went wrong. You may want to ask your instructor for help.

6. For Chapters 4–8 and Chapters 11 and 12, complete the preview questions before you begin the exercises, and complete the follow-up questions after you have completed all of the exercises. These questions will help you evaluate what you learned about the various college subjects that you studied.

When You Finish the Text

When you have finished *Integrating College Study Skills*, you should be ready for the demands of college work. You will be able to read textbooks better, take accurate lecture and study notes, effectively use test-taking practices, and write organized paragraphs and essays explaining what you have learned. Most important, when you have completed this text, you will be able to apply the same reasoning skills to your college reading, listening, and writing and view your college studies as an integrated reasoning activity.

Skills for Beginning Your College Career

In this part of the book, you will become acquainted with the services that your college provides. You will complete schedules for your short- and long-term projects, you will analyze your own learning style, you will learn how to manage your study area, and you will become familiar with the services found in your college library. This information and these skills provide a necessary foundation for your college career.

1 Getting to Know Your College

- ◑ Catalog and class schedule   ◑ Counseling
  - ◑ Financial aid   ◑ Job placement

How to get to know your college

- ◑ Orientation   ◑ First class meeting   ◑ Students you will meet
  - ◑ Class materials   ◑ Class contacts

The first week at a new college is frequently the most hectic. You have to pay tuition and fees, buy books, enroll in classes, and organize a study and work schedule. Many students find colleges, particularly large ones, impersonal. Yet most colleges provide students with materials and services that can make their first semester or their return to college a bit less trying.

College Catalog and Schedule of Classes

Weeks before you enroll in your classes, you can become familiar with your school by obtaining a college catalog and schedule of classes. The catalog is usually published every year. It outlines college policies, gives a short history of the school, lists the services provided to students, names the departments and the courses they offer, and names the faculty of each department. Reading the catalog is a smart way to begin your college career. Look for services that the college provides: scholarships, financial aid, tutoring, and so on. Read through the course offerings in those departments in which you plan to take classes. You will find out how many courses are offered, what kinds of courses are offered, and when during the calendar year specific courses are taught.

After most course titles, the catalog lists the prerequisites and the unit value of each course. Prerequisites are the courses that you must have taken or the exams that you must have passed in order to enroll. Knowing whether you fulfill the prerequisites is important. An introductory chemistry course may give as one of its prerequisites: "appropriate score on placement test." If you do not take and pass this test before the first meeting, you may not be allowed to enroll. Some students enroll in these courses without being aware of the prerequisites and are turned away the first day of class.

The catalog also lists next to the course title its unit value. A unit is usually equal to one hour per week of lecture or discussion. Many courses are three units, so you attend class three hours a week. Some foreign language and science courses are five units and usually require daily attendance or the equivalent of five hours a week. In most cases, if you are enrolled in fifteen units, you will be attending class fifteen hours a week.

The schedule of classes lists each course that will be offered for that semester, the time it is offered, its unit value, and the instructor of the course. The schedule of classes is an important tool for you because it provides all the necessary information that you will need to set up your study list for the semester.

Counseling Services

Most colleges and universities offer some sort of counseling service to all their students. If you are new to the college, you need to make an appointment to see a counselor. At this meeting, discuss your educational and career goals with your counselor. If you have transcripts of course work completed in high school or at other colleges, bring them to this appointment. Ask your counselor what exactly is required to complete a degree or certificate in your chosen major and what your job opportunities are once you graduate.

Your counselor may advise you to take a battery of tests. The results of these tests will often show you which courses you are qualified to take in English, math, and science. Many colleges also have established career centers where you can go any time during the semester to get information about your intended career or any career you may be interested in.

During or after the meeting with your counselor, you may want to set your *long-term goals*—that is, the plans you have for the semester, the year, or your entire college career. Here are some of the questions that will help you in setting these goals:

1. Do I know what I want to study? Or do I want to give myself some time to explore various subjects? Do I know how long it will take to complete my studies?

2. Do I know how my college education is going to be paid for, at least for the year?

3. If I am married or have children, do I know how I am going to spend time with my spouse or children and still have time for my studies?

4. If I'm still living with my parents and have obligations at home, can I juggle these obligations and still have time for my studies?

Be sure your goals are both realistic and specific. For example, finishing a four-year degree in two years is not a realistic goal, and saying that you plan to spend some time with your children each week during the semester is not specific enough. These long-term goals could be more effectively stated as (1) I plan to complete my bachelor's degree in five years, starting this fall semester, and (2) I plan to complete all of my homework for the week by Saturday in order to spend each Sunday this semester with my two children.

Financial Aid

Well before you begin the semester, start planning your finances. This may be one of the long-term goals you considered with your counselor. Many students must drop out of college because they cannot pay all of their school bills. Almost all colleges and universities have a financial aid office. Go to this office before the semester begins to learn of the benefits available to you. If you have already been awarded a scholarship or grant, find out when you will be given the stipend and what grade-point average and unit load you need to maintain to keep your funding. Also find out from the financial aid people what the cost of your education will be each semester or quarter. Then determine whether you can afford your education without having to work.

Job Placement Office

Most colleges and universities also provide job placement services. Many students cannot afford to attend college without having to work. If you are a student without a job and need extra money for school, see what is available at the job placement office.

For most students who are serious about their college studies, being a student is a full-time job. Working full-time and going to school full-time is simply too much for most students. Either school, work, or your health will suffer if you try to do too much. Part-time work of less than twenty hours per week is a reasonable work load for a college student. If you need to work full time, you may want to delay your full-time education until you have adequate savings. Many full-time workers go to school part time, often taking one or two courses at night. Taking twelve units is considered a full load, and you are advised not to work full time if you are also carrying a full load.

Orientation Activities

Many colleges and universities set aside a day or several days before the semester begins for orientation. At this time, new students are given a tour of the campus and are introduced to the various social and cultural activities the college provides. Take part in orientation activities, particularly if the college you have chosen is large. At the very least, on your first day of class you will know your way around the campus. You may also find out about a club or group that interests you.

The First Class Meeting

The first class meeting for any course is an important one. The instructor officially enrolls you and usually gives you the course requirements: topics you will study, reading materials, exam dates, due dates for essays or projects, and the grading policy. Your instructor will also post office hours—hours when he or she will be able to meet with you outside of class. All of this information is usually presented in a syllabus, a calendar of course topics, and a statement of class requirements. Save your syllabus because you will be referring to it all semester.

Class Materials

You should take both pens and pencils to class. Take most of your notes in ink, but use pencil or erasable ink in math and science courses, where you will often be recalculating and erasing. You should have a separate notebook for each class, or at least a separate divider in a three-ring binder. Three-ring notebooks are particularly useful because you can add material for each course at any time during the semester, and you can keep your lectures in chronological order.

Buy your books during the first week of the semester or even before the semester begins. Be sure you know which books are required and which are recommended. Your syllabus will carry this information, and the bookstore will probably post "required" and "recommended" after each book title. After the first week of class, the bookstore may run out of some titles, and you may have to wait several weeks for additional copies to arrive.

If you can afford it, buy new books; but if you buy used books, try to find some that have few or no markings. If you buy a heavily underlined book, you will be reading someone else's comments, which may not agree with yours.

Take to class only those books that you will use during lecture or lab or that you will want to study from during the day. Instructors often read from the textbook or refer to specific pages while lecturing. You will want to read along with the instructor or mark those important pages during the lecture. To carry the books that you will need for the day, you will need a briefcase, an attache case, a large purse or satchel, or a backpack.

Making Class Contacts

During the first week of class, you should get to know at least one reliable classmate in each class. You should get this student's phone number and give yours to him or her. Whenever you cannot attend lectures, you can call this student to find out what you missed. You may also want to read over this student's notes whenever your notes are incomplete.

Most students enjoy studying with a classmate and find that they learn more studying with someone than if they studied alone. Often four to five students form a study group to prepare for a major exam. These groups are especially helpful if your instructor assigns several review questions before an exam. Students in the study group can divide up these questions, then meet to share their answers.

Try working in a study group to see if you learn more easily this way. If you don't find study groups helpful, you may be one of those students who learns best alone. More will be said about various learning styles in Chapter 2.

**The Students You
Will Meet**

You will find that colleges today attract a wide variety of people: young and old, rich and poor. These college students come from all ethnic, racial, and economic groups. Some learners, known as adult students, are over twenty-five; others are married; and some have children. Their needs and time constraints differ from those young, single students who have just finished high school. All come to college with unique desires and interests. As a college student in the 1990s, you need to recognize and appreciate this diversity in the college population and realize that your needs and life circumstances may differ from those of the students you meet, study with, and befriend.

Summary

Preparing for the first day of class takes work. By talking with a counselor, taking placement tests, and attending orientation meetings, you will get a clearer picture of your abilities and of the college you have chosen. The first day of class is also important because you will find out what your instructors expect you to do during the semester or quarter. Finally, getting to know a few fellow classmates early in the semester will help you, so if you cannot attend class, you can call them to find out what you missed.

Summary Box   *Getting Started in College*

What do you need to do?	Why are these activities important?
Read the catalog and schedule of classes	To learn something about your school
See a counselor	To plan your career goals
Establish long-term goals	To develop a better sense of what you can accomplish
Attend orientation meetings	To familiarize yourself with the campus
Obtain the phone number of at least one student in each class	To find out what happened in class when you were absent

Skills Practice

Exercise 1.1
Completing
Important Activities

The following is a list of activities that you need to complete before the semester begins or soon after. When you complete each activity, enter the date. Check the "Does Not Apply" space for those activities that do not concern you.

Does Not Apply	*Date Completed*	*Activity*
1. _____	_____	Buy and read through the college catalog.
2. _____	_____	Buy and read through the schedule of classes.
3. _____	_____	Make an appointment to see a counselor.
4. _____	_____	Take placement tests.
5. _____	_____	Go to the financial aid office.
6. _____	_____	Go to the job placement office.
7. _____	_____	Go to orientation activities.
8. _____	_____	Buy paper, pens, and pencils for classes.
9. _____	_____	Buy textbooks.
10. _____	_____	Get the phone numbers of classmates.
11. _____	_____	Additional activities: _____

Exercise 1.2
Setting Goals for the
Semester

Answer the following questions pertaining to your plans for the current semester. Your answers should help you set reasonable goals for this and later semesters. Write "does not apply" if the question does not pertain to you.

1. What, according to your placement tests, are your strengths and weaknesses?

2. What, according to your career tests, are your vocational interests?

3. What courses have you decided to take this semester as a result of talking to a counselor?

4. What is your intended major?

5. How many units are required for you to complete your major? How many semesters do you need to complete your major?

6. Do you plan to complete all of your course work at your present college, or do you intend to transfer? If you plan to transfer, what school do you intend to transfer to and what are its transfer requirements?

7. Did you find, after meeting with people in the financial aid office, that you are eligible for aid, or do you need to work? If you need to work, how many hours a week do you plan to work?

Exercise 1.3
Setting Goals for an
Incoming College
Student

The following is a description of an incoming community college student—Maria. Read over this description and determine the four most important goals she should consider for her first semester of college. Be sure the goals that you set for Maria are realistic and specific. This activity is best completed in groups of four or five students.

Maria is twenty-five years old. She has been a waitress in Hollywood, California, since finishing high school at eighteen. She wants to change careers and has interests in accounting and business management. She thinks that maybe she can become an accountant for a large restaurant one day or perhaps manage a restaurant herself. Maria has $10,000 in savings, but she does not know how much money it will take to finish her first year of college. She still lives at home with her mother and pays her $200 a month for room and board. She does not know how many courses she should take her first semester or what courses to take. She also does not know whether she should quit her job as a waitress or simply cut down her hours. Maria is single and has been going out on the weekends with the same man for over a year.

The four long-term goals Maria should set:

1. _____

2. _____

3. _____

4. _____

Answers will vary. Share your answers with your instructor and your classmates.

2 Your Learning Inventory: Your Learning Style, Study Time, and Study Area

How to manage your time

- Nonschool activities
- Weekends
- School activities
- Study goals
- Personal time
- Course priority list
- Long-term projects

Studying and organizing your study area

- When to study
- Scheduling longer projects
- How to study
- Analyzing test results
- Where to study
- Tackling difficult assignments
- Studying for tests

Understanding how you learn best

- Getting motivated
- Assessing your learning style
- Coping with stress

Being a successful student is not unlike being a successful executive. And just as an executive needs a calendar to keep track of business and social appointments, you need to keep track of every hour that you spend in and out of school each day so that you can cut down on the number of wasted hours. Students also need to analyze the kinds of learners they are in order to best devise their study program. In addition, students need to examine where they study to see if these study areas are most conducive to concentration.

Both incoming and returning students will find they have many more hours outside of class than they had in high school, where they often had five to six hours of classes to attend each day. Some days a college student may have only two hours of class, and the rest of the day will be free. For this reason, it is especially important for both incoming and returning students to set up schedules that they can and will follow, that will make the best use of their time, and that will minimize stress.

Getting Motivated

Before you analyze your use of time, your learning style, or your places of study, you need to be *motivated*—to have the desire to do your best.

Time	Activity
6–7 am	Shower, get ready for school, eat breakfast
7–7:30 am	Drive to Campus
12–12:45 pm	Eat lunch on Campus
10–11 pm	Exercise and get ready for bed.

Figure 2-1   *Daily activity card.*

Motivation is central, both as you analyze yourself as a learner and in every activity you complete in college. Staying motivated is not a simple challenge, because very few students get up every morning with a desire to complete all the work that is before them. They often complain of being tired, of assignments being too difficult, or of not having enough time to complete assignments.

One effective way to stay motivated is to set goals. You learned about long-term goals in Chapter 1, when you were analyzing your reasons for attending college. Short-term goals will help you stay motivated. *Short-term goals* are those plans you have for the day, week, or month. They include your plans for studying for a test, completing a homework assignment, or fulfilling the requirements of a longer writing or research project.

To be effective, short-term goals must be specific and reasonable. It would be unreasonable to assume that you could study for your business final in one hour and too vague if you simply said that you planned to study for your business final sometime during the week. A reasonable, short-term goal for studying for your business final would be: "I plan to study for my business final for three hours on Friday and three hours on Saturday; then I plan to review for one hour on Sunday."

Much of the time management material you will read in the following sections and subsections involves writing short-term goals—specific and concise plans. Those goals will help you stay motivated to stay on schedule.

Setting Up a Schedule

Your first job in establishing a study schedule is to determine which hours during the day you cannot study. Be detailed. Include the time that it takes for you to get ready for class in the morning and get ready for bed at night, to eat your meals, and to take care of family and personal matters. List all of these activities and the time allotted to each on a 4 × 6 card, as shown in Figure 2-1.

If you do not already follow a routine of getting up at a certain time, eating at set hours, and exercising regularly, start now. You will not be productive if you do not eat, sleep, and exercise well. Students who don't eat breakfast often become exhausted by midday. Similarly, students who do not exercise feel lethargic as the day wears on. Recent studies have shown that exercise gives your body more energy and fights depression. A half-hour to an hour of jogging, swimming, or brisk walking each day is time well spent. Finally, sleeping at least seven hours a night is important. Staying up late catches up with you. Even though it is tempting to stay up late, particularly if you live on campus, try not to; otherwise you will find yourself dozing off in class or sleeping through your morning classes.

School Activities.   Now that you have established regular times to eat, sleep, and exercise, you are ready to identify those hours you can devote to school. First, enter your hours of nonschool activities on a sheet of paper, listing the days of the week and the hours in each day. Also on this list include those hours that you must work, if part-time work is part of your daily schedule. Your schedule should look something like the one in Figure 2-2. In this schedule, the nonschool activities have been listed in the appropriate hours; for the moment, Saturday and Sunday have been left open. By counting the number of blank spaces in each day, you will find that you can devote ten hours (nine full hours and two half-hours) to school.

You now need to include in this schedule the hours that you spend in class. In Figure 2-3, see how this student has included fifteen hours of class time between Monday and Friday.

You will notice on this schedule that the student has spaced the classes. If you do not have to work, spacing your classes is wise. If you are on campus more hours during the day, you will have more time to study. You will also have time to review your lecture notes right after class. If you check the schedule for Monday, you find that this student has the following hours to study: 9–10 a.m., 11 a.m.–12 p.m., 2–6 p.m., 9–9:30 p.m., and 10:30–11 p.m.—a total of seven hours.

Many instructors will tell you that for every hour of lecture you should spend two hours outside of class studying for that course. This may be true, but a more realistic estimate will have to be made by you. For each course, assess your background knowledge; if your background is limited in a particular course, you may have to devote more time to that course than to your other courses. If you are carrying fifteen units, you may need to study fifteen, thirty, or even more hours during the week to be prepared.

It is best to write out a study schedule for each day or for each week. Figure 2-4 shows how this same student has completed a schedule for Monday, including three hours of study on campus. In Exercise 2.1 and Exercise 2.2, you will determine your own study hours for the day and the week.

Daily Assignments.   Each day you will have different school tasks to do. The night before, jot down the work you need to complete for the next

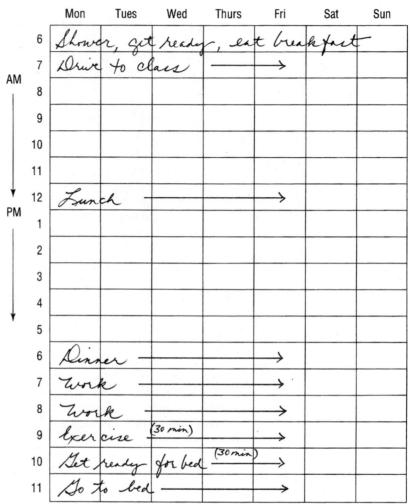

		Mon	Tues	Wed	Thurs	Fri	Sat	Sun
AM	6	Shower, get ready, eat breakfast						
	7	Drive to class	————————→					
	8							
	9							
	10							
	11							
PM	12	Lunch	——————————→					
	1							
	2							
	3							
	4							
	5							
	6	Dinner	——————→					
	7	Work	——————→					
	8	Work	——————→					
	9	Exercise	(30 min) ——→					
	10	Get ready for bed	(30 min) ——→					
	11	Go to bed	——————→					

Figure 2-2   *Weekly schedule with nonschool activities.*

day. Figure 2-5 is a sample list of short-term goals; note that the activities are specific and that each one can probably be completed in an hour.

When you look at a class syllabus at the beginning of the semester, you may feel overwhelmed, thinking that you can never get through all of the assignments. But breaking up large assignments into smaller tasks of no more than an hour each is an effective way of getting things done and of staying motivated. Psychologists call the breaking up of larger activities into smaller tasks *successive approximations.*

Long-Term Projects.   During the semester, you will probably be assigned large projects—term papers, critical papers, lab reports, and so on. You will also have to prepare for midterms and finals—exams that require

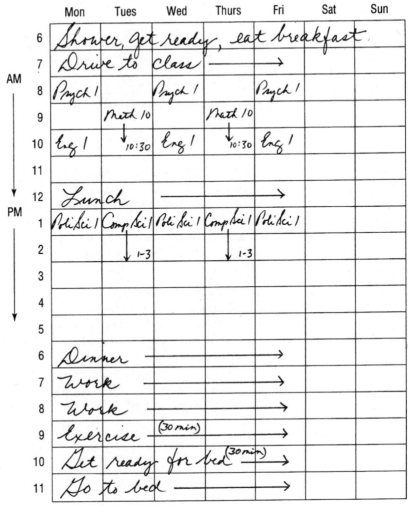

	Mon	Tues	Wed	Thurs	Fri	Sat	Sun
6	Shower, get ready, eat breakfast						
7	Drive to class ——————→						
8	Psych 1		Psych 1		Psych 1		
9		Math 10		Math 10			
10	Eng 1	↓10:30	Eng 1	↓10:30	Eng 1		
11							
12	Lunch ——————————→						
1	Poli Sci 1	Comp Sci 1	Poli Sci 1	Comp Sci 1	Poli Sci 1		
2		↓1-3		↓1-3			
3							
4							
5							
6	Dinner ——————————→						
7	Work ——————————→						
8	Work ——————————→						
9	Exercise —— (30 min) ——→						
10	Get ready for bed (30 min) →						
11	Go to bed ——————————→						

AM ↓   PM ↓

Figure 2-3   *Weekly schedule with school activities.*

Mon	
8	Psych 1
9	Study
10	Eng 1
11	Study
12	Lunch
1	Poli Sci 1
2	Study

Figure 2-4   *Daily schedule showing study hours.*

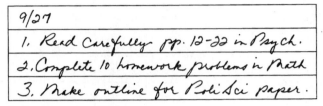

Figure 2-5   *Daily assignment schedule.*

more than just a night or two of study. It is best to place the due dates of these larger tasks on a monthly calendar. You may want to buy a large calendar that you can place on your desk or on the wall near where you normally study. On this calendar, enter the dates of the major projects and tests for that month. Look at how the month of May is marked in Figure 2-6; on May 1, for example, this student has only eight days to finish a research paper but all month to study for a computer final.

Weekends.   If you keep up during the week, your weekends should not end up as study marathons. On weekends, you should relax as well as study; you should complete any late work, get a jump on assignments for the following week, and work on the larger projects. It is best to set aside three or four hours on a Saturday or Sunday to work on an essay assignment. Writing requires concentrated, uninterrupted time.

   If you have to work, weekends are best. With no classes to attend on the weekend, you will be able to work and not feel rushed.

Sun	Mon	Tues	Wed	Thurs	Fri	Sat
MAY						1
2	3	4	5	6	7	8
9	10 Eng 1 paper due	11	12	13	14	15
16	17	18 Critical Poli Sci paper due	19	20	21	22
23 / 30	24 math final / 31	25	26	27	28 Computer final	29

Figure 2-6   *Deadlines marked on the calendar.*

Time for Yourself.   The average student has ample time to study each day. You can therefore set aside some part of each day for fun. Psychologists have shown that students who vary their activities during the day actually retain more than those who study nonstop. So do not feel that you are wasting your time when you are not doing school work. Give yourself some time each day to relax. On weekends, take advantage of the movies, plays, and concerts available to you on or off campus. If you come back to your studies refreshed, you will have a more positive attitude toward the new material.

What has been said so far about scheduling your time, making lists and noting deadlines on a calendar may seem tedious to you, and some of it is. But being organized is one of the most important characteristics of a successful student. If you stick to your schedules and continue to meet your deadlines, you will begin to enjoy the pleasures of being a successful student. Once being organized becomes a habit for you, you may want to dispense with written lists and goals entirely.

You are now ready to consider specific suggestions about your learning style, managing your time, and setting up your study area. With these suggestions, you will be able to make even better use of each study hour.

Your Particular Learning Style

Before you examine how to effectively complete your work in college and where you learn best, you need to look at the kind of learner you are. Then you can modify the following suggestions on study area and test-taking tips to fit your particular learning needs.

You can generally divide up the world of learners into three categories: (1) those who are verbal, that is, very good with language, (2) those who are quantitative, or very skilled with numbers, and (3) those who are spatial, or talented at visualizing. The English professor, the mathematician, and the artist are the most common examples of these three types of learners. A famous Harvard psychologist, Howard Gardner, has identified as many as seven distinct types of intelligence. Along with the three types mentioned above, he includes musical ability, bodily-kinesthetic aptitude, interpersonal intelligence (knowledge of others), and intrapersonal intelligence (knowledge of oneself). For now, consider your abilities in the first three aptitudes mentioned—verbal, quantitative, and visual. You probably have some sense of your strengths in each of these three areas. If not, your counselor can give you more insight into your abilities by analyzing your test scores and previous grades, or by giving you a new battery of aptitude tests.

Each of these three aptitudes helps describe a specific kind of learner in college. A verbal learner generally learns best by taking written notes in lecture, by reading, and by responding to his reading in written responses. A student with a mathematical aptitude generally finds numerical facts and figures easy to remember; she also tends to want to organize material into formulas. Finally, a visual thinker remembers material best if it is in picture form and tends to write notes in diagram fashion.

Obviously, very few learners will rely on only one of these three aptitudes. All learners have varying abilities in each of these three types of thinking. Among the various courses you take in college, you will be asked to demonstrate your abilities in each of these three types of thinking.

These three kinds of learners also rely on different ways of remembering information. Some learners best remember facts—dates, numbers, specific details—as they learn a subject; others are much more adept at remembering the concepts in a subject—the larger or global picture: not when the war began but the three major reasons for the war.

Other learners remember what they hear—they are known as *auditory learners*. They retain material merely by listening to a lecture or by reviewing a tape recording of a lecture. Further, they find that by reading material aloud, they remember much more than if they read the same material silently.

Still others retain material best when they are working with others in study groups. They learn by hearing and responding to what others have to say. This type of remembering is known as *collaborative learning*, and it has become a very popular form of instruction, particularly in humanities courses.

Finally, there are students who learn best not by reading, listening, or working with others, but by doing. They are known as *practical learners*, who learn much like apprentices on the job learn. These learners often do well in subjects that require labs or that include on-the-job training.

As you continue to study and learn in college, it is wise to try out all of these learning styles to see which ones work best for you. Remember that you have some sort of aptitude in each, and one of your goals in college is to see just how you can use each aptitude to succeed in your course work.

Setting Up a Course Priority List

Now that you have been introduced to how students learn, and probably have a better idea of the kind of learner you are, you can more effectively consider the courses you will be taking and the specifics of studying.

At the beginning of each semester, you should look at all your courses and select the one or two that you think are most important. These courses may be the ones in your major or prerequisites to your major. You should list your courses in order of importance and then anticipate the grade you will earn in each. Then you can better predict the time you should devote to each course.

Study the following course priority list, designed by a student majoring in computer science:

Course	*Predicted Grade*
1. Computer Science	A
2. Mathematics 10	A
3. English 1	B

4. Political Science 1   B
5. Psychology 1   C

It is clear that this student will be exerting more effort in the computer science and math courses. Because this student realizes the need to do very well in the computer science and math courses, the anticipated grade of "C" in psychology is realistic. This student is not being pressured to do exceptionally well in all courses.

If you set up such a priority list, you should be able to establish some realistic goals early in the semester. If, during the semester, you are not doing as well as you had predicted, you need to determine what is going wrong. Do you need to study more? Do other activities conflict with your studies? Or have you chosen a major that is not well suited for you?

In Exercise 2.6, you will be able to determine your own priority list.

Making the Best Use of Your Study Time

When should you study for each course? You should study for your priority courses when your mind is freshest. Each student's most productive hours vary. Some find the mornings best, others the evenings or late nights. Find out when you work best, and study for your most important courses then.

How to Study.   In this text, you will be introduced to several study hints and learn a successful study reading system called SQ3R, but first consider the following general study hints:

1. Never study with distractions. Music, though soothing, often is distracting. When you are doing concentrated studying, avoid listening to music.

2. Do not begin studying if you are more concerned about something else. Your study hours need to be concentrated ones. A brisk walk, run, or swim before you study can often clear your mind of daily problems.

3. Try to divide your studying into one-hour blocks. You can take a ten-minute break either at the end or the middle of each hour. Gauge your breaks according to the difficulty of the material. The key to a successful study hour, though, is to put in fifty concentrated minutes of study.

4. After your hour is up, do something different. Either study for a course unrelated to what you have just studied, or do something not directly connected to school. Studying during spaced intervals is more productive than cramming your studying into a few days.

5. Devote some time during your study hours to reviewing what you have learned that day. You need to review your lecture notes or the study notes you have taken from your textbooks. You tend to forget more of what you have learned during the first twenty-four hours, so it is

important to review soon after you have learned something new. More will be said about how to remember in Chapter 14 on Memory Aids.

6. Be sure to complete your reading assignments when they are assigned. Listening to a lecture on completely new material can confuse and frustrate you. So make your reading assignments a study priority item.

How to Tackle Difficult Assignments.   Sometimes your study material is difficult, and studying for a concentrated hour may be exhausting. If this happens, break your studying into shorter activities, or short-term goals. Write these goals out before you begin studying. For example, if you have five difficult math problems to do, you can write out something like the following:

1. Complete problem #1.
2. Read and think about problem #2.
3. Take a four-minute break.
4. Come back to problem #2.

You will find that such goals are attainable if you make them short and realistic. Instead of focusing on five difficult problems, you reward yourself for completing one problem at a time.

How to Study for Tests.   Much will be said in this textbook on how to study for tests, including objective tests (Chapter 15) as well as essay and math or science tests (Chapter 16). For now, read the following time-management hints that apply to preparing for any test.

1. Before you begin studying for a test, you should have completed all of your reading assignments. In addition, you should have reviewed your notes each day.

2. For a weekly quiz, take two days to study—one day to do your reviewing and a second to let the material settle. If the course is difficult, you may need more days to learn the material.

3. For a midterm test, study for three or four days. On the last night, do not cram; review only the general concepts.

4. For a final examination, reserve about a week to study. As with the midterm, review only the general points the night before.

Analyzing Your Test Results.   You can also learn much about your progress as a student by studying your test results, particularly your first test scores of the semester. Study your errors and try to determine why you made them. You may find that you need to study more or study in a quieter area.

By reviewing your results, you can also determine the kinds of tests your instructor gives and which study materials he emphasizes: lecture notes, textbook material, class discussion, and so on. Does the test emphasize details or concepts? Are any of the questions tricky? If the test is essay, what does the instructor seem to be looking for? an organized essay? accurate details? new ideas? the instructor's ideas? By answering these questions, you will probably do better on the next exam.

If you receive a low or failing score, try to figure out what went wrong. Did you not study enough, or do you need to change your studying style for this course? Or is this course too difficult for you? Do you need tutoring, or should you drop the class? Make an appointment to see your instructor. See what he or she has to say. Take these suggestions seriously.

Remember that a test score is more than a grade. By analyzing it, you will become a more successful student.

Making a Schedule for Your Longer Projects.   Do not wait until the last few days of the semester to complete a project like a term paper. You need to divide these larger assignments into smaller tasks—again, short-term goals—and assign deadlines for completing them.

If, for example, you are assigned a 500-page novel to read in ten days, you need to divide the number of pages by the days you have to complete the reading. In this example, you need to read fifty pages a day.

For a research paper, you can divide your work into several smaller tasks: (1) finding library material, (2) taking notes on this material, (3) writing an outline for the paper, (4) writing a rough draft, and (5) writing a final draft. Look at this sample schedule for completing a research paper on the Hopi Native Americans:

Hopi Culture (30-Day Project)

Task	Number of Days
1. Go to the library; make up a bibliography	5
2. Take notes from the book	8
3. Write an outline	2
4. Write a rough draft	7
5. Type a final draft	4
	Total = 26

You may have noticed in the above schedule that, although it is a thirty-day project, the student has estimated twenty-six days for completing the project. The extra four days give him some breathing room in case one task takes longer to complete. Often these projects take longer to finish than you had originally planned. Generally it takes three to four weeks to complete a research paper. Once you complete your first research paper, you will be able to make a more accurate estimate of the time required to complete the next one.

More will be said about the research paper in the next chapter on Using the Library.

How to Cope with Stress at School

The demands of college work—the tests, the projects, listening attentively in class—all take their toll. Very few students do not complain of stress at some time during the semester. Stress is simply the result of not being able to cope with life's demands, and it often manifests itself in physical symptoms: inability to concentrate, nausea, a fast heartbeat, sweating. These symptoms can occur when you are taking an exam or as you are working on a homework assignment. The symptoms of stress often manifest themselves suddenly and may take you by surprise.

There is no hidden cure for combatting stress. As with our learning styles, each one of us has different coping mechanisms; some of us are naturally more prone to stress than others. But there are some ways to help reduce school stress that apply to us all:

1. Try to control your anxiety. When you feel these symptoms coming on, tell yourself that they will only hinder you, wasting your time in studying or finishing a test.

2. During a difficult exam or a stressful study period, take a break for a minute or two. Think of being in a pleasant, relaxed setting; close your eyes and take deep breaths. With your eyes closed, stretch your back, arms, and neck to relax your muscles. These short breaks can avert a stress attack.

3. During an exam or a study period, reward yourself for completing a problem or section of the assignment. The reward can simply be a mental "pat on the back." Confidence both improves performance and reduces stress.

4. Do what is confidence-building first—the easy test questions, the less difficult part of a homework assignment. With more confidence, you can more easily complete the harder sections of the test or assignment.

5. Set reasonable, short-term, goals. Break up difficult assignments into manageable parts—the first three of ten problems on a math exam, a draft of the first paragraph of an extended essay assignment.

For some students, these suggestions do not help overcome stress. Perhaps there are other personal factors causing stress, such as family problems or crises in relationships. If you cannot overcome the stress you experience in school, seek professional help. Your college may have stress counselors or psychologists on their staff, or they may be able to refer you to low-cost professionals if you cannot afford your own private professional. Stress is a psychological problem that can be helped, and only becomes worse if it is not quickly attended to. Psychologists have done extensive research in this field in the last twenty years, and they have devised therapies that frequently offer quick results, such as stress-reducing exercises or biofeedback training involving the monitoring of your brain wave activity.

Setting Up Your Study Area

You may follow all of the previous suggestions and still do poorly in college if you do not have an acceptable study area. Ideally, you should have your own desk in a quiet organized area. On your desk, you need a dictionary, and all the necessary texts and notes that you need to use for a given hour need to be at arm's reach. Your desk should also have scratch paper, lined paper, and typing or computer paper, as well as several pens and pencils. If possible, you should have a typewriter or word processor on your desk. Finally, your chair should not be too comfortable because you want to stay alert while you study. A chair with an upright support for your back is effective. With these materials, you will be able to stay in one place during your study hour.

If these ideal conditions are not possible, you should still be able to create an organized study area. You may be living at home with younger brothers and sisters or with young children of your own often disturbing you. You may be living in a small apartment with several roommates. So your own desk in a quiet area may be an impossibility. But you still can find a large box for all your books and notes for the semester. Keeping all of your material in one area is a must. Students waste precious time looking for books or notes.

If you cannot study without interruption where you live, you need to find a quiet study area, at either a local library or your college library. If you go to the library with friends, sit away from them when you study so that you will not be distracted. If you plan to study in groups, find a quiet area that will encourage your group to get to work and stay focused.

Summary

Setting up schedules is a key to success in and out of school. To organize your time, you must first list those activities not related to school. Once you have listed nonschool activities, you then include those hours when you attend school. Try to space your classes throughout the day. On this same schedule, you can then mark those hours that you reserve for studying. You must plan your hours of study the night before and stick to your plan. Finally, you need to place long-term projects on a monthly calendar so that you know how much time you have to complete them.

Also, knowing the kind of learner you are and the sorts of aptitudes you have will greatly assist you in finding the most effective ways to study in college. Once you have assessed your learning styles, you can begin to devise successful study practices. Set up class priorities to determine which courses you need to concentrate on; then project a grade that you intend to receive in each of these courses. During your study hours, you should concentrate only on your school assignments. When you are working on large projects, you should break them up into smaller tasks, then set up a deadline for completing each one. You need to use stress-reducing activities whenever college work becomes too demanding. Finally, you need to create a quiet study area for yourself, one that has all the necessary materials you need for your study hours.

Summary Box   *Your Learning Inventory*

What is time and study area management?	*Why should you manage your time and your study area?*
A way of analyzing how you spend your day so that you can set aside certain quiet hours to study Devices to help you manage your time and study area: 1. Nonschool schedules 2. On-campus schedules 3. Daily activity schedules 4. Time schedules for longer projects 5. Course priority lists 6. Stress-reducing exercises 7. Analysis of test results 8. Designing of a study area	To develop order in your life as a student To provide time to complete reading assignments, study for tests, and complete term projects To assess your progress in school To get the most out of college

What are learning styles?	*Why should you be aware of your learning styles?*
1. Verbal, quantitative, and visual 2. Factual and conceptual 3. Auditory, social, and practical	To apply these various styles to understand how you learn best

Skills Practice

Exercise 2.1
Setting Up a
Schedule of
Nonschool Activities

Answer the following questions. Then transfer the answers to these questions to the weekly schedule shown in Figure 2-7.

1. When do you get up each morning for school?

2. When do you eat breakfast, lunch, and dinner during the week (excluding Saturday and Sunday)?

3. When do you exercise?

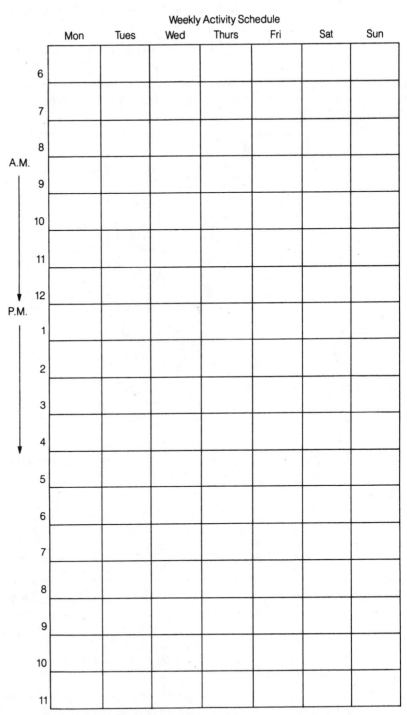

Figure 2-7 *Weekly activity schedule.*

4. When do you go to bed during the week (excluding Saturday and Sunday)?

5. If you work, what are your hours?

Exercise 2.2
Setting Up a
Schedule of School
Activities

Answer the following questions on your school activities. Then transfer the answers to these questions to Figure 2-7.

1. How many units are you carrying this semester?

2. List your classes and the times they meet.

Class Name	*Time Class Meets*

  a.

  b.

  c.

  d.

  e.

  f.

  g.

3. When do you study? In Figure 2-7, shade the boxes of those hours you regularly use for study.

4. How many hours have you reserved for study? Do these hours equal or exceed the number of units that you are carrying? Have you reserved enough hours each week for study?

Exercise 2.3
Making a Calendar
for Long-Term
Projects

In Figure 2-8, you will find a calendar for a typical month. Fill in the current month and the appropriate dates. Then enter the due dates for longer projects and major exams for this month.

  Use this calendar to remind yourself of important due dates. At the end of the month, ask yourself whether this calendar was a useful reminder for you. If you found it helpful, continue using it.

Exercise 2.4
Setting Up Weekly
Schedules

Use the activity reminders shown in Figure 2-9 for the next two weeks. Include no more than two important activities for each day. As with the monthly calendar, include due dates of projects and exam dates. At the end of each week, see how or if the weekly calendar was useful to you.

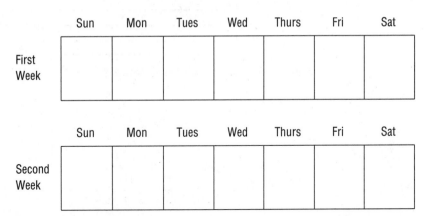

	Sun	Mon	Tues	Wed	Thurs	Fri	Sat
Month:							

Figure 2-8   *Typical month's calendar.*

	Sun	Mon	Tues	Wed	Thurs	Fri	Sat
First Week							

	Sun	Mon	Tues	Wed	Thurs	Fri	Sat
Second Week							

Figure 2-9   *Typical weekly calendar.*

Exercise 2.5
Setting Up Daily
Schedules

Use the activity reminders depicted in Figure 2-10 for the next three days. Remember to write out each task so that you can complete each one in an hour. At the day's end, see if you have completed each task. If you didn't, try to figure out why.

Exercise 2.6
Setting Up Course
Priorities

In this exercise, set up a priority list of your courses. List the courses in their order of importance. Then predict the grade that you will receive in each.

```
┌─────────────────────────────────────────────┐
│  1. First Day    Date: _____ │
│  To Do:                                       │
│  1. _____│
│  2. _____│
│  3. _____│
│  4. _____│
└─────────────────────────────────────────────┘


┌─────────────────────────────────────────────┐
│  2. Second Day   Date: _____ │
│  To Do:                                       │
│  1. _____│
│  2. _____│
│  3. _____│
│  4. _____│
└─────────────────────────────────────────────┘


┌─────────────────────────────────────────────┐
│  3. Third Day    Date: _____ │
│  To Do:                                       │
│  1. _____│
│  2. _____│
│  3. _____│
│  4. _____│
└─────────────────────────────────────────────┘
```

Figure 2-10   *Activity reminders for three days.*

	Course	*Predicted Grade*
1.		
2.		
3.		
4.		
5.		
6.		
7.		

Save this exercise; then, at the end of the semester, compare your predicted grades with your actual grades. If there were differences, try to figure out why.

*Exercise 2.7
Assessing Your Time
Management and
Your Study Area*

Below you will find eleven questions about your ability to manage time and your study area. Read each question carefully; then answer it by circling yes or no. After you have answered all eleven questions, you will be asked to use these results to determine where you need to improve your time management and your study area.

1. Yes   No   Does your mind wander when you study?
2. Yes   No   Do you often take study breaks that are too long?
3. Yes   No   Do you often study for the same kinds of courses back to back?
4. Yes   No   Do you frequently fail to review your reading and study notes?
5. Yes   No   Do you often go to a lecture without having completed the reading assignment for it?
6. Yes   No   Do you become frustrated when you read difficult material?
7. Yes   No   Do you wait until the last day to study for your exams?
8. Yes   No   Do you wait until the last days to complete longer projects?
9. Yes   No   Do you look only at your test score when you get an exam back?
10. Yes   No   Do you sometimes feel overwhelmed by the stress school causes?
11. Yes   No   Is your study area disorganized?

If you answered yes to any of these questions, you need to reread the section in this chapter that applies to the skill in question. Now make a list of those skills that you intend to improve during this semester.

Skills Needing Improvement

1. _____

2. _____

3. _____

4. _____

5. _____

6. _____

7. _____

8. _____

9. _____

     This semester, make it your goal to sharpen those skills that you have listed.

Exercise 2.8
Assessing Your
Learning Style

This activity will help you understand the kind of learner you are. It is best completed with your peers in groups of two or three. Answer the following questions as honestly and completely as you can. If you have any questions, discuss them with your peers and share your responses with the group. Once you have answered the questions and shared them in discussion, complete your learning profile. As you work in your groups, ask your instructor for help when you do not understand any part of this activity.

  1. If I were assigned the following tasks—(1) read a book, (2) do math problems, and (3) draw a picture—which one would I rather do?

     _____

     Why? _____

  2. Do I take written notes easily when I listen to a lecture? _____

  3. Can I complete my reading assignments easily? _____

  4. Do I have a difficult time writing essays or essay exams? Or do I prefer essay tests to other kinds of tests? _____

  5. Has math been an easy subject for me in the past? Am I good at making change, doing my checkbook and taxes, and remembering sports statistics? _____

  6. When I study my notes, is it easy for me to create a diagram of the material? _____

  7. After I have studied, do I tend to remember the specific facts, or the general outlines? _____

  8. Do I remember very much when I listen to a discussion or lecture? Or do I have to write things down in order to remember them? ____

  9. Do I prefer reading silently or orally when I am study reading? ____

10. Do I enjoy using a tape recorder to study? _____

11. Do I learn a lot by watching videos and films and studying photographs when I am taking a history course? _____

12. Do I learn very much in study groups? Or do I study best alone?

_____

13. Am I good at science lab work? _____

14. Do I enjoy hands-on courses like shop? auto mechanics? computer processing? _____

After answering these questions and discussing them in my group, we have decided that I have strengths in:

1. _____ verbal thinking

2. _____ quantitative thinking

3. _____ visual thinking

4. _____ remembering facts

5. _____ remembering concepts

6. _____ remembering by listening

7. _____ remembering by discussing study material with others

8. _____ learning by doing

Some techniques that we have come up with so that I can study more effectively include:

1. _____

2. _____

3. _____

Exercise 2.9
Analyzing a Student
Learning and Study
Profile

Darrell is a thirty-seven-year-old returning student who wants to major in computer technology. He has been a gardener for the past fifteen years, and now wants an entirely new career. This is an excerpt of what Darrell shared with his career counselor.

Read this excerpt over with a group of four or five students. Then determine the kind of learner Darrell is and offer some suggestions to improve his success in college.

I've always liked working with my hands. The out-of-doors appealed to me. But now I want a new challenge. I was good in math in high school and went up to geometry. I tried advanced algebra in college, but I dropped out that semester, when I was twenty. I'm not very good at writing. I have problems with my grammar and saying exactly what I mean. Taking notes has always been hard; teachers always seem to talk too fast for me. I'd much rather copy down math or science problems from the board. I like reading sports magazines and the sports section of the newspaper.

I'm single again, having been divorced for two years now, but I'm living with two roommates, and it's often noisy in my apartment. I'll only have to work part-time, so I'll have two or three extra hours a day to study.

1. Profile of Darrell as a learner: _____

   _____

Answers will vary. Ask instructor for suggested answers.

2. Suggestions for organizing Darrell's study time and area: _____

   _____

3 Using the Library

Using the library

What's in the library?

◑ Computers	◑ Stacks	◑ Reference area	◑ Periodical area
○ On-line	○ Books	○ Dictionaries	○ Newspapers
○ CD-ROM		○ Encyclopedias	○ Journals
			○ Magazines

How are library materials organized?

◑ Dewey decimal system   ◑ Library of Congress system

In Chapter 2, you learned about the various ways you can study effectively and complete longer projects. An important source of information for your studying and the major resource for your longer projects is the library. In this chapter, you will learn about how libraries are organized, how you can use them to obtain more information for your courses and projects, and the basic steps you need to follow to complete a research project. Undoubtedly, your college has one or more libraries, and they are all organized in a similar fashion.

The Main Sections of a Library

Libraries are depositories of information and ideas that will help further your education and enhance your life. Librarians run libraries; their major duties are to select and organize new library materials and to assist you in finding the sources you need in your particular research area.

Libraries are typically divided into three sections. The *reference* section provides you with dictionaries, encyclopedias, and other volumes of brief, specific information that allow you to pursue your research on a particular subject. The *stacks* are where you find those books that you can check out. This is invariably the largest section of the library. And this is where you will spend much of your time in finding particular books on a topic you are studying. Finally, the third section of a library is the *periodical* area, where magazines, newspapers, and journals are found. Here you can locate specific articles on the topic you are interested in studying.

Types of Materials You Will Find in the Library

Libraries contain four types of reading material: books to borrow, periodicals, reference books, and pamphlets. Each type of reading material will advance your knowledge of a topic in particular ways.

Books to borrow are by far the most abundant type of material you will find in the library. These books are arranged on the shelves by subject matter; college libraries generally have more scholarly texts—that is, books that examine a particular topic with more detail and analysis. If you are researching material on the political leader Cesar Chavez, for example, in the stacks you will probably come across books on Chavez's political beliefs, his contributions to the status of the migrant farmer, his biography, and so on. A good college library has both earlier material on Cesar Chavez and recent studies.

Periodicals are newspapers, magazines, and journals that are usually published on a weekly, monthly, or quarterly basis. You will probably find titles of articles on your particular topic in the *Readers' Guide to Periodical Literature,* an index that is published each month and that will tell you what has been published in that time frame on your topic. You then need to determine whether your library has the particular periodical that contains the article. For newspaper articles, you can use the *New York Times Index* or *Los Angeles Times Index* to locate information on your subject. If you are researching a particular book, you can find out what reviewers of that book had to say through the *Book Review Digest.* If your topic is in the arts and humanities, you may want to look through the *Art Index* or the *Humanities Index.* Similarly, if your topic concerns the social sciences, there is also a *Social Science Index.* All of these indexes work like the *Readers' Guide,* telling you what journal or magazine has material on the topic you are studying.

At times you will find the article in question in the magazine or journal. At other times, the article is on microfilm or microfiche, which is a film that has reduced the article in size. You need to use a microfilm or microfiche reader in order to enlarge the material so it can be read.

In the reference section, you may find a host of encyclopedias and dictionaries. General encyclopedias like the *Encyclopedia Britannica* or the *Encyclopedia Americana* provide you with an introduction to the topic you are studying. The articles in these encyclopedia sets are arranged alphabetically by subject, but the index in the last volume is usually the best place to begin searching. The *Encyclopedia Britannica* is an often-used source for general information, while you may want to turn to the *Encyclopedia Americana* for information on issues concerning North America and scientific technological subjects. Finally, the *New Columbia Encyclopedia* is helpful if you want a short summary concerning the subject you are studying. Your library may have a host of other encyclopedias, particularly specialized encyclopedias on art, science, philosophy, and so on. Ask your college reference librarian for the types of encyclopedias your college provides.

You will find several dictionaries in your college library. *Webster's Third International Dictionary of the English Language* is a comprehensive American dictionary on the English language, providing definitions and pronunciations of the words you are interested in. The *Oxford English Dictionary* is another dictionary that you will probably come across in your library. This multi-volume dictionary is unique in that it gives the history, or etymology, of each word in the English language, providing a chronological history of its use in literary and historical texts. And there are a number of briefer or collegiate dictionaries on the shelves in the reference section. You may also find specialized dictionaries on various fields like music, medicine, and law. Again, your reference librarian will provide you with information about the kinds of dictionaries available to you.

Most libraries also carry pamphlets in a special pamphlet file. These are often government or business publications that may provide useful information on a topic that you are interested in. The librarian can help you find any pamphlet on your topic.

How Library Books Are Classified

Library books are commonly organized under two classification systems: the *Dewey decimal* system and the *Library of Congress* system. It is important that you have a general understanding of how these two systems work.

The Dewey decimal system is the older of the two, classifying its books by subject. Each subject has a number that you will find on the outside of the book. The number is usually a whole number and a decimal. Here are the general numbers and their subject classifications:

000—099	General works, including bibliography
100—199	Philosophy and psychology
200—299	Religion
300—399	Social sciences
400—499	Language
500—599	Pure science
600—699	Technology, medicine, business
700—799	The arts
800—899	Literature
900—999	History and geography

Underneath the book's Dewey decimal number, you will find additional numbers and letters that serve as codes for the author and title. All of this is called the book's call number, which identifies where the book will be located. Here is an example of a Dewey decimal classification and an explanation of its abbreviations. The book in question is entitled *The Gang as an American Experience* by Felix M. Padilla:

364.1 — Dewey decimal number for crime

P134g

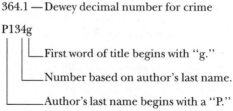

Figure 3-1   *Example of a Dewey decimal classification.*

A second system of classifying books in the stacks is the Library of Congress system. This system provides additional categories for classifying books. Here are the nineteen categories:

A	General works
B	Philosophy, psychology, religion
C–D	History and topography (except America)
E–F	History: North and South America
G	Geography and anthropology
H	Social sciences
J	Political science
K	Law
L	Education
M	Music
N	Fine arts
P	Language and literature
Q	Science
R	Medicine
S	Agriculture
T	Technology and engineering
U	Military science
V	Naval science
Z	Bibliography and library science

Often an additional letter next to the first further divides the topic. PL, for example, would refer to the language and literature of East Asia and Africa. Here is an example of a Library of Congress classification and what each abbreviation means:

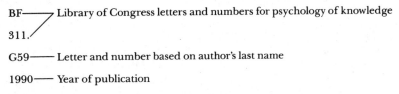

BF——— Library of Congress letters and numbers for psychology of knowledge
311.

G59——— Letter and number based on author's last name

1990——— Year of publication

Figure 3-2   *Example of a Library of Congress classification.*

If you are looking for a magazine or journal article, you will probably be searching in one of the periodical indexes in the reference or periodical section of your library. These guides are generally organized alphabetically around subjects. The information given in each entry is sometimes difficult to understand because much of it is placed in a small amount of space. The following is an excerpt from the *Readers' Guide to Periodical Literature*—the most widely used text. Study all the bibliographical information, and note how the abbreviations are used to condense the information:

Homeless as Authors

Voice for the homeless. B. Marshall. — Author

il | por The Progressive. 55:15 Ag '91
       └— Name of magazine Volume number Page number Date of magazine
     └—Abbreviations for "illustrated" and "portrait"
   └—Title of article

Figure 3-3   *Example of an entry in the Readers' Guide to Periodical Literature.*

Computers in Libraries

Many large college libraries, perhaps even your own, have computerized bibliographical information. These have replaced the traditional card catalogs, which are 3×5 cards listing the books and journals of the library, arranged alphabetically by subject, author, and book title, in rows of drawers. Computerized information is often referred to as an on-line catalog. You gain access to this information by using the keyboards and screens provided in the library. You find information on this terminal by searching for a subject, a title, or an author. Sometimes there is also a printer, which allows you to print the bibliographical information you may need.

What you will find is often the same information that you could find in a card catalog. In addition, however, the computer screen may tell you if the book has been checked out. The advantage to using the computer screen is that you have an up-to-date listing of all library material that has been checked out or purchased. Usually, as soon as a new publication is purchased or material is checked out, the information is automatically added to the on-line catalog. More and more libraries are now going to computer cataloging of their materials, so it is wise for you to learn how to operate the computer commands.

Your library may also have library sources on the computer known as CD-ROM, which is an abbreviation for "compact disc read only memory." This material is different from the on-line computer material in that it is not continually updated. CD-ROM material is on compact discs, so you can read this information much as you would listen to music on a compact disc. CD-ROMs contain bibliographical information on various topics, particularly in the form of book, magazine, and journal titles. Here you will find more extensive listings of titles in the area you are researching.

CD-ROMs are also being used commercially to market encyclopedias that are on computer screens. Unlike the traditional encyclopedias, CD-ROM material can provide video and sound accompaniments to the topic you are researching. You can see, for example, film footage of a particular battle or hear a historical leader's speech as you read about the historical event. Your college library may or may not have this type of CD-ROM material, but you can be certain that CD-ROMs will play a key role in the library research materials of the future.

Moreover, some college libraries now allow you to use their computers to access titles of works in other neighboring libraries. This is known as computer networking. So with the library's computer system—on-line, CD-ROM, and computer networking to other libraries—you can determine just about all that has been written on the topic you are studying.

You will find that your college librarians are particularly helpful in answering any questions that you may have about the library. They frequently provide tours of the library and may even have developed a short-term course that will acquaint you with all aspects of the library, including their computers. Make use of these services before you begin doing any lengthy research.

The Research Project

Throughout your college education, you will find that your college library and neighboring libraries are invaluable when you are doing research projects. These assignments generally call for you to do research in books, magazines, journals, and other related types of material found in the library. Much of the information you have been introduced to in this chapter will help you conduct your research.

You may recall that in Chapter 2 you studied the time-management steps necessary to complete a research project on the Native Americans known as the Hopis. Let's assume that you have chosen this topic to research. There are five important steps to follow to complete a research paper on the Hopis or on any research topic of your choice. You need to: (1) select a topic, (2) locate materials, (3) take notes, (4) evaluate and organize the notes, and (5) draft the paper.

Select a Topic.   The most important step in the research process is select-ing a topic that you can adequately research. Often students begin by selecting a topic that is too general. A ten-page paper on the Hopis would not begin to cover all the important points concerning these people. A full-length book could easily be written on all aspects of the Hopi culture. You need to then ask yourself: What aspect of the Hopi civilization do I want to research: their religion, their migration patterns, their social organization? These examples of subtopics can be adequately covered in a ten-page paper.

Let's assume that you select the topic: The Hopi's Family Structure. You are now ready to share this topic with your instructor and your peers. Ask them whether the topic is still too general and whether they know of materials you can turn to to begin your research.

Before you begin your research, write out the topic you intend to examine—The Family Structure of Hopi Society—so that when you be-gin your research, you will have a more directed sense of the kinds of materials that will help your research, and you will be able to show your topic to librarians whom you ask for assistance.

Locate Materials.   With your topic in mind, you can begin locating your research materials. Start with your college library. Begin looking in en-cyclopedias treating the subject of the Hopis. Encyclopedias are excel-lent places to begin your research, as they can provide you with accurate general information.

Your next step is to begin looking in the various periodical indexes. If you have any questions, consult with the *reference librarian,* whose spe-cialty is tracking down sources. Reference librarians are often very help-ful because they can direct you to areas where you will probably find material for your research and, more important, they can tell you where *not* to look.

Also consider full-length books, whose titles you can find in the card or on-line catalog of your library or in computer networks that direct you to titles in other libraries.

Be creative in tracking down your sources. Think of other titles that might contain material on the Hopis—Native Americans, Native Ameri-cans of the Southwest, Native American Social Structures, and so on.

By the end of your first search, you should have the titles of at least ten sources that will become part of your research.

Take Notes.   It is best to take notes on 4 × 6 cards because they are easy to organize when you begin writing your drafts. Summarize information on the Hopis, and copy down direct quotes that you might consider us-ing in your paper. Each card should have all the necessary bibliographical information on the first and second lines so that, in the event that you must return the book, your source is fully identified. A note card on the Hopis could look like this:

> Serena Nanda *Cultural Anthropology*, 5th ed.
> Belmont: Wadsworth, 1994.   347–348.
> extended matrilineal families: "The Hopi revolves around a central and continuing core of women." (347)
> father's obligations economic.
> mother–daughter relation very close.
> sister relation very strong: children of sisters raised together.

As you continue taking notes, keep asking yourself: Is my topic adequate? Is it too general? Can I rephrase it somehow? As you complete your note-taking, the key points that you want to make in your paper should begin to emerge.

Organize and Evaluate Your Notes.   You should now be able to write out five or six of the most important points you intend to cover. At this time, these points should be used to support a particular argument that you have come upon: The Hopi women exert a strong force on their family, and it is seen in their relationships with their sisters, mothers, and brothers. A beginning list of issues that you may want to cover to support this argument could look like this:

Roles of Women in Hopi Society

— closeness of mothers and daughters
— closeness between sisters
— importance of mother's brother's role
— the economic role that men play

Share this working outline with your instructor and your peers. Take note of their questions, and revise your statements based upon their input. You may have noted that the original topic ''The Hopi's Family

Structure'' has evolved into the more specific concern of ''The Roles of Women in Hopi Society.'' After you have thought through your revised outline, begin attaching sources to each subsection. You may even want to number all of your note cards and refer to each source by number. An excerpt of your outline could look something like this:

— closeness of mothers and daughters. See notes 7-12, 18-21.
— closeness between sisters. See notes 30-35, 47.

With this outline in hand, you can begin to draft your paper.

Draft the Paper.   Now is the time to begin writing. Since this is your first draft, do not fret over a perfect copy at this juncture. Write quickly, incorporating your summaries and relevant quotes. As you write, examine the outline you have set up. Feel free to revise it, rearranging the subtopics or even adding entirely new ones.

As you draft your essay, ask for feedback from your instructor and your peers. Let them read the parts you have completed, and incorporate their suggestions when their comments seem appropriate to you.

Each research project has different requirements, depending on the course you are taking and the conventions the particular discipline uses to do research. Yet what all research projects share is this five-step process: selecting a topic to research, finding appropriate materials, taking notes on these materials, organizing and evaluating the research, and writing the drafts. As you continue to do research, these steps will become habitual.

It is clear, then, that your college library is a significant vehicle for your education. But your college library and your neighborhood library are also places for you to read and browse for pleasure. During those moments when school and work are not too hectic, it is often very relaxing to just browse through the rows of books or the periodical section. As you continue your education, you will find that libraries are those special places that help make learning a life-long experience and pleasure.

Summary

The college library is the campus's central location for the information you need to gather as a student. You will find materials in various sections of the library: reference, stacks, and periodicals. The materials are organized either by the Dewey decimal system or the Library of Congress system. This information is often indexed in a card catalog or on-line computer catalog. CD-ROMs can also provide you with sources of titles for your research that may not be in your college library.

Doing a research project involves five important and sequential steps: locating a topic, finding material, taking notes on the material, organizing these notes, and drafting your paper.

Summary Box   *Using the Library*

What is the college library?	*Why do you use it?*
A central location for scholarly information Materials are located in specific sections: reference, stacks, and periodicals Books are organized according to either the Dewey decimal system or the Library of Congress system in a card catalog, on an on-line computer catalog, or on CD-ROM	To assist your education To provide resources for your college research To allow you to become a more independent learner To build backgrounds for life-long interests and pleasures

What is library research?	*Why do you do it?*
An organized search of the key studies on a particular topic	To learn about a topic by analyzing what researchers have discovered about this topic

Skills Practice

Exercise 3.1
Using the Library to
Locate Sources

Choose a topic that interests you, go to the library, and complete the following activities. You may want to work in groups of four or five and divide up these activities after you have agreed upon a topic:

1. State your topic:

   _____

2. Go to the catalog system (either card catalog, on-line computer, or CD-ROM) and locate five titles that would help you research this topic. Include author and title. Also, be sure you include the Dewey decimal or the Library of Congress call number for each book.

   a. _____

   b. _____

   c. _____

   d. _____

   e. _____

3. Go to the periodical indexes and locate five magazine, journal, or newspaper entries that you could use to research your topic. Include author (if listed), title, and name of periodical, as well as any other bibliographical information that you find in your search.

a. _____

b. _____

c. _____

d. _____

e. _____

4. Now go to your reference librarian with these titles. Ask her/him if there are any other library materials (such as pamphlets or audio-visual material) available to help you with your research topic. List these additional sources.

Score: Answers will vary.

Basic Reading, Listening, and Writing Skills

In this part of the book, you will learn skills that will help you read, listen, and write better. These are very important skills for you to acquire in order to succeed in college. So read each chapter introduction carefully, and do as many of the exercises as you can. When you finish Part Two, you will have some very useful study skills at your disposal.

4 Locating the Main Idea

How to determine the main idea

◑ Find topic   ◑ Look at beginning   ◑ Look at end
◑ Main idea in longer selections   ◑ No stated main idea

Determining main ideas in textbooks and lectures is perhaps the single most important study skill that you can learn. If you do not know what the main ideas are, you cannot follow a writer or lecturer's train of thought. Details can become confusing and meaningless. On the other hand, if you have the main ideas in mind, a textbook chapter or lecture will seem organized and informative. Furthermore, the main ideas will usually stay with you long after you have forgotten many of the details.

Understanding the Role of Main Ideas

Every well-planned lecture and textbook has a series of main ideas. But finding them is not always a simple matter. You often have to know what main ideas do and how they're used in order to find them.

In Relationship to the Topic. The first step in locating any main idea is to determine the *topic* of your reading or lecture material. If you determine the topic early in your reading or listening, you will be on your way to identifying main ideas.

The topic is generally easy to find in a reading selection because it is the title of the material. Most titles clearly tell you what the selection is about. An article with the title "Pollution: Research in the Nineties" is almost sure to tell you what scientists have found out about pollution in this decade. "Pollution: A Hopeless Problem?" will no doubt try to explain why pollution is not yet under control and may never be controlled. It is best to lock the title in your mind before you start reading, to begin examining what the material will cover.

In some articles, the title may be more indirect. For instance, the writer may use a quotation as a title. In this case, you may understand the meaning of the title only while reading or after reading the selection. Let's say an article on pollution uses a question from Henry David Thoreau as its title: "What Is the Use of a House if You Don't Have a Decent Planet to Put It On?" You may not at first understand what this question has to do with pollution. But as you read this article, you may find that the article is not about building houses but about the uselessness of technology if the earth is too polluted to use the technology. When you encounter indirect titles, you may want to begin by jotting down a few notes about what you think the title means.

Locating the topic of a lecture is usually quite easy, because most instructors list the subjects for class meetings in the syllabus, next to the class dates. For example, an environmental studies instructor might write "Monday, June 7—Water Pollution." Write this title on the first line of your page of lecture notes for that day. You should then try to figure out how this topic fits into what your instructor said in the previous meeting. Did she discuss air pollution on Friday, June 4? As you start seeing connections among lectures, you will derive more meaning from each one.

What if your instructor does not provide a syllabus or does not begin the lecture with a stated topic? Then you are responsible for determining the topic. Spend no more than five minutes listening to the lecture to determine the topic. Then write your own title on the first line of your lecture notes.

In Outlines.   With the topic in mind, you are now ready to read or listen for main ideas. Consider main ideas as umbrellas under which all significant details are included. Perhaps you can best see the main ideas as Roman numerals in an outline, where Roman numerals like "I" represent the main idea and capital letters like "A" and "B" represent the supporting details. If you are already familiar with the traditional outline form, you know that the main ideas, preceded by Roman numerals, are placed farthest to the left on your page of notes. You may also have learned that the farther to the right you go, the more details you add. A main idea, then, is more general than its details but more specific than the topic. See how a main idea is sandwiched between the topic and the details of support in the following outline of a lecture on air pollution:

Types of Pollution

I. Air pollution

    A. Types of pollution in the atmosphere
    B. Effects of air pollution on rivers, lakes, and oceans
    C. Effects of air pollution on vegetation

Notice that "I. Air Pollution" is one issue under the topic "Types of Pollution" and that A, B, and C call out specifics of that main idea.

Whether you are reading or listening, see the main idea as the level of information between the topic and the details. Keep this "I, A, B, and C" organization in mind when you are locating main ideas in writing or in lectures. When you are comfortable with the traditional outline structure, you will be able to identify main ideas effortlessly.

Seeing and Hearing Main Ideas

Almost every paragraph or group of paragraphs and list of statements in a lecture should contain one main idea and one or more details. Here are some hints for finding main ideas.

At the Beginning.   In many of the paragraphs you read, you will find the main idea in the first sentence. In the sentences that follow the first sentence, you will usually read details that support this main idea. Study the following paragraph on air pollution to see how the first sentence expresses the main idea and the sentences that follow present details:

> Most air pollution is made up of a combination of gaseous substances. Some of the air pollution is caused by automobile exhaust fumes in the form of carbon monoxide. Other types of air pollution, often found in smog, are made up of chemical oxides. The two most common oxides found in air pollution are nitrogen oxide and sulfur oxide.

Did you notice that the first sentence is the most general, the umbrella under which the other three sentences fall? Did you also notice that in each detail sentence specific types of air pollution are cited? In main-idea sentences you do not usually read a specific fact or figure. In this sense, main-idea sentences are more general. Thus in the main-idea sentence of the sample paragraph, gaseous substances are introduced, not specific gaseous substances.

Similarly, instructors usually present main-idea sentences at the beginning of their lectures or parts of lectures. So you need to listen carefully when they begin a presentation or when they introduce new ideas during the lecture. These introductory remarks will usually be the I, II, and III of your notes.

At the End.   Occasionally, the main idea of a paragraph is presented at the end. In these cases, the detail sentences are presented first. The process of presenting specific information that leads to a general statement is called *induction*. Information is collected, and from this a main idea emerges. Study this paragraph on the sources of air pollution:

> Forest fires occur throughout the world. Wherever there are insects, they disperse pollen. The wind erodes the soil, and it ends up in the atmosphere. Volcanoes erupt and spew their material into the air. All of these are examples of natural events that create air pollution.

Did you notice the specific details in the first four sentences? Did you also notice how these sentences lead to a main-idea sentence at the end? This statement about natural air pollution, like an umbrella, covers all the information about volcanoes, wind, insects, and fires.

This same pattern sometimes occurs in lectures. The speaker presents several details at the beginning of the lecture, and the main idea, or induction, is presented last. In your outline, you need to leave the blank next to item I temporarily empty while you jot down the details (A, B, C) of the lecture. Then, when the speaker presents the main idea, you can go back to fill in the space next to I.

In Longer Selections.   You can also look for the main idea of an entire essay or lecture. In these longer pieces, the main idea can usually be found in the first paragraph of an essay or the first section of a lecture, called the *introduction.* In these longer works, the main idea may be stated in more than one sentence.

In the paragraphs or sections that follow the introduction, which are often called the *body,* details are usually presented to support the main idea. The last paragraph or section—the *conclusion*—is usually as general as the introduction. It either summarizes the main idea of the essay or presents new conclusions that logically follow from the details. So when looking for the main idea in most essays, it is wise to read through the first and last paragraphs and then write out the main idea in your own words.

This outline should help you better understand the relationship between main idea and details in longer works:

I. Introduction: expresses main idea; introduces details

> A. ⎫
> B. ⎬ Body: explains the details more thoroughly in a series of
> C. ⎭ paragraphs or sections

II. Conclusion: either summarizes the main idea or presents a new main idea that follows from the details in A, B, and C.

Through Signal Words.   Several *signal words* may introduce a main idea. You will find signal words most often in the introduction or conclusion of an essay or lecture. Become familiar with these words and phrases: "in general," "generally," "above all," "of great importance," "the main idea is," "the main point is," "the main feature is," "the key feature is," "the truth is." Look at how the following paragraph incorporates signal words into its sentences:

> *Generally,* the most significant cause of pollution in big cities is the emissions that come from automobiles and factories. *The main feature* of pollutants from both these sources is that they do not easily decompose or decay on their own. *Of great importance* is how these pollutants return to the earth in the form of acid rain. It is acid rain that we need to study more carefully next.

Do you see how these signal words introduce the key points this author intends to cover?

The following words and phrases signal main ideas in conclusions: "in conclusion," "to conclude," "to summarize," "therefore," "thus," "consequently," "as a consequence," "as a result," "so," "it can be seen that," "it is suggested that," "it follows that," "from the above reasons," "it is safe to say." Let these words be signals for you to locate concluding main-idea sentences in your reading and in lectures. Authors frequently use these words and phrases to introduce a general statement that you may want to remember. Also, you need to use these signal words when writing conclusions of your own.

Inferring Main Ideas

The preceding suggestions about finding main ideas in first and last sentences cover most of what you will read and hear. In some material, though, you will not find a main idea explicitly stated. In these cases, you need to infer a main idea from the details. You will frequently find paragraphs with implied main ideas in descriptive writing, especially in short stories and novels, where the author is creating a mood or re-creating an experience. Descriptive writing, therefore, does not follow the "main-idea-followed-by-details" pattern.

Read the following description and infer a main idea:

> The leaves on the trees seemed to have been burned by a harmful chemical. The water in the pond was stagnant, and strangely, it did not seem to have any living things swimming in it—no fish, no algae, no insects teeming above the water. All I could see was the stifling, brown air that seemed to hover around everything—the trees, the pond, and me.

Nowhere does the author state that he is describing a dangerously polluted environment, but do you see that all the details lead you to infer that he is? The leaves on the trees are brown, the pond has no living organisms in it, and the air is brown and stifling. The author wants the reader to be disgusted by the details in order to come upon the main idea: how ugly and life-threatening a polluted environment can be.

Applying Main-Idea Rules to Writing

Learning to spot signal words and knowing how essays and lectures are organized will help you locate main ideas. They will also help you write organized essays. You will frequently be asked to write essays as a test of your understanding of reading and lecture material.

Consider these suggestions when beginning a writing assignment. First, use the traditional outline form to jot down notes before you begin writing. Second, use some signal words to introduce your main idea in introductions and conclusions. Finally, fortify your essays with several well-developed paragraphs: an introduction, paragraphs introducing and explaining details, and a conclusion summarizing or synthesizing what you have said. (You will learn more about the extended essay in Chapter 16.)

Are you beginning to see that reading, listening, and writing involve similar processes? The same organizational rules seem to apply to all three activities. The major difference is that when you read and listen, you take in information and consider what it means; when you write, you write down more carefully what you think this new material means to you. Good readers and listeners are often good writers. You will learn more about this reading–listening–writing interconnection throughout this book.

Summary

Determining the main idea of a paragraph and locating the main ideas in a longer passage or in lectures are very important skills for students to learn. About half the main ideas that one reads or hears are found in the first sentence of a paragraph. In fewer cases, the main idea is in the last sentence. Implied main ideas are not stated at all but may be inferred from the details.

Whether the material is spoken or written, the relationship between a main idea and its supporting details can be represented in the outline pattern:

I.

    A.
    B.
    C.

Dividing information into general and specific categories is a mental exercise you should constantly perform when you read, listen, or write. In Chapter 5 you will study the A, B, and C of the outline form—the details.

Summary Box

Main Ideas

What are they?	*Why do you need to use them?*
Key statements made in writing or lecturing, usually found at the beginning and end of material, and implied in most descriptions	To understand the important points in what you read, hear, or write
More specific than topics, less specific than details	To serve as umbrellas for the details that support them

Skills Practice Topic: Environmental Studies

All the exercises in this chapter deal with the issue of environmental pollution, a topic of concern to us all and one that you will examine carefully if you enroll in environmental studies courses in college.

Before you begin these exercises, answer the following questions either by yourself or in small groups to get a sense of what you already know about the environment. Recalling what you already know about a topic is very effective preparation for studying that topic.

1. What does the term *environment* mean?
2. What are the most common environmental problems that we face today?
3. How have human beings contributed to environmental problems?
4. How are environmental problems being dealt with in the world today?

**Exercise 4.1
Determining Stated
or Implied Main
Ideas**

The following paragraphs discuss the ways humans affected the planet in ancient times. The main idea may be found in the first sentence or the last sentence, or it may be implied. Locate the letter of the main-idea sentence, and place it next to the appropriate number in the answer box. If there is no main-idea sentence, write *imp* for "implied" next to the number in the answer box.

Ancient Hunters and Gatherers

(1) (a) For the vast majority of their time on earth, human beings have been hunters and gatherers. (b) They found that some wild plants could be eaten, so they began to gather them to share them with their family. (c) When they found that fish and game were edible, they became hunters. (d) The hunting was generally done by men, and the gathering was performed by women and children.

(2) (a) These early hunters and gatherers formed groups of approximately fifty members. (b) As a group, they worked together to hunt game and gather food in order to feed their people. (c) Once the group grew beyond fifty, it often split up and began forming a second group, which hunted and gathered food on its own. (d) These groups, known as tribes, seemed to be the fundamental social group for hunters and gatherers.

(3) (a) Often these tribes were forced to move from one place to another to find new game and edible plants. (b) The people in the tribes often could not tell how long their supply of game in a particular area would last, which was a source of frustration for them. (c) They also had a difficult time gauging when a particular type of edible plant would no longer be plentiful enough to feed the entire tribe. (d) As nomads, they were also subject to the changes of seasons and were forced to move when the weather proved intolerable.

(4) (a) These tribes soon learned much about coping with weather changes. (b) They also found reliable water sources, even in dry areas. (c) These people eventually became shrewd enough to know which plants were edible and which could serve as medicine. (d) Each tribe also learned to use sticks and stones in preparing its plant and animal foods.

(5) (a) Our current picture of these ancient hunting and gathering tribes calls our modern lifestyle into question. (b) In these tribes of fifty, women and children spent only fifteen hours per week gathering food. (c) The men tended to hunt only one week each month. (d) Further-

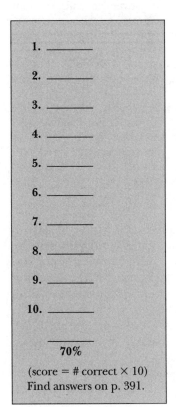

1. _____
2. _____
3. _____
4. _____
5. _____
6. _____
7. _____
8. _____
9. _____
10. _____

_____
70%

(score = # correct × 10)
Find answers on p. 391.

more, our ancient ancestors ate a healthy and varied diet, and the notion of stress was foreign to them.

(6) (a) A negative aspect of the hunter–gatherer lifestyle was their high mortality rate. (b) Many infants died of infectious diseases. (c) For adults, the average life expectancy was about thirty years. (d) Because of this high death rate, the population increased slowly.

(7) (a) The impact of the hunter–gatherer lifestyle on the environment was very slight. (b) Because their population did not grow quickly, they did not deplete the resources in the environment. (c) Also, because these people were nomads, they did not exploit any one area. (d) Finally, these people relied on their own energy rather than on energy resources in the environment to get most of their work done.

(8) (a) About 12,000 years ago, hunters and gatherers began to change some of their behavior. (b) Most important, they improved their tools; cutting tools became sharper, and the bow and arrow were invented. (c) Also, hunters from various tribes began to work together to hunt herds of animals such as bison and mammoths. (d) These people also began to burn some of their inedible vegetation to give the edible vegetation room to grow.

(9) (a) As these hunters developed more advanced skills, some of the forested hunting areas began to turn to grassland. (b) As they became more proficient, these hunters were able to kill off a few more game. (c) The gatherers also changed some of the vegetation patterns by allowing more of the edible vegetation to grow. (d) All in all, though, both hunters and gatherers tended to live in harmony with their neighbors and with nature.

(10) (a) Today people living in industrial areas rarely consider where the piece of meat they eat for dinner comes from. (b) They also tend not to reflect on where or how the vegetables they buy for their salads are grown. (c) They also rarely ask what resources are needed to make the plastics and metal items they use each day. (d) Moreover, people in modern industrial cities often tend to consume more food and purchase more manufactured items than they really need.

*Exercise 4.2
Determining Topics
and Main Ideas*

The following exercise is a series of paragraphs on the history of agricultural societies, continuing the discussion on hunters and gatherers begun in Exercise 4.1. Read the following ten paragraphs carefully; you may choose to reread them. As you read each one, ask the following questions: What is the topic? What is the main idea? Remember that the topic—the subject of the paragraph, usually phrased in two or three words—tends to be more general. The main idea is the point of the paragraph, what all the sentences in the paragraph are about. Choose the correct letter of the topic and main idea for each paragraph and put it in the answer box next to the appropriate number.

Ancient Agricultural Societies

The use of agriculture began about 10,000 years ago. That is when people began to plant crops in one area and began to tame animals so they didn't have to migrate to hunt. What is interesting is that the use of agricultural methods occurred in several parts of the world at about the same time. These methods ultimately made hunting and nomadic living less attractive. Agriculture had some profound effects on how human beings lived.

1. The topic is

   a. the dangers of agriculture
   b. the birth of agriculture 10,000 years ago
   c. hunting and nomadic living
   d. where agriculture was first introduced

2. The main idea concerns

   a. the importance of taming animals
   b. the lack of interest in hunting
   c. the difficulty of introducing agriculture into tribal life
   d. the effect of agricultural methods on social behavior

It is believed that the first cultivation of plants occurred in the tropical areas of Burma, Thailand, and eastern India. The women of the tribes in these areas began to cultivate small vegetable gardens. Anthropologists believe these women realized that their staple food, yams, could be planted and harvested successfully in one area. These pioneering farmers realized that they could clear an area by cutting down the vegetation and then burning it. The ash from the burned vegetation provided rich fertilizer for the yams they planted on this cleared area of land. Food could now be grown and cared for in one area.

3. The topic is

   a. the invention of cultivation
   b. the use of yams in the diet
   c. the value of using rich fertilizer
   d. the ancient people of Burma, Thailand, and eastern India

4. The main idea concerns

   a. new farming methods
   b. the use of ash in cultivating yams
   c. how cultivation changed farming methods
   d. how cultivation kept farming methods the same

These pioneer women farmers invented the notion of *shifting cultivation.* That is, they realized that planting their crops in one area would yield rich harvests for no more than five years. Then they had to clear a new agricultural area. The old agricultural plot needed to remain unplanted, or fallow, for ten to thirty years. During this fallow time, the soil replenished itself; then it was ready for a new round of planting and harvesting. Shifting cultivation is still used by farmers throughout the world.

5. The topic is

    a. the invention of shifting cultivation
    b. rich harvests
    c. keeping land fallow
    d. where shifting cultivation is used today

6. The main idea concerns

    a. the difficulty of shifting cultivation
    b. ways of clearing new agricultural areas
    c. the value of shifting cultivation
    d. how soil replenishes itself

Where the climate was less warm and humid, farmers devised different agricultural techniques. In such areas as East Africa and China, farmers had to clear forested areas; chopping down trees was often quite difficult. Once the area was cleared, the women often planted grains like rice or wheat instead of yams. The farmers in these temperate climates learned the same thing as those in tropical climates: that the area they cleared could yield a successful harvest for only a certain number of years. Shifting cultivation was the most profitable way to get consistently rich harvests.

7. The topic is

    a. temperate climates
    b. the farmers of East Africa and China
    c. the agricultural techniques of farmers in East Africa and China
    d. the planting of rice and grain

8. The main idea concerns

    a. the difficulty of clearing forested areas
    b. the similar agricultural techniques of farmers in tropical and temperate areas
    c. the success of harvesting in temperate climates
    d. the differences between the farmers of temperate and tropical areas

What pioneering farmers in both tropical and temperate climates learned was the value of *subsistence farming.* That is, they learned to harvest enough food to feed their tribe and no more. These farmers did not want to make a profit from any harvest that remained. Subsistence farming proved to be an environmentally sensible type of agriculture, because it used relatively small areas of land. Also, the people did not deplete their area's resources in an attempt to make the farms productive. They used their own strength to clear the farm areas, and they fertilized their farms with burning vegetation grown in the same area.

For these reasons and many more, subsistence farming had little negative impact on the environment.

9. The topic is

   a. the depletion of the environment
   b. the negative effect of subsistence farming on the environment
   c. the nature of subsistence farming
   d. burning vegetation as fertilizer

10. The main idea concerns

    a. the use of land in subsistence farming
    b. subsistence farming as environmentally wise
    c. the profit resulting from subsistence farming
    d. the difficulty of feeding family and tribe

To this day, farmers throughout the world continue to use shifting cultivation and subsistence farming techniques. In Latin America, Southeast Asia, and parts of Africa, up to 200 million people still use these agricultural procedures. Environmentalists call them very sound because they do not deplete the environment. With shifting cultivation, the soil is never wasted; with subsistence farming, no area's resources are ever overused. When these two techniques are not used effectively, the soil becomes depleted, which leads to erosion and sometimes permanent damage to the soil and the surrounding environment.

11. The topic is

    a. farming techniques in Latin America and Southeast Asia
    b. the use of subsistence farming today
    c. the use of subsistence farming and shifting cultivation today
    d. the cause of erosion

12. The main idea concerns

    a. the dangers of soil erosion
    b. the hazards of depleting the environment
    c. soil cultivation and subsistence farming as environmentally sensible today
    d. how poor people farm

Plows were invented about 5000 B.C. These early plows, made of metal, were pulled by tamed animals and steered by the farmer. With a plow, farmers could plant more crops and therefore harvest more food. The plow also allowed farmers to plant in areas that, before introduction of the plow, could not be cleared because the roots in the soil were too deep. Plows also allowed farmers to dig ditches and bring water to dry areas. By helping the farmer harvest more, the plow gave him more food than his family could eat, and he could then sell some of the excess to families with less food.

13. The topic is

a. the invention of the plow
b. the use of water in agriculture
c. the profit resulting from farming
d. how farmers fed their families

14. The main idea concerns

a. the origin of the plow
b. why the farmer dislikes the plow
c. how plows clear roots that are deep in the soil
d. how the plow changed farming in fundamental ways

Farmers' ability to save and sell their product had several effects on society. Because more food was harvested, more people could settle in an area. Because food products could now be bought, not everyone had to be a farmer. Some people began to work in other occupations and use their earnings to purchase food from farmers. After introduction of the plow, jobs began to be specialized. Finally, in part because of the plow, cities emerged, and farming towns grew on the outskirts of these cities. The plow, therefore, had a profound effect on the structure of society.

15. The topic is

a. why farmers lost their power
b. why farming became a popular occupation
c. the emergence of cities
d. the plow's effect on society

16. The main idea concerns

a. the plow's important role in changing occupations and altering city and town life
b. the plow's dangerous effect on society
c. the importance of profit in society
d. why farmers moved out of the city

The separation of cities from farm areas had additional effects on human society. Most important, wealth became a reality. That is, some people had more food and more manufactured products than others had. So there emerged a need for a class of people who could manage the city's wealth. Also, problems emerged between those who had more and those who had less—or the *haves* and the *have nots*. Conflict between these groups and wars between cities were some of the unwanted results of the development of wealth.

17. The topic is

a. the development of city managers
b. the problems caused by war

---

1. _____
2. _____
3. _____
4. _____
5. _____
6. _____
7. _____
8. _____
9. _____
10. _____
11. _____
12. _____
13. _____
14. _____
15. _____
16. _____
17. _____
18. _____
19. _____
20. _____

_____
75%

Ask instructor for answers.

    c. how wealth was given to the people

    d. how wealth came to be

18. The main idea concerns

    a. how wealth restructured society and caused conflict and war

    b. the greed of city managers

    c. why the farmers became wealthy

    d. the occasional need for wars

With increased and more intensive farming came environmental concerns that the hunters and gatherers had never known. City people were
no longer living in harmony with the environment. When more land
was cleared for larger harvests and bigger cities, certain plants and animals were forced out of their natural habitat. Some plants and animals
even died out completely. Overuse of the land led to a depletion of the
soil's riches. What was once fertile territory sometimes became a desert
because of overfarming. Urban or city life generally had a negative effect
on the environment.

19. The topic is

    a. urban life

    b. the death of certain plants and animals

    c. overuse of the land

    d. city life and its effect on the environment

20. The main idea concerns

    a. how cities create deserts

    b. how city dwellers moved the farmers out

    c. how the hunter–gatherer is similar to the city dweller

    d. how city dwellers did not live in harmony with their environment

*Exercise 4.3
Determining More
Topics and Main
Ideas*

The following ten paragraphs address the issue of industrialization and
continue the discussion begun in the previous two exercises. After reading each paragraph, write a topic and a main idea for each. Remember
that the topic is normally expressed in a phrase that can serve as the title
of the passage. The main idea, often stated in the first or last sentence of
the paragraph, expresses the passage's intent. For example, "industrialized countries" can serve as the topic of a paragraph with the main idea
"the pollution caused by industrialized countries." Writing out your own
topics and main ideas is a big part of what you do when you take lecture
and study notes.

How Industrialized Societies Developed

The next big change in human society occurred during the mid-1700s
in England. It was called the Industrial Revolution. Industry seemed to
take over because there were so many inventions in such a short time.

These inventions included the steam engine (1765), the steamship (1807), and the steam locomotive (1829). They made England and most of Europe less farm-based and more urbanized, or city-centered.

1. *Topic:* _____

2. *Main idea:* _____

All of these new inventions had one thing in common: They were driven by natural resources. Coal was the first fuel used to run these machines. Then oil and natural gas were discovered as energy sources to replace human energy. The results were far-reaching, extending the plow's effects on society thousands of years before. Fewer people were needed to do most work, because machines replaced them. Farmers found themselves out of work, and they began to move from the outlying farms to the large cities to find jobs. They often found jobs in large factories.

3. *Topic:* _____

4. *Main idea:* _____

By World War I (1914–1918), machines were becoming more and more sophisticated. These machines helped society in several ways. Because products could be produced in larger quantities, they were often cheaper to buy. Also, the average wage of each working individual went up. Furthermore, farming was more productive, so food was more plentiful. Industrialization also improved practices in medicine, sanitation, and nutrition. Consequently, people tended to live longer. So along with its negative effects on the environment, industrialization had some positive effects on human beings.

5. *Topic:* _____

6. *Main idea:* _____

Industrialization had a negative effect on the environment. Industry tended to create pollutants. The quality of the air, water, and soil was damaged by the waste materials expelled from smokestacks and drainpipes. People soon found that air, water, and soil pollution affected not only their own city but also cities and countries beyond their border. Environmental pollution was no longer a local concern, but a *global* one. That is, people soon began to realize that the actions of a factory in London could affect the entire country and even the world.

7. *Topic:* _____

8. *Main idea:* _____

Industrialization has caused additional social problems. When farmers moved to the cities to find work, the population density of urban areas increased. If the migrants could not find work, the city government had to provide them with some sort of welfare. By increasing the city's population density, these migrants also made the transmission of diseases easier. Furthermore, unemployment and poverty made crime a more serious problem in large cities.

9. *Topic:* _____

10. *Main idea:* _____

How did industrialization affect the city's environment? Like developing cities throughout human history, industrialized cities destroyed topsoil and ate up forests and grasslands. Urban sprawl into the farmlands forced farmers to move farther out. Wildlife was either pushed out of the city or made extinct. What was a city's problem then became a global problem—one that affected all of nature.

11. *Topic:* _____

12. *Main idea:* _____

The Industrial Revolution also affected the economy of the city and the overall economy of the country. Solving each social and environmental problem required money. To cover increased welfare benefits, the city needed to collect taxes. Furthermore, taxpayers needed to address the pollution problems created by large factories. Cleaning up the air and the rivers and lakes took money. So, although the Industrial Revolution improved the average citizen's standard of living, it also made him pay for the social and environmental problems it caused.

13. *Topic:* _____

14. *Main idea:* _____

Today people in industrialized countries throughout the world are asking the same question. Is industrialization helping us or hurting us? Obviously, the Industrial Revolution has made humans more productive. It has increased our standard of living, lengthened human life, and made our life more comfortable. But the Industrial Revolution has also created an unhealthy environment. It has made much of our air unfit to breathe and our water unfit to drink. Environmental pollutants have also created many cancer-related diseases.

15. *Topic:* _____

16. *Main idea:* _____

The Industrial Revolution has also given us an attitude toward nature very different from that of our ancestors. In ancient times, human beings saw themselves as living in harmony with nature. They never took too much from nature and respected the power nature had over them. As human inventions came to the fore, we started seeing ourselves in a much more powerful role. Nature no longer controlled human beings; we controlled nature. Today we often see ourselves as *superior* to nature.

17. *Topic:* _____

18. *Main idea:* _____

It is this superior attitude toward nature that industrialized society needs to question. Yes, in many ways we can control parts of nature. We can build bridges and dams and send satellites outside of the earth's atmosphere. Yet nature still has some power over the organisms that live within it. Our challenge in the twenty-first century is to enjoy the benefits of industrialization but also to respect nature and live in harmony with it. We have to realize that our inventions can make life both better and worse.*

19. *Topic:* _____

20. *Main idea:* _____

70%

(score = # correct × 5)
Find answers on p. 391.

Exercise 4.4
Determining the
Main Idea in a
Longer Passage

To determine the main idea of a passage, you can apply the same rules that you used to determine the main idea of a paragraph. Read the following extended essay on nuclear war and pollution, a major concern of environmentalists, and follow these steps to determine the main ideas:

1. Read the introductory paragraph to determine the main idea of the entire passage.

2. See how the four paragraphs that follow (the body) give details to support this main idea. Locate the main-idea sentence for each of these paragraphs. In two of these paragraphs, the main idea is implied.

After you have taken these steps, answer the five questions that follow the essay. You may look back. Place all answers in the answer box.

Nuclear War and Pollution

(1) Environmentalists generally believe that the biggest threat to our world is a nuclear war. They believe this because of what they know

---

*Exercises 4.1–4.3 adapted from G. Tyler Miller, Jr., *Living in the Environment*, 5th ed. (Belmont, Calif.: Wadsworth, 1988), pp. 25–31.

about the atomic bombs that were dropped at the end of World War II and because they can accurately predict the amount of nuclear destruction countries today possess. Environmentalists have also conducted several studies concerning what would happen to the people and the environment if there were a nuclear war today.

(2) Two atomic bombs were dropped by Americans in August of 1945—one over Hiroshima and the other over Nagasaki in Japan. It is estimated that up to 140,000 people were killed immediately after the blast, and over 100,000 died later from exposure to radiation created by the atomic bomb. The radiation contaminated the dirt in the area of the explosion. This radioactive debris then entered the atmosphere and fell back to the earth as far away as thousands of kilometers from the original explosion.

(3) The threats to humans and to the environment caused by nuclear bombings is much worse than it was at the end of World War II. The damage that could happen today is 952,000 times as great as that to hit Hiroshima almost fifty years ago! One nuclear submarine today can carry enough nuclear warheads to equal 4,570 Hiroshima bombs. By the year 2000 it is predicted that sixty countries will either have nuclear warheads or will have the technology necessary to construct them.

(4) If a nuclear bomb were to explode today, as many as four billion people could die, as much as 80% of the human population. Within two years after the explosion, it is predicted that over 1 billion more people would die of starvation due to the reduced agricultural yields caused by the rdioactive fallout from the atomic explosion. Moreover, the average temperature would suddenly drop to typical fall and winter temperatures.

(5) An atomic explosion would also severely harm the already damaged ozone layer. Environmentalists predict that up to 70 percent of this layer could be destroyed, leading to what they characterize as an ultraviolet summer. This ozone layer reduction would reduce both crop yield and fish harvest. In humans, skin cancers would dramatically increase as well as eye cataracts. Further, those who are prone to infections could die of diseases their immune system would normally have protected them from.*

1. The main idea of paragraph 1 concerns

   a. how an atomic bomb explosion will negatively affect the environment and its people
   b. the effects of the atomic bombs exploded during World War II
   c. environmentalists' predictions
   d. Hiroshima and Nagasaki

2. The implied main idea of paragraph 2 concerns:

   a. The number of people killed in Hiroshima and Nagasaki

---

*Adapted from Miller, *Living in the Environment,* 7th ed., pp. 302–304.

b. the dirt that was made radioactive after the atomic bomb explosion

c. the negative effects on people and the environment of the Hiroshima–Nagasaki atomic bombings

d. the negative effects of an atomic explosion

3. The main idea of paragraph 3 concerns

a. the severity of nuclear bombing

b. the severity of nuclear bombing today compared to nuclear bombings in World War II

c. how many weapons a nuclear submarine can carry

d. the number of countries that will have nuclear capability by the year 2000

4. The implied main idea of paragraph 4 concerns

a. the effects of a nuclear bomb

b. the negative effects of a nuclear explosion on people and the environment, if it were to occur today

c. the number of people who would starve because of a nuclear explosion

d. the drop in temperature due to a nuclear explosion

5. The main idea of paragraph 5 concerns:

a. crop yield and fish harvest

b. the reduction in crop yield and fish harvest after a nuclear explosion

c. the increase in skin cancer due to a nuclear explosion

d. the negative effects on the ozone layer if a nuclear explosion were to occur today

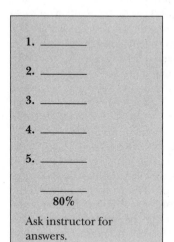

1. _____

2. _____

3. _____

4. _____

5. _____

_____
80%

Ask instructor for answers.

*Exercise 4.5
Determining the
Main Idea in a
Second Longer
Passage*

To determine the main idea of a passage, you can apply the same rules that you used to determine the main idea of a paragraph. Read the following extended essay on the greenhouse effect, another important environmental issue caused by technology, and follow these steps to determine the main idea:

1. Read the introductory paragraph to determine the main idea of the entire passage.

2. See how the four paragraphs that follow (the body) give details to support the main idea. Locate a main-idea sentence for each of these paragraphs.

After you have taken these steps, answer the five questions that follow. You may look back. Place all answers in the answer box.

The Greenhouse Effect

(1) Of the sun's rays that reach earth, 70 percent are absorbed by the land, sea, and air; 30 percent are reflected back into the atmosphere.

When the earth's environment cools, the absorbed heat is released in the form of infrared rays, or heat. Some of the energy escapes into space, and some of it is absorbed by water vapor and carbon dioxide in the atmosphere. The carbon dioxide and water vapor then repeat the cycle, returning some of this energy into the atmosphere and giving some back to the earth. This returning to earth of heat originally absorbed by the carbon dioxide and water of the atmosphere is called the *greenhouse effect.* Because of the greenhouse effect, the earth's temperature has increased about 10 degrees centigrade, or 18 degrees Fahrenheit, from what it would be without water vapor and carbon dioxide in the atmosphere.

(2) This natural cycle is being altered by the burning of coal as a fuel. Coal burning increases the amount of carbon dioxide and water in the atmosphere. This increase then allows for more heat to be returned to the earth because of the greenhouse effect.

(3) What might happen if the greenhouse effect causes average temperatures to rise worldwide? Scientists speculate that an overall increase in temperature will cause rainfall patterns to shift and crop-growing patterns to change. For example, the wheat belt in the United States might shift upward to Canada, where the soil is not so rich. Ultimately, the greenhouse effect might be responsible for less food production.

(4) A second result of an increase in temperature would be melting of the polar ice caps. This melting would increase the water level in the oceans of the world. Scientists now speculate that the sea-level increase would be gradual, probably taking place over hundreds of years.

(5) Despite its potential to flood the land, the greenhouse effect seems to pose greater potential danger to the earth's food-producing capacity. If less food is produced in the next fifty years, the worldwide hunger problem might increase, because in the same fifty-year period the world's population is expected to double.*

1. The main idea of paragraph 1 concerns

   a. how the sun reaches the earth
   b. how the earth cools
   c. how carbon dioxide is created
   d. how the greenhouse effect returns heat to the earth

2. The main idea of paragraph 2 concerns

   a. how coal burns
   b. the value of burning coal
   c. how coal burning increases the vapor and carbon dioxide level
   d. how coal burning decreases the vapor and carbon dioxide level

3. The main idea of paragraph 3 concerns

   a. the difficulty of producing food

1. _____

2. _____

3. _____

4. _____

5. _____

80%

(score = # correct × 20)
Find answers on p. 391.

*Adapted from Miller, *Living in the Environment,* 5th ed., pp. E20–24.

   b. how the greenhouse effect might cause less food to be produced
   c. where the wheat belt is in the United States
   d. why wheat can be grown effectively in Canada

4. The main idea of paragraph 4 concerns

   a. how ice caps are created
   b. the greenhouse effect and its relationship to water level
   c. how fast the polar ice caps are melting
   d. how carbon dioxide affects polar ice caps

5. The main idea of paragraph 5 concerns

   a. the greenhouse effect and food production
   b. food production
   c. world hunger
   d. world hunger and the increase in population

Exercise 4.6
Writing Your Own
Paragraph from
Main Ideas

The excerpt on the greenhouse effect in Exercise 4.5 can easily be outlined in the following way:

I. Main Idea of the Passage (expressed in paragraph 1)

   A.
   B. Supporting details for the main idea of the passage (consisting
   C. of the main ideas of paragraphs 2–5)
   D.

If you are still unclear about what the main idea of each paragraph is, review the correct answers to questions 1–5 in Exercise 4.5.

   Now use the following outline to state, in a phrase, the main idea of each of the five paragraphs in Exercise 4.5.

I. _____

   A. _____

   B. _____

   C. _____

   D. _____

70%

Ask instructor for answers.

With this outline to guide you, answer the following essay question in a paragraph of five sentences (one main-idea sentence and four supporting sentences).

   Essay question: In one paragraph, define the greenhouse effect and discuss its four possible effects on the environment.

Exercise 4.7
Determining the
Main Ideas in a
Textbook Excerpt

The following excerpt is from a textbook chapter on the ozone layer. It relates to the previous excerpt you have read on the greenhouse effect. Read through it quickly to get a sense of the topic. Then go back and read it slowly.

When you finish rereading, answer the five questions that follow the excerpt. You may return to the excerpt in deciding on your answers. Only one important term is not defined in the excerpt—*stratosphere*, which refers to the second layer of the atmosphere extending 11 to 30 miles above the earth's surface.

Depletion of Ozone in the Stratosphere

(1) **THE VITAL OZONE LAYER**   About 2 billion years ago, microorganisms living under water evolved with the ability to carry out photosynthesis. Gradually over millions of years, those organisms began adding oxygen to the atmosphere. As some of that oxygen drifted upward it reacted with incoming ultraviolet radiation and was converted to ozone in the stratosphere. Before this *oxygen revolution* began, life on Earth could exist only under water, where it was protected from the sun's intense ultraviolet rays.

(2) Today, we and many types of plants and other animals survive because this thin gauze of ozone in the stratosphere keeps much of the harmful ultraviolet radiation (specifically ultraviolet-B, or UV-B) given off by the sun from reaching Earth's surface.

(3) **USES OF CHLOROFLUOROCARBONS AND HALONS**   In 1974, chemists Sherwood Roland and Mario Molina theorized that human-made chlorofluorocarbons (CFCs), also known by their Du Pont trademark, Freons, were lowering the average concentration of ozone in the stratosphere and creating a global time bomb. No one suspected such a possibility when CFCs were developed in 1930.

(4) The two most widely used CFCs are CFC-11 (trichlorofluoromethane) and CFC-12 (dichlorofluoromethane). When they were developed, these stable, odorless, nonflammable, nontoxic, and noncorrosive chemicals were a chemist's dream. Soon they were widely used as coolants in air conditioners and refrigerators and as propellants in aerosol spray cans. Now they are also used to clean electronic parts such as computer chips, as hospital sterilants, as fumigants for granaries and cargo holds, and to create the bubbles in polystyrene plastic foam (often called by its Du Pont trade name, Styrofoam), used for insulation and packaging.

(5) Bromine-containing compounds, called *halons*, are also widely used, mostly in fire extinguishers. Other widely used ozone-destroying chemicals are carbon tetrachloride (used mostly as a solvent) and methyl chloroform, or 1,1,1,-trichloroethane (used as a cleaning solvent for metals and in more than 160 consumer products, such as correction fluid, dry-cleaning sprays, spray adhesives, and other aerosols).

(6) Industrial countries account for 84% of CFC production, with the United States being the top producer followed by western European countries and Japan. Worldwide, aerosols account for 25% of global CFC

use. Since 1978, however, most uses of CFCs in aerosol cans have been banned in the United States, Canada, and most Scandinavian countries, mostly because of consumer boycotts. In the United States, CFCs are still legally used as aerosol propellants in asthma and other medication sprays and cleaning sprays for VCRs and sewing machines, and in products such as canned confetti.

(7) The United States accounts for about 25% of the global consumption of CFCs, and per capita use of CFCs in the United States is six times greater than global per capita use. Vehicle air conditioners account for about three-quarters of annual CFC emissions in the United States.

(8) **DEPLETION OF THE OZONE LAYER**   Ozone is destroyed and replenished in the stratosphere by natural atmospheric chemical reactions and is maintained at a fairly stable level. However, there is much evidence that we are upsetting this balance and reducing the levels of life-saving ozone in the stratosphere.

(9) Spray cans, discarded or leaking refrigeration and air conditioning equipment, and the production and burning of plastic foam products release CFCs into the atmosphere. Depending on the type, CFCs are so unreactive that they stay intact in the atmosphere for 60 to 400 years. This gives them plenty of time to rise slowly through the troposphere until they reach the stratosphere. There, under the influence of high-energy UV radiation from the sun, they break down and release chlorine atoms, which speed up the breakdown of ozone (O_3) into O_2 and O.

(10) Over time, a single chlorine atom can convert as many as 100,000 molecules of O_3 to O_2. A single polystyrene cup contains over 1 billion molecules of CFCs. Although this effect was proposed in 1974, it took 15 years of interaction between science and politics before countries took action to begin slowly phasing out CFCs.

(11) Several other stable, chlorine-containing compounds, including widely used solvents such as methyl chloroform (1,1,1-trichloroethane) and carbon tetrachloride, also rise into the stratosphere and destroy ozone molecules. When fire extinguishers are used, their unreactive bromine-containing halon compounds enter the air and eventually reach the stratosphere, where they are broken apart by UV radiation. Each of their bromine atoms destroys hundreds of times more ozone molecules than a chlorine atom. All these compounds, especially CFCs, are also greenhouse gases that contribute to global warming during their trip through the troposphere.

(12) In the 1980s, researchers were surprised to find that up to 50% of the ozone in the upper stratosphere over the Antarctic is destroyed during the antarctic spring from September through mid-October—something not predicted by computer models of the stratosphere. During these two months of 1987, 1989, and 1990, this antarctic ozone hole covered an area larger than the continental United States. Depletion in 1990 was the largest recorded. A new analysis in 1991 suggests that this already-serious seasonal loss of ozone could double in size by 2001.

(13) Measurements indicate that this large annual decrease in ozone over the South Pole is caused when water droplets in clouds form

tiny ice crystals as they enter large streams of air, called polar vortices, that circle the poles in wintertime in both the Antarctic and the Arctic. The surfaces of these ice crystals absorb CFCs and other ozone-depleting chemicals. This greatly increases the rate at which these chemicals destroy ozone and leads to the sharp seasonal drop in ozone over the Antarctic.

(14) After about two months, the vortex breaks up and great clumps of ozone-depleted air flow northward and linger over parts of Australia, New Zealand, and the southern tips of South America and Africa for a few weeks. During this period, ultraviolet levels in these areas may increase as much as 20%. In Australia, which has the world's highest rate of skin cancer, television stations air daily reports on ultraviolet radiation levels and issue warnings for people to stay indoors during bad spells.

(15) Since 1988, scientists have discovered that a similar but smaller ozone hole forms over the Arctic during the two-month arctic spring, with an annual ozone loss of 15% to 25%. When this hole breaks up, clumps of ozone-depleted air flow southward and linger over parts of Europe and North America. This can produce a 5% winter loss of ozone over much of the Northern Hemisphere.

(16) In 1988, the National Aeronautics and Space Administration (NASA) released a study showing that the stratospheric ozone-depletion average over the whole year has decreased by as much as 3% over heavily populated regions of North America, Europe, and Asia since 1969. Unless emissions of ozone-depleting chemicals are cut drastically, average levels of ozone in the stratosphere could drop by 10% to 25% by 2050 or sooner, with much higher drops in certain areas.

(17) In 1990, two Soviet rocket scientists warned that the motors in U.S. space shuttles are contributing to depletion of the ozone layer, with each launch adding 170 metric tons (187 tons) of ozone-destroying chlorine molecules to the atmosphere. Soviet rocket engines use a fuel mixture that is 7,000 times less damaging than the fuel used in American shuttle engines. However, Soviet shuttles still destroy 1,400 metric tons (1,500 tons) of ozone per launch.

(18) **EFFECTS OF OZONE DEPLETION**   With less ozone in the stratosphere, more biologically harmful ultraviolet-B radiation will reach Earth's surface. This form of UV radiation damages DNA molecules and can cause genetic defects on the outer surfaces of plants and animals, including your skin. Each 1% loss of ozone leads to a 2% increase in the ultraviolet radiation striking Earth's surface and a 5% to 7% increase in skin cancer, including a 1% increase in deadly malignant melanoma.

(19) The EPA estimates that a 5% ozone depletion would cause the following effects in the United States:

- An extra 170 million cases of skin cancer by the year 2075. This includes an average of 2 million extra cases of basal-cell and squamous-cell skin cancers a year, and an additional 30,000 cases annually of often-fatal melanoma skin cancer, which now kills almost 9,000 Americans each year.

- A sharp increase in eye cataracts (a clouding of the eye that causes blurred vision and eventual blindness) and severe sunburn in people, and eye cancer in cattle.

- Suppression of the human immune system, which would reduce our defenses against a variety of infectious diseases, an effect similar to that of the AIDS virus.

- Health-care costs in the United States totalling $3.5 billion.

- An increase in eye-burning photochemical smog, highly damaging ozone, and acid deposition in the troposphere. According to the EPA, each 1% decrease in stratospheric ozone may cause a 2% increase in ozone near the ground.

- Decreased yields of important food crops such as corn, rice, soybeans, and wheat.

- Reduction in the growth of ocean phytoplankton that form the base of ocean food chains and webs and that help remove carbon dioxide from the atmosphere. Especially vulnerable are UV-sensitive phytoplankton, which are the base of the principal food web in the Antarctic.

- A loss of perhaps $2 billion a year from degradation of paints, plastics, and other polymer materials.

- Increased global warming from an enhanced greenhouse effect.

(20) In a worst-case scenario, people would not be able to expose themselves to the sun. Cattle could graze only at dusk without eye damage. Farmers might measure their exposure to the sun in minutes.*

1. The topic of this excerpt concerns:

1. _____

2. _____

a. a definition of ozone
b. diseases caused by ozone depletion
c. ozone depletion in Antarctica
d. ozone depletion in the atmosphere and its effects on the environment

3. _____

2. The topic of paragraph 6 concerns:

4. _____

5. _____

a. countries depleting the ozone layer
b. where aerosol cans have been banned
c. who is depleting the ozone layer and laws passed to protect it
d. how ozone relates to VCRs

3. The main idea of paragraph 9 concerns:

a. how CFCs enter the atmosphere and destroy ozone
b. the loss of ozone in the atmosphere
c. the increase in CFCs in the atmosphere
d. how CFCs decompose in the atmosphere

---

*Miller, *Living in the Environment,* 7th ed., pp. 297–301.

4. The main idea of paragraph 13 treats:

   a. ways to measure ozone in the South Pole
   b. how ozone is destroyed in the South Pole
   c. ice crystals in the South Pole
   d. what happens in winter in the South Pole

5. The main idea of paragraph 16 concerns:

   a. what NASA is
   b. ozone depletion in the stratosphere
   c. ozone depletion in the future
   d. the results of NASA's findings on ozone and the atmosphere

   Now go back and reread the excerpt, concentrating on those paragraphs that are referred to in each question. Frame your answers in a phrase or sentence.

6. Reread paragraphs 1 and 2 to determine how ozone protects humans. (1 point)

7. Reread paragraph 17 to determine how space shuttles help destroy the ozone layer. (2 points)

8. Reread paragraph 19, and list two effects of ozone being depleted in the United States by 5%. (2 points)

70%

Ask instructor for answers.

Follow-up on the Environmental Studies Exercises

Now that you have completed these exercises, it may be helpful to see how your reading on this topic has changed some of your ideas about the environment. Another very effective way to remember material is to review it once you have finished studying. You may want to go back to Exercises 4.1–4.7 and reread them just for their content, or for what they have to say about the environment. Then answer the following questions either individually or in small groups:

1. How would you now define the terms *environment* and *environmental studies?*
2. In history, how have human beings contributed to the environmental problem? How have they helped solve some of the problems in the environment?
3. What one environmental problem that you read about in these exercises is of most concern to you? Why?
4. What other issues related to the environment do you now want to study further?

5 Locating Major and Minor Details

Major details

◗ Examples   ◗ Steps   ◗ Characteristics
◗ Causes   ◗ Effects

Minor details

Now that you have practiced locating and writing main-idea sentences, you are ready to learn about detail sentences in reading and lecture materials. You can also use them in your own writing. Details may be either major or minor.

Major Details

Major details are the A, B, C, and so on of the outline format I., A., B., C. They support the main idea, giving examples, steps, characteristics, causes, or effects. Major details often answer the who, what, where, when, why, which one(s), or what kind(s) of a sentence or passage. Also, re-member that major details are usually found in the body of a paragraph, essay, or lecture.

Major Details That Give Examples.   Main-idea sentences often express a point of view, as in the following: "America is experiencing a series of economic problems." In the major-detail sentences supporting this point of view, you would be looking for examples. The examples should answer the question "What kinds of economic problems?" And your answers would be sentences discussing unemployment, inflation, pov-erty, and so on.

Look at how a writer uses examples in the following paragraph:

ex
Business is a study that involves how organizations produce and sell goods and services at a profit. In studying this field, one can analyze many organizations, both large and small. A business analyst can exam-ine how a small organization like a family bakery is operating to make a profit. This same analyst can study how a huge bakery corporation makes its profit. In both studies, the analyst considers the same issues: production, sales, and profit.

Do you see how the business concerns of a small bakery and those of a large bakery corporation become the examples that support the main idea—that business is the study of how organizations produce and sell at a profit?

When you come across the names of persons, places, and things, you probably have found details. The details become the support that you will need when defending a point of view. Start using the abbreviation *ex* in the margins to remind yourself that you are reading or listening to examples. Did you notice that this abbreviation was used in the margin of the previous paragraph to signal the two examples?

Major Details That Give Steps.   Details are sometimes laid out in sequence. For example, your instructor may be discussing the steps involved in reading a graph in an economics textbook, or you may be reading about the steps the federal government took to close down a savings and loan that was going bankrupt. The main-idea sentence that comes before the steps usually alerts you to the number of steps involved. Steps are details that often answer the question "Which ones?"

Consider this main-idea sentence: "There are three steps to remember in reading a graph in business." The details that follow this sentence should include these three steps. Be alert to the following signal words when you read or listen for steps: *first, second, third, and so on, last,* and *finally.*

Look at how the details in the following excerpt provide steps on how to read a graph in business:

steps   There are four basic steps to follow in reading a business graph. *First,* look to see what the horizontal axis represents. *Second,* see what the vertical axis measures. *Third,* study how these two variables relate to each other. *Finally,* study what the graph shows about this relationship.

In this paragraph, the main-idea sentence introduces the number of steps necessary in reading a graph in business. This sentence is general but is followed by specific directions for reading a graph. Did you notice the signal words *first, second, third,* and *finally,* which led you through the four steps? Like examples, steps provide specific information. Unlike examples, steps are more closely interrelated. A writer cannot present step two before step one. A writer presenting examples is usually not concerned with correctly sequencing them. You will learn more about steps as details in Chapter 6, "Identifying Organizational Patterns."

Finally, did you note how the marginal note *steps* in the previous paragraph reminds you of the steps in the excerpt? Marginal notes such as *steps* or *ex* help direct your reading or listening.

Major Details That Present Characteristics.   Some major details are neither examples nor steps. Rather they are descriptive. Major details of characteristics frequently include adjectives or adverbs. Such details may be used to draw a character sketch, be the key points in a film or book review, or be used to define a word. Look at how the following main-idea sentences require characteristics to support their points of view: "Hershey Foods Corporation's recycling activities are interesting ones to study," or "Lee Iacocca is known as an innovative American businessman." Saying that Hershey Foods recycles many of its waste products would not describe the characteristics of Hershey's recycling activities, nor would mentioning that Lee Iacocca brought Chrysler out of its economic hard times necessarily describe the kind of businessman he is. Each of these main-idea statements needs details expressing qualities or feelings that answer the "why" of the main-idea statement.

Look at how the following paragraph on the kind of study business is effectively uses characteristics:

reasons why   Business is a peculiar study in several ways. It is not a pure science like physics, because it studies how people behave in business matters. Yet some of business work is *mathematical* and *formulaic* in that it studies business trends and predicts profits and losses. On the one hand, business is *descriptive* of how people act in business matters; on the other, it is *prescriptive*, in that it tries to show how businesses will respond in certain economic situations.

In this paragraph, do you see that the author does not refer to specific business studies or works? This passage, rather, emphasizes the qualities that make business a unique study. See how the author uses the adjectives *mathematical, formulaic, descriptive,* and *prescriptive* to describe what business is. By placing the comment *reasons why* in the margin, you remind yourself that you are emphasizing the characteristics of business as a discipline.

Major Details That Present Causes and Effects.   A great number of major-detail sentences are closely related to the main-idea sentence. They do not give examples or qualities to support the main idea, nor do they list steps that follow from the main-idea sentence. These sentences of cause or effect are either the reasons for or causes of what the main idea suggests, or they are the results or effects of what the main idea suggests. These sentences usually answer the "what" questions suggested in the main-idea sentence. Words that signal causes include *cause, reason, factor, source,* and *influence*; those suggesting effect are *effect, consequence, result,* and *outcome.*

Read the following paragraph and note how all major-detail sentences provide some suggested causes of poverty:

causes   Some business analysts believe that bankruptcy is *caused* more by economic legislation than by the individual. They contend that a major *source* of bankruptcy is federal and state legislation that influences how a company will survive. They often show that some economic legislation makes it difficult for small companies to make a profit. They contend that a major *reason* for bankruptcy is little or no federal or state contact with the business community concerning the laws it passes.

Do you see how the words *caused, source,* and *reason* signal causes? Do you note as well that these major-detail sentences provide specific information to support the main-idea's point of view that business legislation, not the individual, is the cause of bankruptcy? Finally, note how the word *causes* in the margin reminds you of the kind of information found in this paragraph.

Now look at this paragraph, which deals with the effects of bankruptcy:

effects   Bankruptcy has numerous negative *results* for the individual and society. An individual who files for bankruptcy will have a poor credit rating for several years. *Consequently,* she cannot engage in those business transactions involving bank loans. This in turn *results* in less potential profit for the individual and less taxable income for society. The *outcome* is often a much less confident and secure business person who then shares this insecurity with the larger business community.

Do you see how the signal words, *results, consequently,* and *outcome* suggest a paragraph of effect? Again, note how in the major-detail sentences, you are given specific information concerning the results of bankruptcy. And the word *effects* in the margin becomes your signal that this paragraph is addressing bankruptcy's results.

Major-detail sentences of cause and effect often provide important information. Like steps and examples, they are specific; but unlike examples, causes and effects require you to see relationships in time—how one occurrence may lead to another. You will learn much more about how cause-and-effect details are used in lectures and textbooks in Chapter 6 "Identifying Organizational Patterns."

Remember that in your lecture and reading notes, you should mark major details as examples, steps, characteristics, causes, or effects, as you have done in the previous paragraphs used as illustrations. Actively identifying details gives direction to your reading or listening, and to organizing and connecting information. By identifying details, you will also be able to review this study material for exams.

Signal Words in Major-Detail Sentences.   A number of words and phrases can be used to introduce any type of major detail. Once you become familiar with these words, you will have another way of locating major details in reading materials or lectures.

for example	furthermore	again	last
for instance	moreover	another	of course
in addition	besides	specifically	
also	next	finally	

You should also begin using these words and phrases when you write essays. By using these signal words, you alert your reader to details that you consider important.

Minor Details

By now, you should be able to recognize the four types of major details. So it should be easier for you to locate minor details. You will find minor-detail sentences right after major-detail sentences; minor details provide you with more information about the major detail. When you come upon a minor detail, ask yourself whether you want to include it in your notes. Often, all you need to learn are the main ideas and the major details.

However, you will need to use minor details when you write paragraphs or essays. Adding a minor detail on an essay exam, for example, shows your instructor that you are well prepared. Often a minor-detail sentence picks up a word or phrase that was used in the preceding major-detail sentence.

Look at the following paragraph on inflation, and note that the last sentence further explains the preceding sentences. It is therefore a minor-detail sentence.

> Inflation is defined as a general rise in prices for a long period of time, usually for at least a year. Inflation generally means that what you buy costs more each month, yet your salary does not seem to increase to pay for these higher prices. Therefore, your money does not go as far. *That is, you cannot buy as many items or at the same quality as you did in the previous year.*

Do you see how this last sentence further explains how inflation influences your purchasing power?

You can see more clearly what minor detail sentences are by studying an outline of the previous paragraph. You will note that the minor detail is the material farthest to the right in the outline below—the 1 under B.

I. Inflation—A General Rise in Prices

   A. Items cost more each month
   B. Money does not stretch as far as it once did

      1. You buy fewer items, or they are not as good quality as they once were

Remember that it is the I (main idea) and the A and B (major details) that you often need to write as lecture notes and remember on exams. You may use the 1 (minor detail) more effectively in your essays.

Signal Words for Minor Details. The following words and phrases are frequently used to introduce minor-detail sentences. You should use these words when you introduce minor details in your essays, and you should look for these words to introduce minor details in lectures and textbooks.

a minor point to be made	another way of saying
incidentally	restated
that is to say	namely
in other words	as an aside
of less importance	related to this issue
this is further clarified by	a corollary to this issue
as further clarification	subordinate to this issue

Summary

Major details provide the information necessary to support main ideas. Major details may be examples, steps, characteristics, causes, or effects. They answer the questions "who," "what," "where," "when," "why," "which one(s)," or "what kind(s)." When you can identify the types of major details that are in your reading or listening, you tend to understand the material better. A minor-detail sentence further explains a major-detail sentence that comes before it. Minor details are not often necessary in your reading and lecture notes, but you should use them in essays.

The following summary box should help you see how main ideas, major details, and minor details interrelate.

Summary Box *Main Ideas, Major Details, and Minor Details*

What are they?	Why do you use them?
Main ideas (1): general statements in a paragraph or longer passage	To read and listen more effectively for major and minor details
Major details (A, B, C): support for the main ideas, presented as examples, steps, characteristics, causes, or effects.	To understand the main idea better. To see whether the main idea is based on sound evidence.
Minor details (1, 2, 3): further support for the major-detail sentence that comes before it.	To further explain a major detail. Used in essays, but often not necessary in reading or lecture notes.

Skills Practice Topic: Business

All the exercises in this chapter deal with the issue of business, a topic you may study in college and one you face every day as you make purchases.

Before you begin these exercises, answer the following questions either individually or in small groups to get some sense of what you already know about business matters. Remember that recalling what you know is effective preparation for learning new material:

1. What do you think is studied in an introductory college business course?
2. What are the most common problems facing small and large businesses today?
3. What do you think makes a successful small business?
4. What do you think makes a successful large business or corporation?

Exercise 5.1
Locating Major
Details

Under each of the following ten main-idea sentences are five sentences, three of which support the main-idea sentence. The other two sentences are either minor details or main-idea sentences that would themselves introduce a new topic. Place the letters of the three major-detail sentences in the answer box.

All the sentences in these exercises address the issue of the unincorporated American business, an important introductory concept for students studying business. Unincorporated simply means a business that is not legally separate from its owners.

The Unincorporated American Business

1. *Main-idea sentence:* A business owned by one person is called a sole proprietorship.

   a. This is the oldest form of business.
   b. It is also the most common type of business, with 73 percent of all businesses in the United States being sole proprietorships.
   c. That is, almost three out of four businesses in the United States are sole proprietorships.
   d. There are many advantages to the sole proprietorship business.
   e. Yet sole proprietorships contribute only 6 percent of the total business revenues in the United States.

2. *Main-idea sentence:* There are five basic categories in which sole proprietorships operate.

   a. The largest is the service category, or a business that serves others.
   b. The second largest category includes wholesale and retail trade.

    c. An example of a small service business would be a neighborhood barbershop.

    d. The last three categories, in order of size, include manufacturing, construction, and insurance.

    e. Sole proprietorships are relatively inexpensive to create.

3. *Main-idea sentence:* Sole proprietorships are advantageous because they are easy to operate.

    a. Once a business person has decided on what product to sell or what service to perform, she is ready to start.

    b. There are also very few legal restrictions attached to sole proprietorships.

    c. Finally, as sole owner, the sole proprietor can claim all the profits.

    d. That is, the better the business, the more money the sole proprietor makes.

    e. Yet there are some disadvantages to being a sole proprietor.

4. *Main-idea sentence:* The major disadvantage to being a sole proprietor is that she is liable for anything that may go wrong in the business.

    a. If the business goes into debt, for instance, the sole proprietor must pay what she owes from her own personal savings.

    b. One restaurant owner's business did poorly, and the bank repossessed her car.

    c. Further, the sole proprietor may have limited funds to expand her business.

    d. A sole proprietorship is different from a partnership.

    e. The sole proprietorship may also have limited business and management skills needed to steer her business in the right direction.

5. *Main-idea sentence:* A partnership is another major form of small business where two or more people co-own a business for profit.

    a. In the best of circumstances, each partner brings a different ability to the business.

    b. There are several advantages to a partnership business.

    c. In a partnership, there is often more money to draw from than in a sole proprietorship.

    d. A partnership allows for the members to discuss a business decision before making it.

    e. Incidentally, making the right decision can make or break a small business.

6. *Main-idea sentence:* As with any form of business, there are disadvantages to a partnership form of small business.

    a. As with a sole proprietorship, each partner is liable for the debts the business may accrue.

    b. A partnership may dissolve if one of its members chooses to back out.

c. Moreover, there is often the possibility that partners may begin as friends and then find that they are continually disagreeing.

d. The two types of partnerships are the general and the limited.

e. A joint venture is a special type of partnership.

7. *Main-idea sentence:* A joint venture is a special type of partnership where two or more people agree to complete a specific project.

a. Once this project is completed, the joint venture dissolves.

b. For a general partnership to be dissolved, each partner must agree.

c. A limited partnership has a limited start-up cost.

d. During the joint venture, the partners are responsible for all the debts the venture may accrue, as with a sole proprietorship.

e. One finds joint ventures often in the real estate business.

8. *Main-idea sentence:* Joint ventures are popular in the real estate business for three important reasons.

a. First, each person contributes to the money needed to purchase a property.

b. Second, these members of the joint venture can buy a large piece of property, one they could probably not afford by themselves.

c. Joint ventures are exciting for anyone who wants to quickly enter the business field.

d. Finally, these members of the joint venture can develop, divide, or resell this large piece of property.

e. Any profit derived from a small business is considered income, according to the Internal Revenue Service.

9. *Main-idea sentence:* It is one thing to form a partnership, another to make this partnership successful.

a. Cooperation is the key to any successful business partnership.

b. By cooperation, I mean identifying areas of agreement over how the business should be run.

c. Another way to help a partnership be successful is to establish clear goals for the business.

d. Psychologists have also shown that partners who work well together have a positive attitude toward the success of their partnership.

e. That is, each partner needs to focus on the strengths of the other members of the partnership.

10. *Main-idea sentence:* Not all joint ventures involve individuals with limited capital.

a. Completing short-term projects is the main function of joint ventures.

1. ___ ___ ___

2. ___ ___ ___

3. ___ ___ ___

4. ___ ___ ___

5. ___ ___ ___

6. ___ ___ ___

7. ___ ___ ___

8. ___ ___ ___

9. ___ ___ ___

10. ___ ___ ___

—————
70%

(score = number correct × 10 + ten bonus points) Find answers on p. 392.

   b. The tissue manufacturer, Kimberly-Clark, formed a joint venture
      with a large German tissue manufacturer.
   c. Hewlett-Packard and a large Swedish company worked on a joint
      venture concerning a computer network program.
   d. Finally, the beer company, Anheuser-Busch, teamed up with Ki-
      rin, a Japanese beer company, to boost their sales.
   e. For this venture to get off the ground, Anheuser-Busch provided
      $80 million.*

Exercise 5.2
Identifying Types of
Major Details

The following paragraphs present different kinds of details to support
the main-idea sentences. Your job is to read each paragraph and identify
the kind of detail that is used. Write in the answer box *EX* if the details
are examples, *ST* if the details are steps, *CH* if the details are characteristics, *CS* if the details are causes, and *EF* if the details are effects. The
signal words used in some of the paragraphs should help you recognize
the kinds of details that are used.

All of the paragraphs deal with the business concept of a corporation, which is different from the unincorporated businesses you studied
in the previous exercise.

The Business Corporation

1. A corporation is defined as a legal form of a business authorized by
   a government and considered separate from its owners. One can
   characterize a corporation in the following ways. Most important, it
   is a separate entity not in partnership with its owners, who are called
   shareholders or stockholders. It is human-like in that it can be sued
   or can sue as an independent citizen. In a sense, it is stronger than
   its owners because it does not cease to exist when its owners have
   passed away.

2. How does one form a corporation? The process first involves applying to the appropriate state official for a form titled a Certificate of
   Incorporation. Once this certificate has been approved by the state,
   the corporation has an official charter that describes the corporation's type of business and its purpose. Any change in its purpose or
   business dealings requires the members of the corporation to file a
   separate form, called a charter amendment, with the state.

3. There are three common types of corporations. The first type of
   corporation, called a domestic corporation, does business within the
   state that approved its application. A second type is a foreign corporation, which does business in the other forty-nine states of the

*Adapted from Joseph T. Straub and Raymond F. Attner, *Introduction to Business*, 5th ed.
(Belmont, Calif.: Wadsworth, 1994), pp. 71–87.

United States. Finally, a corporation doing business outside of the United States is known as an alien corporation.

4. How would one describe a closed corporation, that is, one that does not sell its stock to the general public? It is more secretive because it can conceal information about its finances. A closed corporation is less burdened with red tape, or state papers that must be completed by an open or public corporation. Also, the managers of a closed corporation may be more focused on the well-being of their company because they are not required to make formal reports and hold regular meetings with their stockholders.

5. Some closed corporations decide to go public—become open corporations. What are some of the possible results? First, if the economy is good, the stock sold to new shareholders could bring a quick increase in revenues to the corporation. But if the economy is depressed, the stock may yield much less income than the original owners had anticipated. And as an open corporation, the once-closed corporation may also be forced to reveal many of its trade secrets.

6. What are some of the events scheduled on the yearly calendar for a public corporation? First, management must report to its stockholders in an annual or semi-annual report, which discloses the financial condition of the corporation. Afterwards, the public corporation is required to schedule an annual stockholders' meeting whose date each year must be in the corporation's by-laws. Here, the stockholders can question any of the decisions made by the company during that fiscal year.

7. What influences corporations to join with others, as many do each year in the United States and abroad? Some corporations merge with other corporations to increase their profits. Still others point to a need for greater efficiency as their major reason for merging. Finally, most corporations that merge contend that their desire to be more competitive is their primary motivation.

8. A corporate merger occurs when two or more companies become a single company. Major mergers have occurred several times in American history, and they often involve billions of dollars. Powerful companies like United States Steel, DuPont, and Standard Oil are examples of mergers that occurred at the turn of this century. Recently, a part of the telecommunications giant ITT merged with a French corporation for $3.6 billion. In this same year (1992), 2,578 mergers were announced.

9. How would one describe a nonprofit corporation? They are often concerned with educational, religious, charitable, or cultural issues. They cannot make a profit, as their name suggests, but can have a cash surplus, which must be used to improve the corpora-

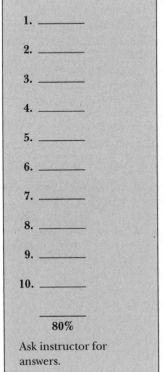

1. _____

2. _____

3. _____

4. _____

5. _____

6. _____

7. _____

8. _____

9. _____

10. _____

_____
80%

Ask instructor for answers.

tion in some way, such as its facilities, services, or personnel. Some of the most successful nonprofit corporations are truly philanthropic, helping those people who cannot help themselves or be helped by government assistance.

10. What are some of the most widely known nonprofit corporations in the United States today? The single largest type of nonprofit organization in the country is private colleges and universities, whose profits must be reinvested in some aspect of the institution. The American Cancer Society, one of the largest cancer research institutions, is also nonprofit. Even the American Automobile Association is a nonprofit organization.*

Exercise 5.3
Identifying Main Ideas, Major Details, and Minor Details

The following paragraphs contain main-idea sentences, major-detail sentences, and minor-detail sentences. Read each paragraph carefully. Then, next to the appropriate number in the answer box, write *MN* for main-idea sentence, *MA* for major-detail sentence, and *MI* for minor-detail sentence. Look for transition words that signal the kind of sentence each one is.

The ten paragraphs define the key business terms involving payments. You will learn how concepts like rent, interest, wages, and profit are related.

Payments and Related Issues

(1) Payments are made to owners of property or business for a variety of reasons. (2) Landowners receive rent. (3) This rent is often paid monthly but may be paid weekly. (4) Owners of businesses receive payments in the form of interest on their investments.

(5) Rent is defined in business as the money one pays for the use of land. (6) Rent is determined by how profitable the land is to the owner and how much the renter is willing to pay. (7) Clearly, owners want to make a profit on their property. (8) Equally clearly, renters want the rent to be less than what the property earns or what they make as wages.

(9) In a business sense, wages are similar to rent. (10) In this case, employers buy the labor of their employees. (11) Employers want to know that their employees are making a profit for the business. (12) That is to say, owners want what the workers do for the company to bring in more money than the cost of their salaries.

(13) But wages do not always work out so neatly. (14) Some people earn more than they are really worth, and others earn less. (15) Some people criticize movie stars' and athletes' high salaries, arguing that they would gladly work for less if others in their field earned less as well. (16) A corollary to this issue is that some athletes earn several million dollars a year.

(17) Some people are blocked from advancing to another job because of racial discrimination. (18) Others are kept in the same unsatis-

1.	_____
2.	_____
3.	_____
4.	_____
5.	_____
6.	_____
7.	_____
8.	_____
9.	_____
10.	_____
11.	_____
12.	_____
13.	_____
14.	_____
15.	_____
16.	_____
17.	_____

*Adapted from Straub and Attner, *Introduction to Business*, pp. 92–115.

18. _____

19. _____

20. _____

21. _____

22. _____

23. _____

24. _____

25. _____

26. _____

27. _____

28. _____

29. _____

30. _____

31. _____

32. _____

33. _____

34. _____

35. _____

36. _____

37. _____

38. _____

39. _____

40. _____

_____
75%

(score = # correct × 2.5)
Find answers on p. 392.

fying position because of their age. (19) Still others do not have the extra money to be trained in a field they are particularly interested in pursuing. (20) All of these job factors are known in economics as *barriers to entry.*

(21) A term related to wages is *capital.* (22) Capital includes products such as tools, equipment, and buildings. (23) Tools and equipment, incidentally, include items used by workers in their particular jobs. (24) A word processor would thus be part of the equipment used by a secretary.

(25) What constitutes the capital of fishermen in a primitive tribe? (26) The nets used to catch the fish would, of course, be part of their capital. (27) The value of a fishnet in business terms is how much profit it can create. (28) That is to say, if a fishnet can allow the fisherman to catch more fish than before, then it is capital that provides for profit.

(29) Profit is different for an independent businessperson than it is for a wage earner. (30) If your concession stand can make you $500 a week, but you can earn $510 a week working for a larger fast-food business, then your stand is not making you a profit. (31) To make a profit in your own business, you must be able to earn more than what you would earn as a wage earner. (32) Analysts believe that independent businesspeople should earn more than wage earners because they are taking greater risks.

(33) How much profit is considered good enough for an independent businessperson? (34) There is no fixed percentage. (35) That is, there is no number that will tell a businessperson that the business is profitable. (36) Psychological factors are involved, such as how much you value working for yourself.

(37) Clearly, rent, wages, profit, and capital are closely related. (38) When people consider the profit of a particular investment, they must factor in issues like rent and wages. (39) They must also determine how much capital they must purchase initially and must replace in time. (40) As an aside, note that it is often the initial cost of capital investments that discourages businesspeople from going into a particular venture.*

_____

*Adapted from Philip C. Starr, *Economics: Principles in Action*, 5th ed. (Belmont, Calif.: Wadsworth, 1988), pp. 22–24.

Exercise 5.4
Writing Effective
Topic Sentences

In composition textbooks, main-idea sentences are often called topic sentences. *Topic sentences* are general statements usually found at the beginning of a paragraph. Like main-idea statements, topic sentences direct the reader to what the paragraph will say.

Effective topic sentences are neither too specific nor too general. They should steer the reader to the details of support and not become details of support themselves.

Look at the following ineffective topic sentences and their revisions:

1. A sole proprietorship is a business. (too general)
A sole proprietorship is a business owned by one person. (acceptable)

Note that the first sentence does not mention the kind of business a sole proprietorship is. Effective topic sentences clearly identify the "what" of an issue.

2. Being a business partner may be disadvantageous. (too general)
Being a business partner may be disadvantageous because one or more of the partners may not agree on important issues. (acceptable)

Note how the revised sentence introduces a reason why a partnership may not succeed. In this case, the revised sentence clarifies the "why" of the general topic sentence.

3. The business partners were taught to take time out when they began to argue. (too specific)
The psychologist provided the partners with a helpful time-out strategy they could use to help resolve their differences. (acceptable)

Do you see that the example of the partners taking time out when they argue would be better used as a supporting detail after the topic sentence introducing the psychologist's strategy?

Your task is to determine whether the following ten topic sentences are too general or too specific. Write in the answer box "general" or "specific." Then revise the topic sentences, making them more effective. These sentences have been taken from the material you have studied in Exercises 5.1–5.3. Review these exercises before or while you complete this assignment to gather information for your responses.

1. Three out of four businesses in the United States are sole proprietorships.

Revision: _____

2. A joint venture is a type of partnership.

Revision: _____

3. A corporation does not cease to exist when its owners have passed away.

   Revision: _____

4. One type of corporation is a closed corporation.

   Revision: _____

5. Public corporations must schedule certain events.

   Revision: _____

6. In 1992, a part of ITT merged with a French corporation for $3.6 billion.

   Revision: _____

7. Another type of organization is a nonprofit corporation.

   Revision: _____

8. A word processor is an example of equipment a secretary uses.

   Revision: _____

9. In business, rent is defined in a certain way.

   Revision: _____

10. Profit is another important business term.

    Revision: _____

1. _____

2. _____

3. _____

4. _____

5. _____

6. _____

7. _____

8. _____

9. _____

10. _____

80%

Ask instructor for answers.

Exercise 5.5
Locating Major and
Minor Details in a
Longer Passage

In this exercise, you will be reading a longer passage that briefly traces the history of American business. It should help you understand how large and small American businesses have changed over the centuries.

Your job is to read for the main idea, major details, and minor details. After you have read the passage, answer the ten questions. You may return to the passage as you answer the questions. Place the answers to the first five questions in the answer box.

A Short History of American Business

(1) American business has changed drastically over the past 200 years. Much of this change has come about because of the technology,

wealth, and power that large American corporations have amassed over these years.

(2) Before 1800, American business was largely structured upon the production and sales of agriculture. American farmers and businessmen did much of their business with England. The Americans often exported precious metals and agricultural products to England in exchange for finished goods like furniture and machines. Most of American industry was based on the cottage system, where goods were made at home.

(3) The Industrial Revolution, which began around 1750, changed the way Americans produced their goods. Large machines were now used, and workers moved from their homes to factories to work. These workers made products in great quantities, a working system known as mass production. Moreover, the reaper on the farms in the Midwest allowed for more grain to be planted and harvested, while the telegraph and the railroad allowed products to be sold and transported more quickly than before.

(4) Between 1850 and 1930, the United States became a modern industrial giant. All types of production were now available within American boundaries, so the United States did not need to rely on Europe to produce its machinery. That is, the United States became more independent industrially. Also, American money was in greater supply because of better banking systems and the development of a national treasury.

(5) Since the end of World War II, the United States has become the leading industrial power in the world. American industry has many strengths. First, it has a sophisticated technology, which allows the United States to produce advanced technical products. It is also a wealthy country so it can produce these products in large quantities and frequently conduct ongoing research to develop new products and improve old ones. Finally, the United States has managerial talent so that its administrators can oversee what is produced and provide for a more efficient business operation.

(6) What recent business developments have suggested to analysts in the United States is that to stay successful, American business must be very sensitive to changes in the market and must be prepared to change quickly to respond to the market's demands. When a business does not respond rapidly to change, it may very soon go out of business. Three American industries that are vitally connected to change are telecommunications, transportation, and computers. That is, in each of these fields, the technology is changing at such a staggering rate that sophisticated technology and accurate marketing research are essential.*

1. The topic of this passage is

   a. change in American history
   b. the power of technology in America

---

*Adapted from Straub and Attner, pp. 20–22.

   c. the historical role of technology, wealth, and power in American business practices

   d. the power of American corporations in the past century

2. The main idea of paragraph 2 concerns

   a. the agricultural emphasis of American business before 1800

   b. agriculture and American business

   c. how Americans exported precious metals to England before 1800

   d. how Americans imported machinery from England before 1800

3. Which is *not* a major detail in paragraph 3?

   a. Large machines replaced small ones during the Industrial Revolution.

   b. The Industrial Revolution changed the ways Americans produced their goods.

   c. Mass production became a popular form of labor during the Industrial Revolution.

   d. The reaper revolutionized the way grain was harvested.

4. A minor detail presented in paragraph 4 is

   a. The United States became an industrial giant between 1850 and 1930.

   b. American money was in greater supply between 1850 and 1930 than in previous years.

   c. Americans were able to construct their own machinery between 1850 and 1930.

   d. The United States developed industrial independence between 1850 and 1930.

5. The first sentence in paragraph 5 is a

   a. major-detail sentence

   b. minor-detail sentence

   c. main-idea sentence

   d. topic for the entire excerpt

6. List one major detail in paragraph 2. ⎯⎯⎯⎯⎯⎯⎯⎯⎯⎯⎯⎯

⎯⎯⎯⎯⎯⎯⎯⎯⎯⎯⎯⎯⎯⎯⎯⎯⎯⎯⎯⎯⎯⎯⎯⎯⎯⎯⎯⎯⎯⎯⎯⎯⎯

7. What is the main idea of paragraph 3? ⎯⎯⎯⎯⎯⎯⎯⎯⎯⎯⎯

⎯⎯⎯⎯⎯⎯⎯⎯⎯⎯⎯⎯⎯⎯⎯⎯⎯⎯⎯⎯⎯⎯⎯⎯⎯⎯⎯⎯⎯⎯⎯⎯⎯

8. List one major detail in paragraph 3. ⎯⎯⎯⎯⎯⎯⎯⎯⎯⎯⎯

⎯⎯⎯⎯⎯⎯⎯⎯⎯⎯⎯⎯⎯⎯⎯⎯⎯⎯⎯⎯⎯⎯⎯⎯⎯⎯⎯⎯⎯⎯⎯⎯⎯

1. ⎯⎯⎯⎯⎯

2. ⎯⎯⎯⎯⎯

3. ⎯⎯⎯⎯⎯

4. ⎯⎯⎯⎯⎯

5. ⎯⎯⎯⎯⎯

⎯⎯⎯⎯⎯
80%
(score = number correct × 10)
Find answers on p. 392.

9. What is the main idea of paragraph 6? _____

_____

10. What type of detail is presented in the last sentence of paragraph 6? What is the signal word or phrase that suggests the kind of detail

it is? _____

_____

Exercise 5.6
Locating Major and
Minor Details in
Second Longer
Passage

In this exercise, you will be reading a longer passage that explains the three major economic systems in our world. It should help explain further how economic terms like *capital, wages,* and *profit* are used in studying a country's economic system.

Your job is to read for main ideas, major details, and minor details. After you have read the passage, answer the ten questions. If necessary, you may return to the passage while you answer the questions. Write your answers to the first five questions in the answer box.

Socialism, Communism, and Capitalism

(1) Today the world seems to be divided into three types of economies: socialism, communism, and capitalism. Communism and socialism seem to be more closely related to each other than they are to capitalism. But careful study reveals that even socialism and communism have important differences.

(2) What are the major features of socialism? In socialism, the government plays an important role, controlling all of the major industries. There are many different kinds of socialism. For example, in France and Italy the government controls many of the major industries. In the People's Republic of China, the government owns and operates much of the country's industry.

(3) One must keep in mind that socialism is not dictatorship. That is, in most socialist countries the people can still vote in free elections. In many socialist countries, the government is trying to control some or many industries in order to provide more jobs for its people and prevent serious economic declines.

(4) Communism can be seen as an extreme form of socialism. In theory, communists believe that the people, not the government, run the country. All of its people work together and take from the country only what they need. Theoretically, no one would want to earn a huge salary. No country has as yet reached this communist ideal. Countries like the People's Republic of China, which is seen by others as a communist country, exert a tremendous amount of government control over their people.

(5) Like communism, capitalism is also an economic system in theory only. In a capitalistic society, people, not government, own property. Also, people are free to choose their own occupation and earn the

amount of money they want. That is, capitalism emphasizes self-interest. Competition is encouraged, not discouraged as it would be in communism.

(6) No capitalistic country follows these ideals to the letter. In capitalistic countries like the United States, the government does control some industries, like transportation and utilities, and wholesale competition is sometimes discouraged if people or industries are treating other people unfairly. Some economists have called this more realistic type of capitalism *mixed capitalism.**

1. The topic of the passage is

   a. a definition of socialism
   b. a description of communism
   c. a definition of capitalism
   d. all of these

2. The main idea of paragraph 2 concerns

   a. socialism in France and Italy
   b. how socialism as an economic system differs from country to country
   c. reasons why the People's Republic of China controls much of its industry
   d. how socialism differs from communism

3. A major detail presented in paragraph 3 is

   a. most citizens in socialist countries can vote
   b. socialism is not dictatorship
   c. socialism provides fewer jobs to its people than dictatorships do
   d. there are never economic declines in socialist countries

4. The major details in paragraph 4 include all *but*

   a. communists believe that the people run the country
   b. the citizens from a communist country take only what they need
   c. in theory, there would be no rich people in a communist country
   d. the People's Republic of China comes closest to being a true communist state

5. The last sentence in paragraph 5 is a

   a. major-detail sentence
   b. minor-detail sentence
   c. main-idea sentence
   d. topic sentence

6. What is the main idea of paragraph 3? _____

_____

1. _____

2. _____

3. _____

4. _____

5. _____

_____

*Adapted from Starr, *Economics*, pp. 29–30.

7. What is the main idea of paragraph 4? _____

_____

8. List one major detail from paragraph 5. _____

_____

9. What is the main idea of paragraph 6? _____

_____

10. List a major detail from paragraph 6. _____

_____

80%

Ask instructor for answers.

Exercise 5.7
Writing Your Own
Paragraph from
Main Ideas, Major
Details, and Minor
Details

Now go back to the passage on economic systems in Exercise 5.6 and locate its main idea (found in paragraph 1); the four major details (found in paragraphs 2, 4, 5, and 6); and the minor detail (found in paragraph 3). Jot down this information in the following outline:

I. _____

    A. _____

       1. _____

    B. _____

    C. _____

    D. _____

From this outline, answer the following essay question. Use only the outline to answer this question.

Essay question: Identify the three major economic systems in the world today, and briefly describe each.

70%

Ask instructor for answers.

Exercise 5.8
Determining Main
Ideas and Major
Details in a Textbook
Excerpt

The following is an excerpt from a textbook chapter on small businesses. It adds more information to the first exercise on the unincorporated business, focusing on how the small businessperson should prepare to launch a successful business. Read through this excerpt quickly to get a sense of the topic. Then go back and read it slowly.

When you finish rereading, answer the following five questions. You may return to the excerpt in deciding on your answers. Place the answers to the first five questions in the answer box.

Small Businesses

Small Business Administration (SBA) A federal government agency started in 1953 to give financial and managerial assistance to owners of small businesses.

(1) The more than 10 million small businesses in the United States account for more than 40 percent of the country's gross national product (these totals do not include farms or farm production). These companies provide livelihoods for their owners and employees while creating goods and services for millions of people.

(2) Small-business owners require a unique combination of characteristics. Seeking economic independence outside the boundaries of traditional jobs and large, formalized employers, these individuals combine courage, determination, resourcefulness, ambition, self-confidence, and optimism into a business enterprise as unique as they are. The pioneer spirit is alive and well in dens, garages, small stores, and utility sheds nationwide.

(3) According to the SBA, small businesses with fewer than 500 employees account for approximately 90 percent of all businesses in the United States and provide more than half of all jobs in existence. The impact that small companies have on employment has become especially significant in recent years. *Fortune* magazine reports that small businesses accounted for 11.3 million of the 16.5 million net new jobs created between 1977 and 1987 and provided nearly all of the 2.7 million net new jobs created between 1988 and 1990. On the other hand, large companies *eliminated* 500,000 jobs during that time. Small businesses, then, form a fundamental and significant pattern in today's economic tapestry.

(4) In this chapter we will discuss starting and maintaining a small business and investigate the pros and cons of franchising. The discussion will be of special value to those who are planning to start their own companies or who have already done so.

A Board of Advisers

(5) Input from an experienced lawyer, a certified public accountant, and an insurance counselor is vital to an infant business, helping pave the way to later prosperity. Few small-business owners are qualified to provide their own legal, accounting, or insurance advice.

(6) Finding a competent professional in each of these fields is a challenge. One way is to ask friends and business acquaintances for recommendations. Local newspapers often interview outstanding local professionals who have earned special awards or recognition. Such service clubs as Rotary or Lions International usually have members who are active in these areas. The business owner must make an organized and thoughtful search; the people selected will be the firm's navigators, advising its owner, the pilot, on the direction he or she should take.

(7) **Lawyer** A lawyer provides in-depth legal advice on choosing forms of business organization. If an owner decides to incorporate, a lawyer can prepare the required forms, using the legal language needed to give the company maximum operating flexibility under its charter.

The lawyer can also help by drawing up a partnership agreement for a business choosing that form.

(8) In addition, a competent lawyer can help the small-business owner avoid legal confusion in such areas as:

- Contracts with outside parties (suppliers, landlords, creditors, customers, and service and repair firms)
- Liability for customer and employee injuries and for injuries caused by a product, service, or operating method
- Compliance with government regulatory agencies (Federal Trade Commission, Department of Justice, Occupational Safety and Health Administration, and others)

(9) **Accountant** An accountant helps ensure the financial success of a business venture. Certified public accountants provide advice on the tax aspects of operating as a sole proprietorship, a partnership, or a corporation and custom-build accounting systems to suit the legal and operating characteristics of a company. More specifically, an accountant helps a business owner:

- Determine how much beginning capital the firm requires
- Make decisions to lease or purchase major fixed assets
- Project cash collections and payouts to ensure that the firm has an adequate supply of cash on hand at all times
- Choose methods for raising short-term and long-term capital
- Manage finances so the owner receives the most favorable federal and state income tax treatment possible

insurance counselor An adviser who recommends a comprehensive program to protect a firm against insurable risks and to meet legal or quasi-legal insurance requirements.

(10) **Insurance Counselor** A business's insurance counselor *is an adviser who recommends a comprehensive program to protect a firm against insurable risks and to meet legal or quasi-legal insurance requirements*, including workers' compensation insurance, mortgage insurance, or insurance required by a building lease. This risk expert should have the same professional concern for a firm's success as its lawyer and accountant. A conscientious insurance counselor should maintain close ties with the owner, recommending changes in coverage when changes occur in the company's size, the kinds of risks it faces, or the owner's personal circumstances.

Starting a Small Business

(11) Entrepreneurs must comply with various legal requirements associated with starting a business and must understand the key factors that affect a company's success and profitability. Each of these elements should be reflected in a comprehensive business plan.

(12) **Legal Requirements** Small-business owners must follow several legal steps before offering a product or service to the public. That includes obtaining any necessary documents and approvals.

zoning ordinances City and county regulations defining the type of business activity that can be conducted at certain locations.

(13) First, the business must meet applicable **zoning ordinances,** which are *city and county regulations defining the type of business activity that can be conducted at certain locations.* The firm must also obtain city and county business permits, and perhaps a state occupational license, if setting up shop as a cosmetologist, realtor, barber, electrician, or some

other state-regulated profession. Local government officials will also inspect a company's building to verify that it conforms to local fire and safety codes. Retailers, who act as sales-tax collection agents for the state, must contact the state revenue department for registration forms and instructions on how to collect and pay sales tax.

(14) The Internal Revenue Service (IRS) has various reporting requirements that affect every type of business. This agency provides a Business Tax Kit that describes the many taxes, deductions, and payment schedules companies must be aware of.

(15) Most firms have to conform to a state's fictitious-name act. This means that if the name of the business is not simply the name or names of its owners, the owners' names must be registered at the county courthouse and published along with the company's name in the Legal Notices section of the newspaper.

(16) Your advisers can provide detailed information on additional steps required in your city, county, and state.

(17) **Factors to Consider**   Infant companies have a fairly high mortality rate. The Dun & Bradstreet Corporation reports that approximately 36 percent of all business failures occur within the first 5 years. The early years, then, are usually the most critical in a firm's life. There are many tasks to accomplish, and the owner's success in doing them will determine the success he or she will enjoy in the business.

(18) EXPERIENCE   Any aspiring business owner should get experience in the line of business. Knowledge of finance, customer relations, marketing, inventory purchasing, personnel requirements, management, and technological developments is essential. Ira H. Latimer, executive vice-president of the American Federation of Small Business, suggests that would-be owners first become an employee in the kind of business they plan to start. They should avoid dead-end jobs that will isolate them from the rest of the organization and strive to become involved in every area of the company's business, however unfamiliar at first.

(19) Experience doesn't have to come through one's main job, of course. A Department of Labor survey of people who worked two jobs revealed that, while 44 percent did so to pay their regular bills, almost 15 percent took a second job to gain career experience or to build a business that they might someday operate as their major source of income.

(20) Dun & Bradstreet reports that 12 percent of all business failures are caused by the owner's inexperience. More than 56 percent of all companies that fail due to the owner's inexperience fail because the owner (1) doesn't know enough about the kind of business he or she has entered or (2) hasn't obtained adequate management experience—intimate, firsthand knowledge of the planning, organizing, staffing, directing, and controlling functions.

(21) Dun & Bradstreet, the nation's major source of statistics on business failures, reported that 96,857 businesses failed in one recent year alone. The effects of these failures extend far beyond the owners themselves, however, because companies never operate in a vacuum. Shock waves from a failed company have an impact on many groups—employees, creditors, suppliers, customers, and governmental bodies

(through lost tax revenue), to name just a few. Those 96,857 failed companies left behind debts of more than $91 billion.

(22) It is not necessary to start small to get the needed experience, though. Many small-business owners learn the basics of sound management in a large firm, then apply them to a small company of their own. Basic management practices remain the same regardless of a company's size. Some business owners have worked for low pay or even as volunteers to learn the basics of an industry, with an eye to the day when they would become their own boss. Keeping a diary of this work experience reinforces learning and helps make the most of the time spent. Courses and self-education supplement the lessons of experience. Business owners can also exchange ideas with one another by participating in service clubs and trade associations.

(23) CAPITAL   It is essential to start with sufficient capital. A company with inadequate financing is like a rowboat with a hole in the bottom: given enough time, it is bound to sink. Some small-business owners dream and save for so long that they reach the end of their patience and open the business come hell or high water. Rather than start a company on a shoestring, it is best either to wait until there is enough capital to ensure success or to begin on a smaller scale than originally planned. Both accountants and trade associations can help potential business owners decide whether they have enough capital to make a sound beginning.

(24) How much capital does a business need? There is no easy answer. It depends on such variables as location, credit terms given by suppliers, distance from markets, and the nature of the product or service. It may take a construction company several months to complete its first projects, for example, but the owner must meet weekly payrolls, buy materials, make payments on leased or purchased equipment, maintain office facilities, and pay insurance premiums, taxes, utilities, and other business expenses in the meantime. These payments demand a large fund of operating capital.

(25) LOCATION   The business owner needs to pick a sound site for operations, a spot that favors the desired type of customer and the product or service that the firm will provide. A wag once declared that the three keys to business success are "location, location, and location." Neighboring businesses should be complementary. Undesirable neighbors can repel traffic, while several businesses with supporting lines or comparable target markets attract more customers than any one of them could alone. Many businesspeople also realize today that there is strength in numbers. This factor accounts for automobile alleys—rows of competing car dealers lined up next to each other—and shopping centers with two or more major department stores.

(26) Site selection decisions often require a traffic study—an analysis of the traffic pattern around a location to confirm what type of person drives by, when, and why. Ideally, many people in the target area will need what the business sells and will find easy access to the premises. Traffic lights, pedestrian safety islands, and other traffic modifcations should make it possible for customers to stop with a minimum of inconvenience. It also helps to consider plans for future street and highway

improvements or business and housing developments. Such changes can make the area the hub or rim of traffic.

(27) LEASE   If a business owner decides to rent a facility, a lawyer should review the lease and explain what the tenant and the landlord are responsible for. Some business owners like to negotiate a short-term lease with an option to renew for a longer period, so they can see how the location actually works out before making a long-term commitment.

(28) CUSTOMER DEMOGRAPHICS   Before business owners can create effective advertising, sales promotion, or personal selling appeals, they must know customers' demographics. These are statistics on such subjects as age, income, marital status, recreational habits, and ethnic customs for people who live within a given geographic area. United States Bureau of the Census tracts help here, providing data on income, social characteristics, and occupations for as broad or as narrow an area as necessary. By combining census data with demographic reports from the chamber of commerce and the city and county government, business owners can define the population features of their trading areas clearly and accurately.

(29) INVENTORY MANAGEMENT   Demographic knowledge enables business owners to identify the most popular items to carry in inventory. Businesspeople who stock excessive inventory use too much storage space and pay too much for recordkeeping and insurance. Furthermore, the dollars invested in unneeded merchandise could be better spent on improved marketing efforts or more modern facilities and equipment. An understocked inventory is just as serious. The business can lose sales, goodwill, and customer loyalty if it cannot satisfy the needs of its clientele.

(30) Major suppliers and trade associations provide information on seasonal trends and buying practices to help retailers stock the correct inventory at the desired levels throughout the year.

(31) COMPETITION   Still another aspect of running a successful small business is analyzing the practices of competitors. What do they do exceptionally well? Where could they improve? An alert newcomer, after observing the ways established competitors do business, can use their most effective practices and procedures from the beginning and avoid measures that they have found too costly, inefficient, or unproductive. One should examine competitors' approaches to such subjects as price, inventory selection, service, customer conveniences, and employee relations before committing oneself to any policy.

(32) CONDITION OF THE BUSINESS   An entrepreneur who buys an existing business rather than starting from scratch must investigate the business thoroughly. The prospective buyer's lawyer and accountant should obtain records that fairly present the business's legal and financial condition. A sole proprietor who claims that a business has earned $35,000 a year should be able to document that claim by showing copies of his or her personal income tax returns, for example. Equipment and merchandise should be physically inspected to verify its age and condition. Responsibility for any repairs should be clearly stated in the sales agreement between the current owner and the prospective owner. One novice restaurant owner who closed a deal without verifying the equipment inventory thought he was buying twenty more chairs

demographics Statistics on such subjects as age, income, marital status, recreational habits, and ethnic customs for people who live within a given geographic area.

than the building actually contained. On top of that, the seller had stopped servicing the equipment, which required expensive overhauling just after the sale was closed.

(33) The buyer also should obtain a clear statement of which items will stay with the business and which will be taken by the seller, covering such things as drapes, special fixtures, paintings, wall hangings, and display equipment.

(34) FINANCIAL RECORDS   Doing it right the first time means keeping accurate and timely financial records. Knowing the current balances of accounts receivable and payable, levels of inventory, sales, expenses, and payment due dates gives an owner a view of the company's financial picture and of marketing trends and overall profitability. A certified public accountant (CPA) can develop an orderly accounting system that a bookkeeper can maintain with minimal effort. Sound and accurate accounting records let you monitor your financial condition from one period to the next and chart a course for success.*

1. The topic of this excerpt concerns:

   a. how small businesses fail
   b. resources for starting a small business
   c. where to set up a small business
   d. the finances necessary to set up a small business

2. The main-idea sentence of paragraph 3 is:

   a. found in the first sentence
   b. found in the third sentence
   c. found in the last sentence
   d. implied

3. A major detail *not* mentioned in paragraph 8 is:

   a. a good lawyer provides important legal advice for a small business owner
   b. a good lawyer interprets contracts with outside parties for the small business owner
   c. a good lawyer can provide information on customer liability for the small business owner
   d. a good lawyer can provide information on government regulatory agencies for the small business owner

4. A major detail *not* mentioned in paragraph 10 is:

   a. a business insurance counselor is an advisor on insurance and legal matters related to the law
   b. a business insurance counselor should be as concerned with the small business as an attorney.

---

*Straub and Attner, *Introduction to Business*, pp. 120–128.

c. a business counselor should keep in close contact with the small business owner.

d. a business insurance counselor is just like a lawyer.

5. A major detail mentioned in paragraph 11 is:

a. when businesses first start up, they have a high rate of failure.

b. Dun & Bradstreet notes that 36% of all businesses fail within the first five years.

c. performance in the early years is not as important to a company's success as was once thought.

d. a business owner should have a thorough knowledge of finance.

Answer these three questions by carefully reading the paragraphs mentioned in each question. Your answers should be in a short phrase or sentence.

1. Reread paragraphs 23–24. Why is capital important in starting up a business? (1 point)

2. Reread paragraphs 28–29. Why are customer demographics so important in the success of a new business? (2 points)

3. Reread paragraphs 32–33. What is meant by the "condition of the business"? (2 points)

Now that you have completed these exercises, it may be helpful to see how your reading of this topic has changed some of your ideas about business. You may go back to reread them just for their content, or for what they have to say about the business field, before you answer the following questions. Answer these questions either individually or in small groups:

1. How would you now define the term *business studies?*

2. Discuss as thoroughly as you can three business issues that you were introduced to in these exercises.

3. What type of American business would you prefer being a part of? Why?

4. What issues in business would you now like to study more?

1. _____

2. _____

3. _____

4. _____

5. _____

70%

Ask instructor for answers.

Follow-up on the Business Exercises

6 Identifying Organizational Patterns

◑ Description   ◑ Comparison–contrast   ◑ Thesis–support

Organizational patterns

◑ Cause–effect   ◑ Problem–solution   ◑ Definition

◑ Sequence of events   ◑ Spatial–geographic

Information is frequently organized in one of a few standard patterns: cause–effect, problem–solution, definition, sequence of events, spatial–geographic, thesis–support, comparison–contrast, and description. If you know what those standard organizational patterns are, you can look for one as you read or listen to lectures and thereby have one more insight into the author or lecturer's meaning. Then you will understand the material better. Main ideas and important details will also be clearer if you understand which organizational pattern is being used.

The Cause–Effect Pattern

Cause–effect is perhaps the most common organizational pattern that you will come across. You will find it in almost every subject that you study, but it is most evident in the sciences and social sciences. You learned something about cause and effect in Chapter 5, which discussed major details. You will now study cause and effect as a pattern that can organize an entire chapter or lecture. Cause–effect sentences, paragraphs, or essays have two parts: the cause, or the source of the change, and the effect, or the result of the change.

In addition, cause–effect relationships can be either direct or indirect. If cause–effect statements are *direct*, they are always true. Look at the following cause–effect statement from chemistry: "When water is lowered to 32 degrees Fahrenheit, it freezes." Do you see that lowering the water's temperature to 32 degrees is the cause and that the water freezing at this temperature is the effect? This relationship is direct because water always freezes at this temperature (at least under normal physical conditions). In your notes, you can show this relationship by using an arrow. "Lowering temperature of water to 32 degrees F. → water freezing."

An *indirect* cause–effect relationship is one whose effect is caused by several factors. Indirect causes are also called *contributory* causes. Indirect cause–effect relationships are often found in the social sciences and the humanities. Consider the following statement from sociology: "Criminal behavior seems to be caused by a deprived social environment." The term of qualification *seems* suggests that this relationship is indirect. A deprived social environment may be one of several influences on criminal behavior. One frequently finds contributory causes in relationships dealing with people and events, and often these relationships are worded with qualifying terms.

The following terms of qualification are often associated with indirect cause–effect relationships:

it appears	perhaps	one can safely say
it seems	probably	one can say with reservation
apparently	likely	there seems to be a link
one can assume	contributing to	there seems to be a relationship

For a more thorough list of terms of qualification, see the lists in Chapter 8 titled "Words and Phrases That Express a Little Doubt" and "Words and Phrases That Express Some Doubt," p. 166. Certain transitional phrases also suggest results, like *consequently, therefore, so, as a result*, and *as a consequence.*

How should you note cause–effect relationships? If you find them in your reading, you may want to separate cause from effect in the margin. From the previous example dealing with crime, you could write:

cause: crime   Criminal behavior seems to be caused by a deprived social environment.
effect:
bad environment

You should also note whether the cause is direct or indirect. You can write the same kinds of comments when you take or review your lecture notes.

*The Problem–
Solution Pattern*

In a sense, the problem–solution pattern is a special type of cause–effect relationship because the solution is the result of the problem. In this pattern, the writer presents a problem needing solution. Early on in their presentation, successful writers of problem–solution material present the problem as clearly and completely as they can, and they are equally clear and specific about the ways they intend to solve the problem. This pattern is commonly used in business and political material because a large part of the work business people and politicians do is finding ways to solve problems: balancing a budget, making a more effective product, developing a product that conforms to environmental and consumer legislation.

Signal words that suggest a problem–solution pattern include: problem, question, issue, solution, answer, explanation, interpretation, decision, findings, suggestion, compromise, plan, proposal, intent.

Look at how the sociological issue of crime prevention is addressed by a politician in the following problem–solution paragraph:

> Teenage crime is rampant; thirteen-year-olds are killing each other with guns and knives, sixth graders are on LSD and cocaine, and teenage car theft is startlingly high. The crime issue will not go away unless we present some concrete proposals. I suggest that we begin discussing crime and its dangerous effects in schools, from kindergarten through high school. We should have police going to the schools and talking about the effects of being picked up for drunk driving or drug possession. Children need to know that these early violations may adversely affect their chances of finding employment later on. Finally, we need to provide federal, state, and private money for counseling families where there is teenage crime.

Do you see how the problem is presented early on, with details of killings, drug use, and car thefts? And do you also see that the solutions are explicitly listed—school programs, police programs, and counseling services? Also note that signal words like *issue, proposals,* and *suggest* alert you to the problem–solution pattern.

The Definition Pattern

You will find definitions in the lecture and textbook material of every course you take. Definitions make up a large part of what you will be asked on examination questions, so you should listen and read carefully when you come upon a definition. Definitions are often expressed concisely, so you should also write down every word of a definition.

In your lecture and reading notes, use the abbreviation *def* as your signal that a definition follows. Look at the following example from sociology:

def: social class   A social class is a particular category of a social system. Working, lower, middle, and upper are the most common classes.

Another successful technique to use when you are learning definitions is to list the general category of the term first, then to give examples or features of the term. See how the above definition of *social class* can be effectively divided into these categories:

Term	*General Category*	*Specific Features*
social class	social system	divided into working, lower, middle, and upper

This method of categorizing is similar to classifying information into main ideas and details. Also, the chart helps you visualize each part of the definition.

When you come upon a definition, you should listen or read more actively. At first you may have trouble remembering all the parts of a definition, because each part tends to be written concisely. But learn to remember definitions, because they are the foundations for any course that you take. They are especially important in your understanding of introductory courses. More will be said about how to remember definitions in Chapter 13, "The SQ3R Study System," and Chapters 15 and 16, which are about examination strategies.

The Sequence-of-Events Pattern

You will find the sequence-of-events pattern in all subjects, but you will often see it in history material, in which dates are presented chronologically. You will also find the sequence-of-events pattern in vocational material, in which you must follow procedures to make or repair an object or to work a machine like a computer. You were introduced to this pattern in the previous chapter, where it was presented as a type of major detail. Now you will see it as a structure that can organize a textbook chapter or a lecture.

The following signal words often introduce a sequence-of-events pattern: *first, second, third,* and so on; *last, now, later, before, often, soon, finally, next.*

When you listen to or read material arranged in a sequence-of-events pattern, you should number the events or steps. Make the number stand out so that, in reviewing your notes, you can picture the sequence in your mind. Look at how information is sequenced in the list that follows this paragraph on a juvenile offender:

> James's history follows a particular pattern that many juvenile offenders seem to fall into. First, he was born to a single parent, a mother who did not work. Second, he did most of his own child rearing, feeding and clothing himself from the age of four. Third, when he began school, he returned home to an empty house. Finally, as a teenager he found himself spending more time on the streets with dropouts than at home.

James's Childhood History

1. Born to a single mother who did not work
2. Began caring for himself at age four
3. Returned from school to an unattended home
4. When he was a teenager, his friends were dropouts

By arranging the sequence of events vertically, you get a clearer picture of the significant moments in James's life.

**The Spatial–
Geographic Pattern**

The spatial–geographic pattern is frequently used in biology and geography courses. In this pattern, you must visualize the various parts of an organism or the relative location of countries, states, or cities on a map.

In biology courses, the following signal words are used to direct you to various parts of an organism:

above	between	inward	anterior	distal
below	upper	external	posterior	
next to	lower	dorsal	medial	
behind	outward	ventral	lateral	

In a biology lecture, your instructor will use these terms along with a slide or diagram. Start associating these terms with what you see. If you can sketch, make a rough picture of the organism during the lecture. In biology textbooks, organs and organ parts are often mentioned in conjunction with a diagram. As you read, refer to the diagram. After you have read the material and studied the diagram, close your book and draw the organ or organism from memory. Your biology instructor may well ask you to label an organism on an exam. On such exams, your spatial–geographic skills will assist you.

The same skills are necessary in geography courses. Your geography instructor may present maps in a lecture and ask you to remember the correct location of various parts. If you can, copy any maps that you see in lectures and important maps that you find in your reading. If you cannot draw well, be sure to use accurate signal words as you take notes. Here are some signal words found in geography readings and lectures:

north	bordering	up
south	adjacent	down
east	next to	opposite to
west		

Let signal words like these help you visualize parts of a city, state, county, or continent. "Southwestern," for example, should be the key word that you hear in the statement "The southwestern border of the city is the area with the most affluent homeowners—the city's upper class."

**The Thesis–Support
Pattern**

The thesis–support pattern is used in all disciplines; its organization is similar to that of the multiple-paragraph essay, which is discussed in Chapter 16. A *thesis* is a point of view expressed by a speaker or writer. Usually the thesis is in the first paragraph of an essay or at the beginning of a lecture.

When you locate a statement that seems to be the thesis, write *thesis* in the margin; then summarize it. For example, if your sociology instructor begins a lecture with a statement like "Power is a fundamental drive that seems to organize all types of society," you could write something like this:

<u>Thesis</u>: power—a basic drive organizing societies

Underline the term "thesis" so that, in reviewing your notes, you will remember to reread this statement. On exams, you are expected to know well the thesis of a lecture or an article.

Be sure that you can distinguish between a thesis and a fact. Like a main idea, a thesis expresses an opinion that needs support. Like a detail, a *fact* may support a thesis. Unlike a thesis, a fact does not ask you to question it. Which of the following two statements is the thesis and which is the fact that supports it? (1) "Power is expressed in the amount of money and capital an individual possesses." (2) "Members of the upper class always possess more money than the classes below them do." Do you see that in the second statement the writer is not presenting an argument, merely a fact? But in the first statement, you may question whether money is the only indicator of power.

Once you have located the thesis, you need to analyze its details. Remember that a thesis is only as good as its details. Some details are well chosen; others are not. Start training yourself to look for the well-chosen detail. Make marginal comments in your textbook or when taking lecture notes, stating whether the details support the thesis well. If a sociology instructor said that social power is expressed in several ways, you would be correct in wanting to know what is meant by "several." Are there three ways or thirteen? In your notes, you should identify important details with the abbreviation *det.*

Here are some signal words that introduce a thesis–support pattern:

the thesis is	for example	especially
it is theorized that	for instance	one example is
the hypothesis is	specifically	the idea is supported by
it is my belief that	in particular	proof is found in

You can use these same signal words in writing your own thesis–support essay.

The details used to support a thesis may be causes, effects, spatial or geographic words, or descriptions. The thesis–support pattern is the most general of the seven and may include other organizational patterns.

The Comparison–Contrast Pattern

The comparison–contrast pattern is used in all disciplines. Like the thesis–support pattern, it may be made up of several paragraphs, and it may include other organizational patterns. The comparison–contrast pattern asks you to find similarities and differences in what you read or hear.

Here are some of the most common signal words for the comparison–contrast pattern:

Contrast

but	on the one hand	although	opposed
however	on the other hand	while	opposing
yet	contrary	different from	conversely
nevertheless	on the contrary	differently	whereas
at variance	in contrast	oppositely	
otherwise	rather	opposite	

Comparison

and	similar	as	parallel to	exactly like
also	similarly	just as	much the same	analogous
like	as if	resembling	comparable	analogously

Use these signal words not only to recognize comparison–contrast patterns but also to write essays that show comparison or contrast. Use them to highlight the similarities and differences that you present in your writing.

When you take reading and lecture notes that show comparison or contrast, you can best show these similarities or differences in a chart like this one:

Similarity or Difference

Topic	*Topic*
1.	1.
2.	2.
3.	3.

In this chart, you can neatly place similarities and differences side by side and thus more easily see how the various pieces of information relate. As you listen to a lecture or read textbook material, be sure that you can identify the topic or topics that explore particular similarities or differences. You studied ways to locate and express topics in Chapter 4. It is only with an accurate topic in mind or with appropriate categories of comparison and contrast that you can create a useful comparison–contrast chart.

Look at the following information taken from a sociology lecture; then see how a chart can be used to explain the material.

> Capitalism and socialism begin with different ideologies. While capitalism implies private ownership, socialism assumes state ownership of certain property. Capitalism allows people to pursue economic gain; socialism controls the economic gains of people.

Differences

Capitalism	Socialism
1. Private ownership of property	1. State ownership of most property
2. Economic freedom for people	2. Economic control of people

Do you see how this chart highlights the differences between socialism and capitalism?

A lecturer or an author of a textbook may present similarities and differences by using such a chart. If you come upon comparison–contrast patterns and the information is presented in paragraph form, you may want to create your own chart. Sometimes you will read or hear material that presents both similarities and differences. Here you can create two charts next to each other showing similarities in one and differences in the other. These charts often allow you to remember compare–contrast information more easily. More will be said about comparison–contrast charts in Chapter 15 and 16 on preparing for objective and essay exams.

The Descriptive Pattern

The descriptive pattern is different from the other organizational patterns. You will find it most often in literature: short stories, novels, poems, plays. Descriptive patterns re-create experiences through the suggestiveness of language and often use characteristics as details. Your job is to see how description awakens your senses. In your notes, comment on how well the description re-creates an experience.

Read this excerpt about a young man fleeing from the law, from John Edgar Wideman's *Brothers and Keepers*:

visual images

Johnny-Boy wasn't from Pittsburgh. *Small, dark, greasy,* he was an outsider who knew he didn't fit, ill at ease in a middle-class house, the meandering conversations that had nothing to do with anyplace he'd been, anything he understood or cared to learn. Johnny-Boy had trouble talking, trouble staying awake. When he spoke at all, he *stuttered* riffs of barely comprehensible ghetto slang. When the rest of us were talking, he'd *nod off.* I didn't like the way his *heavy-lidded, bubble eyes* blinked open and searched the room when he thought no one was watching him.

Do you see how the descriptions *small, dark, greasy* and *heavy-lidded, bubble eyes* present a clear picture of this young fugitive? Also, *stuttering* and *nodding off* are vivid actions that describe him. If you were reading this novel, a marginal comment like *vivid picture* would be helpful as you reread the work.

In any literature course you take, you will come upon the descriptive pattern. Your literature instructor will probably give you reading suggestions to use in analyzing descriptions. When you read any descriptive passage, remember to study the words and what they suggest rather than analyzing the thesis and details of support.

Summary

Organizational patterns are used by speakers and writers to present their ideas more clearly and to show the structure of their arguments. Recognizing which organizational pattern is being used and knowing how that pattern works will help you better understand the material. Organizational patterns often overlap; that is, several structures may be used by a lecturer or writer. Don't expect each paragraph you read or each lecture you hear to use only one organizational pattern. The eight most common organizational patterns are cause–effect, problem–solution, definition, sequence of events, spatial–geographic, thesis–support, comparison–contrast, and descriptive. Each organizational pattern has its own logic and signal words that show you how the material is organized. Being familiar with these eight organizational patterns will make your reading and lecture notes clearer and will improve your writing.

Summary Box   *Organizational Patterns*

What are they?	*Why are they used?*
Structures used in writing and speaking to explain ideas, describe experiences, or show the logic of an argument Eight common patterns: cause–effect, problem–solution, definition, sequence of events, spatial–geographic, thesis–support, comparison–contrast, descriptive	To help a reader or listener understand an argument better and take better reading and lecture notes To help a writer compose logical and organized essays

Skills Practice Topic: Sociology

All the exercises in this chapter deal with some issue from sociology, a subject you will probably study sometime during your college career.

Before you begin these exercises, answer the following questions either individually or in small groups to get some sense of what you already know about sociology:

1. What do you think sociology covers?
2. What are some of the problems that you currently see in society?
3. How do you think these problems should be addressed?

4. Why do people in society act the way they do? Are they born to act in a certain way? Or does society teach them?

Exercise 6.1
Identifying Thesis
Statements

Some of the following ten statements express a point of view and would qualify as thesis statements; others are statements of fact. All of the statements discuss what sociology is, so they should provide you with an introduction to this discipline. In the answer box, write ''thesis'' or ''fact'' on the appropriate lines.

Some Introductory Statements About Sociology

1. Sociology is the study of how people make agreements and how they organize, teach, break, and change them.
2. Sociology is a less difficult discipline than psychology.
3. Sociology also studies how people come to disagree.
4. People who study sociology usually become dissatisfied with society.
5. Sociology is a scientific study of how people agree and disagree.
6. Sociology tests what it knows by carefully measuring and analyzing how people behave.
7. Sociology is the most intelligent discipline to have emerged in the past fifty years.
8. Sociology focuses on action, or on what people do.
9. People tend to accomplish goals more by acting than by speaking.
10. Actions are shaped by what has come before, or previous actions.

The following five paragraphs on social activities each have only one thesis statement. Write in the answer box the letter of the sentence that is the thesis statement.

Social Activities

11. (a) A conversation is one of the most amazing examples of human social activity. (b) People meet, and they exchange glances. (c) They shake hands. (d) And they proceed to get to know one another by sharing experiences in their lives.

12. (a) A fistfight is an example of social interaction. (b) A mugging is also a type of social activity. (c) The mugger points a gun at you and demands your money. (d) Some social interactions are painfully inharmonious.

13. (a) Sociologists study many interesting aspects of social interaction. (b) They may focus on spoken communication. (c) They may specialize in aggressive behavior. (d) Still others may specialize in aggressive behavior manifested in speech.

14. (a) When two people interact, they establish a system of roles. (b) These roles may be learned before the interaction or as the interaction occurs. (c) During the interaction, the particular roles a

Answer box (left margin):

1. _____
2. _____
3. _____
4. _____
5. _____
6. _____
7. _____
8. _____
9. _____
10. _____

11. _____
12. _____
13. _____
14. _____
15. _____

_____
75%

(score = # correct × 5 [1–10] + # correct × 10 [11–15])
Find answers on p. 392.

person plays may even be challenged. (d) These roles form the basis of human relationships, which are the fundamental ways people express meaning to one another.

15. (a) In the roles people play, status relationships are set up. (b) One person may feel more important than another and act accordingly. (c) One's status in a relationship determines the respect or lack of respect received from the other partner. (d) Status has proven to be a very important way of wielding power over others.

Exercise 6.2
Locating Steps in an
Argument

Read the following paragraphs on how sociologists conduct their research. Then reread them and list in correct sequence the steps presented in each paragraph.

Research Methods in Sociology

1. Some sociologists use deductive reasoning in their research. A deduction starts with a general idea—for example, "All people will eventually die." Then the deduction moves to a particular case: "John is a person." It then applies the general premise to the particular case and comes upon a new idea: "John will eventually die."

   Three Steps in a Deduction

   1.

   2.

   3.

2. Sociologists more often use inductive reasoning in their research. It involves three basic steps. The sociologist observes a particular human action. She then begins to record those actions that seem to follow a particular pattern. From a study of these observations, known as *data*, the sociologist comes upon a general statement or idea. Inductions move from the specific observation to the general conclusion, but deductions start at the general level and move to the specific conclusion.

   Three Steps in an Induction

   1.

   2.

   3.

3. The general ideas developed from inductions are also called *hypotheses*. To determine whether a hypothesis is accurate or valid, sociologists do what is called *hypothesis testing*. The first step in this procedure is to state the hypothesis clearly. Then the researcher studies the data she has collected and sees if they follow a pattern. She usually sets up graphs to see what kind of pattern the data show. Finally she studies the graph to see if the hypothesis is supported by what the graph shows.

Steps in Hypothesis Testing

1.

2.

3.

4. Sociologists often study what large groups of people do. The first question they ask is which population they are studying. Once they have answered the "which" and have observed this group, they put their observations into categories. Finally, once the data have been put into categories, they are analyzed, and researchers then draw conclusions about the group in question.

Steps in Studying Large Groups

1.

2.

3.

Now read the following four paragraphs, and look for the proper sequence of events in each. Before you list the steps, write an appropriate title.

5. Random sampling is sociologists' way of determining what a large group of people will do, even though they study a small number. In studying attitudes toward abortion, for example, sociologists often select telephone area codes at random and numbers from all over the area they are focusing on. They then check to see if these numbers are random by testing them with mathematical equations. Finally, they publish their conclusions, usually in the form of percentages and graphs, to report how most people in that area feel about abortion.

6. Some sociologists engage in field research. In field research, they both observe a particular action in society and participate in this activity in some way. During this activity, sociologists gather data. They use the data to write a report—which is often a case study, or an in-depth report on a particular social event.

7. Sociologists also conduct surveys to try to answer a particular sociological question—for example, "Are schoolteachers satisfied with their jobs?" Once the overall question has been formulated, researchers devise more specific survey questions. The people they question are asked to respond either over the telephone or in writing.

80%

Ask instructor for answers.
---

8. Most sociological studies, then, follow a set sequence. The researcher begins with an interest in a particular social activity—crime, for example. This interest then leads to an unsupported idea or intuition: "Society creates criminals." Finally, this intuition is tested and made into a theory: the social theory of criminal behavior.*

Exercise 6.3
Understanding
Definitions

The following ten statements define sociological terms that you have read about in Exercises 6.1 and 6.2. After reading each statement, separate the definition into a general category and an example. Be brief. Place all of your information in the columns that follow the statements. Use the following definition of *survey research* as a model: "A sociological research method is one using questionnaires that people answer, either on their own or with the help of an interviewer. Asking a large number of people about their attitudes on tax increases is an example of a survey question."

Term	General Category	Examples
survey research	determining a group of people's attitude on a topic	tax increases

*Adapted from Thomas R. Dye, *Power and Society*, 5th ed. (Belmont, Calif.: Wadsworth, 1990), pp. 23–30.

Key Sociological Terms

1. Conflict theory is the aspect of sociology that studies why people disagree; sociologists who study crime often use conflict theory.

2. A deduction (as used in sociology) is a logical process that moves from a general idea to a theory about a specific person or group. A sociologist who contends that women are discriminated against on the job might deduce that female executives receive a smaller salary than male executives.

3. Demography is a careful sociological look at population—what it is and why it acts the way it does. A study of the movement of Mexicans into California in the 1990s would be a demographic study.

4. An empirical study involves gathering data from what the researcher observes. A sociologist observing how American males greet each other would collect empirical, or observational, data.

5. In sociology, field research requires going into the natural setting to observe a particular activity. Carefully observing political rallies would qualify as field research in sociology.

6. A hypothesis in sociology is a conclusion that a researcher draws through either observation or intuition. Assuming that criminals are victims of society is a hypothesis.

7. An induction in sociology is a conclusion that a researcher draws based on the careful study of data, or observations. A sociologist who concludes after studying a statewide survey that New Yorkers are not in favor of increased state taxes is using inductive logic.

8. In sociology, a population is a group or category of people that merits careful study. Students in community colleges nationwide are an example of a sociological population.

9. Random selection is a sociological research tool designed to ensure that a large group of people are selected for a study by chance and not through a particular researcher's bias. Random selection can be achieved by asking a computer to select a group of people through the use of random numbering.

10. Social interaction is defined as the way one person directs the responses of another person or persons. A conversation is an excellent example of social interaction.*

---

*Adapted from Earl R. Babbie, *Sociology: An Introduction,* 2nd ed. (Belmont, Calif.: Wadsworth, 1980), pp. 574–584.

Term	General Category	Examples

1.

2.

3.

4.

5.

6.

7.

8.

9.

10.

*Exercise 6.4
Identifying
Comparisons and
Contrasts*

The following ten statements compare various disciplines to sociology or compare pairs of terms used in sociology. In a one-sentence explanation of each statement, identify the issue that is compared or contrasted. Be sure that you use the word "compare" or "contrast" in your explanation. Here's an example:

> Although inductions and deductions are both ways by which sociologists explain their data, they begin with very different ways of looking at the data.
> *Explanation:* This statement contrasts inductions and deductions as ways sociologists interpret their data.

1. Sociology and psychology are different in that psychology generally studies what an individual does and sociology analyzes what occurs between people.

   Explanation: _____

2. The major difference between sociology and anthropology is that until recently anthropology studied preliterate peoples, those unable to read and write, and sociology generally studied literate people. The distinctions between these two studies have recently been blurred.

   Explanation: _____

3. Economics and sociology share a focus on how people relate and interact. Economics specifically focuses on financial interaction.

   Explanation: _____

4. Political science differs from sociology in that it specifically addresses how people use power. In sociology, power is just one of many areas that is studied.

   Explanation: _____

5. Social welfare and sociology are very similar disciplines, except that social welfare focuses on how to help people and sociology considers ways to study them.

   Explanation: _____

6. Socialism is not sociology. Socialism is an economic system in which most industry is controlled by the government; sociology studies how humans interact. Socialism could, therefore, be a topic studied in sociology.

   Explanation: _____

7. Furthermore, sociology is not synonymous with social reform. Social reformists want to make the world better; that is not the goal of sociology, which merely studies social behavior.

   Explanation: _____

8. Sociology differs from history in that history records, narrates, and interprets human experience. Sociology focuses exclusively on interpreting human interaction.

   Explanation: _____

9. Racial inequality and sexual inequality can be considered similar in that both express how a group of people—a race or women—have been treated unfairly by the ruling class.

   Explanation: _____

10. Urban life is characterized by large numbers of people living in a concentrated area, whereas rural life is characterized by fewer people and more space between groups of people.

    Explanation: _____

The following five paragraphs present either comparisons or contrasts of terms used in sociology. Read over the paragraphs carefully. Then complete the comparison and contrast chart that follows each paragraph. In paragraphs 13–15, you need to provide the topics as well.

11. There are several similarities between the upper-class population and the middle-class population. For one, both are future-oriented; that is, they are constantly making plans for a better life. Both groups are self-confident, believing that they have reasonable control over the experiences in their lives. Finally, both are also willing to make financial investments that will improve their future financial status.

Similar Beliefs

	Upper Class		*Middle Class*
1.		1.	
2.		2.	
3.		3.	

12. The differences between the working class and the lower class are minor. The working class generally works to pay the bills for themselves and their family; the lower class often does not work, and when they do they often move from one job to another. Working-class families are often married couples, but lower-class families are more often run by single women. Finally, a working-class person often belongs to and regularly attends church; the lower-class individual attends church infrequently.

Differences

	Working Class		*Lower Class*
1.		1.	
2.		2.	
3.		3.	

13. An issue that continues to surface in sociological studies is the difference between *nature* and *nurture*. Believers in the influence of nature contend that heredity, or one's genetic makeup, determines one's actions. Proponents of the influence of nurture assume that social forces—family, friends, environment—determine how one acts. Nurture theorists would say that one's mother is a dominant force in one's behavior. Nature theorists would say that some of a mother's genetic makeup is given to her child and that is why the child behaves in a particular fashion. In studying twins that were separated at birth, a nature proponent would be looking for evidence of similar behavior. A nurture theorist, in contrast, would be looking for proof that their behavior is different because it is shaped by a different environment.

How Their Ideas Differ

1.   1.

2.   2.

3.   3.

14. There are three differences between the liberal and the conservative positions in the United States today. Whereas liberals favor federal aid for education, health, and Social Security, conservatives work toward cutting funds in these areas. Conservatives believe in spending more on defense; liberals see military spending as too high and want to cut it. Finally, conservatives often favor aid to foreign countries; in contrast, liberals frequently fear that aid to foreign countries will lessen the amount spent on the needs of the American people.

Different Beliefs

1.   1.

2.   2.

3.   3.

15. Are urban and suburban lifestyles and environments different? Suburbs tend to be less densely populated than their urban counterparts. Homes in the suburbs tend to be built on larger parcels of land than urban dwellings, which are often built on smaller pieces of land and are several stories high. Violence is also an important factor for those who decide to move from a large city to a suburb. Suburban violence tends to be less common than that experienced in large cities.*

---

*Adapted from Dye, *Power and Society*, pp. 5–9, 76–77.

Differences in Lifestyle and Environment

1.	1.
2.	2.
3.	3.

*Exercise 6.5
Identifying
Organizational
Patterns*

The following ten paragraphs discuss the sociological issues of heredity versus environment and the sense of self, expanding on the issue of nature and nurture that you read about in Exercise 6.4. Each paragraph is structured according to one of the organizational patterns described earlier. Read each paragraph; then identify the organizational pattern that describes it. Some paragraphs use more than one organizational pattern; in this case, choose the one that seems to dominate the paragraph. Place the appropriate code in the answer box: *C-E* = cause–effect, *DEF* = definition, *C-C* = comparison–contrast, and *SEQ* = sequence of events.

Heredity, Environment, and the Self

1. What is the nature–nurture controversy? Some sociologists believe that we are the product of our genes, or nature, and that our sex, our race, and our physical characteristics are qualities we inherit at birth. Others believe that nurture, or our upbringing, is more important. Our ability to use language and our attitudes toward politics and religion, they argue, are shaped by our environment.

2. Identical twins have been studied carefully for answers to the nature–nurture question. Some studies have asked what causes intelligence. Identical twins, even if they are raised apart, seem to show very similar intelligence quotients (IQs). This result would suggest that heredity greatly influences intelligence.

3. What are the social forces that a typical child faces in the first seven years of life? During the first weeks, months, and sometimes years, a child is cared for by her mother. In our present society, this child is then often cared for by baby-sitters or day-care workers. Then, at the age of three, she is often enrolled in preschool, where she experiences the influence of teachers and a large group of peers. Finally, at five she moves to a formal schooling experience, interacting with a teacher and a large group of peers in a self-contained classroom.

4. Two studies have offered different views of how intelligence is shaped. One study, using evidence from identical twins who have been raised apart, suggests that intelligence is transmitted genetically. Another study of foster children suggests that environment plays a key role in intelligence. This study shows that foster children,

who are not related biologically to their parents, have an IQ similar to that of their foster parents.

5. Related to this issue of nature–nurture is the sense of self, which seems to develop in identifiable stages. A newborn has no sense of self apart from his attachment to his mother. Before the child begins to speak, at about the age of one, he begins to see himself as separate, often pointing to himself in the mirror. By the age of three, the child often is able to use language to explain who he is in relationship to others in his family.

6. What is the sociological meaning of the self? The self is one's sense of being, apart from one's occupation or social position. It is the continuous sense of who one is, in private, at work, and in social interaction. Some sociologists are finding that this continuous sense of oneself cannot be separated from the society feeding this self.

7. How does socialization affect the sense of self? As children mature, they learn to wear various masks—one at school, one at church, and so on. As they interact more with society, they learn that each occasion calls for a different side of themselves. Their notion of who they are thus becomes more and more complex.

8. Socialization, then, is a process in which the individual learns to use a variety of social selves. It is also a process by which these social selves become integrated with one another. Socialization thus gives to each individual both a personal and a social identity.

9. Sigmund Freud did much to help us understand the concept of self. He was interested in the effect of childhood experiences on adult behavior. He believed that people held many of their painful childhood experiences in what he called the *unconscious*. These unconscious memories often caused individuals to express themselves in strange, unexplained ways. These strange behavior patterns often led troubled individuals to seek help from psychoanalysts like Freud.

10. Both Sigmund Freud and Erik Erikson were psychologists interested in the development of the self, what they both termed the *ego*. Freud and Erikson differed slightly in their concept of how the ego developed. Freud believed that the ego resulted from a constant battle between the unconscious (the *id*) and the *superego* (society's values). In slight contrast, Erikson believed that the ego developed as a result of the individual's sense of sameness, or continuity, from one experience to the other. When there is a sharp contrast between who the individual thinks she is and who society thinks she is, the ego faces a crisis.*

1. _____

2. _____

3. _____

4. _____

5. _____

6. _____

7. _____

8. _____

9. _____

10. _____

80%

(score = # correct × 10)
Find answers on p. 393.

*Adapted from Babbie, *Sociology*, pp. 127–132.

Exercise 6.6
Identifying More
Organizational
Patterns

The following ten paragraphs concern the sociological issue of groups—what they are and how they operate. This discussion ties in with the previous discussion of the self. Again, these paragraphs are structured around various organizational patterns. Your job is to identify the organizational pattern that best describes each paragraph. If more than one pattern seems to apply, choose the pattern that seems to dominate the paragraph. Place the appropriate code in the answer box: *S-G* = spatial–geographic, *T-S* = thesis–support, *DES* = descriptive, and *C-E* = cause–effect.

A Sociological Look at Groups

1. In general speech, the term *group* has several meanings. A teacher can refer to a group gathered outside the classroom door. A spokesperson for the manufacturer of a sports car can refer to a group that consistently buys that car. And a rock star can mention the "groupies" who follow her from concert to concert.

2. What is key to understanding groups in sociology is how each group fits into a particular category. Brown-eyed Americans constitute a category. So do college professors. And so do people who buy the same sports car. What is common among all these groups is that, although the people in them belong to a particular category, they do not necessarily know or interact with one another.

3. How do groups influence behavior? Sociologists would argue that your membership in a group determines to a large degree your sense of self, or who you think you are. The friends you had in school determine how you see yourself as a student. Whether you thought you were part of the "in-group" or the "out-group" also determines how successful a student you see yourself to be.

4. To be part of an in-group is meaningful only if you see that another group—an out-group—is not as successful as the group you identify with. The in-group often refers to the others in the group as "we" and to those in the out-group as "them." In schools, students are often categorized as athletes (the "jocks") and academic types (the "nerds"). Each one of these groups sees itself as part of a "we" that is unlike, and in conflict with, the "them."

5. What do in-groups provide people? By being in an in-group, you develop a sense of being wanted. Your group members support you and are loyal to you. Being part of an in-group gives you a sense of stability and, as Erik Erikson would argue, this stability lets your ego develop without conflict.

6. A *reference group*, or the group that one looks up to as a standard, gives individuals ways to improve. If you are a "B" student in sociology and your close and respected friend consistently receives "A"

grades, she may provide you with a reference point for how well you are doing and for how much better you may want to become. Her "A" may very well prod you to study more for the next sociology examination. Reference groups are important because people need to see themselves in a better light if they are ever to develop their abilities.

7. But comparing yourself to others can also lead to what sociologists call *relative deprivation*—or doing poorly because others are doing better. Instead of looking up to a successful person or group, an individual may develop feelings of inadequacy whenever she compares herself to the more successful peer or acquaintance. This feeling of inadequacy may prevent the individual from trying her hardest. In extreme circumstances, relative deprivation can lead to feelings of apathy or even depression.

8. In-groups and reference groups can be visualized as two or more floating platforms, with individuals on each. The people below can look up at the other individuals above them. They see them as happy and somehow more comfortable. In contrast, the people above—the in-group—can look down and feel better because the out-group seems to be more crowded and uncomfortable, wishing in vain that they could join the in-group. But if the in-group looks up from where they are, they will invariably see still another group—even less crowded and more comfortable, enjoying life even more than they do.

9. One sociology student described herself this way in a journal entry: "In college, I usually have not felt part of an in-group. I've always looked to others and envied who they were. I envied them for their grades and for how well they could speak up in class and get the teacher to listen. I see myself as a shy student who still has a long way to go before I can feel comfortable expressing myself in class and with other students outside of class. I want to be like these more successful students. They are becoming my models."

10. Another student had this to say about his first day in college: "I was born in Taiwan and went to school there until I was thirteen. This college is big. The buildings are large, and there is much land between buildings. I still have not gotten used to how much of everything there is here. There are three cafeterias in this school and five libraries. The parking lots are as large as the land that my elementary school was on in Taiwan. I still feel a little strange when I compare my college to the schools back home."*

1. _____
2. _____
3. _____
4. _____
5. _____
6. _____
7. _____
8. _____
9. _____
10. _____

_____
80%

Ask instructor for answers.

---

*Adapted from Babbie, *Sociology*, pp. 201–204.

*Exercise 6.7
Recognizing
Organizational
Patterns in a Longer
Passage*

Read the following passage on *stratification* (a sociological term that treats a person's relative ranking in society). The discussion of stratification is a further elaboration of the discussion of in-groups and out-groups in the previous exercise. Make marginal comments on the major organizational patterns that you come across. Then answer the questions that follow the passage. You may go back to review it as you answer the questions. Place the first five answers in the answer box; then answer the rest of the questions in the spaces provided.

Various Views on Stratification

(1) Sociologists refer to inequalities in society with the term *social stratification*. Each stratum in society is made up of a group of people who have a similar social rank. Sociologists have found that social rank depends on factors that vary from one culture to another. Some of the most common criteria for assigning social rank are status within the family, possessions, occupation, education, and religion.

(2) In most cultures, newborns achieve a particular status because of the family they are born into. If a child is born into a rich family, that child is automatically part of the rich stratum of society. A child who is born into a royal family automatically becomes part of a royal stratum at birth. Some families are considered morally upright, and a child born into such a family will have high social standing as long as he continues to practice the values of his family and the community continues to share these respected values.

(3) In the United States, money seems to give an individual the greatest social status. Many types of wealth define a rich American: a high salary, expensive possessions, a lot of property. Alongside these physical manifestations of wealth are the people of equal wealth whom a rich American knows. High status is assured if the rich American belongs to exclusive clubs or is selected to be a member of an exclusive organization. The number of wealthy contacts one has in a society that values possessions automatically increases one's status as a wealthy person.

(4) One's occupation also plays an important role in status. Interestingly enough, the amount of money one makes is not always the only criterion for assigning rank. Some of the most prestigious occupations are Supreme Court justice, doctor, scientist, governor, and college professor. Although doctors and governors often earn a high salary, scientists and college professors sometimes do not. So clearly, in some cases, factors other than salary are often involved in assigning status to an individual's occupation.

(5) In many cultures, particularly developed ones, education is a consistently important way to improve one's social status. People in most cultures seem to assign value to an educated individual, even if that individual does not earn a lot of money. Something about education confers instant respect on an individual. And this has been true throughout history. In most cultures, the wise person has been awarded a special place in the community.

(6) The same value seems to be given to people who choose a religious vocation, like priests. Although religious people tend not to earn

a big salary, and some even live in poverty, society consistently seems to rank religious vocations high on their list of respected occupations. Society seems to believe that both educated and religious people possess valuable knowledge. In a sense, spiritual or intellectual possessions are as important as the physical possessions of the wealthy.

(7) The issue of social stratification is a difficult one to understand, because it seems that many factors are involved. Material wealth, education, religious knowledge—all seem to give certain individuals a privileged position in society. The reasons for assigning social status, like so many expressions of group behavior, are mysterious and the result of many different motivations.*

1. The bulk of the sentences in paragraph 1 fit into the organizational pattern of

   a. sequence of events
   b. description
   c. cause–effect
   d. definition

2. The last sentence in paragraph 1 is a

   a. topic sentence
   b. main-idea sentence
   c. minor-detail sentence
   d. major-detail sentence

3. The major organizational pattern of paragraph 2 is

   a. description
   b. sequence of events
   c. definition
   d. thesis–support

4. Paragraph 2 presents three

   a. topic sentences
   b. minor-detail sentences
   c. major-detail sentences
   d. none of these

5. The main idea of paragraph 3 concerns

   a. the value of knowing rich people in the United States
   b. the value of belonging to exclusive clubs in the United States
   c. the value of wealth in achieving social status in the United States
   d. the number of wealthy people one knows

1. _____

2. _____

3. _____

4. _____

5. _____

80%

(score = # correct × 10)
Find answers on p. 393.

---

*Adapted from Dye, *Power and Society*, pp. 66–69.

Answer each of the following five questions in a short phrase or sentence.

6. What is the main idea of paragraph 4?

7. Find a major detail in paragraph 4.

8. What organizational pattern does paragraph 4 seem to fit into?

9. What is the main idea of paragraph 6?

10. What organizational pattern does the entire excerpt seem to fit into?

Exercise 6.8
Writing an Effective
Paragraph Using
Organizational
Patterns

Now that you have read the selection on stratification in Exercise 6.7, go back and reread it. As you do, complete the following outline:

I. Main Idea of the Excerpt:

II. Factors That Influence Social Status

    A. Family:

    B. Wealth:

    C. Occupation:

    D. Religion and education:

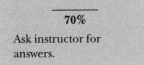

70%

Ask instructor for answers.

Refer only to this outline in answering the following:

> *Essay question:* In an organized paragraph, define social stratification. Then show how it applies to one's family and one's occupation.

Exercise 6.9
Determining Main
Ideas, Major Details,
and Organizational
Patterns in a
Textbook Excerpt

The following is an excerpt on deviant behavior from a sociology textbook. This material further explains the previous exercise on heredity, environment, and the self.

Read through the excerpt quickly to get a sense of its organization. Then go back and reread it slowly. When you finish, answer the five questions that follow. You may refer to the excerpt in deciding on your answers. Place your answers to the first five questions in the answer box.

Deviance and Conformity

Biological Theories of Deviance

(1) For centuries humans have wondered why some people are chronic deviants—why some people cannot be trusted to conform to important norms. Virtually every facet of life has been blamed by someone as a

cause of crime and deviance. But perhaps the oldest claim about deviance is that some people are just "born bad": Some people have an inborn personality flaw that stimulates misbehavior or prevents them from controlling their deviant urges. This view became very influential in the 1870s, when an Italian physician, Cesare Lombroso (1836–1909), began to gather systematic data on prison and jail inmates and to develop a biological theory of criminal behavior.

(2) **"Born Criminals"**   Lombroso believed he had found the key to criminal behavior in human evolution. His years of careful observation and measurement of prison inmates convinced him that the most serious, vicious, and persistent criminals (who he believed made up about one-third of all persons who commit crimes) were "born criminals" (Lombroso-Ferrero, 1911). Born criminals were less evolved humans who were biological "throwbacks" to our primitive ancestors, according to Lombroso. The born criminal is "an atavistic being who reproduces in his person the ferocious instincts of primitive humanity and inferior animals."

(3) Lombroso believed that, because of their genetic makeup, born criminals could not restrain their violent and animalistic urges. Because the trouble was biological, he argued, little or nothing could be done to cure born criminals; society could be protected only by locking them up. However, because their criminality was not their fault, born criminals ought to be treated as kindly as possible in dignified, decent prisons.

(4) Lombroso and his students presented a great deal of evidence to support his theory. He claimed that criminals tended to be more apelike than normal people, having abnormal skulls, huge jaws, flat noses, and long arms. Because Lombroso developed a testable theory, we know today that his theory was incorrect. His error lay in examining only prisoners and assuming that they displayed a higher proportion of physical abnormalities than nonprisoners did. However, when the British physician Charles Goring (1913) measured nonprison populations, he found the same incidence of physical abnormality as Lombroso had found among convicts. Thus, Goring showed that there was no correlation between these physical characteristics and committing crimes. As Chapter 3 made clear, something cannot be the cause of something else if the two are not correlated. Lombroso's theory was therefore disproved.

(5) However, even though criminologists have known for more than seventy years that Lombroso was incorrect, they have not dismissed the possibility that human biology plays a role in crime and deviance. Indeed, in his book that exposed Lombroso's faulty methods, Goring reaffirmed his belief that criminals can be distinguished from noncriminals on the basis of body build and physiology. And throughout this century researchers have continued to try to discover and demonstrate such biological differences (Wilson and Herrnstein, 1985).

(6) **Behavioral Genetics**   In Chapter 5 we examined the new field of behavioral genetics, which has attempted to assess the role of heredity in various forms of human behavior. As we saw, studies of twins have been a primary research method for behavioral geneticists. One study done in Denmark examined 3,586 twin pairs (Christiansen, 1977). The researcher checked each twin through the criminal record files of the

Danish police, recording only serious offenses. The results were highly suggestive. For identical (or monozygotic) twins, if one twin had a serious criminal record, the odds were 50 percent that the other twin did too. But for fraternal (dizygotic) twins (using male sets only, to eliminate gender differences within pairs), if one twin was a criminal, the odds were only 21 percent that the other twin also was a criminal. Because each set of twins grew up in the same home, their environment was held constant, and thus these differences suggest that the more genetically similar, the more similar the pattern of deviance or conformity. Adoption studies also have sustained interest in a hereditary component in criminal behavior. In terms of criminal records, adoptees much more closely resemble their biological than adoptive parents (Mednick et al., 1984).

(7) Keep in mind that even if there is a genetic "predisposition" to break the law, much more is involved in criminal acts. For one thing, such actions, like all human behavior, must be learned. Spiders may be genetically programmed to spin webs, but no human is born with instincts to break into houses or to write bad checks. Moreover, geneticists still have a long way to go to discover just *what* people inherit that can predispose them to deviance. Wilson and Herrnstein (1985) have suggested that much deviant behavior results because some people seem unable to control their impulses or to consider long-term costs versus short-term gains. Perhaps genetic aspects of the nervous system play a role.

(8) In any event, most sociologists are uncomfortable with the idea that a tendency to commit crimes might be partly rooted in physiology and genetics. On the other hand, they long have been puzzled by the marked gender and age differences in patterns of deviant behavior, traits having obvious physical as well as social aspects. Then Walter Gove suggested a new synthesis of biology and sociology.

Walter Gove: Age, Gender, Biology, and Deviance

(9) Walter Gove began with three well-known, but little understood, facts about crime and deviance. First of all, no other variables influence criminal activity as much as do gender and age. In all societies for which data exist, males are far more likely than are females to commit crimes (South and Messner, 1987). Moreover, arrest rates decline very steeply with age and this same pattern holds in all societies on which data are available (Hirschi and Gottfredson, 1983).

(10) However, both the age and sex effects are far more significant for some kinds of crimes than for others (Steffensmeier et al., 1989). Table 7-3 shows that U.S. and Canadian women make up a far larger proportion of those arrested for property crimes such as larceny-theft, forgery, embezzlement, and fraud than of those arrested for crimes of violence. Table 7-4 shows that the arrest rate for robbery and homicide falls very rapidly with age but that arrests for larceny-theft decline much more gradually.

(11) Many social scientists have attributed gender differences in crime rates to socialization, claiming that females are socialized in ways that make them more law abiding (Bowker, 1981). This may well be true, but it doesn't help to explain why gender differences are so much

Table 7-3 *Percent of Females Among Persons Arrested for Various Crimes*

Offense	Percent Female	
	United States	Canada
Robbery	3.6	7.0
Burglary	7.5	3.9
Homicide	13.1	11.8
Aggravated Assault	13.4	11.0
Larceny-theft	30.3	31.8*
Forgery	33.8	†
Embezzlement	38.0	†
Fraud	39.5	24.1
Shoplifting	†	43.0
All violent crimes	10.7	9.7
All property crimes	23.5	20.0

Sources: U.S. Department of Justice, *Uniform Crime Reports*, 1985;
Canadian Centre for Justice Statistics, 1984.
*Theft.
†Not reported as a separate category.

smaller for some crimes than for others. Presumably a well-socialized person should be as unwilling to write bad checks as to rob stores. In similar fashion, attachments often have been invoked to explain the decline in criminality as people get older. Thus, as people marry and begin to have children they have more to lose by being detected in deviant behavior (Sampson and Laub, 1990). While this explanation has considerable merit, it does not address the question of why age has so

Table 7-4 *Arrests per 100,000 Male Population (United States)*

Age	Arrest Rates			
	Homicide	Robbery	Larceny-Fraud	Larceny-Fraud Arrests per Robbery Arrest
16–19	47	408	2532	6.2
20–24	39	299	1441	4.8
25–29	24	204	1075	5.3
30–34	17	129	903	7.0
35–39	13	74	712	9.6
40–44	10	36	471	13.1
45–49	7	19	306	16.1
50–54	5	9	209	23.2
55–59	4	5	145	29.0
60–64	3	2	109	54.5
65 and over	1	1	63	63.0

Source: U.S. Department of Justice, *Uniform Crime Reports*, 1990.

much greater impact on some offenses—homicide and robbery, for example—than on others, such as larceny-theft.

(12) Pondering these issues Gove concluded that the common factor linking these patterns is that *crimes differ in the extent to which they involve aggressive and physically demanding behavior.*

(13) At this point Gove assessed a growing literature that links aggressive or assertive forms of deviance to physique. Beginning with the work of Sheldon (1940) in the 1930s, through studies by Cortés and Gatti (1972) and Cortés (1982), research has found that an athletic (or mesomorphic) body build is conducive to these forms of behavior. This is not to suggest that being muscular causes people to commit assault or robberies but that it requires some degree of strength and self-confidence to act in these ways: The proverbial 98-pound wimp does not make a successful mugger. Moreover, the life-style of the drunk or the addict is often very physically demanding as well. Consider the testimony of this heroin addict:

> [It was] the worst period of my life. I found myself wandering around the streets of New York filthy all the time. I had no place to stay. I slept on rooftops, in hallways, in damp cellars, any available place and always with one eye open. . . . I was really low then, not eating . . . and cold all the time. (Tardola, 1970)

Finally, Gove was ready to put these pieces together.

(14) Why do these forms of deviance rapidly decline at around age 30? First of all, because *physical strength* peaks in the early twenties and then declines. Secondly, *physical energy* also peaks in the twenties. Gove postulates two aspects of energy. The first is endurance, or conditioning. We remain strong enough to perform various actions to a later age than we retain the endurance or conditioning to do them for a long time. An aging boxer may still be a dangerous opponent for a few rounds but may be forced to try for an early knockout, knowing he will tire badly in later rounds. A second aspect of energy, according to Gove, is the ability to *rebound*, or recover, from injury and exertion; for example, an older alcoholic will recover more slowly from a drunken spree. Thirdly, Gove argues that *psychological drives*, especially those sustained by the production of such hormones as testosterone and adrenaline, decline suddenly too.

(15) This line of theorizing leads easily to explaining the differential patterns of male and female deviance. Gove suggests that females are so much less likely than males to commit certain acts simply because they are weaker and smaller. He notes that the differences shown in Table 7-3 indicate the need to explain not simply why women are less likely than men to commit crimes but also why the difference is so much greater for the high-risk, physically demanding crimes. Moreover, among both males and females, those with more muscular builds are more prone to these forms of deviance, and both genders show a notable drop in these behaviors as they begin to pass their physical prime. Gove concluded with the observation that, at the age when some people are winning Olympic medals, others their age are busy committing assaults, robberies, rapes, and burglaries and that both groups consist of "young adults who withdraw from the field as they age."

(16) Although Gove's new approach may help explain certain aspects of deviance, it leaves many others unaddressed. Most people do not stop committing risky and physical crimes as they pass their prime because *most people never commit these offenses at any age.* What distinguishes those who do from those who don't? Let's turn to other theories of crime and deviance in search of answers.

Personality Theory

(17) Despite an immense amount of research, efforts to link various forms of deviant behavior to abnormal features of the personality have been disappointing (Sagarin, 1975; Liska, 1981). An assessment of ninety-four studies, which were conducted between 1950 and 1965 and meant to distinguish between criminals and noncriminals by using various personality tests, found the overall results to be weak and contradictory (Waldo and Dinitz, 1967).

(18) The most promising line of psychological research has been on extremely aggressive behavior. Hans Toch (1969) found that *men who repeatedly assaulted others* had very weak self-esteem. This trait made them extremely resentful of even slight criticism or discourtesy, especially if it occurred in the presence of others. The violent rages of these men stemmed from the fear of loss of face, combined with the belief that others already held them in low esteem.

(19) In-depth interviews with men frequently convicted of assault led Leonard Berkowitz (1978) to expand on Toch's position. Berkowitz concluded that these men had such fragile self-esteem that they flew into uncontrollable rages even when no one except the offending person was present. An audience might spur them to even wilder reactions, but they could suddenly become violent even without such a spur.

(20) Berkowitz's respondents consisted of sixty-five white males between the ages of 18 and 43; most were in their late twenties. Each was serving time in an English jail for assault, and most had served many previous sentences for violent behavior—one had twenty-seven prior convictions. Another, with fourteen previous convictions for assault, had gotten into an argument with a policeman and knocked him down. Then the man ran into his house, got a machete, and battled eight cops, wounding two of them. Why had he done it? His answer was, in effect, Why not? The cop "just got on me back. . . . That was it, [I] just elbowed him, brought him over me shoulder, and stamped him with me foot."

(21) Arguments were the most common preliminary to violent outbursts by these men. The interviews showed remarkably little sign of rational calculation—of deciding whether or when to hit someone. Of course, men in jail may wish to deny responsibility for the act that got them there. Still, that these same men had repeated such behavior so often despite jail sentences strongly suggests that there is truth to their claims that these things just seem to happen to them. As one man with a long record of assault convictions put it, "At the time I'm not thinking at all, you know. It's afterwards I think this all out, but at the time I don't stop to think. At the time it seems the natural thing to do or the right thing to do" (Berkowitz, 1978).

(22) Whatever the psychological dynamics involved, social scientists now agree that some people are extremely prone to committing violent acts. For example, recent research conducted on all men born in Copenhagen, Denmark, between Jan. 1, 1944, and Dec. 31, 1947—a total of 28,884 men—found that 147 of them (or 0.5 percent) accounted for 20 percent of the violent offenses committed by the entire group (Brennan, Mednick, and John, 1989). Each of these men had been arrested repeatedly for violent crimes. Had these offenses occurred during the commission of a property crime—when, for example, a robber pistol-whips an uncooperative victim or a mob "enforcer" beats up someone as a tactic to make him pay a debt—issues of psychopathology need not arise, even if such a person repeatedly offends. But the existence of people who repeatedly commit violent acts that seemingly have only psychological motives encourages many social scientists to keep exploring the psychological processes of such people.

(23) However, noting that violence always involves at least *two* people, some sociologists have shifted their attention to *interpersonal* processes that precede violence. These often are defined as "character contests" in which two people having very poor interaction skills and very "thin skins" find themselves trapped in a situation in which they must escalate the level of abuse and insult until they find it necessary to become violent or suffer unbearable humiliation (Luckenbill, 1977; Luckenbill and Doyle, 1989).

(24) An additional approach to studying aggression through personality analysis suggests not only that the inability to control rage is a frequent cause but also that *too great* control over rage may lead to extreme violence. Thus, very passive, mild-mannered people who suppress their anger during a long period of provocation may cause others to provoke them excessively; eventually the quiet people erupt in acts of extreme retribution. Had they been less controlled, they might have prevented the increased mistreatment. Instead, they took it as long as they could and then earned newspaper headlines as the person who "wouldn't hurt a fly" but who suddenly took an axe to a spouse or a neighbor or went to the office one morning with a shotgun (Schultz, 1960; Megargee, 1966).

(25) Later in this chapter we shall see that some forms of deviant behavior do seem to be acts of sudden impulse. We shall also see that sociological theories are not well suited to deal with these forms of deviance, which are probably best understood through psychology.

(26) However, *most of the deviant acts that prompt so much interest in criminology are not acts of impulse.* And at least so far, personality theories have not helped much in explaining acts of deviance involving conscious choices. We shall return to these matters toward the end of the chapter. Now we should see just what sociologists think they know about deviance.*

---

*Rodney Stark, *Sociology*, 4th ed. (Belmont, Calif.: Wadsworth, 1992), pp. 174–177.

1. The main idea of the entire excerpt seems to be about

    a. how biology affects deviant behavior
    b. how personality types affect deviant behavior
    c. how men tend to be more violent than women
    d. how biology and personality influence deviant behavior

2. The main idea of paragraph 2 concerns

    a. Lombroso's theory that criminals are less evolved human beings
    b. the instincts a criminal has
    c. Lombroso's theories on crime
    d. Lombroso's studies of prisoners

3. The major organizational pattern of paragraph 5 seems to be

    a. thesis–support
    b. cause–effect
    c. sequence of events
    d. definition

4. The major organizational pattern of paragraph 6 seems to be

    a. cause–effect
    b. definition
    c. spatial–geographic
    d. sequence of events

5. The organizational patterns that seem to structure paragraphs 17 and 18 are

    a. sequence of events and cause–effect
    b. compare–contrast and cause–effect
    c. thesis–support and cause–effect
    d. definition and cause–effect

---

1. _____

2. _____

3. _____

4. _____

5. _____

_____
70%

Ask instructor for answers.

Read the following three questions. Then go back and reread the excerpt. Answer these questions in a phrase or sentence without looking back.

1. What was Cesare Lombroso's theory of criminal behavior? (2 points)
2. What does the twins study suggest about heredity and crime? (2 points)
3. Why does Walter Gove believe that there is a relationship between age and crime? (1 point)

Follow-up on the
Sociology Exercises

Now that you have completed these exercises, it may be helpful to see how your reading of this topic has changed some of your ideas about social issues. You may want to go back to these exercises to reread them just for their content or for what they have to say about sociology. Then answer the following questions either individually or in small groups:

1. How would you now define *sociology*?
2. What sociological issue that you read about interests you the most? Why?
3. Where do you stand on the issue of nature versus nurture?
4. What theory of crime seems the most convincing to you? Why?

7 Summarizing and Paraphrasing

Summarizing

❶ Locate main idea   ❶ Locate major details

Paraphrasing

❶ Look up difficult words   ❶ Break up difficult sentences

Being able to summarize information from textbooks, lectures, and lecture notes is one of the most important skills to master. Organized summaries will provide helpful study sheets for exams. A *summary* is an accurate restatement of material, presented in condensed form. The key terms to remember are *accurate* and *condensed*. Inaccurate summaries are useless, while lengthy summaries are much like the original.

Summarizing, like note-taking and critical reading, is a complex activity that improves with practice. So do not expect to be an expert summarizer right away.

How to Summarize

To be able to summarize efficiently, you need to identify main ideas and major details, both in lectures and in reading textbooks. As your summaries improve, you will be choosing the significant major details. In summaries, you rarely include minor details.

For now, follow these steps when you summarize textbooks and lecture material. Most of these hints apply to summarizing written material. In Part Three you will learn more about how to summarize while listening to lectures.

1. In each paragraph of text or on each page of lecture notes, locate the main idea, which is often the first sentence. You must include these main ideas in your summary. Underline the main idea twice or use a curved line. And underline the important parts of the sentence. Look at this example:

   <u>Anthropology</u> is a study that <u>compares</u> human <u>societies and cultures</u>, attempting to analyze, <u>describe</u>, and explain different ways of life in different parts of the world.

2. Sometimes main ideas are implied, and often in textbooks two or three shorter paragraphs work like one big paragraph. If you read several paragraphs and cannot locate a main-idea sentence, write your own in the margin.

3. Underline one or two major details in each paragraph of text or section of lecture notes. Do not underline the entire sentence, just the important words. Underline these details once to differentiate them from main ideas. See how the major detail is highlighted in this sentence:

> Cultural anthropology focuses mainly on human behavior that is learned rather than behavior that is transmitted genetically and considers what is typical in a particular group or society

Which details should you include? This choice may be difficult at first; just keep asking yourself: Which are the important details? Which most directly support the main idea? The layout of the textbook should help you. Main ideas and certain major details are often in boldface print or in italics. In lectures, listen for such comments as "I want you to remember this," "It is important to remember," or "I repeat." Also, note what the instructor writes on the blackboard; these are his clues that he is presenting key points.

4. When you have finished five or six paragraphs of textbook material and have underlined main ideas and major details, stop reading. Also, when you have marked a page or two of lecture notes, put your pen down. Then, write a summary of five or six sentences or phrases either in outline form or in a short paragraph. It is often better to put your summaries in outline form because you can separate main ideas from major details.

Put this summary in your own words. By putting the information in your own words, you make it easier to learn. When you are copying from a textbook or from your lecture notes, you are not actively thinking, and you will probably not remember what you have copied. Only when you read or hear a definition, should you copy. Here, the exact wording is necessary for you to understand the term. Learning research consistently shows that when you make material your own by using the words familiar to you, you have a much greater chance of remembering it. You will learn more about summarizing text material in Chapter 13 on the SQ3R study system.

Read the following five-paragraph excerpt on the study of anthropology. See if you can locate the main ideas and significant major details by effective underlining. Then place your summary in the outline skeleton that follows the excerpt. Use your own words wherever possible.

(1) Who were the Nacirema? How did they live? What accounted for their extreme ideology of remaking the natural environment? Why did they disappear? What can we learn from a study of their culture?

(2) Anthropology, the comparative study of human societies and cultures, provides some answers to questions like these. The aim of anthropology is to describe, analyze, and explain the different ways of life, or cultures, through which human groups, or societies, have adapted to their environments. Anthropology is comparative in that it attempts to understand both similarities and differences among human societies, in both the past and the present. Only by the study of humanity in its total variety can we understand the origins and development of our species.

(3) Anthropologists study our species from its beginnings several million years ago right up to the present. We study human beings as they live in every corner of the earth, in all kinds of physical environments. Some anthropologists are now trying to project how human beings will live in outer space. It is this interest in humankind throughout time and in all parts of the world that distinguishes anthropology as a scientific and humanistic discipline. In other academic disciplines, human behavior is studied primarily from the point of view of Western society. "Human nature" is thought to be the same as the behavior of people as they exist in the modern industrial nations of Europe and the United States.

(4) Human beings everywhere consider their own behavior not only right, but natural. For example, both "common sense" and Western economic theory see human beings as "naturally" individualistic and competitive. But in some societies, human beings are not competitive, and the group is more important than the individual. Anthropologists see the Western idea of "economic man"—the individual motivated by profit and rational self-interest—as the result of the particular socioeconomic and political system we live in. It is not an explanation of the behavior of the Arapesh hunter in New Guinea, who makes sure he is not always the first to sight and claim the game, so that others will not leave him to hunt alone (Mead 1963:38). In anthropology, more than any other discipline, concepts of human nature and theories of human behavior are based on studies of human groups whose goals, values, views of reality, and environmental adaptations are very different from those of modern, industrial Western societies.

(5) In their attempts to explain human variation, anthropologists combine the study of both human biology and the learned and shared patterns of human behavior we call culture. Other academic disciplines focus on one factor—biology, psychology, physiology, or society—as the explanation of human behavior. Anthropology seeks to understand human beings as whole organisms who adapt to their environments through a complex interaction of biology and culture.*

I. Anthropology

   A. Definition: _____

---

*Serena Nanda, *Cultural Anthropology*, 4th Ed. (Belmont, Calif.: Wadsworth, 1991), p. 5.

B. Three basic aims: _____

C. How anthropology is different from other disciplines:

_____

D. Two studies anthropology combines: _____

_____

Compare your underlining and summary with that on pp. 393–395.

Now that you have completed your underlining and summary and checked it with the answer key, read the following comments about the excerpt.

1. Paragraph 1 is basically meant to catch your attention; your note-taking should begin with paragraph 2.

2. In paragraph 2, did you notice that the first sentence defines anthropology and the next sentences address the specific concerns of anthropology?

3. Paragraphs 3 and 4 focus on the differences between anthropology and other disciplines.

4. Paragraph 5 emphasizes those studies anthropology relies on to conduct its research.

This excerpt has a fairly straightforward organization—general information usually comes before the details. Even when the organization is difficult to follow—when the main idea is implied—you are still following the same procedure as you summarize. You look for the general statement made by a paragraph or paragraphs; then you locate the specific information that supports it.

As you continue working through this book, you will be completing several summaries. As you complete each summary, your abilities will improve.

How to Paraphrase

Instead of dealing with several sentences, a paraphrase may focus on a single sentence. Often you cannot understand this sentence because either it is long or the vocabulary is difficult. When you paraphrase, you try to make sense of a difficult sentence. A *paraphrase* is a simply worded, accurate restatement of a phrase, sentence, or sentences. Unlike a summary, a paraphrase may be longer than the original statement.

Here are some steps that you need to follow when you paraphrase. Most of these suggestions apply to what you read:

1. Read each difficult sentence carefully. Reread the sentence that comes before it and after it. You do this to place the difficult sentence in its proper context.

2. If the sentence has difficult words, look them up in the dictionary or in the glossary of the textbook. Often your confusion abates when you understand the terminology. But don't simply find synonyms for words you do not know and plug them into your paraphrase. Let your understanding of any difficult words help you take a fresh look at the entire sentence. You may want to reread the sentence you are paraphrasing once you have looked up and understood a difficult word.

3. Divide long sentences into phrases or clauses. Phrases and clauses are often set off by commas, semicolons, colons, and dashes. If you hear a particularly long sentence in a lecture, listen for the pauses.

4. Determine the subject and verb of the sentence. The subject and verb should give you the core meaning of the sentence.

5. If the statement is written, reread the phrases and clauses; even read these parts aloud if you have to.

6. Be sure your paraphrase is complete and that no part of the sentence has been omitted.

7. As much as possible, write your paraphrase in your own words, as you do with your summaries. By using your own words in your paraphrase, you have a better chance of understanding the difficult sentence because you will not be tied to the voice and style of the original sentence.

8. Write your paraphrase in the textbook margins or on the left-hand side of your notes.

Look at the following italicized sentence, and use these eight steps to paraphrase it correctly. It's the fourth sentence in paragraph 4 from the excerpt in anthropology that you just summarized. You are also given the preceding sentence and the one that follows:

> But in some societies, human beings are not competitive, and the group is more important than the individual. *Anthropologists see the Western idea of "economic man"—the individual motivated by profit and rational self-interest—as the result of the particular socio-economic and political system we live in.* It is not an explanation of the behavior of the Arapesh hunter in New Guinea, who makes sure he is not always the first to sight and claim the game, so that others will not leave him to hunt alone.

Write your paraphrase here: _____

_____

After writing your paraphrase, see whether you used some of the following practices:

1. You notice that the sentence before refers to societies in which competition is unimportant, and the sentence after describes the behavior of the New Guinea hunter. Your sentence concerns the notion of the economic man in the Western world.

2. You may have looked up the word *rational* to find that it means logical or reasoned and *Western* to refer to European and American history and civilizations.

3. You note that the sentence is broken up by dashes, with a description of economic man within the dashes. Without this parenthetical material, the sentence is quite clear.

4. You note that the subject of the sentence is *anthropologists* and the verb is *see*. You then ask: What do anthropologists see? Your answer is that anthropologists see something about economic man in the West.

5. It is the object of this sentence—what anthropologists see—that is confusing, mainly because this part of the sentence is long and written in a complicated syntax. After rereading this part of the sentence, you realize that economic man has the following characteristics: he focuses on himself in a desire to make money and this desire is shaped by his culture.

Once you have completed these steps, you are ready to write your paraphrase, which should say something like: "Anthropologists see economic man to be reasoned and self-centered in his desire to make money, and he is like this because of the particular environment that influences all Western people."

Paraphrasing may seem tedious, but as you continue to paraphrase, you will find that your critical reading practices will improve. Most students who cannot paraphrase simply ignore difficult passages and thus have poorer comprehension of the material, often incorrectly summarizing the material they read. As your paraphrasing abilities improve, you will be able to determine whether your difficulty in comprehension is due to difficult words or to long and involved sentences. In this way, you will begin to analyze the author's style. In some cases, you will find that your paraphrase is a simple statement after all—that in the original passage, the author used big words and many words to express a simple idea. In others, your paraphrase will allow you to uncover an essential and difficult concept in your reading. Finally, you will discover that as you learn more in a particular subject, it will be easier for you to paraphrase difficult sentences in that field.

Summary

Summarizing and paraphrasing are necessary practices in reading textbooks, in listening to lectures, and in reviewing your notes. Both are sophisticated, critical activities. In summarizing, you locate main ideas and important details. It is an active process of sorting out the important from the less important and the unimportant. When you paraphrase, you attempt to understand a difficult sentence or sentences. Paraphrasing involves seeing a sentence in its context, looking up new words, and dividing the sentence into phrases and clauses. Finally, when you summarize and paraphrase, you are putting information into your own words and thus have a better chance of remembering it.

Did the summary of this introduction separate the significant from the less significant? Was it worded differently? Do you think it was a successful summary?

You are now ready to practice these two activities in the following exercises, which also deal with anthropology, and in Part Three on note-taking.

Summary Box   *Summarizing and Paraphrasing*

What are they?	*How do you use them?*	*Why do you use them?*
Summarizing: accurate restatement of material in fewer words.	Locate main ideas and significant details and put this information in your own words.	To remember more easily large chunks of information.
Paraphrasing: accurate restatement of difficult material to put it more simply.	Read sentence in its context; look up new words; divide sentences into smaller chunks.	To understand difficult sentences that you would otherwise skip over.

Skills Practice Topic: Anthropology

All the exercises in this chapter focus on anthropology, a subject you may study in your college career.

Before you begin these exercises, answer the following questions either individually or in small groups to get some sense of what you already know about anthropology:

1. How would you define the study of anthropology?
2. What is meant by the term *culture*?
3. Are there any topics in anthropology that you have already studied?
4. How do you think an anthropologist would study religion?

Exercise 7.1
Summarizing a
Longer Passage

The following excerpt is from an anthropology textbook, and it explains how anthropologists study religion. Your job is to underline main ideas and major details. Then, based on your underlinings, complete the five questions that follow. Remember not to underline entire sentences, just the important parts.

The Functions of Religion

The Search for Order and Meaning

(1) One of the most important functions of religion is to give meaning to and explain those aspects of the physical and social environment that are important in the lives of individuals and societies. Religion deals with the nature of life and death, the creation of the universe, the origin of society and groups within the society, the relationship of individuals and groups to one another, and the relation of humankind to nature. Anthropologists call this whole cognitive system a cosmology, or world view. Human societies create images of reality, often in symbolic ways, that serve as a framework for interpreting events and experiences, particularly those that are out of the ordinary. These "different realities" emerge as a way of imposing order and meaning on the world within which humans live and of giving humans the feeling that they have some measure of control over that world.

(2) Science and religion, which are often opposed in Western thought, are similar in that both involve "the quest for unity underlying apparent diversity; for simplicity underlying apparent complexity; for order underlying apparent disorder; for regularity underlying apparent anomaly" (Horton and Finnegan 1973). But where science provides explanations that are open to new data and explicitly acknowledges a possibility of various alternatives, religious systems tend not to be open to empirical testing.

(3) The separation between religion and science in our own society corresponds to our sharp separation of the supernatural and the natural. In other societies, these two concepts are less sharply separated. The supernatural can be seen as part of the natural and as intervening in all aspects of life. Thus, the kin group includes both living relatives and dead ancestors; power and leadership are often believed to have divine origins; rules of behavior are given divine sanction; and breaches are punished by the gods. The success of even ordinary undertakings in the physical world is ensured by enlisting the help of supernatural powers. Natural disasters, illness, and misfortune are believed to be caused by extrahuman or supernatural spirits. Natural and supernatural, human and natural, past, present, and future may be perceived as a unity in a way that violates the logic of Western thought. This makes it difficult for us to understand many non-Western religions and accounts for our ethnocentric labeling of them as "irrational," "contradictory," or the products of faulty thinking.

(4) **Reducing Anxiety and Increasing Control**   Many religious practices are aimed at ensuring success in carrying out a wide variety of human activities. Prayers and offerings are made to supernatural beings in the hope that they will aid a particular individual or community. Rituals are performed to call on supernatural beings and to control forces that appear to be unpredictable, such as those in the natural

environment upon which humans depend for survival. One of the wide-spread practices used to control supernatural forces is magic. Although magical practices exist in many societies, magic seems to be more prominent in those in which there is less predictability in the outcome of events and thus less feeling of being in control of the social and physical environment. In the Trobriand Islands, for example, magic is not used for ordinary canoe trips within the lagoons, but only when the Islanders undertake the long-distance and dangerous canoe trips to other islands in their kula trade. Magic is also prevalent in sports and games of chance.

(5) Even if magic cannot "work" from the standpoint of Western science, it may be effective in achieving results indirectly, mainly by reducing the anxiety of the individuals and groups that practice it. This reduced anxiety allows them to proceed with more confidence, and the confidence may lead to greater success. Where technological advance and science are able to increase predictability and control over events and human relations, magic tends to become less important.

(6) **Maintaining the Social Order** Religion has a number of important functions that either directly or indirectly help maintain the social order and the survival of a society. To begin with, religious beliefs about good and evil are reinforced by supernatural means of social control. Thus, religion is a powerful force for conformity in a society. Furthermore, through myth and ritual, social values are given sacred authority and provide a reason for the present social order. Religious ritual also intensifies solidarity by creating an atmosphere in which people experience their common identity in emotionally moving ways. Religion is also an important educational institution. Initiation rites, for example, almost always include the transmission of information about cultural practices and tradition.

(7) By supporting the present social order and defining the place of the individual in society and in the universe, religion also provides people with a sense of personal identity and belonging. When individuals have lost a positive identity, or when life has no meaning because of the disintegration of a traditional culture, religion can supply a new and more positive identity and become the basis for a new adaptation. Religion can also provide an escape from reality; in the religious beliefs of an afterlife or the coming of a Messiah, powerless people who live in harsh and deprived circumstances can create an illusion of power through the manipulation of religious symbols. Religion in these circumstances is an outlet for frustration, resentment, and anger and is a way of draining off energy that might otherwise be turned against the social system. In this way, religion indirectly contributes to maintaining the social order.

(8) In summary, religion has both instrumental and expressive functions. The instrumental aspect of religion has to do with actions performed in the belief that, if people do certain things, they can influence the course of natural or social events to their advantage. The expressive aspect of ritual refers to the ways in which religious symbolism is used to express ideas about the relation of humans to nature, self to society, or group to group. In its expressive aspect, religion is an important force for social integration.*

*Nanda, *Cultural Anthropology*, pp. 361–363.

1. The main idea of paragraph 1 is:

   a. anthropology can effectively study religion.
   b. cosmology is a world view.
   c. religion serves to give meaning to and explain what is important in a particular society
   d. religion serves to give its members control of their world.

2. Paragraph 2 serves to:

   a. define science
   b. introduce the similarities and differences between religion and science
   c. show how religion tends to organize that which is disorganized in life
   d. show how religion is not scientific

3. The main idea of paragraph 3 concerns:

   a. the separation of the natural and supernatural in our society and their connection in other societies
   b. the power that the dead exert in other cultures
   c. how common practices rely on the supernatural for their success
   d. the irrational side of non-Western religions

4. The last sentence in paragraph 6 is a:

   a. main-idea sentence
   b. major-detail sentence
   c. minor-detail sentence
   d. none of these

5. Which of the following is *not* a main idea of this excerpt?

   a. Religion serves to ensure the success of a culture's activities.
   b. Magic tends to create anxiety among the peoples who practice it.
   c. Religion helps maintain the social order.
   d. Religion helps people derive a sense of belonging.

1. _____

2. _____

3. _____

4. _____

5. _____

_____

(score = # correct × 20)
Find answers on p. 397.

Exercise 7.2
Summarizing a
Second Passage

The following is a second excerpt from an anthropology textbook, focusing on how a New Guinea tribe uses religion to satisfy several of its needs. As in the previous exercise, underline the main ideas and significant details in each paragraph. Underline only key sentence parts. From your underlinings, finish the partially completed outline that follows.

Religious Ritual and Adaptation

(1) Recent research has shown that religious belief and ritual not only indirectly contribute to the survival of a society but may also directly affect the relationship between a social group and its physical environment. A study by Roy Rappaport (1967) of the Tsembaga of New Guinea

shows how religious belief and ritual may produce "a practical result on the external world."

(2) The Tsembaga, who live in the valleys of a mountain range in New Guinea, are swidden cultivators who also raise pigs. Small numbers of pigs are easy to keep, as they eat anything and help keep residential areas free from garbage. Although pigs can ruin gardens in the early stages of planting, after the trees are well established, pigs are allowed to root in the gardens, where they actually help cultivation by eating seeds and tubers (sweet potatoes). If pig herds grow very large, however, feeding them becomes a problem, and it becomes necessary for extra food to be harvested just to feed the pigs. Furthermore, when pig herds become too large, they are more likely to invade gardens and require more supervision. The Tsembaga kill pigs only on ritual occasions—either at pig feasts or in times of misfortune such as illness, death, or warfare.

(3) The Tsembaga have a ritual cycle that they perform, they say, in order to rearrange their relationships with the supernatural world. This cycle can be viewed as beginning with the rituals performed during warfare. In Tsembaga warfare, opponents generally occupy territories next to each other. After hostilities have broken out, each side performs certain rituals that formally designate the other group as the enemy. Fighting may continue on and off for weeks, sometimes ending with one group's being routed. In this case, the survivors go to live with their kinsmen, and the victors destroy the losers' gardens, slaughter their pigs, and burn their houses. The victors do not occupy their land, however, as this is believed to be guarded by the ancestors of the defeated group.

(4) Most Tsembaga warfare ends in truce, however, with both groups remaining on their territory. When a truce is declared, each group performs a ritual called "planting the rumbin." The rumbin is dedicated to the ancestors, who are thanked for helping in the fight. At this ritual planting, there is a wholesale slaughter of adult pigs. Some of the meat is eaten by the local group itself, and the rest is distributed to other groups that have helped it fight. After this feast, there is a period in which the fighting groups are still considered to be in debt to their allies and their ancestors. This period will not end until the rumbin plant is uprooted. This ritual also requires a pig feast and occurs when there are sufficient pigs.

(5) The question is: How many pigs are sufficient? It is when pig herds reach over four per woman caretaker that they become too troublesome to manage and begin to compete with humans for food. Thus, it is the wives of the owners of large numbers of pigs who begin agitating for the ritual to uproot the rumbin. This ritual, which is followed by a pig festival lasting about a year, involves much entertaining among villages. Food is exchanged, and hosts and guests spend the nights dancing. At this time, future alliances may be set up between hosts and guests. At this time, also, much trade takes place, involving such items as axes, bird plumes, and shell ornaments. For one festival, Rappaport observed that between 4,500 and 6,000 pounds of pig meat were distributed over 163 occasions to between 2,000 and 3,000 people in seventeen local groups. The pig festival ends with another pig slaughter and the

public presentation of a salted pig belly to one's allies. This concludes the ritual cycle. A local group would now consider itself free to attack its neighbors, knowing that assistance from both human allies and ancestors would be forthcoming because their obligations to feed them pork has been fulfilled.

(6) This ritual cycle among the Tsembaga shows a number of functions of religion. It adjusts the man-land ratio, as survivors in a defeated group seek refuge in other local groups. It also facilitates trade through the markets and exchanges that take place during the year of the pig festival. Most directly in terms of survival, however, it ensures the distribution of local surpluses of pig meat, which is a source of high-quality protein, throughout the whole Tsembaga region. The ritual cycle also helps to maintain an undegraded environment, as pigs are killed when there get to be too many of them and when they threaten the source of human food.*

I. Tsembaga's use of pigs

Answers will vary. Ask instructor for sample underlinings and outline.

   A.

   B.

   C.

II. The Tsembaga ritual cycle

   A.

   B.

   C.

III. Description of "planting the rumbin" _____

IV. Description of pig festival _____

  V. Functions of ritual cycle

   A.

   B.

   C.

   D.

_____

*Nanda, *Cultural Anthropology*, pp. 364–365.

***Exercise 7.3
Summarizing a
Third Passage***

This third excerpt deals with the anthropological examination of various kinds of beliefs. In this excerpt, several important terms related to belief are introduced and explained. As with the previous two exercises, underline main ideas and significant details. Then complete an outline—this time without any help—summarizing the main ideas and major details.

Kinds of Beliefs: Animism and Animatism

(1) A basic distinction in types of religious beliefs is that between animism and animatism. **Animism** is the belief that not only living creatures but also inanimate objects have life and personality; these supernatural persons are referred to as spirits, ghosts, or gods. Such beings are believed to behave as people do: They are conscious, they have will, and they feel the same emotions as human beings feel. Such spirits may reside in features of the physical environment, such as trees or stones, or they may reside in animals. In hunting societies—for example, the Lele of Africa and the Inuit—the spirits of animals are worshipped because it is believed that a hunt will be successful only if an animal allows itself to be killed. Souls, which may also reside in human bodies, are believed to be able to leave the body at will, temporarily during sleep or permanently as in death. Spirits or souls that leave the body at death turn into ghosts, which come in a variety of forms and relate in various ways to the living in different cultures.

(2) The distinction between a spirit and a god is mostly one of scale. A god is a supernatural being of great importance and power; a spirit is a lesser being. **Polytheism** is the term used for a religion with many gods, and **monotheism** refers to a religion with only one god. Whether a religion is polytheistic or monotheistic is not so clear-cut in real cultures, however. In so-called polytheistic religions, the many gods may be just so many aspects of the one god. In India, for example, it is said that there are literally millions of gods; yet even an uneducated Indian will understand that in some way (which does not confuse him or her, though it may confuse us), these are all aspects of one divine essence.

(3) The Nuer are another culture in which the distinction between the Great Spirit and lesser spirits is fuzzy to the outsider. The Nuer, of course, have no difficulty in understanding the different contexts in which different aspects of the Great Spirit are invoked. E. E. Evans-Pritchard (1968) describes a ceremony held to end a blood feud. All the speakers, representing both clans and including the Leopard Skin chief, addressed the various gods: Great Spirit, spirit of the sky, spirit of our community, spirit of the flesh (this refers to the divine power of the Leopard Skin chief), and spirit of our fathers. Each clan representative appealed to God not only as God but also as God in relation to the group he represented. The Leopard Skin chief referred to God in his special relation to his religious role as mediator, as well as to the priestly lineage he belonged to.

(4) Just as in polytheistic religions, in which all gods and spirits may be reflections of one god, so in monotheistic religions, the one god may have several aspects. In the Roman Catholic religion, for example, there is God the Father, the Son, and the Holy Ghost, in addition to a number of lesser supernatural spirits such as the saints, ghosts, the devil, and the

souls of people in heaven, hell, and purgatory, as well as the souls of those living on earth.

(5) **Animatism** is the belief in an impersonal supernatural power. *Mana* is perhaps the most widely known term for this power. **Mana**, or supernatural power, may be inherent in the universe but may also be concentrated in individuals or in objects. We have seen earlier that Polynesian chiefs had a much higher degree of mana than ordinary people did. Mana is the key to success, but it can also be dangerous. That is why the belief in mana is so frequently associated with an elaborate system of taboos, or prohibitions. Mana is like electricity; it is a powerful force, but it can be dangerous when not approached with the proper caution.

(6) A cross-cultural approach seems to indicate that mana, or power, is often found in those areas (spatial, temporal, verbal, or physical) that are the boundaries between clear-cut categories. Hair, for example, is believed to contain supernatural power in many different cultures (remember the Old Testament story of Samson and Delilah). Hair is a symbol of the boundary between the self and the not-self. It is both part of a person and can be separated from the person. Hence its ambiguity and its power. Doorways and gates are also familiar symbols of supernatural power. They separate the inside from the outside and can thus serve as a symbol of moral categories such as good and evil, pure and impure. Because these symbols of boundaries contain supernatural power, they are frequently part of religious ritual and are surrounded by religious taboos.*

Write your outline of this passage here.

Answers will vary. Check your underlinings and outline with the sample underlinings and outline on pp. 397–398.

Exercise 7.4 Paraphrasing Sentences in Paragraphs

Four paragraphs on practices and rituals follow, and you will be able to apply what you have learned so far about religion and anthropology to the concepts of ritual and prayer. In these paragraphs, you will be asked to paraphrase five sentences. Before you answer these questions, read through the excerpt to get a general understanding of it. Then, apply the rules for paraphrasing to these sentences. Read through the four paraphrasing choices and select the paraphrase that is most like yours. Place all of your answers in the answer box.

*Nanda, *Cultural Anthropology*, pp. 367–369.

Practices and Rituals

(1)   [1]A religious ritual is a patterned act that involves the manipulation of religious symbols.   [2]Most religious rituals use a combination of the following practices to contact and control supernatural spirits and powers: prayer, offerings and sacrifices, manipulation of objects, telling or acting out myths, altering the physiological state of the individual (as in trance and ecstatic experiences or through drugs), music, dance, and drama (Wallace 1966).

Prayers and Offerings

(2)   [3]Prayer is any conversation held with spirits and gods. [4]Prayer can involve a request or a pleading; it can be in the form of a bargain or consist of merely praising the deity.   [5]In many religions, it is common to make a vow in which the individual promises to carry out a certain kind of behavior, such as going on a pilgrimage or building a temple, if the gods will grant a particular wish.   [6]Other forms of prayer are less familiar to the Westerner. In some cultures, gods can be lied to, commanded, or ridiculed.   [7]Among the many Northwest Coast tribes of North America, the insulting tone used to one's political rivals was also used to the gods.   [8]In these ranked societies, the greatest insult was to call a man a slave; when calamities fell or their prayers were not answered, people would vent their anger against the gods by saying, "You are a great slave" (Benedict 1961:221).

(3)   [9]Making offerings and sacrifices to supernatural beings is also a widespread religious practice.   [10]Sometimes these offerings consist of the first fruits of a harvest—grain, fish, or game.   [11]Sometimes the offering of food is in the form of a meal for the gods; among the Hindus, the gods are given food that they eat behind a curtain.   [12]After the gods have eaten, this food is distributed among the worshippers.

(4)   [13]In some societies, animals or humans may be sacrificed as an offering to the gods.   [14]Among cattle pastoralists of East Africa, such as the Nuer and the Pokot, cattle sacrifices are an important part of religious practices.   [15]The essence of the East African "cattle complex" is that cattle are killed and eaten only in a ritual and religious context, which seems to be an inefficient use of resources.   [16]This ritual use of cattle in sacrifice has always been of interest to anthropologists, and at one time it was given as a common example of how religious practices interfere with rational exploitation of the environment.   [17]More recent research has shown, however, that the sacrifice of cattle in a ritual context may be quite adaptive.   [18]Cattle sacrifices are offered in community feasts that occur on a fairly regular schedule, averaging once a week in any particular neighborhood.   [19]The feasts are thus an important source of meat in the diet.   [20]Furthermore, the religious taboo that an individual who eats ritually slaughtered meat may not take milk on the same day has the effect of making milk more available to those who have no meat, or conserving milk, which can be consumed as sour milk on the following day.   [21]In addition, the Pokot prefer fresh meat, which is also healthier than meat that is not fresh.   [22]Because one family could not consume a whole steer by itself, the problem of how to utilize beef most efficiently without refrigeration techniques is solved by offering it

to the community in a ceremonial setting.   [23]In this way, meat can be shared without fighting over the supply, because the portions are distributed according to age and sex by a rigid formula (Schneider 1973).*

1. An effective paraphrase for sentence 8 is:

   a. These tribes disliked the term *slave*.
   b. In anger, these tribes would insult the gods by accusing them of being slaves.
   c. For these tribes the term *slave* was insulting, and during bad times even the gods were accused of being slaves.
   d. The greatest slave was often considered to be the one who defied the gods somehow.

2. An effective paraphrase for sentence 15 is:

   a. In this case, cattle is only eaten when a religious service is practiced.
   b. This East African practice requires that cattle be killed and eaten during a religious experience, but this seems to be a wasteful practice.
   c. Cattle are eaten in a ritualized context, which makes use of the resources.
   d. The basis of cattle killing for these tribes must be ritualized and religious.

3. An effective paraphrase for sentence 16 is:

   a. The use of cattle in a ritualized sacrifice is of interest to anthropologists because it was evidence that religion was in conflict with a reasoned use of the environment.
   b. Destroying the environment is often not in agreement with the practices of ritual.
   c. Anthropologists see that religion interferes with the correct use of the environment.
   d. Sacrificing cattle is an interesting phenomenon for anthropologists studying the respectful uses of the environment.

4. An effective paraphrase for sentence 22 is:

   a. Eating an entire cow is difficult, even for a tribe.
   b. How to keep meat cold was a problem in keeping the beef from spoiling.
   c. Since one family could not eat all of the cow, offering the cow as a sacrifice to the rest of the tribe solved the problem of the meat keeping.
   d. The consumption of an entire cow was indeed a problem, especially since refrigeration was unknown to this tribe.

1. _____

2. _____

3. _____

4. _____

5. _____

_____
70%

Ask instructor for answers.

*Nanda, *Cultural Anthropology*, p. 369.

5. An effective paraphrase for sentence 23 is:

   a. Distributing the meat was logically solved by the tribe.

   b. The young as well as the old got an equal portion of the meat, so fighting was avoided.

   c. Thus, meat can be eaten harmoniously because a mathematical system is established.

   d. Thus, meat is divided up without conflict because a clear system has been established that takes into consideration the age and sex of the community members.

Exercise 7.5
More Paraphrasing
of Sentences in
Paragraphs

The following paragraphs continue the discussion of practices and rituals, this time focusing on human sacrifices. Read through the paragraphs carefully; then, using your paraphrasing skills, write appropriate paraphrases for the numbered sentences that come after the paragraphs. If you did not complete the previous exercise, read it through to get a sense of where this excerpt begins.

Human Sacrifices

(1) ¹Human sacrifice has also been a widespread practice, although it was often stamped out by European colonial governments. ²The Aztecs of Mexico, for example, had a religion in which human sacrifice was an important element, as we saw in the opening passage of this chapter.   ³The Aztec gods, such as the jaguar and the serpent, were bloodthirsty and fierce and required human victims to appease their appetites.   ⁴The victims, most of whom were captured in war, were ritually killed at the top of a pyramid built for this purpose.   ⁵Although Aztec cannibalism was limited to the ruler, nobles, and those who had captured victims in a war, it was practiced on a rather grand scale, perhaps totaling about 20,000 victims a year.

(2)   ⁶A wide-ranging debate has occurred in anthropology over the meanings and purposes of Aztec cannibalism.   ⁷Michael Harner (1977) proposes an ecological interpretation of Aztec sacrifice and cannibalism.   ⁸He holds that human sacrifice was a response to certain diet deficiencies in the population.   ⁹In the Aztec environment, wild game was getting scarce, and the population was growing.   ¹⁰Although the maize-beans combination of food that was the basis of the diet was usually adequate, these crops were subject to seasonal failure.   ¹¹Famine was frequent in the absence of edible domesticated animals.   ¹²To meet essential protein requirements, cannibalism was the only solution. ¹³Although only the upper classes were allowed to consume human flesh, a commoner who distinguished himself in a war could also have the privilege of giving a cannibalistic feast.   ¹⁴Thus, although it was the upper strata who benefited most from ritual cannibalism, members of the commoner class could also benefit.   ¹⁵Furthermore, as Harner explains, the social mobility and cannibalistic privileges available to the commoners through warfare provided a strong motivation for the "aggressive war machine" that was such a prominent feature of the Aztec state.

(3)   [16]A more symbolic approach to understanding Aztec cannibalism has been suggested by Marshall Sahlins (1978) and Peggy Sanday (1986).   [17]According to Sahlins, materialist anthropologists such as Harner have focused too much on Aztec cannibalism and have not paid enough attention to the context of human sacrifice.   [18]For the Aztecs, the consumption of human flesh was less emphasized than the sacred character of the sacrificial rite, the aim of which was to bring humans into communion with the gods.   [19]Without the proper nourishment of human hearts and human blood, the gods could not work on behalf of humans.   [20]The gods depended on human sacrifice for energy, without which the sun would not come up, the sky would fall down, and the universe would return to its original state of chaos.   [21]The sustenance given to the gods in the sacrificial offering and to humans in their houses ensured the regeneration of every individual and of Aztec society.

(4)   [22]Sanday's cross-cultural study, appropriately named Divine Hunger, emphasizes the ritual context of Aztec and other forms of cannibalism, viewing it "as a system of symbols and ritual acts through which human beings explore their relationship to the world, to other beings, and to being itself" (1986:31).   [23]Thus she, like Sahlins, sees Aztec cannibalism as making a statement about the sources of life and death and how these sources can be controlled by human beings.   [24]While both Sanday and Sahlins agree that the practice of cannibalism involved political and economic factors, as well as relations of the Aztec state with its enemies, both see Harner's materialist approach as too simplistic and partly as a projection of the American cost-benefit ideology.

(5)   [25]Other criticisms of the materialist approach have also been offered.   [26]To begin with, some anthropologists question whether the Aztecs even practiced ritual cannibalism, and there is no agreement about the extent of this practice.   [27]Harner, for example, bases his arguments on the evidence from early Spanish chroniclers such as Cortez, who wrote journals and letters describing Mexican customs.   [28]But as one critic (Ortiz de Montellano 1978) points out, the Spanish conquistadors did not necessarily write straightforward accounts of what they saw; they slanted their descriptions to make the Aztecs seem like barbarians in order to convince the king of Spain to support the conquest and undertake a large conversion effort by the Roman Catholic church.   [29]Ortiz de Montellano further argues that Aztec cannibalism can be fully explained by religious ideology and the desire to achieve status.   [30]He holds that neither the need for a dietary supplement nor the significance of the dietary contribution of human flesh has been convincingly demonstrated by Harner.   [31]The point here is not to prove one side of the argument or the other but to indicate some of the ways in which anthropologists have tried to "make sense" out of (to us) seemingly bizarre religious practices, by relating them to the sociocultural systems of which they are a part.*

---

*Nanda, *Cultural Anthropology,* pp. 370–372.

Paraphrase the following numbered sentences:

15. _____

18. _____

21. _____

24. _____

31. _____

Exercise 7.6
Using Summarizing
and Paraphrasing
Skills in a Longer
Passage

The following excerpt contains several paragraphs on magic and sorcery from an anthropologist's perspective. The sentences in italics will require paraphrasing on a separate sheet of paper or in the margins. When you have completed your reading, answer the five questions that follow. In answering the questions, you may refer to the passage. Place all your answers in the answer box.

Magic and Sorcery

(1) Magic and sorcery play major roles in the religious practices and rituals of many cultures throughout the world. Magic and sorcery are slightly different practices—magic more concerned with supernatural forces, sorcery with the harming of a specific individual.

(2) It is worthwhile to do a careful study of magic in order to understand how it differs from sorcery. Magic is defined as the attempt to control supernatural forces. By practicing magic, the magician is suggesting that he or she can control the supernatural world. *In this sense, magic is different from prayer because the magician is not asking a higher power to intervene.*

(3) There are two kinds of magic—imitative and contagious. In imitative magic, the magician copies the action she wants to happen: drawing a picture of a captured animal before a hunt or reciting lines like "Water is cold. Snow is cold." to stop one's pain caused by a burn. Contagious magic differs because it uses a part of an object that the magician wants to influence. For example, if a magician wants to cure an individual, she may use the individual's fingernail to cure the entire person.

(4) Magic is common practice in many countries. The Asoro society in New Guinea buries a new-born infant's umbilical cord so that the sorcerer cannot harm the infant. In courting his first girl, the young boy is taught to use love magic, which may cause the girl to see him as another boy to whom she is attracted. In this same society, pigs are supposedly tamed by blowing smoke into their ears. In this way, the magician tries to cool down the pig's hot temper.

(5) In many cultures in the East and the West, divination is practiced. Divination is defined as the method of deriving information from a supernatural figure. The Naskapi tribe on the Labrador Peninsula scorch the shoulder blade of an animal's skeleton. The magician then reads the information on this scorched bone to determine where the tribe can hunt by seeing the lines on the charred bone as a map. In Western society, the flipping of a coin is an example of divination because a higher power is invoked in determining "heads or tails."

(6) Sorcery—the magical practice used to harm an individual—is performed in tribes of Melanesia. The sorcerer throws a stick in the direction of the person he intends to hurt. He performs this act in a tone of anger and passion.

(7) There are several documented cases where sorcery seems to be successful. *Anthropologists attribute the success of a sorcerer's magic to the susceptibility of the victim.* If the victim believes that sorcery is powerful, she may succumb to it. Some common symptoms of a victim giving in to sorcery include general sadness, loss of appetite, and even starvation.

(8) *Sorcery and magic are becoming more popular supernatural practices in the United States because it seems Americans feel more vulnerable and they often have fallen away from the consolation that traditional religion used to provide them.* A witch cult in San Francisco has been studied by an anthropologist. This cult provides its members with curses which they can use on their enemies. In this particular cult, the recipient of the curse may also have his name written on lamb skin by the cult leader. This high priest then burns the name at the altar while he chants dangerous threats against the victim. As with victims of sorcery in Melanesia, if the victim is made aware that he is a target of sorcery, he may develop symptoms of illness.*

1. An effective summary of paragraph 2 is:

   a. Magic is different from prayer.
   b. Magic attempts to control the supernatural and, unlike prayer, is not asking a higher power for assistance.
   c. The magician can control the supernatural and has greater powers than those who pray.
   d. Magic and sorcery are entirely different forms of supernatural power.

2. The best summary of paragraph 3 is:

   a. Imitative magic mimics in action what the magician wants to happen.
   b. Contagious magic uses a part for the whole in making its magic happen.

---

*Adapted from Nanda, *Cultural Anthropology*, pp. 372–374.

   c. The two forms of magic are imitative and contagious—imitative copies the desired action; contagious uses a part of an object to achieve its result.

   d. Fingernails are often the materials used by magicians performing contagious magic while pictures are used by those performing imitative magic.

3. A major detail in paragraph 4 is:

   a. In New Guinea, pigs are tamed by blowing smoke into their ears.

   b. Magic is commonly practiced in many countries.

   c. The Asoro tribe is found in New Guinea.

   d. All of these.

4. The main idea of paragraph 5 is:

   a. Divination is practiced in many cultures.

   b. The Naskapi tribe practices divination on dead animals.

   c. Divination is the method of getting information from a supernatural figure.

   d. The flipping of a coin is a kind of divination.

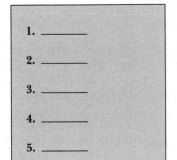

1. _____

2. _____

3. _____

4. _____

5. _____

5. The best summary for paragraph 6 is:

   a. Sorcery is performed in Melanesia.

   b. Sorcery is magic used to harm a person.

   c. Sorcery is magic with the intent of hurting an individual, an example being a sorcerer throwing a stick at a person he wants to harm.

   d. By throwing a stick at a person, a sorcerer is able to harm an individual that he is practicing sorcery on.

Answer the following five questions in a short phrase or sentence.

6. Reread paragraph 1. List the two points that this excerpt intends to cover.

7. Reread paragraphs 7 and 8. What are the reasons given for the sorcerer's supposed success?

8. Paraphrase the underlined sentence in paragraph 2.

9. Paraphrase the underlined sentence in paragraph 7.

_____
80%

Ask instructor for answers.

10. Paraphrase the underlined sentence in paragraph 8.

Exercise 7.7
Writing a Paragraph
Using Summarizing
and Paraphrasing
Skills

Your job is to go back to the excerpt on magic and sorcery and to find the information to answer the following questions. Much of this information is to be found in your paraphrases and your answers to the summary questions. From your responses to these questions, answer the essay question that follows. Write as much as you can in your own words.

1. Define magic and sorcery.

2. Provide two examples of magic.

3. Provide two examples of sorcery.

70%

Ask instructor for answers.

Essay question: In one paragraph, define magic and sorcery as these terms are used in anthropology. Then provide an example of each, preferably one from the West and another from a non-Western culture.

Exercise 7.8
Using Summarizing
and Paraphrasing
Skills on a Textbook
Excerpt

The following is an anthropologist's view of how religions are organized, analyzing the four different categories of religious practices. Read through the excerpt quickly to get a sense of its organization. Then go back and read it slowly, paying particular attention to longer sentences that you may want to paraphrase. You also may want to underline the key main ideas and major details. When you finish, answer the five questions that follow and place your answers in the answer box. You may refer to the excerpt in deciding on your answer.

The Organization of Religion

(1) Like other human behavior, religious behavior is patterned and organized. A useful way of examining religious organization is in terms of the degree of specialization of religious personnel—those who conduct ceremonies and perform rituals. On this basis, Anthony Wallace (1966) identifies four patterns of religious organization: individualistic cults, shamanistic cults, communal cults, and ecclesiastical cults. Although all patterns can be found in complex societies, simple hunting and gathering societies may have only individualistic and shamanistic cults. Communal cults are characteristic of horticultural and tribally organized societies, and ecclesiastical cults are found in state societies.

Individualistic Cults

(2) In **individualistic cults**, each person may be a religious specialist, seeking contact with the supernatural directly according to his or her own experience and psychic needs. An example of an individualistic religious cult is the *vision quest,* a pattern of seeking contact with the supernatural found among many Indian groups of North America. In these cultures, an individual was able to develop a special relationship

with a particular spirit that would give the person power and knowledge of specific kinds. The spirit acted as a personal protector, or guardian. The vision seeker was under a strong emotional impulse and by various means, such as fasting, isolation in a lonely spot, or self-mutilation, intensified his or her emotional state.

(3) The Thompson Indians of western Canada had a vision quest that included most of the traits typical of this pattern. When a boy, usually between the ages of twelve and sixteen, became old enough to dream of an arrow, a canoe, or a woman, he began his search for a guardian spirit. Before the actual quest itself, the boy had to run, with bow and arrow in his hands, until he was exhausted. Then he was made to plunge into cold water. He did this four times a day for four days. His face was painted red, and he put on a headband of cedar bark and tied ornaments made of deer hoof to his knees and ankles. He also wore a skin apron decorated with symbols of the life occupation for which he sought the spirit's assistance. The nights prior to undertaking the quest were spent in dancing, singing, and praying around a fire on some nearby mountain peak.

(4) The boy then went on lonely pilgrimages into the mountains, eating nothing for several days on end. He intensified his physical suffering by sweating himself with heated rocks over which he threw water and also by whipping his body with nettles. During all this time, he also threw rocks and ran for miles to ensure against disease, laziness, and bad luck. This strenuous regimen continued until the boy had a dream of some animal or bird and received the inspiration for a spirit song that he would then always use to call upon his protector. He also prepared a medicine bag of the skin of the spirit animal and filled it with a variety of objects that had taken on symbolic significance for him during his quest. These became the symbols of his power (Pettitt 1972).

(5) Although the vision quest was an intensely individual experience, it was nevertheless shaped by culture in a number of ways. Among the Crow Indians, for example, several informants related the same vision and interpretation to the anthropologist Robert Lowie (1963). They told of how on their lonely vigil they saw a spirit or several spirits riding along and how the rocks and trees in the neighborhood turned into enemies who attacked the horsemen but were unable to inflict any harm. They interpreted this to mean that the spirits were making the visionary invulnerable. This motif is part of Crow mythology and is unconsciously worked into their experience by the vision seekers. Another cultural influence is that most Crow Indians obtained their spiritual blessing on the fourth night of their seclusion, and four is considered a mystical number among the Crow.

Shamanistic Cults

(6) A **shaman** is socially recognized as having special supernatural powers that are used on behalf of clients for a variety of activities: curing, divination, sorcery, and reading fortunes, among others. Among Inuit coastal communities, the shaman's most important service is to make a yearly spiritual trip to the bottom of the sea to persuade the sea goddess (Sedna), who is the keeper of the sea animals, to release the game so that the Inuit can live through one more year. Inuit shamans are also

frequently called upon to cure illness; this is done by discovering which supernatural being has been offended by a broken taboo and caused the illness. Frequently, the illness is treated by extracting a confession from the victim, and through a ritual procedure, the possessing spirit is then exorcised.

(7) A typical shamanistic curing performance among the Netsilik Inuit is described by the ethnographer Asen Balicki:

> The shaman, adorned with his paraphernalia, crouched in a corner of the igloo . . . and covered himself with a caribou skin. The lamps were extinguished. A protective spirit called by the shaman entered his body and, through his mouth, started to speak very rapidly, using the shaman's secret vocabulary. While the shaman was in trance, the *tupiliq* (an evil spirit believed to be round in shape and filled with blood) left the patient's body and hid outside the igloo. The shaman then dispatched his protective spirits after the *tupiliqs;* they, assisted usually by the benevolent ghost of some deceased shaman, drove the *tupiliqs* back into the igloo through the entrance; the audience encouraged the evil spirits, shouting: "Come in, come in, somebody is here waiting for you." No sooner had the *tupiliqs* entered the igloo than the shaman, with his snow knife, attacked them and killed as many as he could; his successful fight was evidenced by the evil spirits' blood on his hands. (1963:385)

In case the patient died, it was said that the *tupiliqs* were too numerous for the shaman to kill or that after the seance evil spirits again attacked the patient.

(8) Shamanistic activity has important therapeutic effects for individual clients, who are often relieved of illness through the cathartic effects of the ritual. Shamanism also has important integrating functions for the society. Through a wide variety of symbolic acts, shamanistic performances bring together various beliefs and religious practices in a way that dramatically expresses and reinforces the values of a culture and the solidarity of a society. Such performances frequently involve participation by the audience, whose members may experience various degrees of ecstasy themselves. These performances are cathartic in the sense that they release the anxiety caused by various disturbing events affecting individuals or the community as a whole. The forces of nature and the supernatural, which have the power to do evil in a society, are brought under control; seemingly inexplicable misfortunes are given meaning within the traditional cultural pattern; and the community is better able to carry out its normal activities.

Communal Cults

(9) In **communal cults**, groups of ordinary people hold rituals or ceremonies for the entire community or parts of it—for example, age groups, sex groups, kinship groups, castes, or neighborhoods. These ceremonies may use ritual specialists, but the basic responsibility lies with ordinary people who on this occasion take on specialized sacred roles and perform sacred acts. Communal cult institutions include many different kinds of rituals. Some are not connected with the supernatural, such as Fourth of July celebrations in the United States. Most of these

rituals can be conveniently divided into rites of passage and rites of intensification.

(10) **Rites of Passage** Rites (rituals) of passage mark the transition of an individual from one social status to another. One of the most important functions of religion is to help individuals and society deal with the crises of life. In almost all societies, transitions in social status—conception, birth, puberty, marriage, death—are surrounded by religious ritual. As I mentioned earlier in the chapter, rites of passage tend to have three phases: separation, transition, incorporation. In the separation phase, the individual is removed from his or her old group or status. The rituals of this phase symbolize the loss of the old status or personality—having the head shaved or casting off one's old name. In the transition stage, the individual is between stages; although cut off from the old status, he or she has not yet been incorporated into the new one. At this point, the individual may be treated as sacred, in recognition of the power and the danger of this in-between position. In the third stage, the individual is incorporated into the new group or status. The rituals and symbols of this stage frequently are those of rebirth.

(11) The Kaguru, a matrilineal tribe living in East Africa (Beidelman 1971), have initiation rites for both boys and girls. The Kaguru view initiation as necessary in order to convert irresponsible, immature minors into morally responsible adults. Kaguru male initiation includes both circumcision and moral instructions. Kaguru initiates learn how they will be expected to conduct themselves as adults. The physical distress of initiation makes the difference between the old life of the child and the new life of the adult more dramatic and leads to a greater acceptance of a new code of behavior.

(12) Ideally, a group of boys is initiated together, both to increase the prestige of the ceremony and to divide the costs; also, it is felt that the boys will bear the pain of circumcision and learn better if they are in a group. The most important persons in charge of putting the boy through initiation are his father and his mother's brother, who plays an important role in all matrilineal societies. A professional circumcisor is hired for the operation. He is chosen for his skill in cutting and the effectiveness of his medicines, which protect the boy from both physical and supernatural dangers.

(13) The themes of danger and vulnerability are dominant in the ritual. On the announced day, the boys, some senior male kin, and their circumcisor are led into the bush. The boys are stripped of their clothing and shaved of all body and head hair. This symbolizes the separation from their previous statuses. The boys are told that they may die from the circumcision. The boy's elder kinsmen hold him down in a sitting position while he is circumcised. It is considered admirable not to flinch or cry out, but those who do so are not condemned. The cutting is accompanied by songs and ritual. The foreskin is cut off, removing the "low, dirty," femininelike part of the boy. The bloodied objects are buried secretly. The boys are led to a shed to rest and be fed by elders. During the healing time, they are considered to be helpless, like babies.

(14) When the boys recover physically, each day they are allowed to go farther back into the camp. The boys are told that if they reveal the secrets of initiation, they will be devoured by wild beasts. During this

time, the kin of the boys are also on their best behavior, because their actions may supernaturally endanger the boy's life. When the boys have finally recovered, they are sent out into the forest to perform some task. Everything in the initiation camp is then burned or buried. When the boys return, they are told that the elders have swallowed everything. After staying up all that night, the youths, singing to show they have "conquered" the bush, are led out of the camp the next morning by their friends and kinsmen. After a feast and dance, the boys will be considered fully initiated. During this feast, the boys are blessed and given new names associated with certain kinsmen, both living and dead. The youth is now considered a fully responsible member of society. He may engage in an adult sex life, court girls, and consider marriage. He will require a full funeral when he dies and will become a true ancestral ghost.

(15) Funerary rites from our own and other societies indicate that death is a rite of passage. Rituals of the first stage, in which grief may be demonstrated by family and friends, mark the loss of the social person. In this stage, the remains of a deceased person may be buried. In the transitional period, the soul of the dead, as well as the corpse itself, is believed to be dangerous. It can take the form of a ghost and can wander among the living and cause illness and other misfortunes. In the third stage, the deceased is ritually removed from isolation or "limbo" and incorporated into its new status, perhaps as an angel in heaven or as reunited with ancestors. This stage is marked in some societies by unearthing the bones of the dead, ritually treating them, and burying them again. With this phase of the ritual, the deceased is no longer dangerous to the living.

(16) **Rites of Intensification** Rites of intensification are directed toward the welfare of the group or community, rather than the individual and have explicit goals: increasing the fertility of the land in agricultural societies or the availability of game among hunting and fishing groups. These rites are also performed when there is a crisis in the life of the group, as in the transfer of power or in the loss caused by death. Funerary rites directed at moving the deceased individual from death to a new life have corresponding rituals that must be observed by the survivors. In the first stage, the survivors ritually express their bereavement for the loss of the deceased; in the interim stage, they are in a period of limbo (mourning); finally, with the performance of rituals that end the mourning period, they resume normal social activity. Rites of intensification are also carried out to maintain the ties between the dead and the living, as in the case of ancestor worship, or to express the unity between humans and nature, as in the case of totemism.

(17) Totemism is a prominent feature of the religion of the Australian aborigines, who believe that people and nature share a common life and belong to one moral order. Just as human society is divided into mutually dependent and reciprocating groups, so too is nature. Each human group is linked with some species or object in the natural environment, which is its totem and with which it is mutually interdependent. By rules of birth and locality, people are grouped into "societies" or "lodges," each of which is associated with a different totem. This

totem is their Dreaming. The Dreaming refers to the name of the totem species, to a cult hero, to the myths that tell of the deeds and sacred places of the totem species or hero, and to the rituals organized to represent the myths. In order to join the cult for which he is eligible, each male must undergo an initiation symbolizing death and rebirth. Only after this initiation is knowledge of the myth, ritual, and sacred objects that make up the Dreaming gradually given to him. The chief object is the bull-roarer, the symbol and voice of the sky hero or of the totemic Dream Time heroes.

(18) In desert areas of Australia, the most important aboriginal rites are for the increase of the totemic species. These rites are connected with centers associated with the cult heroes. Natural objects, mostly rocks, are said to be transformed bodies or parts of heroes or totemic species that appear in the cult myths. Myths are sung, actors recreate the heroic scenes, and human blood is applied to the stone symbol. As a result, the natural species increases, as the spirits of the species go forth to be reincarnated. Except for an annual ritual occasion, the members of a totemic group do not eat its totem species, although members of other totem groups are allowed to do so. Thus, each group denies itself one type of food and depends on other groups for the ritual increase of foods it does eat. In addition to increasing rites, there are also ceremonies held at temporarily sacred places. Here, the past of the Dream Time heroes is reenacted. As they realize the presence of the Dreaming, onlookers and performers become carried away in a state of ecstasy. Through these rituals, the community maintains continuity with the past, enhances the feeling of social unity in the present, and renews the sentiments on which cohesion depends (Elkin 1967).

(19) The totem rites of the Australians clearly point up the social functions of religion. According to Emile Durkheim (1961; originally published 1915), a French sociologist, it was this function of religious ritual that was most important. When people worship their totem, which is a symbol of their common social identity, they are actually worshipping society—the moral and social order that is the foundation of social life. Durkheim believed that totemism was the origin of religion, because the aboriginal populations of Australia are technologically among the world's simplest societies. Although this aspect of his theory is no longer considered correct, his analysis of the social function of religious rites in terms of heightening social solidarity is an important contribution to anthropology.

(20) Religious ritual can also promote social solidarity by channeling conflict so that it does not disrupt the society. In all societies, there are conflicts of interest and unconscious hostility between groups who are in unequal power relationships. Many societies have *rituals of reversal* during which people in the different groups ritually reverse their relationships. In the Zulu society in Africa, one day in the year women act as men and men act as women. The women chase and beat the men and act sexually aggressive toward them. In India, the celebration of Holi, which is primarily a harvest festival, includes a ritual reversal between dominant and inferior castes, as well as between men and women.

(21) We are familiar with such reversals in Sadie Hawkins Day and Leap Year rituals, when in our own society it is considered permissible

for women to ask men to marry them. In many high schools and colleges, one day is set aside when freshman are allowed to harass the senior class, or students take over the classrooms and teachers take the role of students. Rituals of reversal contribute to social stability by allowing the channeled release of tensions that build up when one group of people is in a permanently subordinate position to another.

Ecclesiastical Cults

(22) An **ecclesiastical cult** has a professional clergy that is formally elected or appointed and that devotes all or most of its time to a specialized religious role. These people, called priests, are responsible for performing certain rituals on behalf of individuals, groups, or the entire community. Individuals have access to supernatural power only through these intermediaries. Where ecclesiastical cults exist, there is a clear-cut division between the lay and priestly roles. Laypeople participate in the ritual largely as passive respondents or audience, rather than as managers or performers. Ecclesiastical cults are most frequently associated with gods who are believed to have great power; these cults may be part of a religion that worships several such high gods, as in the religion of the ancient Greeks, Egyptians, and Romans, or just one high god, as in the Judeo-Christian tradition and Islam. Ecclesiastical cults are usually found in politically complex state societies. In these socially stratified societies, the elite may invoke religious authority in order to control the lower classes. The priesthood and religion act not only as a means of regulating behavior, which is a function of religion in all societies, but also as a way of maintaining social, economic, and political inequalities.

(23) In societies where an ecclesiastical cult is the established religion of the state or the upper classes, the religious practices and beliefs of the poor or lower classes may be different from those of the elite. Powerless segments of society may use religion to rationalize their lower social position, and they may place more emphasis on an afterlife in which they will receive more rewards than will those who had power. Sects and cults among the poor may have a millenarian outlook—they may be focused on the coming of a messiah who will usher in a utopian world. In many of these cults, members participate in rituals that give individuals direct access to supernatural power by experiencing states of ecstasy heightened by singing, dancing, handling of dangerous objects such as snakes, or using drugs. There are many such sects and cults in the United States.

(24) One of the most well known is that of the serpent handlers, whose churches are spread over southern Appalachia. Serpent handling is justified in these fundamentalist congregations by reference to Mark 16:17–18, in the King James Bible:

> And these signs shall follow them that believe: In my name shall they cast our devils; They shall speak with new tongues; **They shall take up serpents**; and if they drink any deadly thing, it shall not hurt them; They shall lay hands on the sick, and they shall recover.

For those who are members of these churches, the above signs are demonstrations of the power of God working in those individuals who, through their belief, become his instrument. When a person receives the power of the Lord, he or she is able to handle poisonous snakes without being bitten. In these church services, members of the congregation pick up handfuls of poisonous snakes, thrust them under their shirts or blouses, hold on to them while dancing ecstatically, and even wrap them around their heads and wear them like crowns. The ritual of serpent handling takes up only part of the service, which includes in addition the singing of Christian hymns, dancing, spontaneous sermons, faith healing, and "speaking in tongues," all of which are part of the holiness movement in Appalachia.

(25) Weston LaBarre, writing about these churches in *And They Shall Take Up Serpents* (1969), suggests that to the extent that these religious experiences create an illusion of power and stop people from making real changes in their lives, these sects and cults are maladaptive. They are adaptive at the level of the whole society, however, because they channel dissatisfaction and anger so that the larger social structure is left intact.*

1. An appropriate summary of paragraph 2 is:

    a. In an individualistic cult, the individual has a personal experience with the supernatural, a common example being the vision quest where the individual develops a special relationship with a spirit.
    b. In the vision quest, the individual has a strong relationship with the spirit, but has to experience pain to achieve this relationship.
    c. In the individual cult, each believer has the power to achieve a spiritual vision, so in this sense, each believer is his or her own priest.
    d. In the vision quest, the spirit becomes the individual's guardian, but the spirit asks the participant to perform very painful tasks.

2. The main idea of paragraph 3 concerns:

    a. the Thompson Indians of Canada
    b. how the young boys of the Thompson Indian tribe dance, sing, and pray
    c. the search for a guardian spirit among the adolescent boys
    d. the vision quest of the Thompson Indians of Canada, whose adolescent boys must perform certain specified activities.

3. The main idea of paragraph 5 concerns:

    a. the Crow Indians
    b. how the vision quest is shaped by the culture
    c. the mystical number *four* among the Crow Indians
    d. Crow Indian mythology

---

*Nanda, *Cultural Anthropology*, pp. 375–382.

4. A major detail in paragraph 6 is:

a. the supernatural powers of the shaman
b. how the shaman helps his clients
c. The Inuit shaman makes an annual trip to the bottom of the sea to ask the sea goddess's blessing.
d. how the shaman can read fortunes

5. What is the main idea of paragraph 9?

a. a definition of the rite of passage
b. a definition of the rite of intensification
c. The Fourth of July can be seen as a ritual celebration.
d. how communal cults perform ceremonies for the community, not just for the individual

Read the following questions; then go back and reread the excerpt. After you have reread the excerpt, answer the following questions without looking back.

6. Paraphrase this sentence from paragraph 16: "Rites of intensification are directed toward the welfare of the group or community rather than the individual and have explicit goals: increasing the fertility of the land in agricultural societies or the availability of game among hunting and fishing groups." (2 points)

7. Paraphrase this sentence from paragraph 17: "Just as human society is divided into mutually dependent and reciprocating groups, so too is nature." (2 points)

8. What is the major difference between a communal cult and an ecclesiastical cult? (1 point)

1. _____
2. _____
3. _____
4. _____
5. _____

_____
70%
Ask instructor for answers.

Follow-up on the Anthropology Exercises

Now that you have completed these exercises, it may be helpful to see how your reading of this topic has changed some of your ideas about what anthropology as a study is. You may want to go back to these exercises and reread them just for their content, or for how they introduce the various ways anthropologists study religion. Then answer the following questions either individually or in small groups.

1. How would you now define anthropology?
2. From an anthropologist's perspective, what are the major functions of religion?
3. In what ways are religious practices in non-Western cultures different from those in the West?
4. What issue or issues in anthropology do you now want to study further?

8 Reading and Listening for Inferences

Making inferences

◑ Terms of qualification ◑ Word choice: connotations ◑ Details
  ○ General?
  ○ Specific?

Now that you have begun to identify various organizational patterns in writing and speech and you are summarizing and paraphrasing what you read and hear, you are on your way to reading and listening more critically. But sometimes knowing the main idea, the details, and the organizational pattern is not enough. Books and lectures often leave much unsaid, and you must "read between the lines." Making judgments and drawing conclusions about what is suggested is called *making inferences*. The effective student is an efficient inference maker, gleaning important points from what is suggested. It is the correct inference that instructors are looking for on exams and essays. You can make inferences about most material by looking for the terms of qualification in a sentence, the author or speaker's word choice, and the kinds of details used.

Terms of Qualification

A single word or phrase can change the message of a sentence. It can give strong support for a statement or add doubt. A *term of qualification* is a word or phrase that limits the truth of a statement. In most cases, the speaker or writer will not tell you the degree of certainty intended in a statement; you need to infer this certainty from the term of qualification.

Terms of qualification can be divided into four categories: terms expressing no doubt, terms expressing a little doubt, terms expressing some doubt, and terms expressing much doubt.

Words and Phrases That Express No Doubt

all	surely	assuredly	there is no doubt
none	conclusively	undoubtedly	without reservation
never	clearly	absolutely	without hesitation
always	unequivocally	constantly	it is a proven fact
certainly	precisely	undeniably	it is undeniable
definitely	plainly	without a doubt	without question

Let these words and phrases become signals to you that what you are reading or listening to carries certainty. You can also use them when you write particularly strong statements.

See how the use of the word *absolutely* adds conviction to the following statement: "Mozart is absolutely the most brilliant musician ever to write classical music." The writer here evidently has positive feelings about Mozart and uses *absolutely* to establish these positive feelings. Sometimes, when you find such strong terms of qualification, you may want to underline them and make a marginal comment like "strong statement."

Now consider terms that express a small degree of doubt:

Words and Phrases That Express a Little Doubt

most	seldom	there is little doubt	it is believed
mostly	rarely	almost never	almost always
usually	slightly	with little reservation	
consistently	one can safely say	the consistent pattern	

When you find such words and phrases, ask yourself what the exceptions to the statement might be. These exceptions are often not discussed by the author. By failing to notice the term of qualification, you might wrongly conclude that the statement has no exceptions.

Consider how in the following statement the word *usually* plants a question in your mind: "College students usually find Mozart's opera *The Marriage of Figaro* to be the most exciting work they study in the course." If the author does not discuss the exceptions, it would be wise for you to underline the term of qualification and write in the margin something like "When do students not enjoy this opera?" Also begin using these terms in your own writing when you want to show a little doubt.

Now look at this list of terms expressing some doubt. If these terms are used, you need to consider the exceptions, which are often not elaborated upon by the writer.

Words and Phrases That Express Some Doubt

many	ostensibly	it seems
frequently	apparently	one can infer
often	somewhat	one can say with some
may	likely	reservation
might	this might mean	the hypothesis is
perhaps	this could mean	the theory is
one would assume	the results imply	it is possible that
the assumption is	possibly	it is probable that
one would infer	at times	
it is suggested that	it appears	
seemingly		
generally		

The following sentence uses the term of qualification *it appears*. How does this term alter the meaning of the statement? "It appears that rock music will continue to be an important musical experience for teenagers." Because the writer includes *it appears* in this statement, you cannot conclude that rock music will always be teenagers' preferred form of music. In a marginal comment, you might ask "What are the author's reservations?" You can also start using these terms in your own writing when your statements are not definite.

Finally, consider the following words, which suggest much doubt. When you see or hear these words, you should question the truth of these statements.

Words and Phrases That Suggest Much Doubt

supposedly	it is suspected that
it is guessed that	it is rumored that
it is conjectured that	

Look how *it is rumored that* makes the following statement questionable: "It is rumored that the federal government is trying to ban rock concerts that sell over 10,000 tickets for one show." Because this statement is rumor, you cannot include it in any serious discussion of rock concerts. Many irresponsible speakers and publications use rumor as the basis for their arguments. Never cite these speakers or publications as sources in a serious essay or speech.

Word Choice

You can make many inferences about a passage by analyzing the kinds of words that a speaker or author uses. *Connotations,* the hidden meanings of words, tell you whether an author or speaker has a positive, neutral, or negative attitude toward the topic. Authors and speakers often do not directly tell you their attitude toward the topic because they do not want to be accused of being biased. But you can infer these attitudes from the connotations of their words.

Look at the following sentence on Duke Ellington and see if you can locate the word with a strong positive connotation: "Duke Ellington continues to be one of the most revered figures in the history of American jazz." Do you see that *revered* is a positive word, suggesting that Ellington still commands a great deal of respect among jazz historians? To be revered is to be greatly respected, almost worshipped. In a marginal note about this sentence, you could include a comment like 'Revered' suggests great respect, almost worship."

Look at the use of *destructive* to see how it gives negative associations to this sentence about heavy metal music: "Heavy metal music clearly has a destructive effect on the behavior of young people, particularly at concerts." Do you see that *destructive* has antisocial and violent associations? Although the author does not directly state that young people lose their sense of right and wrong, such a meaning is suggested in the connotations of *destructive*. A marginal comment noting the connotations of this word would help you remember the author's intent.

Some statements avoid using words or phrases with obvious connotations. Notice how this statement uses neutral language: "The swing era in jazz lasted for about fifteen years, from 1935 to 1950." Do you see that the author uses no words suggesting that the swing era was either a positive or negative musical event? Here the author may be purposely using neutral language so as not to express an opinion about swing.

The total effect of an author's choice of words on a particular passage is called its *mood*, or the feeling that a reader gets from the words used in a passage. A passage's mood can leave the reader with positive, negative, or neutral feelings toward the topic. After you read a work, ask yourself what overall feeling it gives you. Then try to see what type of language in the work makes you feel this way.

Details of Support

In longer written passages or in longer lectures, you can infer something about the author or speaker from the details that are presented. If the details are presented logically, you can infer that the speaker or author is in command of the material. But if the details are disorganized, you can infer that the speaker or author is poorly prepared. You also can infer something by studying the sources used in the work. If known publications or experts are cited, you can more likely value the argument. If the speaker or author does not mention sources, you would be justified in questioning the thesis. Again, the author or speaker will probably not comment on the nature of the details; it is up to you to determine the value of the work from the nature of the details.

Look at the following paragraph on the Beatles. What do the details say about the competence of the writer?

> The Beatles were a very famous rock group several years ago. There were four of them, and they acted and dressed strangely. Their appearance and behavior made people like them even more. They made their first appearance in the United States in the early sixties on a popular television show.

Even if you agree with the thesis of the excerpt, the evidence is vague. The author does not name who these Beatles were, nor does she mention how they acted and dressed. The author also does not name the show they appeared on. Because these details are vague, you can infer that the writer, although logical, is not well prepared. Therefore her argument is not convincing.

Study the details of this second passage on the Beatles, and again try to infer something about the author:

> The Beatles were decidedly the most famous rock group to emerge from England in the sixties. There were four of them: John, Paul, George, and Ringo. Fans in America and Europe loved them for their long hair and their often irreverent sense of humor. They gained great notoriety in the United States in 1964 when they appeared on the "Ed Sullivan Show," the most popular variety show on television at the time.

Doesn't it seem that the author of this excerpt has done more research on the subject? She knows the names of each member, how they acted and looked, and the name of the show that made them famous in the United States. You will probably read this writer carefully, because the material is both logical and detailed.

When you write your own critical essays, be sure to cite your sources and present accurate details. If you do, your reader will read your work more carefully. You will learn more about effective essay writing in Chapter 16.

Summary

An *inference* is an insight you gain from something that is not stated directly. By making correct inferences, you better understand the material. You make inferences by noting terms of qualification, word choice, and the nature of the details. You should make marginal comments on your inferences.

The more you read and listen, the more sophisticated your inferences will become. You will begin comparing past knowledge with what you are currently learning. And your learning will be that much more rewarding.

Summary Box   *Inferences*

What are they?	How do you make them?	Why do you need them?
Insights or deductions made by a reader or listener but not directly stated	By studying terms of qualification, word choice, and details	To give more meaning to your reading and listening To become more questioning of what you read and hear

Skills Practice Topic: Music History

All the exercises in this chapter deal with the issue of music history, a course that you might one day take in college. Before you begin these exercises, answer the following questions either individually or in small groups to get some sense of what you already know about music history.

1. How would you define *music history*?
2. What do you know about classical music? Who are some of the great classical composers?
3. Are rock music and jazz in any way like classical music?
4. What is your favorite type of music? Why?

Exercise 8.1
Making Inferences
from Details

You can make inferences from the examples an author uses. If the examples are accurate, you can infer that the author is credible; if the examples are inaccurate, you can infer that the writer is unprepared.

Read the following paragraphs carefully, and determine whether the author is being detailed or vague. All of the paragraphs describe musical instruments. Write *D* in the answer box if the paragraph is detailed and *V* if the paragraph is vague.

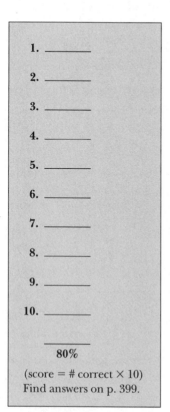

1. _____

2. _____

3. _____

4. _____

5. _____

6. _____

7. _____

8. _____

9. _____

10. _____

80%

(score = # correct × 10)
Find answers on p. 399.

The Instruments of the Orchestra

(1) The string instruments are very important to an orchestra: They make up about half of all of the instruments. They include the violin, viola, cello, and double bass. What makes these instruments different is their relative size. Their differing sizes produce different pitches or sounds.

(2) How does a string instrument make sound? Part of the instrument is hollow. Another part transmits the sound to the body. Then the body changes the sound. This change in sound makes each instrument different.

(3) Woodwinds are another type of orchestral instrument. As their name suggests, these instruments rely on wind to make their sound, and each one is made of wood. Examples of woodwind instruments are the flute, piccolo, oboe, English horn, clarinet, and bassoon. Each of these instruments has a hollow body and holes along the length that let air in and out.

(4) The flute is a peculiar instrument. In recent times the material it is made of has changed. The flute and piccolo produce a particular sound. This sound is made by air moving and colliding with other air. The flute also has a particular sound range.

(5) The oboe is another interesting orchestral instrument. The wood that oboes are made of is specially treated. The reeds used in oboes are an important part of the instrument's sound. The range of sound that the oboe produces is not very wide.

(6) The saxophone is sometimes included in an orchestra. It is considered part of the woodwind family, even though its body is made of

metal. What makes it like other woodwind instruments is the reed that it uses to produce its distinctive sound. Although it is only an occasional member of the orchestra, the saxophone is always part of concert and jazz bands.

(7) Brass instruments make up another musical family. They are unlike woodwinds. The unique sound of a brass instrument is its buzzing. Brass instruments come in various sizes, and the size of each instrument can be changed.

(8) What types of brass instruments does the orchestra use? In most orchestras, three trumpets, four French horns, two tenor trombones, one brass trombone, and one tuba are included. Of these instruments, the trumpet has the highest pitch. Its pitch is altered by changing the length of its tubing. There are three piston valves in a trumpet that alter its size and therefore its range.

(9) Another instrument in the brass family is the cornet, which is similar to the trumpet. The cornet's tube is shaped like a cone. It produces a mellow sound. Finally, a cornet is also equipped with a mute, which softens its tone even more.

(10) The trombone has a different sound from the trumpet. It is also shaped differently from the trumpet. Also, the trombone's sound is powerful. Its sound is unique but very difficult to describe.*

Exercise 8.2
Locating and
Analyzing Terms
of Qualification

The following paragraphs discuss Johann Sebastian Bach (1685–1750), one of the great classical composers. In these paragraphs are five terms of qualification, which are underlined. In the spaces provided, explain how each term of qualification alters the meaning of the sentence. Comment on whether the term makes the statement stronger or casts doubt on it. You may want to refer to the lists of terms of qualification on pp. 166–167.

Example: Almost every student of music knows Bach's work and is impressed by it.

Explanation: This is a strong statement about Bach's abilities, but the use of "almost" suggests that not all students of music find him to be great.

Johann Sebastian Bach

(1) Most students of music would say that Johann Sebastian Bach is one of the greatest composers of all time. Bach's life was uneventful. The most important biographical detail is that he was part of an extremely talented musical family that spanned six generations.

(2) What is Bach's appeal? Why is he an undeniably dominant figure in music history? Scholars of music constantly refer to his skill in writing counterpoint. The way that he ordered musical relationships, it seems, has a pleasing effect on the listener's mind.

---

*Adapted from Charles R. Hoffer, *The Understanding of Music*, 6th ed. (Belmont, Calif.: Wadsworth, 1989), pp. 52–57.

(3) The *fugue* is Bach's greatest musical contribution. In a fugue, lines of music imitate each other in carefully organized ways. Scholars <u>generally</u> agree that the fugue evolved over several generations and with several composers.

(4) Analyzing a Bach fugue shows how fugues are <u>frequently</u> structured. Bach's Fugue in C Minor begins with a melody <u>divided into</u> four parts. This main melody is called the subject, and this subject is expressed by various imitations called voices, which constantly reinterpret the subject.*

1. *Term:* _____

 Explanation: _____

2. *Term:* _____

 Explanation: _____

3. *Term:* _____

 Explanation: _____

4. *Term:* _____

 Explanation: _____

5. *Term:* _____

 Explanation: _____

Now read the following series of paragraphs, continuing the discussion on Bach. In these paragraphs are five additional terms of qualification. This time they are not underlined. Locate them and determine their effect on the sentence. Place each term and explanation on the lines provided at the end of the excerpt.

(5) The fugue is certainly not the only form of music that Bach wrote for the organ, although perhaps it can be seen as the most important. Two others known as the *chorale variation* and the *chorale prelude* also use the fugue format, but these two musical forms vary the main musical theme each time it is introduced into the composition.

(6) Another type of music Bach wrote for the organ is called the *passacaglia*. This musical form continues one musical theme throughout but adds variations over it. The passacaglia is usually seen as a fascinat-

*Adapted from Hoffer, *Understanding of Music*, pp. 185–188.

ing, demanding listening experience. Without question, one of Bach's finest works is the Passacaglia in C Minor.

(7) There is no doubt that anyone interested in seriously studying European music will spend time experiencing this amazing composer—J. S. Bach.*

6. *Term:* _____

   Explanation: _____

7. *Term:* _____

   Explanation: _____

8. *Term:* _____

   Explanation: _____

9. *Term:* _____

   Explanation: _____

10. *Term:* _____

   Explanation: _____

80%
Ask instructor for answers.

Exercise 8.3
Commenting on Word
Choice in Sentences

The following paragraphs describe the life and music of Wolfgang Amadeus Mozart (1756–1791), a German composer who came after Bach. The writer of these paragraphs has a definite attitude toward Mozart. Read these paragraphs carefully to determine what he is saying about Mozart and what his attitude toward him is; then go back and reread the underlined words to see how they alter the meaning of the sentence in which they appear. As you complete this exercise you may want to consult a dictionary or thesaurus to determine the meanings of the underlined words. Place your explanations on the lines provided at the end of the excerpt.

Example: Mozart was one of the <u>dazzling</u> composers of the eighteenth century.

Explanation: To dazzle is to overpower by intense light. The author is suggesting that Mozart was clearly an overpowering and brilliant composer of his time.

---

*Adapted from Hoffer, *Understanding of Music,* pp. 185–188.

Mozart's Music and Life

(1) Wolfgang Amadeus Mozart is nothing less than a musical miracle. His compositions are consistently clear, delicate, and simple, yet they defy a simple musical analysis.

(2) Mozart was a child prodigy, composing his first pieces at the astonishing age of five. He was performing at six, and by the age of thirteen, he had written concertos, symphonies, and an opera.

(3) Mozart had a phenomenal musical memory. He was able to do the seemingly impossible task: compose entire musical pieces in his mind. He has been quoted as saying that when he committed a musical piece to paper, he had worked it all out in his mind beforehand.

(4) Although Mozart possessed an unfathomable musical gift, his personal life was disastrous. He was naive when it came to his finances and consistently found himself in debt. At thirty-five he died of uremic poisoning, and he did not have the money for a respectable funeral. This musical giant died a pauper.

(5) His short life notwithstanding, Mozart completed a remarkable number of musical compositions. He explored many musical genres: operas, symphonies, concertos, and string quartets. With each type of music he composed, Mozart left an indelible musical style. His works consistently reveal different aspects of his musical genius, so he continues to be studied by musical scholars, performers, and musical composers today for what he has to say about classical music.*

1. *Explanation:* _____

2. *Explanation:* _____

3. *Explanation:* _____

4. *Explanation:* _____

5. *Explanation:* _____

6. *Explanation:* _____

7. *Explanation:* _____

8. *Explanation:* _____

9. *Explanation:* _____

10. *Explanation:* _____

70%
(score = # correct × 10)
Find answers on p. 400.

---

*Adapted from Hoffer, *Understanding of Music*, pp. 210–212.

Now go back and reread the passage. What do you think is the overall mood of this passage? What words suggest this mood?

_____

_____

Exercise 8.4
Making Inferences
in a Longer Passage

In the following passage on rock music, you will be asked to make inferences based on details, word choice, and terms of qualification. Read the passage carefully, marking the text for main ideas and major details as well as commenting on any word choice that seems particularly interesting to you. Then answer the questions that follow. You may refer to the passage when answering the questions. Place all answers in the answer box.

Rock Music in the Fifties and Sixties

(1) It seems that rock music got its start in 1955 when Bill Haley and the Comets sang "Rock Around the Clock" in the movie *Blackboard Jungle.* This film was about a group of rowdy teenagers in an urban high school. The simple blues-like music of the Haley song, coupled with the feelings of discontent among teenagers, seem to have laid the foundation for rock music, a kind of music that seems to speak to almost all teenagers today.

(2) Elvis Presley soon followed on the heels of Bill Haley. His striking good looks and sexually suggestive movements as he performed added more excitement to his singing. Songs like his "You Ain't Nothing but a Hound Dog" continued the simple yet catchy beat of "Rock Around the Clock." Presley was undeniably the most significant contributor to rock music in the fifties. Although he has been dead for over fourteen years, his legacy lives on in both the now middle-aged fans who remember him and the teenagers who know him today through his music.

(3) Rock music in the sixties became a more complex, more thoughtful type of music. There seemed to be a singing style for everyone in this decade: Motown, the Beatles, the Rolling Stones, as well as the folk music of balladeers like Bob Dylan and Joni Mitchell. By the sixties, some rock music had developed a keen social conscience. Good looks and physical movement would no longer always sell a lyric. Singers and songwriters like Bob Dylan and the Beatles began to introduce social questions into their lyrics. Many antiwar rock songs emerged as a response to the war in Vietnam, which began to escalate in the sixties and create violence and discontent in the entire nation.

(4) What defined rock music in both the fifties and the sixties was a clear beat and an often refreshing experimentation with musical form. Moreover, the musical instruments that rock employed were decidedly different from those used before the fifties. The saxophones and trumpets of the forties gave way to electronic instruments, especially guitars and organs. Rock music also often used music technology in interesting

ways, amplifying the sound and playing with it through the engineer's skillful use of mixing and multiple tracks.

(5) What seemed to separate rock music of the fifties from that of the sixties was the electrifying popularity of the group in the sixties over the solo performer. The advantage of the group was that it was able to play several instruments—particularly electric guitar, electric organ, and drums—as it sang. Fans could now select their favorite group member among the several who performed in concert and on television.

(6) Thanks to the contributions of performers in the fifties and sixties, rock music seems to be here to stay. Its variety today seems to have provided for a larger listening audience—from teenagers, its original audience, to young adults and middle-aged adults who grew up and in a sense were nourished on rock.*

1. What terms of qualification are used in paragraph 1?

   a. *seems* and *got*
   b. *seems* and *almost all*
   c. *almost* and *kind*
   d. *simple* and *this*

2. Which word from the following sentence in paragraph 2 has positive connotations? "His striking good looks and sexually suggestive movements as he performed added more excitement to his singing."

   a. looks
   b. movements
   c. performed
   d. striking

3. What term of qualification is used in the following sentence in paragraph 2? "Presley was undeniably the most significant contributor to rock music in the fifties."

   a. significant
   b. contributor
   c. undeniably
   d. fifties

4. Which word or words from this sentence in paragraph 3 have positive connotations? "Rock music in the sixties became a more complex, more thoughtful type of music."

   a. complex
   b. thoughtful
   c. both a and b
   d. neither a nor b

---

*Adapted from Hoffer, *Understanding of Music*, pp. 511–516.

5. Which word or words in the last sentence of paragraph 3 has negative connotations?

a. emerged
b. discontent
c. response
d. nation

Now answer the following five questions with a short phrase or sentence.

6. What do you think the writer means in paragraph 4 by the phrase "an often refreshing experimentation with musical form"?

7. Locate a word in the last sentence of paragraph 4 that positively describes the music engineer.

8. What do you think the writer means in paragraph 5 by the phrase "electrifying popularity of the group"?

9. What term of qualification is used in the first sentence of paragraph 6? How does it alter the meaning of this sentence?

10. What do you think is this author's overall attitude toward rock music in the fifties and sixties? Which words or statements help suggest this attitude?

1. _____

2. _____

3. _____

4. _____

5. _____

80%

Ask instructor for answers.

Exercise 8.5
Writing Your Own
Paragraph Using
Main Ideas and
Major Details

Your job in this exercise is to go back to the passage on rock music in Exercise 8.4 and determine the major characteristics of rock music in the fifties and sixties. As you locate this information, jot it down in the outline below. From the information in the completed outline, answer the essay question in one paragraph.

I. Characteristics of Early Rock Music

A. In the fifties: _____

_____

B. In the sixties: _____

_____

70%

Ask instructor for answers.

Essay question: Rock music developed in interesting ways in its first two decades. What were the characteristics of rock music in the fifties and sixties? In what ways was the music in these two periods similar? How was it different?

Exercise 8.6
Determining Main
Ideas and Major
Details, and Making
Inferences from a
Textbook Excerpt

The following is an excerpt from a textbook on jazz, an American musical movement that came before rock. Read through the excerpt quickly to get a sense of its organization. Then go back and read it slowly, paying particular attention to the way jazz is described. You will not need to know the various technical terms to answer the questions that follow. You may refer to the excerpt in deciding on your answers.

Jazz

(1) Various types of popular music, especially jazz and rock, are among America's most recognized contributions to the world of music. Travelers to other countries—Japan, Thailand, France, Greece, and so on—hear American popular music (often with the lyrics still in English). Each type of popular music has its promoters and detractors, and most of the styles have developed under a cloud of doubt about their musical quality. Regardless of their artistic merits, or lack of them, no presentation of American music can be complete without some discussion of jazz and other popular music.

Traditional Jazz

(2) The roots of jazz reach back to black Americans' African heritage. But other elements have also influenced jazz: minstrel show music, work songs, field hollers, funeral marching bands, blues, French-Creole and Spanish-American music, and, more recently, West Indian music. Jazz did not develop until about the beginning of the twentieth century. Basin Street in New Orleans is traditionally considered its birthplace, although clearly jazz did not just pop into being in one spot and at a fixed historical moment. It was brought to public attention by the funeral procession. On the way back from the cemetery the band played tunes in a way quite different from the somber sounds that accompanied the march to the gravesite. The players shifted the emphasis from the strong to the weak beat and launched into a decorated version of the melody. When Storyville, the New Orleans red-light district, was closed down in 1917, many jazz musicians lost their jobs and sought work in other cities. Jazz moved up the Mississippi River through Memphis and St. Louis to Chicago and the rest of the United States.

(3) Two types of Afro-American folk music existed before and during the early years of jazz and later merged with it. One of these was **ragtime**. It featured the piano, occasionally in combination with other instruments. The music sounds like a polished, syncopated march with a decorated right-hand part. Early musicians associated with ragtime are Scott Joplin in Sedalia, Missouri, and Ben Harvey, who published his *Ragtime Instructor* in 1897.

(4) The other type of music involved with early jazz was the folk **blues**. Its musical characteristics will be discussed shortly. Some of the most famous names associated with blues are Leadbelly, whose real name was Huddie Ledbetter; W. C. Handy, who was known for his "Memphis Blues" and "St. Louis Blues"; and Ferdinand "Jelly Roll" Morton, whose first published blues appeared in 1905—the "Jelly Roll Blues."

(5) Like folk music, jazz was created by generally untutored musicians who could not have written down what they played or sang, even if they had wanted to. Jazz is different from most folk music in two respects, however. It has sprung from the cities rather than the fields and forests; it is an urban form of music. And for most people, it is a spectator experience. Usually only a few people perform, although listeners may contribute a little hand clapping and foot stomping.

(6) **Musical Elements of Jazz**   What is traditional jazz? It has several elements.

(7) *Melody*   The most significant feature of jazz melodies is the **blue note**. These notes are derived from an altered version of the major scale. The blues scale merely lowers the third, fifth, and/or seventh steps. Many times the performer shifts between the regular note and its lower alternative as if searching for a sound, which in a sense is what is happening. The blue-note interval is an approximation of a microtone, roughly half of a half step in this case. African music is the influence behind its use in jazz. Blue notes are a source of subtle color. Their effect in jazz is further enhanced by the fact that the chord in the harmony usually contains the particular note at its expected pitch while the lowered blue note is sounded in the melody. This combination creates an interesting and characteristic dissonance.

(8) *Harmony*   Traditional jazz harmony is as conservative as any church hymn. The typical chords are the same three that form the backbone of traditional tonal harmony: tonic (I), dominant (V), and subdominant (IV). More recently, sophisticated types of jazz have employed the advanced harmonic idioms of Debussy, Bartók, and Stravinsky. The appeal of jazz, however, does not lie in its harmony.

(9) *Rhythm*   Rhythm is one of the most important features of jazz. Although its meter is nearly always two beats per measure, with irregular meters occurring only rarely, the jazz musician employs an endless variety of syncopated patterns and rhythmic figures over this regular pulse. Syncopation—the redistribution of accents so that the rhythmic patterns do not occur as the listener expects—is the lifeblood of jazz.

(10) Jazz rhythms do not fit well into the usual divisions of time into sixteenths, eighths, and quarters. Jazz musicians perform rhythm with small deviations of timing and accent that cannot be rendered in notation. Players even make slight alterations of the patterns of conventional notation when reading them. These deviations in rhythm are one reason why traditionally trained musicians often cannot achieve an authentic jazz sound.

(11) *Timbre*   The basic timbre sought by jazz instrumentalists is perhaps an unconscious imitation of the black singing voice: a bit breathy with a little vibrato (rapid and slight variance of pitch on a single tone). Certain instruments, therefore, have become associated with this idiom. The saxophone was intended to be a concert instrument, but it was taken up by jazz musicians because it can produce the desired quality. Mutes—metal or fiber devices inserted in or over the bell of brass instruments to change the tone quality—are often used, and their names are as distinctive as the sounds they produce: *cup, wahwah,* and *plunger* (like the end of a rubber sink plunger). Many jazz trumpeters use a particular type of mouthpiece that helps them produce a more

shrill sound and makes high notes easier to play. In jazz style the clarinet is played in a manner that produces a tone quality like that of the saxophone. The timbres of other instruments also vary according to whether they are playing orchestral music or jazz.

(12) Some jazz timbres, like the bongo and conga drums and the Cuban cowbell, are from Afro-Cuban sources, while others, such as the Chinese woodblock, cymbals, and vibraphone, have an Oriental flavor.

(13) *Repetition of Material* Jazz has no form that is true for all its styles. Generally it is a series of stanzas based on the chords to a popular tune. The form of the blues is more definite. A line is sung and immediately repeated; then a third line concludes the stanza. Sometimes the singer does not sing all the way through a section, and an instrumentalist fills in with a short solo called a *break*.

(14) *Text* The metrical scheme of the text is often one of the standard poetic meters. It is not uncommon to find iambic pentameter in verses of the blues. The texts seldom have literary value, but some are quite moving.

(15) *Improvisation* Improvisation is a fundamental component of jazz. Traditionally jazz is not written down because it is made up on the spot. This extemporaneous creativity is what gives jazz its ever-fresh quality. Sometimes people confuse a sexy or "hot" popular song with jazz. Jazz does not exist unless someone improvises on a tune.

(16) What happens is this: The musicians agree that they will play a certain song in a certain key. They also agree generally on the order of each player's featured section. Then the first player, while keeping in mind the harmonies and melody of the song, improvises a part that reflects the rhythmic and melodic characteristics of jazz. This procedure is followed as each player takes a turn. In the final chorus, all play together in simultaneous, semi-accidental counterpoint. It is like an improvised musical conversation. Throughout the number, no player knows exactly what the others will do, but each plays according to musical instinct so that every part fits in with the others. Nor are the individual players entirely certain what they themselves will do, because a player taking a "ride" on a number plays it somewhat differently each time.

(17) Sometimes there seems to be so much improvisation that the melody is no longer identifiable. Why does that happen? Because the player improvises on the basic harmony as well as the melody. For example, if the song starts on the tonic chord, as it often does, and if the piece is in the key of C, then the notes of the tonic chord are C E G. The improviser may play any or all of these three notes plus tones that are nonharmonic in relation to that chord. In other words, other pitches can be woven around the notes of the chord, which may rather obscure the tune.

(18) The particular song may get lost for another reason. Most popular songs have simple chord patterns and there is little difference between the chords of one popular song and another. When the melody is being improvised upon, the harmony is often not distinguishable from that of other songs. The rhapsodic nature of jazz improvisation also leads to a sameness of mood that makes it more difficult to distinguish the basic song.

(19) **Types of Jazz**   The 1920s saw the real emergence of jazz, which was given impetus in 1918 by Joe "King" Oliver's famous Creole Jazz Band in Chicago. Other musicians soon became prominent: Bix Beiderbecke, who started "white" jazz with his cornet and a band called the "Wolverines"; Paul Whiteman, whose band presented the first jazz concert in 1924, featuring the premiere of George Gershwin's *Rhapsody in Blue*; Bessie Smith, the famous blues singer; Fletcher Henderson and his band; and the notable Louis Armstrong. Through his trumpet playing and vocal renditions, Armstrong had much influence on the basic sound and style of jazz

(20) *Dixieland*   The prevailing style in the 1920s was dixieland. It is characterized by a strong upbeat, a meter of two beats to the measure, and certain tonal and stylistic qualities that are impossible to notate. It has a "busy" sound because there is simultaneous improvisation by perhaps four to seven players. The result is a type of "accidental" counterpoint that is held together only by the song's basic harmony and the musical instincts of the players. The presence of simultaneous improvisation in both African music and jazz can hardly be a coincidence. Dixieland style is often described as "hot"; it is rather fast and usually loud.

(21) *Boogie-Woogie*   During the depression of the 1930s the hiring of bands became prohibitively expensive. So pianists enjoyed increasing popularity, especially as they developed a jazz piano style called boogie-woogie. It features a persistently repeated melodic figure—an ostinato—in the bass. Usually the boogie-woogie ostinato consists of eight notes per measure, which explains why this type of music is sometimes called "eight to the bar." Over the continuous bass the pianist plays trills, octave tremolos (the rapid alternation of pitches an octave apart), and other melodic figures.

(22) *Swing*   The swing era in jazz lasted from 1935 to about 1950. It featured intricate arrangements and big bands of about seventeen players under the leadership of such musicians as Benny Goodman, Count Basie, and Duke Ellington. It was also the era of the featured soloist—Gene Krupa, Fats Waller, and Tommy Dorsey, to name a few. Other notable figures from the period include Artie Shaw, Harry James, Glenn Miller, Coleman Hawkins, and Fletcher Henderson. Musically, swing has four beats to the measure and rhythm with a "bounce." The swing era was one in which the audience danced. Its "concert halls" were such places as the Roseland Ballroom in New York and the Hollywood Palladium.

(23) There were many great bands and arrangers during the swing era. The most enduring, and the one probably still heard today more than the others, is Duke Ellington and his orchestra. Ellington's group spanned nearly five decades and produced varied and interesting music. "Take the 'A' Train" was one of Ellington's more popular works, and it demonstrates well the style of the bands in the swing era. The melody is taken in four rather fast beats per measure. There is a contrasting phrase to the eight bars in the example. The remainder is the same sixteen measures repeated with new improvised solo material or played in a different key. The chord symbols in the example indicate the chords on which the soloists improvise.

(24) ***Bop***   Following World War II there emerged a style called be-bop, or more commonly, bop. It was developed chiefly by Charlie "Bird" Parker (see pages 508–9) and Dizzy Gillespie, who once defined the term by saying that in bop you go *Ba-oo Ba-oo Ba-oo* instead of *Oo-ba Oo-ba Oo-ba*. What he was describing was the nearly continuous syncopation that occurs in bop. It also features dissonant chords and freely developed melodies. Often the performers play in unison at the octave instead of presenting the traditional improvised counterpoint. In bop the fifth step of the scale is lowered, which is a carry-over of the blue notes discussed earlier. The bass drum does not sound all the time—a change from earlier styles. Instead, the double bass is given the responsibility for keeping the beat. Bop bands were much smaller than the bands of the swing era.

(25) ***Progressive and Free Form Jazz***   Stan Kenton was the leader of progressive jazz, which is characterized by big bands and highly dissonant chords. In a sense, the progressive style is an updated, intellectual version of the swing style that prevailed about fifteen years earlier. With Miles Davis, the Modern Jazz Quartet, and Dave Brubeck, jazz turned toward a "cool" style, still intellectual and well ordered, but performed by much smaller groups. Charlie Mingus, Ornette Coleman, and John Coltrane led a movement toward free form jazz, in which all restraints were removed. No longer was improvisation held together by the harmony.

(26) Over the years jazz has become more of a listener's type of music, in contrast to its early history. Gone is much of jazz's image as a "music of the people." It has matured in the sense that it is not always played just for fun, at least not by many jazz musicians. It is now serious business, performed by musicians who have studied Stravinsky and Bartók. One need only listen to works by jazz composers such as Miles Davis, Dave Brubeck, Herbie Hancock, and Chuck Mangione to hear how far jazz has progressed from what its "founding fathers" started.

(27) Jazz represents the rediscovery of the art of improvising, which was largely neglected after the time of Bach and Mozart. Perhaps it was a better counterbalance to the deadly seriousness of nineteenth-century music than were the arty, chic attempts at ridicule by Satie and his followers.*

Place the answers to the first five questions in the answer box.

1. The first paragraph

    a. discusses jazz's roots

    b. focuses on the influence of the African-American culture on jazz

    c. discusses the types of jazz

    d. both a and b

---

*Hoffer, *Understanding of Music*, pp. 501–510.

2. In the first sentence of paragraph 4, what term of qualification is used?

a. jazz
b. untutored
c. generally
d. not

3. What word in the last sentence in paragraph 6 has a positive connotation?

a. combination
b. dissonance
c. interesting
d. creates

4. The main idea of paragraph 7 is

a. jazz has a conservative harmony
b. jazz's attraction is not based on the type of harmony it uses
c. jazz has used some of the music styles of Debussy and Stravinsky
d. both a and c

5. The last sentence in paragraph 8 uses a word with a positive connotation. The word is

a. lifeblood
b. listener
c. rhythmic
d. accents

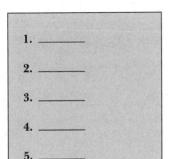

1. _____

2. _____

3. _____

4. _____

5. _____

Read the following questions, then go back and reread the excerpt. Finally, without looking back, answer the following questions in phrases or short sentences.

6. Describe three of the seven most important characteristics of jazz. (3 points)

7. Briefly describe two types of jazz. (2 points)

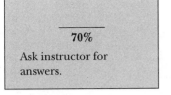

70%

Ask instructor for answers.

Follow-up on Music History Exercises

Now that you have completed these exercises, it may be helpful to see how your reading of this topic has changed some of your ideas about music history. You may want to go back to these exercises and reread them just for content or for what they have to say about music history. Then answer the following questions either individually or in small groups:

1. How would you now define *music history*?
2. What do you now know about Bach and Mozart?
3. What do you now know about rock and jazz? How are they similar? different?
4. What area in music history would you now want to pursue further?

9 Reading Graphs, Charts, and Tables

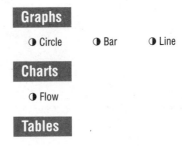

Reading graphs, charts, and tables is a necessary college reading skill. A graph and a chart are visual representations of information; a table presents information compactly. If you learn more easily visually, graphs and charts should help you learn. For each kind of graph, you need to apply specific practices.

Circle Graphs

Circle graphs show how the whole is broken up into recognizable parts. The entire circle equals 100 percent, and the divided sections represent the parts. When you study circle graphs, you must first determine the subject. Then you should see how the various parts relate to this subject and to each other.

Look at the graph in Figure 9-1 on the various elements in the earth's crust. Answer the following questions as you study this graph:

1. What does the whole circle represent?
2. How are the parts organized—smallest percentage to largest and largest percentage to smallest?
3. Can you remember the three most plentiful elements in the earth's crust?

In studying this circle graph, you should have noted that the entire circle represents the composition of the earth's crust, or its ten most

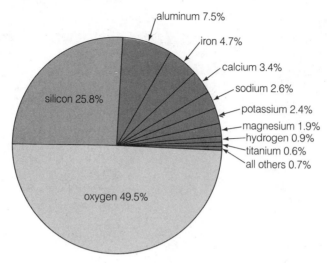

Figure 9-1   *Earth's crust. (Source: G. Tyler Miller, Jr.,* Living in the Environment, *4th ed. [Belmont, Calif.: Wadsworth, 1985], p. 235. Used by permission.)*

plentiful elements. You should have then noticed that as you move clockwise, the percentages become smaller, from the most plentiful oxygen to the least plentiful titanium. If on an ecology exam, for example, you had to remember the elements making up the earth's crust, this circle graph would have helped you.

Bar Graphs

Bar graphs are usually a series of rectangles comparing the parts of a whole, much like circle graphs. Each rectangle represents 100 percent, and the rectangle is often divided into parts of this 100 percent. You should ask the same questions that you would when studying a circle graph:

1. What is the subject?
2. How do the parts relate to this subject?
3. How do the parts relate to each other?

Look at the bar graph in Figure 9-2 on the crops of the world. Determine the subject, what each bar represents, and how these bars relate to each other.

In studying this material, you should have determined that this graph represents the relative production of various crops in the world,

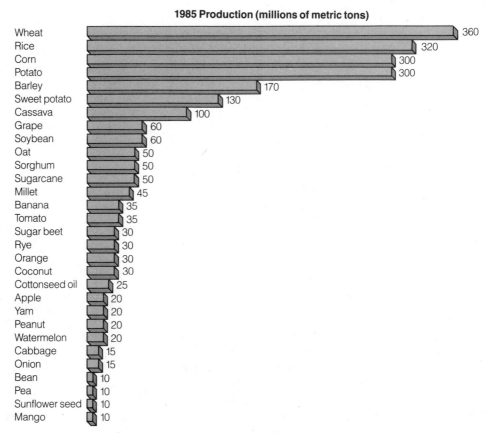

1985 Production (millions of metric tons)

Wheat	360
Rice	320
Corn	300
Potato	300
Barley	170
Sweet potato	130
Cassava	100
Grape	60
Soybean	60
Oat	50
Sorghum	50
Sugarcane	50
Millet	45
Banana	35
Tomato	35
Sugar beet	30
Rye	30
Orange	30
Coconut	30
Cottonseed oil	25
Apple	20
Yam	20
Peanut	20
Watermelon	20
Cabbage	15
Onion	15
Bean	10
Pea	10
Sunflower seed	10
Mango	10

Figure 9-2   *World food crops (1985 production in millions of metric tons). (Source: G. Tyler Miller, Jr.,* Living in the Environment, *5th ed. [Belmont, Calif.: Wadsworth, 1988], p. 235.)*

each bar representing the crop's supply in millions of metric tons. Did you determine that five crops—wheat, rice, corn, potato, and barley—account for most of the world's crops?

Bar graphs are effective study aids when you need to remember a great deal of information.

Line Graphs

Line graphs may be more difficult to grasp than circle or bar graphs. Line graphs are made up of three important parts: (1) the vertical axis, or the line going up and down; (2) the horizontal axis, or the line going from side to side; and (3) the diagonal line, or the line going either up, down, or parallel to the horizontal axis. Line graphs always illustrate relationships, usually cause–effect relationships. In business or economics material, the line graph often shows how the supply of a particular

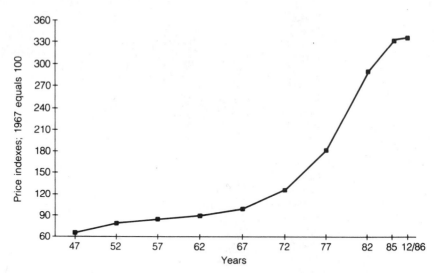

Figure 9-3   *Consumer price indexes, 1947–1986. (Source: Adapted from Philip C. Starr,* Economics: Principles in Action, *5th ed. [Belmont, Calif.: Wadsworth, 1988], p. 215.)*

product affects its demand—how, for example, lowering the supply increases the demand; in biology material, the line graph often shows how a biological activity is affected by a particular variable or change—how, for instance, temperature (a variable) affects cell movement (a biological activity).

As with circle and bar graphs, you need first to determine the subject of the graph and what the numbers on the vertical and horizontal axes mean. Unlike circle and bar graphs, you then need to study the vertical and horizontal axes as well as the diagonal line to determine the nature of the relationship. Determining this relationship is crucial, because without it, you will not understand what the details of the line graph mean or the meaning of the diagonal line's movement up, down, or parallel to the horizontal axis.

Look at the line graph in Figure 9-3 on the consumer price index, which shows how prices fluctuated in the United States from 1947–1986. First, determine what the numbers on the vertical and horizontal axes represent. Then decide what the diagonal's upward movement suggests.

Having studied this graph, did you determine that the consumer price index increased over this time span, that it almost doubled between 1947 and 1972, and that it more than tripled between 1967 and 1985?

With line graphs, you may not be able to determine precisely where the diagonal meets each axis. Using a small, six-inch ruler to locate a particular point on the diagonal will help your calculation. Use

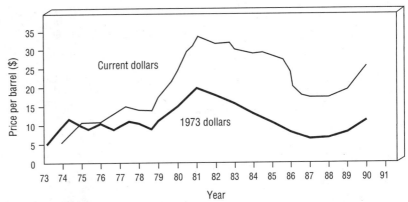

Figure 9-4   *Average world crude oil prices, 1973–1990. (Source: G. Tyler Miller, Jr.,* Living in the Environment, *7th ed., [Belmont, Calif.: Wadsworth, 1992], p. 15. Data from Department of Energy and Department of Commerce.)*

a ruler to find the consumer price index for 1977. Did it help you to locate 180?

Sometimes line graphs are more complicated because there are two or more diagonals or variables for you to consider. And sometimes these diagonals intersect. No matter how complicated the line graph, though, your practice should be the same as in reading a line graph with one diagonal: (1) determine the subject of the graph, (2) determine what the numbers on each axis represent, and (3) determine how the diagonals relate to each other.

Look at the line graph in Figure 9-4 on crude oil prices in the United States. Determine the subject, what the numbers on each axis mean, and how the two diagonals relate to each other.

Having studied this more complex line graph, you should have determined that it is comparing the price of crude oil between 1973 and 1990 in terms of 1973 dollars and 1990 dollars. The vertical axis measures the price per barrel, while the horizontal axis lists the years from 1973 to 1991. The diagonal lines suggest that oil prices went up sharply in the years 1979 through 1981, then proceeded to decline rather sharply until 1989, when they began to increase once again. Further, because of inflation, the purchase of a barrel of oil with 1990 dollars was much more expensive than with 1973 dollars. In 1981, for example, purchasing a barrel of oil with 1990 dollars cost almost twice as much as in 1973.

By carefully reading a line graph such as this one, with two or more diagonals or variables, you can extract a great deal of information.

Charts

Charts are another way to present information visually and compactly. They are often used in the business field to categorize information and

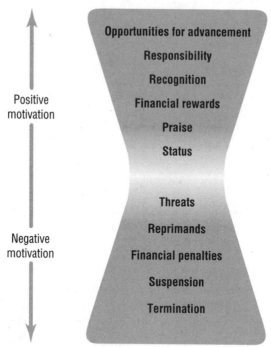

Figure 9-5   *Motivation continuum. (Source: Joseph T. Straub and Raymond F. Attner,* In-troduction to Business, *5th ed. [Belmont, Calif.: Wadsworth, 1994], p. 283.)*

present procedural sequences and in the history field to show time se-quences. Business analysts often use charts in their oral presentations to summarize important information and make it more understandable to their audience. Look at the figure on motivation (Figure 9-5) to see how various elements of positive and negative motivation are represented in these two, connected, four-sided shapes, with the arrows indicating the degree of positive and negative motivation. Such a chart can be effec-tively used at the end of an oral presentation on motivation as a memory and summarizing device. As you study charts like this, ask yourself the following questions: (1) How do the shapes relate to the material? Do larger shapes represent greater relative importance and smaller shapes lesser importance? (2) How is the material positioned? Does the posi-tioning suggest relative importance? Do you see how the chart on moti-vation is set up so that the more important terms are in the larger parts of the shape, farther up and down the arrows?

Flow charts have become particularly popular in the business and computer field to show the sequences of various procedures. Note how Figure 9-6 depicts the steps in purchasing a product, with the first step at the top, the last step at the bottom, and each step connected by curved arrows. Flow charts can also be used to portray more complicated pro-cedures. In Figure 9-7 you see how, after a product is created, its market-

Figure 9-6   *A typical purchasing procedure. (Source: Joseph T. Straub and Raymond F. Attner,* Introduction to Business, *5th ed. [Belmont, Calif.: Wadsworth, 1994], p. 355.)*

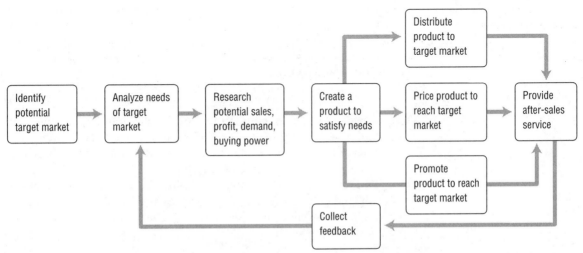

Figure 9-7   *The process of marketing a product. (Source: Joseph T. Straub and Raymond F. Attner,* Introduction to Business, *5th ed. [Belmont, Calif.: Wadsworth, 1994], p. 355.)*

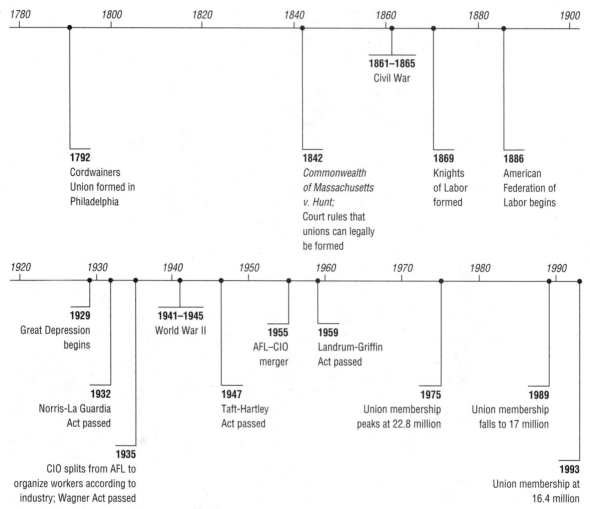

1780   1800   1820   1840   1860   1880   1900

1861–1865
Civil War

1792
Cordwainers
Union formed in
Philadelphia

1842
*Commonwealth
of Massachusetts
v. Hunt;*
Court rules that
unions can legally
be formed

1869
Knights
of Labor
formed

1886
American
Federation of
Labor begins

1920   1930   1940   1950   1960   1970   1980   1990

1929
Great Depression
begins

1941–1945
World War II

1955
AFL–CIO
merger

1959
Landrum-Griffin
Act passed

1932
Norris-La Guardia
Act passed

1947
Taft-Hartley
Act passed

1975
Union membership
peaks at 22.8 million

1989
Union membership
falls to 17 million

1935
CIO splits from AFL to
organize workers according to
industry; Wagner Act passed

1993
Union membership at
16.4 million

Figure 9-8   *Important events in the history of labor-management relations. (Source: Joseph T. Straub and Raymond F. Attner,* Introduction to Business, *5th ed. [Belmont, Calif.: Wadsworth, 1994], pp. 302–303.)*

ing activities branch out into three steps—distribution, pricing, and promotion—all of which lead to after-sales service. Then note how after-sales service requires collection of feedback and analysis of needs, so the chart loops back to the second step.

With flow charts be sure that you follow the arrows very carefully so that you are familiar with the sequence presented, and study particularly thoroughly those more complicated flow charts that loop back into a previous step or procedure.

In history material, charts known as time lines present sequences of historical events in chronological order, usually in a left-to-right design, with the material on the right being the most recent and that on the left the earliest. Note how the time line in Figure 9-8 shows the history of labor management. See how the time line gives you a sense for the time relationships among historical events that you might not grasp as well by simply reading about these events.

All these charts are effective ways to organize material and also serve as visual designs to help you remember what you are studying. In Chapter 11, you will create your own charts, known as study maps or advanced organizers, in order to make more comprehensible the material you read and hear.

Tables

Unlike graphs, tables are not visual. They simply present information concisely. Tables are especially helpful study aids because they present much information in a small space. When you read tables, as you did with graphs, first determine the subject; then establish what each category and subcategory represent. If you do not know what a particular part of a table means, you may not be able to use the table efficiently. Unlike a line graph, whose diagonal shows a trend (up, down, or staying the same), a table does not spell out these trends for you; you need to make these inferences from the data in the table. If you note a trend in a table, make a marginal note stating what that trend seems to be.

Look at Table 9-1 on the damage caused by plants and animals imported in the United States. Note the categories of the table, and note the order of each entry. What inferences can you draw from the data? What conclusions do you come to?

The table presents five causes of damage (mammals, birds, fish, insects, and plants) as well as where each cause came from, how it was brought over to the United States, and the type of damage that it caused. The agents causing damage seem to have come from Asia, Europe, and Latin America. Insects and plants appear to have caused the greatest damage—the camphor scale insect damaging 200 species of plants, the chestnut blight destroying nearly all American chestnut trees, and the Dutch elm disease killing almost all the elms.

Do you see how densely packed with information this table is? Most tables that you will come across are equally informative. As you continue to read tables, you will be able to make more subtle inferences and determine more patterns that are suggested by the data. You will also begin to rely more frequently on tables for study purposes.

Summary

Graphs are visual, concise means of presenting information. There are three kinds of graphs: circle, bar, and line. Line graphs show relationships among two or more variables and are sometimes difficult to understand. Charts are visual ways of presenting material in order to show

Table 9-1   *Damage Caused by Plants and Animals Imported into the United States*

Name	Origin	Mode of Transport	Type of Damage
Mammals			
European wild boar	Russia	Intentionally imported (1912), escaped captivity	Destruction of habitat by rooting; crop damage
Nutria (cat-sized rodent)	Argentina	Intentionally imported, escaped captivity (1940)	Alteration of marsh ecology; damage to levees and earth dams; crop destruction
Birds			
European starling	Europe	Intentionally released (1890)	Competition with native songbirds; crop damage, transmission of swine diseases; airport interference
House sparrow	England	Intentionally released by Brooklyn Institute (1853)	Crop damage; displacement of native songbirds
Fish			
Carp	Germany	Intentionally released (1877)	Displacement of native fish; uprooting of water plants with loss of waterfowl populations
Sea lamprey	North Atlantic Ocean	Entered via Welland Canal (1829)	Destruction of lake trout, lake whitefish, and sturgeon in Great Lakes
Walking catfish	Thailand	Imported into Florida	Destruction of bass, bluegill, and other fish

Source: G. Tyler Miller, Jr., *Living in the Environment,* 5th ed. (Belmont, Calif.: Wadsworth, 1988), p. 302. From *Biological Conservation* by David W. Ehrenfeld. Copyright © 1970 by Holt, Rinehart and Winston, Inc. Modified and reprinted by permission.

relationships, particularly procedures and time sequences. Tables are not visual; rather, they present information in categories. In reading a table, you need to make inferences and draw conclusions regarding the patterns that emerge from the data.

Graphs, charts, and tables are often effective study aids because much information is presented in a small amount of space. You may choose to create your own graphs, charts, and tables when you want to condense the material you are studying.

Name	Origin	Mode of Transport	Type of Damage
Insects			
Argentine fire ant	Argentina	Probably entered via coffee shipments from Brazil (1918)	Crop damage; destruction of native ant species
Camphor scale insect	Japan	Accidentally imported on nursery stock (1920s)	Damage to nearly 200 species of plants in Louisiana, Texas, and Alabama
Japanese beetle	Japan	Accidentally imported on irises or azaleas (1911)	Defoliation of more than 250 species of trees and other plants, including many of commercial importance
Plants			
Water hyacinth	Central America	Intentionally introduced (1884)	Clogging waterways; shading out other aquatic vegetation
Chestnut blight (a fungus)	Asia	Accidentally imported on nursery plants (1900)	Destruction of nearly all eastern American chestnut trees; disturbance of forest ecology
Dutch elm disease, *Cerastomella ulmi* (a fungus, the disease agent)	Europe	Accidentally imported on infected elm timber used for veneers (1930)	Destruction of millions of elms; disturbance of forest ecology

Table 9-2   *Persons Below the Poverty Level as a Percentage of Total Population by Race*

	Race			
Year	White	Black	Other*	Everyone
1965	13.3	NA	NA	17.3
1970	9.9	33.5	NA	12.6
1975	9.7	31.3	26.9	12.3
1980	10.2	32.5	25.7	13.0
1984	11.5	33.8	28.4	14.4

Source: Philip C. Starr, *Economics: Principles in Action*, 5th ed. (Belmont, Calif.: Wadsworth, 1988), p. 172. Data from *Statistical Abstract of the United States, 1982–83* and *1986*.
*Includes people of Spanish origin and people of all other races.

Summary Box   *Graphs, Charts, and Tables*

What are they?	Why use them?
Graph: a visual way to present information in circles, bars, or lines.	Graph: To present information visually and to help you learn material more easily

Chart: a visual way of representing relationships, especially procedures and time sequences	Chart:
	  to condense information into a visual, easy-to-remember form
	  to create your own for studying and remembering lecture and textbook material

Table: a concise way to relate information by setting up categories and subcategories	Table:
	  to present information concisely
	  to show relationships among facts and figures
	  to gain insights about the material you are studying
	  to help you remember information for exams

Skills Practice

**Exercise 9.1
Reading Graphs,
Charts, and Tables**

Use the reading skills you have just learned to answer the following questions concerning graphs, tables, and charts on topics that are familiar from the exercises you have completed in previous chapters. Place all answers in the answer box.

1. Table 9-2 concerns:

   a. poverty
   b. persons by race above the poverty level
   c. the poorest and the richest people of the United States
   d. the percentage of various races under the poverty level in the United States

2. The race in America that seems to have the largest percentage below the poverty level is:

   a. other
   b. white
   c. black
   d. none of these

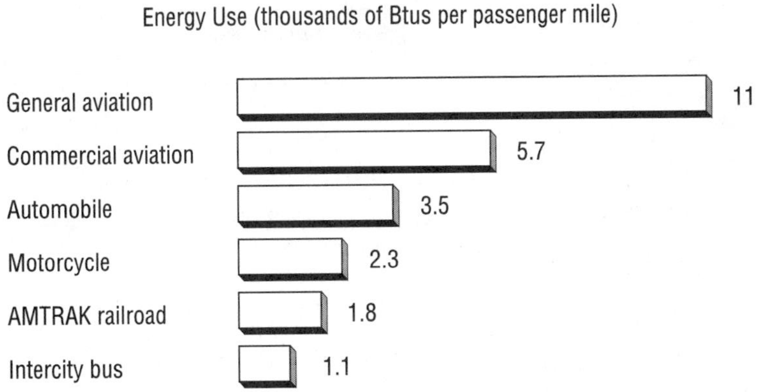

Energy Use (thousands of Btus per passenger mile)

General aviation — 11

Commercial aviation — 5.7

Automobile — 3.5

Motorcycle — 2.3

AMTRAK railroad — 1.8

Intercity bus — 1.1

Figure 9-9   *Energy efficiency of various types of domestic transportation. (Source: G. Tyler Miller, Jr., Living in the Environment, 7th ed. [Belmont, Calif.: Wadsworth, 1992], p. 443.)*

1. _____

2. _____

3. _____

4. _____

5. _____

6. _____

7. _____

8. _____

9. _____

10. _____

_____
80%

(score = # correct × 10)
Find answers on p. 400.

3. What can you conclude about poverty among all Americans between 1965 and 1984? The percentage of people below the poverty level has:

a. increased
b. gone down considerably
c. gone down somewhat
d. none of these

4. The subject of the bar graph in Figure 9-9 is:

a. energy use
b. how efficiently various types of transportation use energy
c. how much energy automobiles use in the United States
d. how railroad transportation compares in energy use to automobiles

5. Which form of transportation uses ten times as much energy as the intercity bus?

a. motorcycle
b. automobile
c. commercial aviation
d. general aviation

6. Which is the third most energy-efficient form of transportation?

a. AMTRAK railroad
b. motorcycle
c. automobile
d. commercial aviation

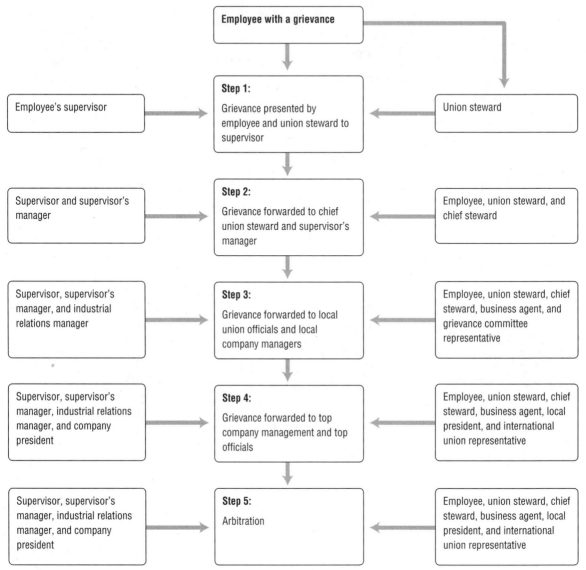

Figure 9-10   *Steps in a grievance procedure. (Source: Joseph T. Straub and Raymond F. Attner,*
Introduction to Business, *5th ed. [Belmont, Calif.: Wadsworth, 1994], p. 318.)*

7. If you were an environmentalist studying these figures, what recommendation would you make?

   a. Intercity buses should not be allowed on the streets.
   b. Automobiles should be commended for their very efficient use of energy.

   c. The airlines should find ways to build more fuel-efficient air-
planes.

   d. all of these

8. In the flow chart (Figure 9-10), which procedure is *not* mentioned?

   a. management personnel involved in the grievance

   b. union personnel involved in the grievance

   c. employee agrees to salary increase

   d. movement of the grievance

9. You can conclude that, as the grievance progresses,

   a. fewer personnel are involved

   b. more personnel are involved

   c. the same number of personnel are involved

   d. the employee filing the grievance must finally represent herself

10. At what step would a grievance be sent to the President of the
company?

   a. Step 2

   b. Step 3

   c. Step 4

   d. Step 5

Exercise 9.2
Reading Graphs and
Tables

Here are two more graphs and another table from topics familiar to you,
each followed by questions. Place your answers in the answer box.

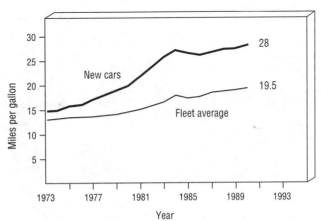

Figure 9-11 *Increase in average fuel efficiency of new cars and the entire fleet of cars in the United
States between 1973 and 1990. (Source: G. Tyler Miller, Jr., Living in the
Environment, 5th ed. [Belmont, Calif.: Wadsworth, 1992], p. 443. Data from U.S.
Department of Energy and Environmental Protection Agency.)*

1. From Figure 9-11, determine the difference between the miles per gallon for new cars in 1990 and the fleet average in 1990:

   a. 8.5
   b. 9.5
   c. 10.5
   d. 11

2. What was the fleet average for miles per gallon in 1973?

   a. 10
   b. 11
   c. 12
   d. 13

3. What can you conclude about the relationship between the miles per gallon averages and fleet and new car gas use?

   a. Fleet cars are less efficient.
   b. New cars seem to be improving more than fleet cars.
   c. both a and b
   d. Graph does not say.

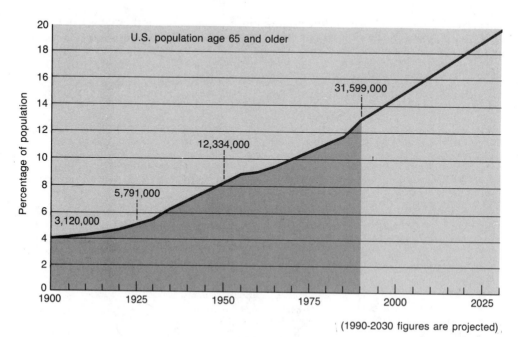

(1990-2030 figures are projected)

Figure 9-12   *The graying of America (1990–2030 figures projected). (Source: Thomas Dye,* Power and Society, *5th ed. [Pacific Grove, Calif.: Brooks/Cole, 1990], p. 265. Data from* U.S. Bureau of the Census, Statistical Abstract of the United States 1988 *[Washington, D.C.: U.S. Government Printing Office, 1988], p. 15.)*

4. What is the main point of the line graph in Figure 9-12?

    a. As time goes on, there are more older Americans.

    b. In 1900, there were less than 3 million Americans over 65 years of age.

    c. The number of older Americans seems to double every 25 years.

    d. The number of older Americans will decrease after the year 2000.

5. What does the shaded area represent?

    a. a 90-year representation of the numbers and percentages of older Americans

    b. a 50-year representation of the numbers and percentages of older Americans

    c. the increase in percentage of older Americans over a 75-year period

    d. the decrease in percentage of older Americans over a 90-year span

6. A conclusion you can draw regarding older Americans between 1900 and 1990 is that their percentage has:

    a. doubled

    b. tripled

    c. quadrupled

    d. increased fivefold

7. The projections for the years 2000–2025 suggest that:

    a. the number of older Americans will decrease.

    b. the number of older Americans will increase, but their percentages will decrease

    c. older Americans will increase to about 32 million

    d. the percentage and numbers of older Americans will continue to increase

8. Table 9-3 lists:

    a. the sales of the twenty largest U.S. multinational corporations

    b. the profits of the twenty largest U.S. multinational corporations

    c. the number of employees in each of the largest multinational corporations

    d. the twenty largest U.S. multinational corporations in terms of sales, profits, assets, stock equity, and employees

9. Which of these companies has the fewest employees?

    a. Chevron

    b. Mobil

    c. Amoco

    d. Dow Chemical

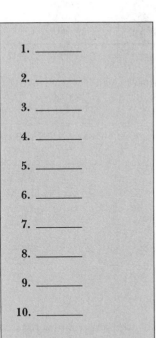

1. _____

2. _____

3. _____

4. _____

5. _____

6. _____

7. _____

8. _____

9. _____

10. _____

_____

80%

Ask instructor for answers.

Table 9-3   *The Twenty Largest U.S. Multinationals.*

Rank/Company	Sales ($ Millions)	Profits ($ Millions)	Assets ($ Millions)	Total Stockholders' Equity ($ Millions)	Employees
1 General Motors	132,774	(23,498)	191,012	6,225	750,000
2 Exxon	103,547	4,770	85,030	33,776	95,000
3 Ford Motor Co.	100,785	(7,385)	180,545	14,752	325,333
4 IBM	65,096	(4,965)	86,705	27,624	308,010
5 General Electric	62,202	4,725	192,876	23,459	268,000
6 Mobil	57,389	862	40,561	16,540	63,700
7 Philip Morris	50,157	4,939	50,014	12,563	161,000
8 Chevron	38,523	1,569	33,970	13,728	49,245
9 E. I. duPont de Nemours	37,386	(3,927)	38,870	11,765	125,000
10 Texaco	37,130	712	25,992	9,973	37,582
11 Chrysler	36,897	723	40,653	7,538	128,000
12 Boeing	30,414	552	18,147	8,056	143,000
13 Procter & Gamble	29,890	1,872	24,025	9,071	106,200
14 Amoco	25,543	(74)	28,453	12,960	46,994
15 PepsiCo	22,083	374	20,951	5,355	371,000
16 United Technologies	22,032	(287)	15,928	3,370	178,000
17 Conagra	21,219	372	9,758	2,232	80,787
18 Eastman Kodak	20,577	1,146	23,138	6,557	132,600
19 Dow Chemical	19,080	(489)	25,360	8,074	61,353
20 Xerox	18,089	(1,020)	34,051	3,971	99,300

Source: Joseph T. Straub and Raymond F. Attner, *Introduction to Business,* 5th ed. (Belmont, Calif.: Wadsworth, 1994), p. 690. Data from Ani Hadjian and Lorraine Tritto, "Another Year of Pain," *Fortune,* July 26, 1993, pp. 191–193. © 1993 Time Inc. All rights reserved.

10. Which of these companies has the second largest number of employees?

a. PepsiCo
b. Ford Motor Co.
c. IBM
d. Amoco

Exercise 9.3
Writing a Paragraph
with a Main Idea
and Supporting
Details from
Information in a
Graph

In this writing exercise, you are to use only the information presented in the circle graphs and bar graphs in Figure 9-13 to answer the following essay question. This material concerns the Hispanic population in America and comes from a sociology textbook.

Use the following outline to jot down notes you will use in your paragraph.

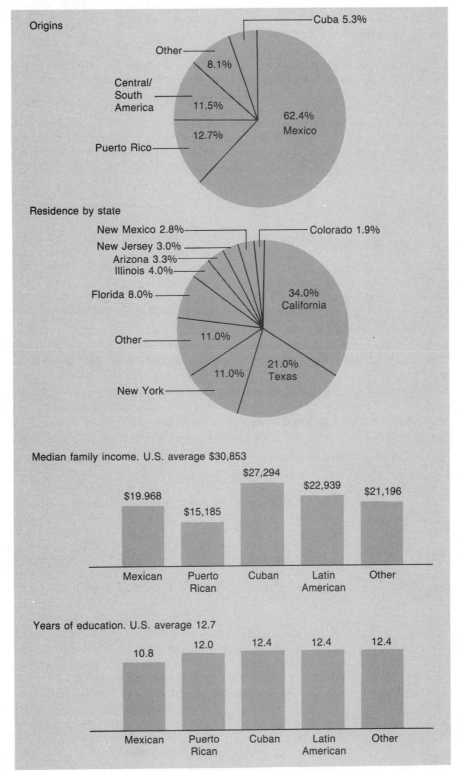

Figure 9-13 *Hispanic Americans. (Source: Thomas Dye,* Power and Society, *5th ed. [Pacific Grove, Calif.: Brooks/Cole, 1990], p. 241. Data from U.S. Bureau of the Census,* Statistical Abstract of the United States 1988 *[Washington, D.C.: U.S. Government Printing Office, 1988].)*

I. Basic Information on Hispanics in the United States

A. Where Hispanics generally come from: _____

B. Where they live: _____

C. Income: _____

D. Education: _____

Essay question: In an organized paragraph, discuss where most Hispanics have come from, the most populated Hispanic areas in the United States, the Hispanics with the highest and lowest incomes, and their educational levels compared to the U.S. average. Where appropriate, provide specific figures. Start with a topic sentence discussing where Hispanics generally live and how their lifestyle compares to the average American's.

Exercise 9.4 Determining Main Ideas and Major Details and Interpreting Charts and Tables in a Text Excerpt

The following is an excerpt from a college business text on the ways consumer products are distributed. Read through the excerpt quickly to get a sense of its organization. Then go back and read it slowly, paying particular attention to the four charts and two tables and their relationship to the excerpt. When you finish, answer the following five questions. You may refer to the excerpt in deciding on your answers.

Distribution Strategy

(1) Distribution strategy and pricing strategy are the third and fourth ingredients in a company's marketing mix. When these elements are "blended" with product and promotional strategy, the organization has created its marketing strategy to reach the selected target market. In this chapter we will examine the importance, objectives, and components of distribution strategy. We will also investigate pricing: its objectives, methods of determination, and potential strategies.

The Importance of Distribution Strategy

(2) Distribution strategy encompasses physical distribution systems and the channels used to place the product in the customer's hands. It is responsible for getting the product to the right place at the right time. A firm can have the best products in the world (product strategy) and people can know about them and want them (promotional strategy), but all this will be useless if people cannot get the products when and where they want them.

(3) Distribution involves (1) the routes goods take and the people involved in that process and (2) the activities involved in getting the goods to the consumer—a physical distribution system. Element 1 deals with the channels, choices of channels, and channel members. Element 2 deals with the actual components of a physical distribution system—transpor-

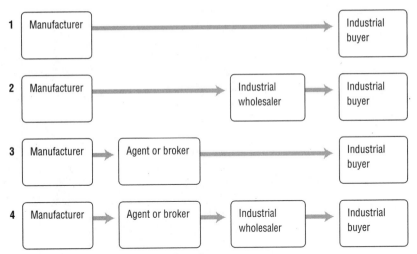

Figure 9-14 Distribution channels for industrial goods.

tation, warehousing, order processing, materials handling, and inventory control.

Channels of Distribution

(4) A channel of distribution, or marketing channel is *a route that goods follow on their journey from manufacturers to consumers.* Distribution channels are composed of organizations or people known as channel members, middlemen, or intermediaries: **wholesalers**—*those who sell products to other sellers of goods*—and **retailers**—*those who sell products to the ultimate consumer.* The channels and the organizations that comprise them serve as pipelines by which the manufacturer moves goods to the final customer—either an individual consumer or industrial buyer.

(5) Based on these two types of customers, there are two major distribution channel categories by market: the industrial goods market and the consumer goods market.

Channels for Industrial Goods

(6) Industrial goods channels tend to be more direct than consumer goods channels—many industrial goods are designed solely for the end user. For example, Otis Die and Casting Company designs and manufactures tool dies for Cummings Tool. But in other instances—accessory equipment, supplies—longer channels are required. Figure 9-14 illustrates the four main distribution channels that producers can use to reach the industrial goods market. Let's discuss each of them:

(7) 1. *Manufacturer to industrial buyer.* The shortest and sometimes most practical way for a manufacturer to distribute industrial goods is to sell them directly to industrial customers. Direct distribution is used if goods are awkward to handle, the market segment is small, the seller must train the buyer's employees to operate the product, or, as

channel of distribution *or* marketing channel A route that goods follow on their journey from manufacturers to consumers.
wholesalers Those who sell products to other sellers of goods.
retailers Those who sell products to the ultimate consumer.

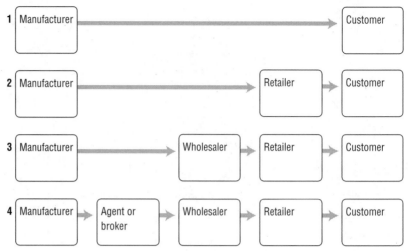

Figure 9-15   *Distribution channels for consumer goods.*

previously noted, the product is specifically designed for the end user. Computers, textile manufacturing equipment, and iron ore often are distributed in this way.

(8) 2. *Manufacturer to industrial wholesaler to industrial buyer.* Industrial goods with a broad market, such as welding rods, printing paper, and construction materials, need wider distribution. They utilize a distribution channel featuring wholesalers known as *industrial distributors.* These distributors resell to the industrial buyer.

(9) 3. *Manufacturer to agent or broker to industrial buyer.* In some instances the product being sold does not require the intermediate warehousing service provided by a wholesaler but still needs some intermediary to sell the products. An agent or broker can serve as the contact point for the manufacturer without taking possession of or title to the goods and can provide the necessary sales support.

(10) 4. *Manufacturer to agent or broker to industrial wholesaler to industrial buyer.* Small manufacturers often need to contract with an agent or broker to represent products to wholesalers. This agent serves the purpose of bringing the wholesaler and manufacturer together but does not take title to the goods.

(11) **Channels for Consumer Goods**   Consumer goods channels tend to be longer and more complex than industrial channels. Because a large number of consumer goods are low-priced convenience goods, by necessity more middlemen need to be involved. Chewing gum, razor blades, and paper plates cannot be effectively marketed directly from the manufacturer to the consumer. Figure 9-15 shows the four distribution channels that manufacturers of consumer goods can use. Let's examine each:

(12) 1. *Manufacturer to consumer.* Although the direct channel is favored for reaching industrial users, only approximately 5 percent of consumer goods are moved in this way. Such products as plants at nurseries, vegetables at farmers' markets, and arts and crafts items at fairs are often sold directly to consumers. Firms such as L. L. Bean, Omaha

Steaks, Wolverman's (muffins, bagels, crumpets) sell direct through their mail-order catalogs.

(13) 2. *Manufacturer to retailer to consumer.* Some manufacturers choose to select their own retail outlets to represent them. Automobiles and large household appliances are products that traditionally are distributed directly to retailers without the need for wholesalers.

(14) 3. *Manufacturer to wholesaler to retailer to consumer.* Some products—magazines, combs, lipstick, hair spray—need a broad channel of distribution. This is provided by incorporating a wholesale and retail link in the channel. The wholesaler aids in allocating the product to the retailers in order to have the product available when and where needed by the consumer. The success of consumer product manufacturers such as Gillette and Schick is related directly to the distribution networks the firms have developed. As convenience goods, the products are placed in supermarkets, convenience stores, drug stores, and discount stores across the country.

(15) 4. *Manufacturer to agent or broker to wholesaler to retailer to consumer.* When goods are produced by a large number of small companies—canning, frozen-food packing, meat packing—an agent or broker brings the buyers and sellers together. In some cases the agent or broker contacts the wholesalers, who in turn buy from the producers. In other instances the wholesaler may be seeking a source of supply.

(16) **Selection of a Distribution Channel**   Which of these distribution channels should a manufacturer use? The decision is based on a number of variables, such as:

(17) • *The market segment.* As we have seen, a major factor in the decision is whether the product is intended for the consumer or industrial market. Industrial purchases normally deal directly with the manufacturer, while consumers make most purchases at retail stores.

(18) • *The size and geographic location of the market segment.* A market that is large and geographically dispersed, as in the case of many consumer goods, requires the use of marketing intermediaries. On the other hand, a direct channel is more effective when the manufacturer's potential market is small and geographically concentrated.

(19) • *The type of product.* Product type also dictates channel selection. Convenience goods require broad distribution to have them available where the consumer wants them—therefore a long channel with multiple intermediaries. Specialty goods are distributed directly to retail stores.

(20) • *The ability to perform the marketing functions.* A critical factor is whether the manufacturer can perform the required marketing functions (selling, transporting, storing, financing, risk bearing) or has the need for others—intermediaries—to do so. If a company has adequate resources—managerial, financial, marketing—it feels less pressure to use intermediaries.

(21) • *The competitor's distribution strategy.* Sometimes it is necessary to respond to a competitor's distribution strategy. Dell Computers, by bypassing retail outlets and going directly to the consumer, revolutionized computer sales and forced similar actions by IBM.

(22) • *The degree of market coverage.* Adequate market coverage—the number of dealers or outlets where the good can be purchased—for some

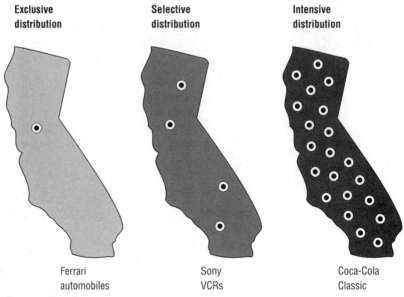

| Exclusive distribution | Selective distribution | Intensive distribution |

| Ferrari automobiles | Sony VCRs | Coca-Cola Classic |

Figure 9-16 *Degrees of market coverage.*

intensive distribution Widespread market coverage that utilizes a large number of wholesalers and retailers.

selective distribution Utilizing a moderate number of retailers and wholesalers.

exclusive distribution Limiting distribution to one retailer or wholesaler in a geographic area.

products could mean one store for 70,000 people, while for another it may mean one store for 200,000. As seen in Figure 9-16, there are three degrees of market coverage: intensive distribution, selective distribution, and exclusive distribution. A firm that markets convenience products will want **intensive distribution**, *widespread market coverage that utilizes a large number of wholesalers and retailers.* Another manufacturer that markets shopping goods may wish to emphasize image and a good sales volume through **selective distribution**, *utilizing a moderate number of retailers and wholesalers.* Finally, for a specialty good, a manufacturer may use **exclusive distribution**: *limiting distribution to one retailer or wholesaler in a geographic area.*

(23) With these factors in mind, let's examine the roles of the two major channel members.

Channel Members

(24) As mentioned earlier in the chapter, the various channels of distribution we have examined are composed of organizations or people known as *channel members, middlemen,* or *intermediaries.* These intermediaries perform the marketing functions of buying, selling, storing, transporting, risk taking, and collecting marketing information for the manufacturer. In addition, marketing intermediaries are vitally important in creating time, place, and possession utilities. The intermediaries ensure that products are available when and where they are needed.

(25) Two types of middlemen operate between the manufacturer and consumer or industrial user: wholesalers and retailers. In the next sections we will discuss each.

(26) **Wholesaling Middlemen**   Wholesalers are middlemen who sell goods to retailers, to other wholesalers, and to industrial users, but who do not sell in significant amounts to the final consumer. As shown in Figure 9-17 [p. 210], if wholesalers did not exist, retailers would have to spend a great deal of time dealing with many different manufacturers, attempting to coordinate numerous product orders and shipments, and acquiring and maintaining huge stock inventories.

(27) Not all wholesalers are the same. Some take title to the goods (merchant wholesalers); others do not (agents and brokers). Some provide a full range of services. As shown in Table 9-4 [p. 210], full-service merchant wholesalers provide credit, store and deliver, and provide sales and promotional assistance. On the other hand, limited-service merchant wholesalers simply resell goods and provide little or no service. Table 9-5 [p. 211] provides a sampling of the various types of wholesalers and their characteristics.

(28) **Retailing Middlemen**   Retailers are the last stage in the channel of distribution: they perform the business activities involved in the sale of goods and services to the ultimate consumer for personal use. The activities may include buying and selling of products, transportation or delivery, storage of inventory, financing, and risk bearing. Retailers can be classified by type of ownership and where business is conducted.*

1. _____

2. _____

3. _____

4. _____

5. _____

1. The main idea of paragraph 1 suggests that:

   a. Distribution strategies are often inefficient.
   b. Distribution strategies must focus on delivering goods on time at the right location.
   c. Product strategy and promotional strategy are extremely important in understanding distribution.
   d. Distribution strategies have often been incompletely studied by business analysts.

2. The main idea of paragraph 11 is that consumer goods channels:

   a. move items like chewing gum and razor blades
   b. move inexpensive items
   c. generally have four types of distribution
   d. are more complicated and time consuming than industrial channels

3. Which is *not* a major detail in paragraph 14?

   a. Lipstick is one product that needs a broad distribution.
   b. Gillette and Schick have successfully implemented a broad distribution strategy.
   c. Some products require a broad distribution.
   d. Products like magazines are distributed to supermarkets, drugstores, and discount stores across the country.

---

*Joseph T. Straub and Raymond F. Attner, *Introduction to Business*, 5th ed. (Belmont, Calif.: Wadsworth, 1994), pp. 438–445.

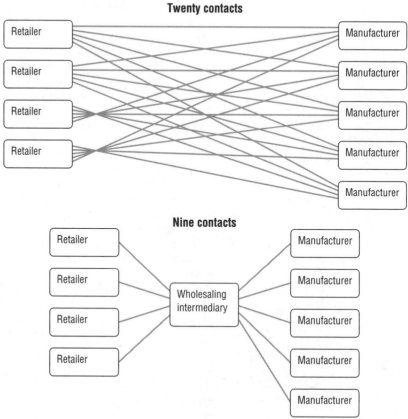

Figure 9-17   *The value of the wholesale middleman.*

Table 9-4   *Typical Services Provided by Full-service Wholesalers.*

Services to Manufacturers	*Services to Retailers*
Relay market information from retailers	Advise retailer on layout, promotional activities, bookkeeping practices, inventory planning, and sources of credit
Employ sales force to sell products	
Save manufacturers work by extending credit to retailers	Tell of new products that manufacturers are bringing to market
Store products before resale and deliver them when sold	Deliver merchandise faster and in smaller quantities than producers are willing to do
Bear risk of market changes that may reduce demand for the product	Simplify retailers' recordkeeping and inventory-handling activities by gathering many manufacturers' products into a single delivery and billing

Table 9-5   *Types of Wholesalers and Their Characteristics*

Wholesaler	Characteristics	Takes Title
Manufacturers' agent*	An agent who sells products made by several manufacturers Has little authority to approve customer requests for price concessions, expedited delivery, or credit	No
Selling agent*	An agent who sells a producer's entire output Usually has broad authority to approve customer requests for price concessions, expedited delivery, or credit	No
Auction house*	Brings buyers and sellers together in one location Allows buyers to inspect products before purchase	No
Commission merchant*	An agent who represents producers Sells products for the best price possible; takes possession of goods Sells agricultural products	No
Broker	An agent who represents either buyer or seller for a commission on sales or purchases made Arranges for products shipped directly to the purchaser Distributes such products as coal, grain, and produce	No
Rack jobber	A type of consumer-goods wholesaler Sets up manufacturers' point-of-purchase displays in stores and restocks them as needed Distributes such products as magazines, panty hose, and candy	Yes
Drop shipper	An intermediary who does not take physical possession of goods Provides selling and credit Does not provide advertising or merchandising support Distributes primarily raw materials	Yes
Truck wholesaler	An intermediary who sells and delivers goods at the same time on a regular sales route Provides merchandising and promotion support Distributes potato chips, bakery, and dairy products	Yes

*Manufacturers' agent, selling agent, auction house, and commission merchant are all categorized as *agent* channels of distribution.

4. The first flowchart (Figure 9-14) suggests that:

    a. Some products go directly from the manufacturer to the consumer.

    b. Other products need a retailer.

    c. The most complicated distribution pattern requires three channels before it gets to the consumer.

    d. all of these

5. What can you conclude from the chart showing degrees of market coverage (Figure 9-16)?

    a. Exclusive distribution requires many distribution sites.

    b. Intensive distribution seems to market popular, inexpensive products.

    c. Sony VCRs require exclusive distribution.

    d. Selective distribution often markets extremely expensive items.

    Now reread various sections of this text excerpt and then answer the following questions in a phrase or sentence.

6. Reread paragraphs 24–28. What is the difference between a wholesaling middleman and a retailing middleman? (1 point)

7. Study the table that lists the typical services provided by full-service wholesalers (Table 9-4). Without looking back at the table, list two services full-service wholesalers provide manufacturers and two services they provide retailers. (2 points)

8. Study the table that lists the types of wholesalers and their characteristics (Table 9-5). Without looking back at the table, list the characteristics of two of these wholesalers. (2 points)

70%

Ask instructor for answers.

Taking Lecture and Study Notes

In this part, you will learn several note-taking skills that you can successfully use in listening to lectures and in study reading. You will find that when you take effective notes, you are using several of the reading and listening skills that you acquired in Part Two. When you can effectively use these note-taking techniques, studying for exams will become both organized and worthwhile.

10 Characteristics of Lectures

Characteristics of lectures

❶ Who is the speaker?   ❶ What are the students'
❶ What is the subject?   obligations?

Lectures are a special kind of communication. A lecture is a dialogue between you and the speaker. Your response to the lecturer is often in the form of notes rather than oral comments. Accurate notes are important, for they are your only record of what your lecturer said. In this part of the book, you will learn how to write useful notes. Consider the following aspects of a lecture: the lecturer's speaking style, the subject of the lecture, and your obligations as a listener.

The Speaker

Lecturers' speaking styles are as varied as writers' styles. Some lecturers speak loudly, others softly. Some lecturers speak quickly, others slowly. It is up to you to adjust your listening practices to the speaker's style. The average lecturer speaks at 125 words per minute, whereas the average reading rate is 250 words per minute. With a lecturer who speaks quickly, you may have a difficult time writing down all of the information. With a lecturer who speaks slowly, your mind may wander and you may become bored. But whatever the lecturer's style, you need to focus on the main ideas and the major details of the material.

If a lecturer presents too much information, consult with classmates, who may have written down some of the information that you did not get. If a lecturer speaks slowly and presents too little information, you need to concentrate on the important points of the lecture.

Also, you should realize that most instructors are not professional speakers. Their delivery will usually not be polished and humorous. Lecturers are not entertainers; they are trained to impart information, not to be comedians. Some students have even commented that the entertaining lecturers are generally not the most informative.

Most instructors present organized lectures, so your focus must be on the instructor's organization, which often centers on general and specific bits of information. Instructors often use the same signal words in their lectures that you find in written material. In fact, good lecturers use these signal words to direct you to important information. Good lecturers realize that students can reread what is in writing, but that "relistening" without a tape recorder is impossible. Successful lecturers also understand that lectures are not as formal as written discourse. So they repeat themselves and make obvious comments such as "This is important" or "Write this down."

Along with repeating themselves and using signal words, lecturers use visual and vocal signals to punctuate their speaking. A lecturer's most effective visual aid is the chalkboard. When an instructor writes a term on the board or draws a chart or map, be sure to write this material down. A lecturer may also list important steps on the board or say "There are three steps to remember." Jot these steps down. In addition, a lecturer's tone of voice or rate of speech may change when an important point is made. Lecturers who speak rapidly often slow down when they say something important. Lecturers who normally speak softly may present a key point in a louder tone. Get acquainted with each lecturer's speaking style, and look for the verbal signals.

Finally, lecturers may sometimes read directly from the textbook. You should write down the page number of these passages, because they are probably important points.

A few lecturers are disorganized in their presentation, making your note-taking a difficult chore. They may not consistently present main ideas and major details in proper proportion, and they may digress often so that main ideas lose their focus. Unfortunately, you will need to compensate for this lack of organization by noting what information is missing. You will then need to rely more on your textbooks and on library material. You may also need to consult with classmates who may have understood more of the lecture.

The Subject of the Lecture

All of the skills you have learned so far in this book should be used when you take notes. Lecturers will organize their material around main ideas, major details, and minor details as well as the eight patterns of organization. Thus you should listen for the words that signal a particular organizational pattern. You will also use your paraphrasing skills when a lecturer speaks in difficult sentences, and you will need to make appropriate inferences when a lecturer is being indirect.

Although you will be using all of these skills when you listen to lectures, you also need to know how lectures are different from writing. Lecturers are often repetitive, whereas writing is not. Consider repetition in lecture as a kind of rereading; what a lecturer repeats is often important and difficult to understand the first time.

A lecturer may also *digress*, or stray from the main point. A lecturer may occasionally relate a humorous anecdote that is related to the lecture. These digressions would not make sense if you were to read them. Because writing is often concise, digressions in writing are seen as flaws. When you hear digressions in lecture, you should see how they apply to the topic as well as enjoy them. See digressions as unique to speaking, a feature that makes speech more intimate than writing.

The subject matter of the lecture also dictates the kinds of notes you will take. You will often take notes using main ideas and major details in the arts and humanities, the social sciences, and some biological sciences. In a history lecture, for example, you will often group your information around main ideas and details of support. On the other hand, in physical science and math courses, you will need to copy down solutions to problems and ignore the traditional note-taking format. The successful note taker in a math or science course accurately writes down the steps in a problem. Finally, in a foreign language course you will be responding orally, so your notes will be brief—a grammatical rule or a new vocabulary word. With each course, you need to be flexible and devise a note-taking style that best fits the subject matter.

Student Obligations

The key to successfully listening to lectures finally rests on you. You must see listening to lectures as a concentrated activity. You must anticipate the instructor's comments and determine the structure of the lecture.

Here is a list of hints that should help you become a more effective note taker. Some of these points have already been discussed in this chapter, but it will help if you see them put together.

1. Listen attentively for the topic, the main idea, and details of support. Train yourself to hear both general and detailed statements. Keep asking yourself: Is this the topic? the main point? What details relate to this main idea?

2. Listen for signal words that introduce a particular organizational pattern. When you identify the proper organizational pattern, you will better understand the logic of the lecture.

3. Look for visual cues and listen for auditory cues—what the lecturer puts on the board and when and why the lecturer's tone of voice changes. These cues often suggest important points.

4. Familiarize yourself with the topic before you begin listening to the lecture. If an instructor assigns a chapter before she lectures on it, read the material even if you do not understand all of it. The more exposure students have to a topic, the less difficult they tend to find the material. Attending a lecture without having done the assigned reading is unwise.

5. Listen attentively during class discussions. Do not assume that because a student is speaking you do not need to listen. What students ask or say often are the same questions and answers that you have. Sometimes, even student comments deserve a place in your notes. Also, listen to the instructor's response to student comments. You will learn a lot about your instructor by listening to his responses to students' ideas. You may find that a particular instructor likes original

thinking, while another is looking for the conventional answer. These inferences can help you in studying for exams in these courses.

6. Try to see the lecture material from the instructor's point of view. You have every right to disagree with the instructor, but only after you have listened to what he or she has said. Students often tune instructors out when they do not agree with their point of view. By not listening to the several points of view on each topic, they are being unfair both to the material and to the instructor.

Mastering these hints may take some time. But once you have fully embraced these suggestions, you will be able to anticipate the direction of the lecture—knowing beforehand when the lecturer will introduce a new topic or main idea or what organizational pattern the instructor intends to use. When you are able to anticipate information and structure, you will find that listening to lectures becomes both interesting and challenging.

Your other obligation is to assess the value that is assigned to lecture material in each of your courses. By the second or third week of the semester, you should have determined the value of notes in each of your courses. You should have determined whether the lectures are like or unlike the material in textbooks. And by the first examination, you should have determined how much of the exam came from your notes. You will find that some instructors rely on the textbook when making up an exam. Others rely on their lecture notes, and some formulate many of their questions from class discussion. Most instructors divide up their exam questions evenly between textbook, lecture, and discussion material. It is you who must resolve all of these issues, and you should do so early in the semester.

Some students think that attending lectures is a waste of their time— that they can learn everything from the textbook and from the notes of others. Except for the very bright student, not attending lectures is a bad idea. Even if most of the instructor's lectures follow the textbook, by attending lecture you will develop an appreciation for the subject that you cannot get from your textbook. You will also get to know your instructors from their lectures—both their personality and their attitude toward the material. If your instructor loves the subject, some of this enthusiasm will rub off on you. From the very best lectures, you will learn details and hear anecdotes that you cannot find in textbooks. And it may be in a particularly exciting lecture that you will decide to major in that subject—a decision that can affect the rest of your life.

Summary

Lectures are dialogues between the instructor and you. When you attend lectures, you must remember that speech is different from writing. Instructors repeat themselves in lectures, and they may digress. You should use all of the reading skills that you have learned to listen to lectures effectively. Each course you take requires a different listening and note-taking style, which you must determine early on in the semester.

Attending lectures gives you an appreciation for a particular course that reading will not give you. If you listen critically to lectures, you will have another important educational tool at your disposal.

Summary Box   *Lecture Material*

What is it?	*Why do you need it?*
An oral means of transferring information from the speaker to you A dialogue between the speaker and you Information that is usually organized around main ideas and major details Information that is not as concise as writing and that requires active listening	To gather information in a particular area To record the speaker's attitude toward a subject To appreciate a subject—something you cannot acquire just by reading your textbook

Skills Practice

Exercise 10.1
Inventorying a
Lecture

Choose an instructor whose lectures are difficult for you. Then complete the following inventory on one of his or her lectures. This inventory may help you understand why you are having difficulty taking notes on the lecture material.

1. Name of instructor: _____

2. Name of course: _____

3. Place a check next to those qualities that describe your instructor's lecture style:

_____ a. speaks rapidly

_____ b. speaks slowly

_____ c. speaks loudly

_____ d. speaks softly

_____ e. does not use the chalkboard

_____ f. is disorganized

_____ g. makes statements you do not agree with

_____ h. other: _____

The following are some suggestions for dealing with the characteristics that you checked in item 3, lettered to correspond to the list of problems.

a. If the instructor speaks too fast, you must try to keep up with the pace. Don't get upset if you cannot write down all of the important points. Just keep listening for main ideas and supporting details. Check classmates' notes to see what you may have missed.

b. If the instructor speaks too slowly, you may get bored, and your mind may wander. Keep listening for the lecture's focus: main ideas and details of support.

c. Notice when the instructor's voice becomes softer or louder. A change in loudness may signal that an important point is going to be made.

d. If the instructor speaks softly, you need to listen more actively; try to find a desk nearer to the instructor. Notice when his or her voice changes volume and see whether this change signals important information.

e. If your instructor doesn't use the chalkboard to highlight important points, see whether he or she uses any other cues. Does your instructor repeat key words and phrases or use hand gestures that signal important material?

f. If your instructor is disorganized, you will need to listen more carefully, jotting down those questions that your instructor leaves unanswered. In this case, you will need to rely more on your textbook, library material, and your classmates.

g. If your instructor makes remarks you disagree with, try to follow his or her train of thought. You are free to disagree with your instructor, but you need to follow his or her line of argument first.

h. Bring any other problems that you may have to your study skills instructor. You may even choose to present your complaint to the instructor who is giving you difficulty. State what your criticism is and what you would like to see changed. Some instructors will take your criticisms seriously and try to change their lecture style.

Exercise 10.2
Inventorying Your
Notes

Choose one course whose notes you are not entirely satisfied with. Then complete the following inventory.

1. Name of course: _____

2. Place a check next to those qualities that describe your note-taking style:

_____ a. too brief

_____ b. too wordy

_____ c. disorganized

_____ d. inaccurate

_____ e. messy

_____ f. any other problem: _____

The following are some suggestions for dealing with the problems that you checked in item 2, lettered to correspond to the list.

a. If your notes are too brief, you need to listen for supporting details. You are probably concentrating too much on main ideas. Remember, you also need to recall supporting details. Keep in mind that supporting details may be examples, characteristics, steps, causes, or effects. So listen carefully for names, places, and numbers. However, remember that brief notes are acceptable in a foreign language course.

b. If your notes are wordy, you are probably trying to write down everything. Remember that minor details usually do not need to be part of your notes. Wordy notes obscure main ideas and supporting details. Before writing, ask yourself: Is this statement significant? Will it give support to the main idea? Is this statement a restatement of something I've already written? Does this statement further elaborate on a previous detail? Approximately two to three written pages of notes in an hour's lecture is adequate.

c. If your lecture notes are disorganized, you probably cannot differentiate well between main ideas and supporting details. You will learn more about this issue in the next chapter. For now, remember that separating general from specific information is a key to learning and remembering. You may want to review Chapters 4 and 5, which treat main ideas and supporting details.

d. If your notes are inaccurate, you must start listening more carefully. Inaccurate notes are often caused by a daydreaming note taker. Inaccuracy is especially problematic in a math or science course, where the right number or correct sequence is essential to a correct solution. Leave your personal life outside of class, so you can listen to the lecture material with full concentration. Anyone can listen more attentively; it just takes discipline.

e. If your notes are messy, go over them soon after class is over and rewrite any words that are hard to read. If your handwriting is poor, you may need to write more slowly, even if you write less. Notes with less information are better than those that you cannot read.

f. If you have any other problems with your notes, speak with your study skills instructor.

11 Commonly Used Note-taking Techniques: Numeral–Letter, Indenting, and Cornell

Commonly used note-taking techniques		
◑ Numeral-letter format	◑ Indenting format	◑ Cornell

Ways to take notes efficiently	
◑ Condense	◑ Abbreviate

Now that you have made an inventory of your strengths and weaknesses as a note taker, you are ready to study the note-taking tips and techniques that have helped many students. The three most common techniques are the numeral–letter format, the indenting format, and the Cornell system. All find ways to present verbal material efficiently. You will discover that taking notes in math and science courses requires different note-taking practices. With all these techniques, you can condense information and use abbreviations to save time writing. You can apply these suggestions both to your lecture notes and to the notes you take as you study.

Numeral–Letter Format

The numeral–letter format is a commonly used note-taking system. You have already studied it in the beginning chapters on main ideas and major details. In this format, you identify main ideas with Roman numerals (I, II, III) and place them farthest to the left of your margin. You identify major details with capital letters (A, B, C) and indent them to the right of the Roman numerals. Look at the following example:

I. Two major sources for advertising

    A. Television
    B. Newspapers and magazines

In some cases you may want to include a minor detail. You represent minor details with Arabic numerals and place them to the right of your major details. Study the following example:

I. Two major sources for advertising

    A. Television

        1. Particularly prime-time television ads

There are many rules that go along with the numeral–letter format. In taking lecture notes, you do not need to know all of them. If you try to follow all of the rules, you may get confused. The main rule you should follow is that main ideas should be placed to the left of your paper, major details to the right. By now, you should realize that main ideas and major details organize so much of what you read and hear. Main ideas must be attached to major details; both bits of information are meaningless unless you place them in a general and specific context. Knowing that the business department offers a series of college courses is meaningless unless you know that business includes many disciplines, like consumer behavior, finance, and accounting. On the other hand, knowing that consumer behavior is a course of study does not make sense unless you connect this detail to the more general statement that it is part of the larger study of business.

You need to adhere to two minor procedures when you use the numeral–letter format. First, be sure to place a period after the numeral or letter (I. or A.) By using a period, you separate the number or letter from the words you write. The period thus shows that the numbers and letters are divisions and not part of your comments. Second, skip a line between Roman numerals (the main ideas). By separating main ideas, you give more emphasis to them, and you will be able to locate them more easily when you study your notes. Look at the following example:

I. Fields related to the study of consumer behavior

    A. Psychology
    B. Sociology
    D. Anthropology

II. Psychology and consumer behavior

    A. Focus on the psychology of motivation
    B. Focus on learning theory

By creating a space between I. and II., you make "Fields related to the study of consumer behavior" a different chunk of information from "Psychology and consumer behavior."

Don't expect to write all of the major details that you hear. As with summarizing, write down only the significant details, or those that most directly support the main idea. If for some reason you miss a few major details in lecture, ask to see a classmate's notes.

Indenting Format

The indenting system, another popular format, does away with letters and numbers entirely. You simply place main ideas to the left, major details to the right, and minor details to the right of major details. You separate general from specific statements by their positioning on your paper. Here is an example:

Topics in the study of mass culture
  Investigations of subcultures
    Example of elderly subculture

As you can see, the information becomes more specific as you move to the right. Many students prefer this format to the numeral–letter format because they do not have to remember the correct sequence of numerals and letters. They do not need to go back to their notes to see if their previous main idea, for example, was a II. or a III. Some students also complain that the numerals and letters clutter their notes.

Remember that both formats rely on the same idea. The farther to the right you put information, the more specific this information is. Try both techniques to see which one fits your listening and writing style.

The Cornell Note-taking System

A system developed at Cornell University incorporates several of the practices used in the numeral–letter and indenting formats and includes a successful recall technique. To use this system correctly, follow these ten steps:

1. When taking notes, use spiral-bound notebook paper and place all of your lecture notes in chronological order in a loose-leaf notebook. By using these two items, you can include material without destroying the sequence of the lectures. Also, title and date each lecture on the top line.

2. Draw a vertical line 2½ inches from the left edge of the page. You will have the remaining 6 inches of paper to write down your lecture notes.

3. During lecture, take notes in any format you prefer—numeral–letter, indenting, or even short paragraphs.

4. Concentrate on writing only main ideas and significant details during lecture.

5. Skip lines between main ideas, and use only one side of the paper.

6. Read through your notes after class, filling in any incomplete information and rewriting any illegible words.

7. As you review your notes, underline or box all main ideas.

8. After you have reviewed your notes once, jot down in the 2½ inch margin key phrases that summarize what you have learned. In this left-hand section, you may also want to formulate questions on this material that you believe may be on an exam.

9. Cover up the 6-inch side of your notes to see whether you can recall the important parts of the lecture with only the key phrases and questions on the left side of your notes as clues.

10. Continue this procedure until you can easily recall the important parts of the lecture.*

Look at the following lecture notes dealing with advertising. This student has correctly employed the Cornell system:

← 2½ inches →	← 6 inches → ***Major Characteristics of Ads***
def of ad	Def: "Persuasive message intended to sell a product."

2 forms	Found in:
	     print: newspapers and magazines
	     broadcast: radio television

What are 3 goals of ads?	Used to:
	     create awareness of product
	     establish new product
	     immediately buy product

The student in the above excerpt first used the indenting format; then she applied the Cornell system, as seen in the marginal comments. In reviewing her notes, this student was able to identify the definition, forms, and goals of advertising. In this way, she was able to further organize this lecture material. In some ways, the Cornell system is a refinement of the numeral–letter and indenting formats. Once you can easily work through the steps of the Cornell system, you will be able to organize and retain large amounts of study material in an efficient and intelligent manner. You will be asked to use this Cornell system in many of the exercises that follow.

Taking Notes in Mathematics and Math-Related Courses

In math and science courses, you will often find that the numeral–letter, indenting, and Cornell formats are inappropriate note-taking forms. Math and science instructors often present solutions to problems on the board, writing each step in sequence. With these solutions, you cannot

*Adapted from Walter Pauk, *How to Study in College*, 2nd ed. (Boston: Houghton Mifflin, 1974), pp. 126–132.

separate main ideas from major details. In a sense, every step to the solution is a main idea.

Consider the following hints for taking notes in math and science courses:

1. Listen carefully when your instructor presents laws, axioms, theorems, or properties. When possible, write these statements down word for word, as you would a definition. In the margin, identify the particular statement as a law, axiom, theorem, or property. Look at the following example:

associative $a + b = b + a$ $\bigg|$ $5 + 3 = 3 + 5$
property $a \times b = b \times a$ $\bigg|$ $5 \times 3 = 3 \times 5$

Numbers may be added or multiplied in any sequence.

2. When an instructor solves a problem on the board, copy it down step by step. The problems an instructor writes on the board are probably important ones. These solutions will often be like homework problems and problems on exams. Number each step, and make comments after any step that is unclear to you. Put question marks next to those steps that you cannot follow. Try to answer these questions before you come to the next class. Look at this example:

Problem 3: $2(5x + 5) + 4x = 80 - 2x$. Solve for x.

Do operations in   (1) $10x - 16 + 4x = 80 - 2x$
parentheses first.   (2) $14x - 16 \qquad = 80 - 2x$
                       (3) $16x = 96$
+ 2x balances   (4) $x = 6$
both sides of the
equation.

3. Leave spaces next to the problems you did not complete. When you review your notes, try to complete them.

4. Leave extra spaces between problems or draw a line across your page of notes to show where one problem ends and another begins.

5. Reread your notes after every lecture. Math and science are disciplines that build upon information you have previously learned. If you are unclear about Monday's solutions, Wednesday's will be even more confusing.

6. Use the numeral–letter and indenting formats whenever the instructor presents material not requiring problem solving.

Note-taking Tips

Now that you have studied the numeral–letter, indenting, Cornell, and math–science outlining formats, you are ready for the following note-taking tips that apply to all the note-taking systems you have learned so far.

1. The notes you take for each course should be written in a separate, bound notebook or in a three-ring notebook with dividers for each class. Three-ring notebooks are especially useful because you can add supplementary material to your notes, you can take out material when you want, and you can insert notes for a lecture that you may have missed. Also, you can keep all of your lecture notes in chronological order. You may think that all of this organization is a waste of time, but you will find that such preparation will pay off when you have to study for an exam. You do not want to be one of those students who has difficulty studying for the exam because lecture notes are missing or disorganized. Divide your notebook into two sections—one for your lecture notes and another for your study reading notes. More will be said about preparing reading notes in Chapter 13 on the SQ3R study system.

2. Put the title of each day's lecture at the center of the top line of a clean sheet of paper. Put the date at the top right-hand corner of the same page. Look at the following title:

Consumer Behavior Terminology   *11/24/95*

3. Use a ball point, fountain, or felt-tip pen when you take notes in courses that use traditional outlining formats. For math and science courses, which require figuring and refiguring, use pencil or an erasable pen.

4. Write on only one side of the page. As you review your notes, you may need the back side to write additional information.

5. In addition to posing key questions and summarizing your notes, you can also use the left-hand margin during lecture to remind yourself of important due dates: when a project is due, an examination date, and so on. By placing this information where you normally place important points of summary, you will be less likely to forget these dates. Look at how a test date is incorporated into the following lecture excerpt on purchasing:

	The Purchasing Process
	I. Three major stages
What are 3 stages?	A. Intentional
First test 3/18	B. Buying
	C. Post purchasing

6. Identify the kinds of details that you include in your notes, either during or after lecture. The abbreviations that you will most commonly use are: *def* for definition, *ex* for example, *eff* for effect, and *char* for characteristic. *Cause* and *step* have no abbreviations. As you identify the details, you will better understand the lecture's organization. See how the abbreviation *ex* is used in the following lecture excerpt on buyer satisfaction:

> ### Buyer Satisfaction
>
> *Ex:* | Buyer is so pleased with his new car, he tells his neighbor why she should buy the same model.

7. Do not recopy your notes. Recopying does not require much thinking, and it is time that you can better spend doing other assignments. Merely rewrite any words or phrases that are hard to read. You must edit your notes, though. After class or within twenty-four hours, reread your notes, summarizing and answering key questions, as you learned in the Cornell system. Reviewing information right after it has been introduced helps you to remember it.

8. Write legibly, even if you write less; students lose time trying to decipher their handwriting.

Condensing Information

Learning to condense information will help you write down more information in a shorter period of time. You can condense information when you use any of the note-taking systems you have been introduced to so far. When you summarize, you locate main ideas and major details from long passages; when you *condense*, you write the key elements in a sentence and delete unnecessary words and phrases. What you usually write down are the subject, verb, and object of a sentence. Often you reduce a complete sentence to a phrase. Look at the following sentence, and see how it is condensed: "In an important sense, consumers respond to ongoing signals in their environment" is condensed to "Consumers respond to signals." In condensing, you are often left with the *who* or *what* and the *what was done* of the sentence. In this sentence, the who are the consumers and the what was done is their response to signals. In lecture, then, listen for names and for what these names accomplished.

Sometimes it is preferable to copy information exactly as it is stated. You have already seen the importance of copying down a mathematical or scientific law or theorem or the steps in a solution. When you hear a definition, try to write it exactly as you hear it. Definitions are the tools for understanding a subject, so it's best to write down their exact meanings, as in the example below:

I. Market

    A. *Def:* A group of potential customers with the authority and ability to purchase a particular product*

With the exception of definitions and mathematical solutions and laws, you will often not be copying information exactly as you hear it. So condensing is a key skill to learn, as important as summarizing. You cannot write down everything the instructor says unless you know short-hand. By condensing each sentence into the "who" or "what" and the "what was done," you uncover the significant elements of the lecture. You will have several opportunities to condense lecture and textbook material in the exercises in this chapter and in those that follow.

Using Abbreviations

Now that you have learned various note-taking systems and have been introduced to the essentials of condensing, you are ready to use abbreviations to save even more time when you take notes. You can use these abbreviations for both lecture and study notes. Like condensing, abbreviations reduce words to their essential letters.

Abbreviation Symbols   Here is a list of commonly used symbols that students use when taking notes; commit them to memory.

Symbol	Meaning
=	equals
=ly	equally
≠	does not equal
" "	when you repeat the same information
⟶	causes
⟵	is caused by
⟶ ⟵	is both cause and effect
>	greater than
<	less than
+ or &	and or more
−	less or minus
∴	therefore
⊃	imply or suggest
#	number
%	percentage
¶	paragraph
//	parallel

---

*Adapted from Joseph T. Straub and Raymond F. Attner, *Introduction to Business*, 4th ed. (Boston: PWS-Kent Publishing Company, 1991), p. G-9.

See how the following sentence can be rephrased with an abbreviation:

With this product, the teenage market is greater than the adult market.

teenage market > adult market

Words Commonly Abbreviated   Below are abbreviations for words and phrases that you will commonly see in textbooks and hear in lectures. Study these abbreviations; then commit them to memory.

• Words denoting quantities, time periods, or geography:

Word(s)	*Abbreviation*
amount	amt
centimeter	c
century	cy
foot/feet	ft
gram	g
inch	in.
meter	m
mile	mi
north, south, east, west	N, S, E, W
pound	lb
yard	yd
year(s)	yr(s)

• Words denoting conditions, trends, or degrees:

Word(s)	*Abbreviation*
decrease	decr
general(ly)	genl
important	imp't
include/including	incl
incomplete	inc
increase	incr
large	lg
logic(al)	log.
main	mn
major(ity)	maj
maximum	max
minimum	min
necessary	nec
negative	neg
original(ly)	orig
positive	pos
principal	prin
significant	sig
usually	usu

• Words used to clarify concepts and ideas:

Word(s)	Abbreviation
antonym	ant.
compare	cf
conclusion	concl
continued	cont'd
definition	def
feminine	fem
first, second, third	1st, 2nd, 3rd
for example	eg
introduction	intro
masculine	masc
plural	pl
specific(ally)	specif
spelling	sp
synonym	syn
that is, that is to say	ie
through	thru
versus, or against	vs
with	w
without	w/o

• Other commonly used words:

Word	Abbreviation
America(n)	Am.
chapter	chpt
company	co
department	dept
each	ea
mountain	mt
page	p
pages	pp
point	pt
regarding	re
subject	subj

If you study this list carefully, you will find that four words end with a period (in., Am., ant., log.). You need to use a period after an abbreviation if the abbreviation spells out an actual word. The period corrects the confusion. For example, "ant" without a period could be mistaken for an insect rather than an antonym.

    Once you have learned these abbreviations, you will be able to take down more information during lectures. See how the following statement can be written concisely. "A large increase in advertising time usually results in greater profits." "lg incr ad time usu → greater profits."

Once you have memorized these abbreviations, they become easy to read and do not slow down your reading rate.

Rules to Follow When You Create Your Own Abbreviations.   Here are a few guidelines for creating your own abbreviations:

1. If the word is one syllable, write it out. It takes about as much time to write "tax" as it does "tx."

2. When you decide to leave out letters, leave out vowels rather than consonants. You recognize a word more easily if you see the consonants. You will probably recognize the abbreviation "bkgd" as "background" because you have kept the consonants.

3. Use the first syllable of a long word if that first syllable gives you enough information to identify the word. In your history class you might use "fam" for "famine" without getting confused. But "ty" does not easily equate with "tyranny," so write out two syllables, "tyran."

4. You can sometimes use an apostrophe to delete a syllable or syllables of a word. For example, "requirement" can be written as "requir't" or "unnecessary" can be abbreviated to "unnec'y."

5. To make an abbreviation plural, add an "s" to it as you would normally add to the entire word. For example, "wds" would be the plural for "words."

6. Generally, use a number instead of writing it out. You can write "65" more quickly than "sixty-five." But "45 million" (or "45 mil") is easier to write than "45,000,000." In writing numbers, choose the method that will save you the most time.

7. Often you will be writing down a key word or a phrase several times during lecture. Early in the lecture, make up an abbreviation for that word or term. The first time you use the term, write this abbreviation and the complete word in the left hand margin. For example, if you are studying consumer behavior in a marketing lecture, you could abbreviate consumer behavior to CB, and in your margins write: "consumer behavior = CB."

8. Quickly learn the symbols and abbreviations that your math and science instructors use. You will be regularly using these abbreviations and symbols when you read the textbook, take lecture notes, and solve problems.

9. When you edit your notes, be sure that you completely write out any abbreviated words that are not immediately clear to you. Edit your notes soon after the lecture. If you wait too long, you may not be able to decipher your abbreviations.

10. Use abbreviations even more when your lecturer speaks quickly or presents a great deal of information. In such lectures, you are pressed for time; using abbreviations will help you get down more information.

11. Do not overuse abbreviations. You do not want to begin reading over your notes only to find out that you do not know what the abbreviations stand for.

Summary

The three most common note-taking techniques—the numeral–letter, indenting, and the Cornell system—are similarly organized. All place main ideas to the left of the margin and details to the right. Cornell helps you further organize your notes as you review them. Main ideas and major details are key elements to your notes. You should train yourself to be alert for details when you hear a main idea. With practice, you should be able to balance main ideas properly with major details. Do not expect to write down all of the details, only the significant ones. Try to condense whatever you hear to the "who" and the "what" of each statement.

Notes in math and science courses are structured differently. In these courses, you do more copying, mainly of solutions to problems. You should comment on the steps to a solution that you do not fully understand.

Remember to review your notes daily, making comments and corrections. Because you will be using these notes all semester, they need to be legible.

You will find that abbreviations help you to write down more information. Abbreviations are either symbols or shortened words. Memorize the most common abbreviation symbols and abbreviated words. In reviewing your notes, be sure that you write out the complete word or phrase for those abbreviations that you cannot immediately read.

Summary Box   *Note-taking Techniques*

What are they?	*Why do you use them?*
Numeral–letter format: places main ideas (I) to the left and major details (A,B,C) to the right	To give order to your lecture notes and separate main ideas from major details
Indenting format: places main ideas to the left and major details to the right; no numerals or letters are used.	To write down significant information from lectures
Cornell: further organizes your notes and allows you to begin studying them	To help you remember important material for exams
Math–science format: accurately lists and describes the steps necessary for solutions to problems and allows marginal comments when a step is not understood	
Abbreviations: shortened words or symbols for words or phrases	To write down more information
	To save time when taking notes

Skills Practice Topic: **Consumer Behavior**

All the exercises in this chapter deal with consumer behavior. Before you begin these exercises, answer the following questions, either individually or in small groups, to get some sense of what you already know about the field of consumer behavior:

1. What is consumer behavior?
2. What kinds of questions do you think researchers in consumer behavior ask?
3. How do you think a knowledge of consumer behavior benefits the customer?
4. Do you think consumer behavior research can really predict what a customer will buy?

Exercise 11.1
Condensing Sentences
from a Lecture

The following ten sentences are taken from an introductory lecture on consumer behavior. Your job is to read each sentence and then condense it into a phrase in which only the essential information remains. You will find that sentences from a lecture tend to be wordy, a style much different from what you normally read. Use the abbreviations "def" and "ex" where appropriate.

1. We must first define the term "consumer behavior." Let's say it is what people do when they are involved somehow with market items—in buying, selling, or producing.

   _____

2. I want to emphasize that consumer behavior as a study is part of many other studies—that is, it is interdisciplinary, and I think it relies heavily on such fields as sociology, anthropology, and psychology.

   _____

3. How is sociology involved in the study of consumer behavior? I think in its focus on group behavior patterns, sociology helps us understand how consumers act.

   _____

4. Psychology also plays a role in our study. In its focus on the individual, psychology shows us how people typically act when they buy something. "Motivation" is an example of a psychological term that we can apply to an individual consumer's activities.

   _____

5. How do you think anthropology is related to our study of consumer behavior? Anthropology, I think, gives us a picture of the culture that determines a person's buying behavior. Ethnic preference is an example of how we use anthropological knowledge in our study of consumers.

   _____

6. Another term that we must define early in this semester is "consumer." Let's say for now that a consumer is anyone who purchases or uses a product.

   _____

7. How should we define "purchasing"? It is a more complicated term. I want to focus on one part of its meaning today. Purchasing on one level simply refers to obtaining an item from someone who sells.

   _____

8. In this course we will later pursue other areas of consumer behavior—specifically where people buy particular products and how they use them. I want to explore these topics only after we have a better understanding of certain key terms.

_____

9. Other issues that I think you will find of interest in consumer behavior involve psychology and economics: how frequently people tend to purchase certain products and the decisions they use in deciding on a particular purchase.

_____

70%
(score = # correct × 10)
Find answers on
pp. 400–401.

10. Finally, I want you to place yourselves in these particular explorations of consumer behavior. Analyzing how you purchase certain items will assist you in understanding your sociological, psychological, and anthropological motives.*

_____

**Exercise 11.2
More Condensing
Sentences from a
Lecture**

Here are ten more sentences, again from an introductory consumer behavior lecture. Condense these sentences into phrases that pick up the significant information. Where necessary, use the abbreviations "def" and "cause."

1. Often consumer behavior scholars first look at the cultural influences of a particular group's purchasing choices. This is often defined as the macro perspective.

_____

2. In contrast, the micro perspective is often seen as what the individual in a group decides to purchase and the reasons why.

_____

3. I also want to add that an additional discipline I did not consider in the last lecture is economics. It influences consumer behavior in several ways, but particularly it shows us how an economic system like ours distributes its wealth.

_____

_____

*Adapted from Harold W. Berkman and Christopher C. Gilson, *Consumer Behavior: Concepts and Strategies* (Belmont, Calif.: Dickenson, 1978), pp. 5–6.

4. Now I want to begin a new section to my introductory remarks on consumer behavior—its history. Did you know that consumer behavior as a serious study is very young, emerging in the late 1940s?

_____

5. Since the late forties, scholarship in consumer studies has increased tremendously.

_____

6. I think the most important cause of increased studies in our field is the many uses we have found for the computer, so that we can now project with the help of the computer what a consumer will likely do in particular situations.

_____

7. We now have several journals that study consumer behavior, and they have added a greater seriousness to our field.

_____

8. What has also been a major factor in making consumer behavior a serious study is how we have recently begun to use theory to explain how consumers behave.

_____

9. Often consumer behavior scholars study theoretical models. I would define a model in our field as the application of a certain behavioral theory to a particular problem in consumer behavior.

_____

_____
80%
Ask instructor for answers.

10. I would say that the most popular study that we use to develop theoretical models is the discipline of psychology. I will be talking later on in the semester about various behavioral models that are based on psychological theory.*

_____

Exercise 11.3
Using Note-taking Techniques on Short Lecture Passages

Read the following lecture excerpts on the cultural and social influences on consumer behavior. After you have read and condensed the information into main ideas and major details, complete the outlines that follow. Use the Cornell System to add comments in the left-hand margin.

_____

*Adapted from Berkman and Gilson, *Consumer Behavior*, pp. 6–7.

Because you are reading an instructor's lecture, you will find some of it repetitious.

1. I want to start today's lecture by focusing on how our American culture influences what we in the United States tend to buy. From a consumer standpoint, the one aspect of our culture that seems to go beyond particular ethnic groups is our interest in purchasing material goods. This goal of wanting material wealth is also tied in to other values that seem to be American. I'm thinking about our belief in the self and our basic optimism for the future. We also seem to value order over disorder.

   I.

      A.

      B.

      C.

      D.

2. But can we really say that these values define American culture? Is there really such a thing as an American culture? In some ways Americans seem to be moving away from a focus on material wealth. And though we are not a poor country, the recent economic problems we have seem to make some of us question whether the American culture is still as optimistic as it was, say, twenty years ago. Also, some consumer scholars have argued that the American focus on self-reliance has made some Americans terrified of being alone and of facing life's problems alone. Also, many people interested in the environment have begun to question just how valuable it is to be ordered. Worded differently, we can ask: Has the order of technology created disorder for the environment?

   I.

      A.

      B.

      C.

      D.

3. There are also a great number of ethnic groups in the United States today who seem to call into question just what we mean by an American culture. African Americans and Hispanics, I think, provide a huge marketing challenge. In determining what these groups purchase, we find that many African Americans and Hispanics fit into what sociologists traditionally think is typically American. Yet in many ways we can see that their buying interests show a different set of values.

   I.

      A.

      B.

      C.

4. Along with cultural questions, the student of consumer behavior must also see if class influences people's purchasing decisions. Do the values of the lower, middle, and upper classes shape what the people in each of these groups purchase? Or is this question just as difficult to answer as the question of culture and buying in the United States? Does income influence what a person buys? Or does a person's income determine what sorts of beliefs she or he holds? These are just a few of the puzzling questions that we will try to find answers to as the semester goes on.

   I.

      A.

      B.

      C.

      D.

5. Another issue closely related to what people buy is where the family fits into these decisions. The family seems to have much to say about what people buy. The family gives to its members certain values. Yet purchasing decisions are also influenced by which members the product will serve. And purchasing is further complicated by who tends to be more powerful—the father, the mother, or the children. And we must also consider how these decisions change as the family gets older—I mean, as parents and children mature.

I.

    A.

    B.

    C.

    D.

Now use the indenting format to complete the following lecture material on consumer behavior and the individual. Again, use the Cornell System to add marginal comments. This time you will be given no outline format.

6. Now that we have talked briefly about some of the questions that consumer behavior researchers have about culture and society, we can turn to how the individual influences consumer behavior. Consumer behavior researchers begin by assuming that people learn to buy in certain ways. That is, they are not born to be a certain kind of consumer. The most important way for us to determine how an individual will react is to look at his or her past experience. Because of habit and experience, marketers try very hard to develop what they call brand loyalties, or a consumer's consistent buying of certain products.

7. Another individual factor that I want to talk a little bit about today is how perception affects what somebody buys. Marketers now realize that each person perceives a product differently. For some, price is the major concern. For others, it is the look or image that the product presents.

8. As in our discussion of class, society, and culture, an individual's choice in purchasing leads to no definite conclusions. What we do know is that the question of personality does affect what someone buys. Certain personalities tend to choose a sports car over a station wagon. A woman's personality type also helps determine the shade of lipstick she will buy.

9. Another individual factor that I want to talk about is attitude and buying. That is, how does a person's attitude affect what he or she buys? Here, marketers often try to use sports figures or actors to help sell a particular product. Marketers realize that these stars conjure up many positive and negative attitudes in the viewer. And these attitudes help sell a product.

10. Marketers have found that attitudes, unlike other parts of an individual's makeup, are difficult to change. Yet, this fact in itself becomes a marketing challenge. Can a marketing campaign change a person's attitude? And can this changed attitude make an individual buy a product she would normally not buy? Researchers still do not know how effective a marketing campaign can be in changing a person's attitudes. Your reading assignment will pick up this topic in much greater detail.*

70%

(score = # correct × 2, + 6 bonus points) Find answers on pp. 401–402.

Exercise 11.4
Using Note-taking
Techniques on More
Short Lecture
Passages

For the following three lecture excerpts on consumer behavior terminology, your job is to read each excerpt and then use the numeral-letter format to record notes. An outline is provided for these excerpts. As in Exercise 11.3, condense the information, and use Cornell to provide comments in the margins.

1. I want to introduce a few more terms today that should round out the most important terms that we will be using for this course. I want to talk a bit about micromarketing. A definition for this term is the business of marketing. Some of the areas that we will consider in micromarketing include managing a marketing campaign, researching marketing behavior, and creating profitable marketing campaigns.

---

*Adapted from Berkman and Gilson, *Consumer Behavior*, pp. 8–12, and Straub and Attner, *Introduction to Business*, pp. 628–629.

In the study of micromarketing, the most important concern is looking for new markets. The challenge today is that new markets are not that easy to come by because today's consumer tends to be more educated and less susceptible to earlier marketing strategies. With each product, marketers need to ask similar questions: Is the market young, or is the market becoming younger? Is the market ethnic or becoming culturally diverse? Marketers need to be secure in the data they receive in answer to these questions. As I have said many times before, these are not easy questions to answer.

I. Def.:

    A.

    B.

II.

    A.

    B.

    C.

    D.

2. In an attempt to make their job more manageable, some marketers have looked closely at the audience that would most likely buy a particular product. The segment of the market that a marketer looks at may be very small or very large. It may be a market directed at a restricted group, like retirees interested in golfing, or a large group, like teenagers between the ages of thirteen and eighteen.

    Magazine executives can tell marketers what segment of the population tends to buy their magazines. This is the population that marketers may want to target for the sale of a particular product. Magazines often provide what is called a demographic profile. What does a demographic profile consist of? It often includes the age span of the magazine audience and its average income, as well as readers' educational level. So in a strange way, marketers are finding that sometimes, if they restrict their buying population for a particular product, they are actually allowing for greater profit. Why is this so? By targeting a market well, marketers then have a better chance of attracting a greater percentage of that segment to buy their product.

I.

    A.

    B.

II.

    A.

    B.

    C.

3. I'd also like to talk about the concept of macromarketing. Macromarketing, unlike micromarketing, is concerned with consumer behavior on a larger social level. You might find macromarketers asking questions like these: How is advertising deceptive to the public? How does a particular product adversely affect the environment? How can society be trained to recycle?

In some ways, macromarketing begins with different premises than micromarketing does. I think micromarketers see the consumer as someone they need to persuade so they can sell a particular product. The macromarketer begins by assuming that the consumer is often deceived by advertisements and that his role is to help the consumer not be deceived. A healthy market comes about, I think, when macromarketers keep the micromarketers in check. What do you think?

    I. Def.:

      A.

      B.

      C.

    II.

      A.

      B.

      C.

Now use the indenting technique to take notes on the following two passages on the value of studying consumer behavior. This time, you are not provided with skeletal outlines.

4. Thus far I have been presenting you with an overview of our course in marketing. We have discussed important terms and important marketing concepts that we will pursue this semester. I want to talk a little bit today about the value of the study of consumer behavior. I'll try to be as brief as I can.

   Because we are a capitalist society, we as a country focus a lot of our energy on consumer behavior. We have studied many reasons why consumers act the way they do and how culture and society affect their purchasing. In a way, consumer behavior studies also help sociologists and psychologists understand their fields a little better.

   Let me be more specific about what I mean about the relationship between our discipline and others. When we study consumer perception, we help psychologists understand their research on perception better. And when we explore how class affects purchasing, then we help sociologists understand just what they mean by class. In this way I want you to see consumer behavior as an excellent interdisciplinary study. I'm going to be showing how our field relates to other disciplines throughout the course.

5. I also want to repeat that we have two types of consumer behavior studies: micromarketing and macromarketing. But I will be focusing on the micromarketing studies, except for a few lectures at the end of the course.

   Before you can appreciate these micromarketing studies, we must go over other preliminary material. This time we'll be talking about how these studies are organized. So we'll first be looking at theories and models as they relate to consumer behavior. Then we'll be looking at the measurement techniques that our field uses to interpret these models. In this part of the course, we'll be learning some elementary rules about flowcharting, and we'll examine and practice some very common formulas in statistics.*

80%

Ask instructor for answers.

---

*Adapted from Berkman and Gilson, *Consumer Behavior*, pp. 14–16, and Straub and Attner, *Introduction to Business*, p. 526.

Exercise 11.5
Writing
Abbreviations from
Memory

Go back to the section called "Using Abbreviations" (pp. 230–232) to review all of the abbreviations that are listed. Then, without referring to those pages, complete the following questions. Place all answers in the answer box.

Write the abbreviations for the following:

1. equals
2. greater than
3. and
4. implies
5. regarding

6. necessary
7. positive
8. increase
9. large
10. maximum

Now write the correct word or words for these abbreviations:

11. w/o
12. cf
13. vs
14. inc
15. imp't

16. prin
17. cont'd
18. #
19. ∴
20. →←

1. _____

2. _____

3. _____

4. _____

5. _____

6. _____

7. _____

8. _____

9. _____

10. _____

11. _____

12. _____

13. _____

14. _____

15. _____

16. _____

17. _____

18. _____

19. _____

20. _____

_____
80%

(score = # correct × 5)
Find answers on p. 402.

Exercise 11.6
Making Your Own
Abbreviations

For the following twenty words and phrases relating to consumer behavior, write your own abbreviations, using the rules given on pages 233–234. Your answers may vary from those devised by other students. Discuss your answers with your instructor and classmates. Place all answers in the answer box.

1. behavior
2. advertising
3. *Wealth of Nations* (used several times)
4. social class acceptance
5. persuasiveness
6. affluence
7. competitive
8. urbanize
9. cognitive dissonance (used several times)
10. consumer behavior (used several times)
11. consumption
12. cultures
13. customers
14. industrial
15. labeling
16. law of diminishing returns (used several times)
17. perception
18. reinforcement
19. marketing
20. macromarketing (used several times)

1. _____
2. _____
3. _____
4. _____
5. _____
6. _____
7. _____
8. _____
9. _____
10. _____
11. _____
12. _____
13. _____
14. _____
15. _____
16. _____
17. _____
18. _____
19. _____
20. _____

_____
80%
Ask instructor for answers.

Exercise 11.7
Reading and Writing
Abbreviations in
Sentences

Assume that the following abbreviated sentences on international marketing techniques are from your consumer behavior lecture notes. Your job is to rewrite each as a complete sentence, changing the abbreviations to words.

1. Mrktng bcmng an international actvty.

   _____

2. Easy to make lrg mistakes in this interntl mrkt.

   _____

3. Mny mrktrs do not undrstnd cultrl setting.

   _____

4. Anthroplgy helps cnsmr beh to undrstnd cultrs.

   _____

5. Anthrplgsts use stdy called cross-cultural resrch (CCR).

   _____

6. CCR studies how cultrs are same and diff.

   _____

7. CCR studies atts re love in cltrs.

   _____

8. CCR also works w politcl power in ea cultr.

   _____

9. CCR studies cultrl mng of color.

   _____

10. In some cultrs blk & gray = good.

    _____

Now write your own abbreviated sentences from the sentences on international marketing techniques that follow. Be sure to condense and to make up your own abbreviations when necessary.

11. Cross-cultural research has shown that the colors yellow, white, and gray are weak everywhere.

_____

12. Red and black seem to be strong colors in every country.

_____

13. Some marketers see each culture as unique.

_____

14. This belief suggests that we focus on local marketing campaigns.

_____

15. Other marketers believe in standardized marketing plans.

_____

16. These marketers believe in looking at cultural uniformity in the world.

_____

17. Therefore, they see several countries as one possible market.

_____

18. Tourism and the mass media have caused some similar marketing needs.

_____

19. These marketers see Europe as one country rather than several.

_____

20. The answers to these questions may have a positive or negative impact on each advertising campaign.*

_____

80%

(score = # correct $\times$ 10 [1–10]; answers will vary for 11–20)
Find answers on p. 403.

---

*Adapted from Berkman and Gilson, *Consumer Behavior*, pp. 93–94.

Exercise 11.8
Outlining Lecture
Excerpts and Using
Abbreviations

The following lecture excerpts discuss particular markets and the strategies marketers use to sell their products to them. Use all your note-taking skills (condensing, abbreviating, and the numeral–letter format and Cornell System) to outline the first three excerpts.

1. We talked last time about the marketing needs of the single person. Today I want to focus on the marketing strategies used for the elderly and the poor. With the elderly, I think we need to know something about how they live and where they live. In past generations, the elderly usually lived with their children; now they often live away from them. Some live in communities for the elderly. Florida, as an example, has become a popular site for the elderly, where they live away from their children.

2. Here are some more vital statistics about the elderly. Today the elderly tend to be better educated than they were in the past. They often have greater incomes than they had in years past. They tend to be better and smarter shoppers. Also, many do some sort of part-time work. They also tend to want to enjoy their retirement years more. Therefore, you see more elderly traveling than you did in the past.

3. What are some of the markets that speak directly to the elderly? There are several, and I want you to list them in order. First, the elderly have unique housing needs. Second, their health needs are different in many ways from those of the rest of the population. Furthermore, they have a different set of insurance needs—both health and life insurance. To a degree, we can target particular foods that the elderly would tend to buy. Finally, the elderly have a unique set of travel needs. I want to emphasize that these six needs provide marketing challenges for the nineties.

Now use the indenting and Cornell formats to outline the following excerpts on marketing strategies for the poor. Be sure to condense information and use abbreviations where appropriate.

4. I want to turn now to another market. That is the market that concerns the poor. What are the unique needs of the poor? What is their particular profile? We know that the poor tend to spend a larger share of their income on life's necessities. These necessities include such things as food, housing, and medical care. What do you think the poor spend less on? Transportation and clothing are not areas where they spend much of their money. Researchers have also found that the poor spend a large amount of their income on sturdy items, like stoves and refrigerators. In terms of automobiles, the poor tend to buy used rather than new cars, as you would expect. In terms of furniture, the poor often buy sets of furnishings rather than individual pieces.

5. What sorts of foods do the poor often purchase, and how do they pay their bills? Of course, they tend to buy low-cost food. They often look for low-cost fresh items rather than prepackaged foods, especially in rural areas. They rarely buy more expensive convenience foods. What about credit? More and more people are using credit cards, but the poor tend to use credit and installment buying more often than the middle and upper classes do. Some researchers have even shown that poor families often have a credit debt that is twice that of higher-income families.

6. Finally, what can we say about the shopping behavior of the poor? Some of these statistics are surprising, I think. Poor urban people tend to pay more—not less—for products than those who live in wealthier areas. Also, there are fewer supermarkets in the poor urban

areas for shoppers to choose from. The poor also tend not to be shrewd shoppers. They often listen to what their family members, friends, or the media say rather than looking into programs that provide reduced rates or reading newspaper ads carefully. Also, the poor often shop in areas close to their homes because transportation is often harder to come by for them. Therefore, their consumer options tend to be restricted.*

> Answers will vary. Ask instructor for sample answers.

Exercise 11.9
Taking Notes on a
Longer Lecture
Passage and Using
Abbreviations

The following is a longer lecture excerpt on consumer behavior and social responsibility. Your job is to take notes on this passage. Use the indenting and Cornell formats, condense information where necessary, and abbreviate where appropriate. After you have taken your notes, give the lecture an effective title.

Title: _____

(1) In this part of the course, I want to talk about issues that have not concerned us up to now. How does consumer behavior relate to ethics? That is, how should consumer behaviorists be concerned with treating the consumer correctly? I want to talk specifically about the key consumer issues relating to ethics: truth in marketing, product quality, and product safety. I will talk about each separately, then come to some conclusions about this issue of ethics and consumer behavior, both for the consumer and for the marketer and producer.

(2) Marketers have an obligation to be honest in their presentation of a product. The Federal Trade Commission monitors advertisements to ensure that they are not fraudulent. The Commission has uncovered and put a stop to many mail-order frauds. Recently, the question of packaging and labeling has become an important concern. For example, what does it mean for a product to be low in fat or low in cholesterol? What does it mean for a product to be fat-free? The Federal Trade Commission has now written specific requirements that spell out what these packaging statements mean, and marketers and producers are going to have to follow these regulations.

---

*Adapted from Berkman and Gilson, *Consumer Behavior*, pp. 133–135, 136–138.

(3) The next issue that consumers need to consider is how reliable a product is. What can a consumer do if a product fails to operate as promised, or if a product becomes a hazard? Consumers need to read what the warranty promises. Often the warranty insists that consumers either exchange a product or get a refund. Particularly when consumers buy an expensive item, they need to see just what the warranty promises and does not promise, so they will not be surprised if the product somehow fails.

(4) What happens when the consumer is not satisfied with the warranty, or if the seller does not live up to the warranty? Does the consumer have any options? The customer can go to court and sue. But this process is lengthy and can prove to be expensive.

(5) Some companies have responded to consumer complaints in a positive way. I want to emphasize here that by serving the customer politely and honestly, many companies have increased, not decreased, their profits. So it can pay to be honest. What some companies have done is to ask customers to be very frank about their complaints.

(6) How can complaints serve both the customer and the company? An honest complaint provides useful information for the decisions a company makes in the future. Furthermore, complaints can make the company rewrite its warranties, so future customers will be even more satisfied with the product and the company. When a customer tells her family and friends that a company actually listened to her complaints and even changed policies because of her, they will often become customers of that company as well.

(7) I want to emphasize here that ethics works both ways. If there are unethical companies, so are there unethical customers. For the marketplace to work well, the company and the consumer need to respect each other. What companies and customers need to realize is that honesty on the part of both parties goes a long way to solidify long-term business dealings. I want to repeat that it does pay to be honest. Profits on the part of the producer and satisfaction on the part of the consumer can result if producer and consumer trust each other.*

Answers will vary. Find sample answers on pp. 403–404.

Exercise 11.10
Using Lecture Notes
to Answer an Essay
Question

Now use only your lecture notes from Exercise 11.9 to answer the following essay question. Begin with a main-idea sentence, and support it with relevant details from the lecture.

Essay question: In what ways are customers protected from fraudulent companies? In what ways can companies serve their customers even more efficiently? Be specific by using evidence from the lecture.

80%
Ask instructor for answers.

*Adapted from Straub and Attner, *Introduction to Business*, pp. 604–606, 617–618.

Follow-up on the
Consumer Behavior
Exercises

Now that you have completed these exercises, it may be helpful to see how your reading on this topic has changed some of your ideas about consumer behavior. You may want to go back and reread these exercises before you answer the following questions. Answer them either in small groups or individually.

1. How would you now define *consumer behavior*?
2. In what ways do you now think that a knowledge of consumer behavior can benefit marketers and consumers?
3. What are the most interesting areas of consumer behavior for you?
4. What areas would you like to study further?

12 Visual Note-taking Techniques: Laddering and Mapping

Now that you have studied three common note-taking techniques, you will find the visual techniques of laddering and mapping helpful. Both laddering and mapping are visual note-taking systems. You can best use these two techniques when you are editing your notes, much as you use the Cornell system when you study your notes. Laddering and mapping offer visual ways of understanding new material.

What Is Laddering?

Laddering is a visual note-taking system that ties main ideas to main ideas and details to details. Laddering is best used when you are editing your notes and see relationships emerging.

Here is how laddering works. Draw a solid vertical line just to the right of your main ideas. You should use a different color pencil or pen so the line stands out. Then draw a perpendicular line from this vertical line to each main idea, so that the main ideas are connected. The vertical and horizontal lines then look like part of a ladder. Look at the main ideas concerning early childhood development in Figure 12-1 to see how laddering brings these ideas out.

You follow this same procedure with the details under each main idea. As it does with main ideas, laddering groups supporting details under each main idea. Place all major detail ladders under the same plane, so that your eyes see one solid vertical line for main ideas and a broken vertical line for supporting details. See how details are grouped through laddering in Figure 12-2, and how laddering brings out main ideas and major details in Figure 12-3.

What Is Mapping?

Mapping is a note-taking technique that uses geometric shapes, pictures, and arrows to show the relationship of main ideas to their details. Mapping is individual; you choose your own design to show the relationship

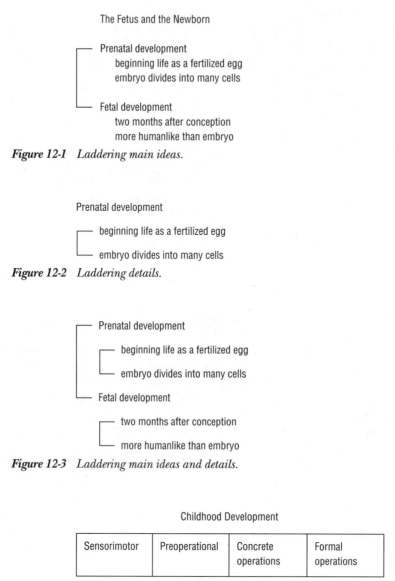

The Fetus and the Newborn

Prenatal development
    beginning life as a fertilized egg
    embryo divides into many cells

Fetal development
    two months after conception
    more humanlike than embryo

Figure 12-1   *Laddering main ideas.*

Prenatal development

beginning life as a fertilized egg

embryo divides into many cells

Figure 12-2   *Laddering details.*

Prenatal development

    beginning life as a fertilized egg

    embryo divides into many cells

Fetal development

    two months after conception

    more humanlike than embryo

Figure 12-3   *Laddering main ideas and details.*

Childhood Development

Sensorimotor	Preoperational	Concrete operations	Formal operations

Figure 12-4   *Mapping sequential stages.*

between general and specific information. The most commonly used shapes are circles, squares, rectangles, and radiating lines. Because maps are individual, they help you to retain the material more easily. Maps, often called study maps or advanced organizers, reduce large amounts of information to the essentials; so they are ideal when you study for exams.

Maps may be large or small. If they are large, they need to be put on a separate sheet of paper. If you place additional information on this

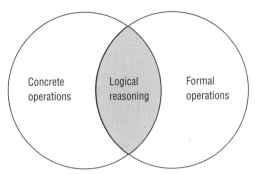

Figure 12-5   *Mapping similarities.*

page, you take away from the study map and distort the visual picture of main ideas tied to details.

Let's say you are studying your notes in early childhood development and you come across the following statement: "Jean Piaget identified four stages in childhood development: sensorimotor, preoperational, concrete operations, and formal operations." You can map this statement in the way shown in Figure 12-4. In this map, you see childhood development as the general category, with the four stages as the distinct steps.

Let's say you want to show how the later stages in childhood development share the ability to reason logically. You can map what these stages have in common by using intersecting circles. Intersecting circles are an effective way of mapping similarities. See Figure 12-5.

Mapping is also effective in showing sequences. Arrows can join one step to the other. If you came across this statement in your childhood development notes, how could you map it? "The sensorimotor stage beings at birth and ends at one-and-a-half years; the preoperational goes from one-and-a-half years to seven years, concrete operations from seven to eleven, and formal operations eleven and above." See Figure 12-6. Do you see how this map shows both the stages and their sequence?

A map using arrows is similar to a flow chart, a visualization often used by programmers to set up the logic of their computer program. Flow charts are now widely used by people outside programming to list the steps in a procedure. You studied flow charts in Chapter 9. Look at Figure 12-7, which shows an individual's responses to stimuli and how they can be conditioned, or changed. Psychologists have conducted experiments studying the behaviors people cannot control—unconditioned stimuli (UCS) and unconditioned responses (UCR)—and those they can control—conditioned stimuli (CS) and conditioned responses (CR). Follow the two sets of arrows—both top and bottom—to see how an individual can learn a particular response. Note how the bottom sets have two instead of three steps. Do you see how this flow chart economically presents the theory of stimulus and response, showing that certain stimuli can automatically create a certain emotion in an individual?

Stages of Childhood Development

Figure 12-6   *Mapping a sequence.*

Flow charts may also provide you with complex steps and procedures presented in a visual manner. Look at Figure 12-8, which shows the career ladder in a computer company. Follow the arrows from bottom to top, each pointing to a high-level position. Also note that some arrows

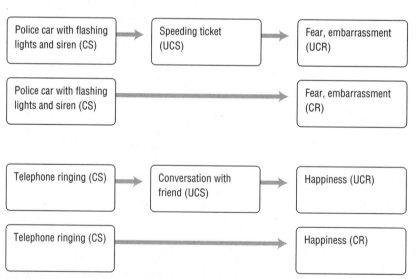

Figure 12-7   *Mapping cause-and-effect sequences. (Source: James W. Kalat,* Introduction to Psychology, *3rd ed. [Belmont, Calif.: Wadsworth, 1993], p. 282.)*

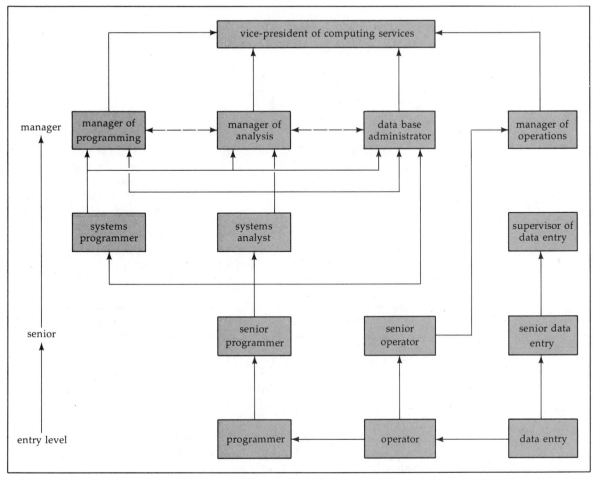

Figure 12-8   *Laddering a potential career progression. (Source: Perry Edwards and Bruce Broadwell,* Data Processing, *2nd ed. [Belmont, Calif.: Wadsworth, 1982], p. 560. Used by permission.)*

are joined by broken lines and point in two directions, suggesting the double career option for a person at this level.

In your own studying and note-taking, you can also create larger maps that tie together larger chunks of information such as several lectures or an entire textbook chapter. Pretend that you are reviewing your notes on Piaget's developmental stages in child development, and you want to map this information. Your map could look something like the one shown in Figure 12-9. This map reduces several paragraphs into a compact rectangle, listing each developmental stage and noting its important characteristics.

More complex advanced organizers can also show the relationships among topics, main ideas, and supporting details. The topic is usually in

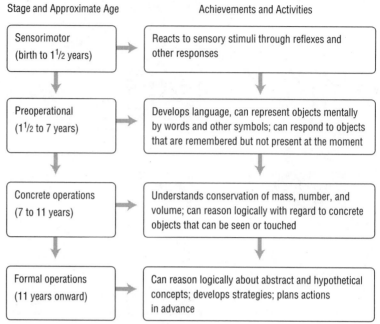

Figure 12-9 *Mapping lecture notes on a sequence of stages. (Adapted from James W. Kalat, Introduction to Psychology, 3rd ed. [Belmont, Calif.: Wadsworth, 1993], p. 233.)*

the center, the main ideas branching out from the center, with details of support branching from the main-idea lines. See Figure 12-10. These study maps can be used to summarize an entire lecture or a complete textbook chapter.

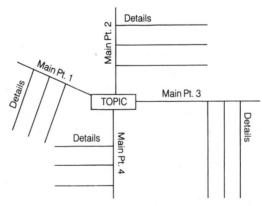

Figure 12-10 *Diagram of a study map.*

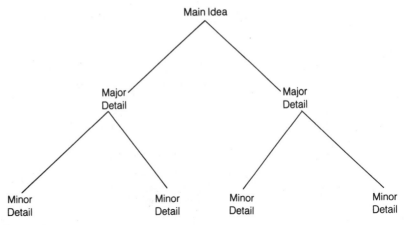

Figure 12-11 *Tree study map.*

A second way of presenting a great deal of information in a study map is through a tree diagram. The main idea is at the top of the tree, the major details branch out from the main idea, and the minor details in turn branch out from the main ideas. Figure 12-11 shows a tree study map.

Many students have found that these larger maps are effective study aids for midterm and final examinations. These maps encourage students to condense and see relationships between general and specific types of material. Further, the visual nature of the study map allows students to "see" the whole and its parts when they take their exams.

Keep in mind that mapping requires few rules and is for the most part individual. If you have a visual aptitude, create study maps as you edit your notes. Even if you don't have strong visual abilities, begin using study maps to help you review for exams because they allow you to economically grasp a host of information.

Summary

Laddering and mapping are visual note-taking techniques. You can use them most effectively when you are editing your notes. Laddering works by placing horizontal and vertical lines next to main ideas and major details. Mapping is individualistic, allowing you to create your own shapes to illustrate relationships. Mapping also reduces information to its essentials and serves as an excellent review for exams. These two systems work best if you have a visual aptitude, but all students will benefit if they use these visual techniques as study aids. Like the commonly used note-taking systems, mapping helps you see the relationships between main ideas and supporting details.

Summary Box   *Visual Note-taking Techniques: Laddering and Mapping*

What are they?	*Why use them?*
Laddering: vertical and horizontal lines join main ideas to main ideas and supporting details to supporting details. Mapping: shapes relate general and specific information; information reduced to its essentials.	To show visually how main ideas relate to major details.

Skills Practice Topic: Early Childhood Development

All four exercises in this chapter deal with early childhood behavior. Before you begin these exercises, answer the following questions, either individually or in small groups, to get some sense of what you already know about the psychology of childhood behavior.

1. How would you describe a child from a psychological point of view?
2. What sorts of topics do you think psychologists studying children investigate?
3. What are a child's most important needs?
4. How do you think children learn to talk?

Exercise 12.1
Mapping Statements
from Lectures

The following ten statements are taken from lecture notes on infancy and childhood studies. Your job is to create, on a separate sheet of paper, a map for each statement that will show the relationship between main ideas and major details. Remember that mapping is individual, so do not expect your maps to be exactly like the ones in the answer key.

Infancy and Childhood

1. A child forms attachments to his parents for two important reasons: first, if his biological needs are met and, second, if his emotional needs are nourished.

2. Infants often engage in parallel play; that is, infants play at the same time, and at the same place, but independently.

3. One can identify three types of children who play: (1) the popular ones, who have many friends, (2) the rejected ones, who, as you may guess, have few other friends, and (3) the controversial ones, whom some like and others do not.

4. How do older siblings influence their younger brother or sister's behavior? They can have a positive influence by playing with them and serving as teachers for them. They can also have a negative influence. If the older sibling has emotional or physical problems, the healthy younger child may become aggressive because he has not been given enough attention by the parents and the sick brother or sister.

5. Let's talk a bit about birth order. Psychologists say that birth order affects a child in two important ways. First, every child because of her order in the family experiences the environment differently. Second, each child gets different prenatal care. By that I mean to say that the mother is in a different state of health with each child she carries.

6. There are two significant theorists in the area of early childhood development. The first is Jean Piaget—the Swiss psychologist working in the first half of this century—and the second is Erik Erikson, who was a pioneer in childhood psychoanalysis.

7. For Erik Erikson, the newborn is in a stage he calls basic trust versus mistrust. What are some of the newborn's needs at this stage? Let's put them on the board in terms of questions the child would ask if he could talk: (1) Is my world predictable? (2) Do my parents care for my needs? (3) Do my parents love or nurture me? All of these needs shape the newborn's personality, according to Erikson.

8. The second stage for Erikson is called autonomy versus shame and doubt. Autonomy simply means being able to take care of oneself. This stage is the age of the toddler—ages 1–3. The child learns to be independent or dependent as she performs the following activities: walking, talking, being toilet trained, responding to instructions, and making choices.

9. The third stage for Erikson is called initiative versus guilt, for ages 3–6. There is a major contrast between this stage and autonomy versus shame which, you will recall, is the second stage. In this third stage the child does not ask, Can I do it? as he would in stage two, but Am I good or bad? Here you will see that the child begins to develop a morality.

10. Let's list some of the characteristics of the fourth stage, for ages 6–12—what Erikson calls the industry versus inferiority stage. Here the child deals with questions of self worth. They move their interests

---

70%

(score = # correct × 10)
Find answers on
pp. 404–406.

from their family to the larger society. They also begin to compete with their peers, or children their same age.*

Exercise 12.2
Applying Laddering
and Cornell to a
Lecture Passage

In the following ten-paragraph lecture excerpt on Jean Piaget, you will be asked to use the indenting system to outline the material. Once you are finished, apply the laddering technique and the Cornell system to highlight the significant concepts and main ideas and major details.

This lecture continues the discussion of childhood development, focusing on Jean Piaget's four major stages of intellectual development.

Jean Piaget's Four Intellectual Stages

I want to begin my discussion today of the major intellectual stages that Jean Piaget introduced. I will be talking about them in detail, but let me introduce them now. They are: (1) sensorimotor, (2) preoperational, (3) concrete operations, and (4) formal operations. Piaget emphasized that these stages are not exact and that children develop at various rates. Some, he noted, never reach the last stage of formal-operations.

Let's begin with the sensorimotor stage. Its years are from birth to age one-and-a-half. What characterizes this stage? This is the stage of simple motor responses like sucking and grasping. The infants at this age, and this is important, respond to their surroundings, not to what they remember. Piaget emphasized that children at this stage cannot respond to what they remember; they merely respond to what they see, hear, feel, and touch at the moment. Is this maybe why we have so few memories of our early childhood?

At the end of this first period, some important changes occur. The infant begins to talk. When this happens, toddlers can begin to talk about what they do not see. This ability Piaget referred to as object permanence. Please write this term down. Infants at the end of the sensorimotor stage also begin to recognize who they are. Experiments show that babies at this time who see themselves in the mirror can recognize who they are. Often they will touch their noses as an indication that they recognize what they see in the mirror. This action seems to say: "I know who that person is!" Also at the end of this stage, babies can show embarrassment. And this is another piece of evidence that the infant knows him or herself.

Now let's turn to the preoperational stage. It is a long stage—from one-and-a-half years to seven years, or a five-and-a-half-year span. What characterizes this stage is the tremendous development in language that the child experiences. Yet it is not the language of adults, and I want to emphasize this point. These children use many words, but they do not

---

*Adapted from James W. Kalat, *Introduction to Psychology*, 3rd ed., pp. 247–252.

understand the complex meanings of many of them. Piaget talks about this use of language as reversal. Let me give you an example. If I fully understand the meaning of the word father, I know that my father also had a father. For Piaget, this means that the speaker can reverse the operations, so he calls this ability reversal. A child in this preoperational stage lacks this operation to reverse. That is, she cannot understand how her father can also be the son to someone else.

Piaget also presents another important term for this preoperational stage. He says that the child from one-and-a-half to seven is egocentric. Let's define this term. An egocentric child sees the world as being totally for himself. You can say that he cannot put himself in someone else's shoes. Piaget has shown that this egocentric state is not absolute, and he has provided examples of children who are preoperational who do show some understanding of others. In an experiment with a card having a different picture on each side, a child of three or four can say that what the adult sees on the opposite side of the table is different from what she sees.

There is another key concept that I want you to learn, and that word is conservation. In the preoperational stage, Piaget has shown that children lack the concept of conservation. What is conservation? Children do not understand that an object conserves certain properties such as number, length, volume, area, and mass. What do I mean by this? If you were to put the same volume of colored liquid in two containers, one long and thin and the other short and fat, the child would say that there is more water in the long and thin container even though he has seen the same amount of water poured from the fat container to the thin one. Because the child sees the water within a longer shape, he is sure that there is more of it than when it was in, what it appeared to him to be, a smaller container. That is the concept of conservation.

Let's now go to the concrete operations stage. Remember that this is the stage from about seven to eleven. At this time, the child begins to understand the concept of property, or conservation, which she didn't understand in the preoperational. Like all the stages, this one also does not happen all at once. So a five-year-old may know that a ball of play dough may be shaped differently but have the same mass but may not understand that water in different containers has the same volume.

Why does Piaget call this period concrete-operations? He uses this term because the child from seven to eleven likes to deal with the concrete world—sizes, shapes, and numbers. You could say that she understands all that she can sense. Yet the child at this stage has a difficult time playing with these concrete realities. If you were to ask a seven-year-old where she would like a third eye, she would likely say "Between the other two." She does not have the ability to understand the abstract abilities of seeing. Older children are much more creative with a question like this and say something like "At the back of my head so I can see what is going on behind me."

We now turn to the last Piagetian stage—formal operations, and, remember, that it happens at about age eleven, at or around the onset of puberty. In this final stage, the child is able to begin thinking in abstractions. What do I mean by abstractions? Abstractions are those thoughts that go beyond the concrete. A friend is a concrete being, but friendship is an abstraction—a concept for the idea of a friend. To abstract requires logical and systematic practices. These are practices that take a lifetime to develop. And please remember that Piaget said that not all children develop into adults who can successfully use formal-operations.

Let's look at an experiment done to identify when a child has entered the formal operations stage. The problem is to have students produce a yellow liquid from five bottles of liquid of various colors. The goal is to get the right combination of liquids. What do you think children in the concrete operations stage did? They started mixing the liquids haphazardly, picking any combination of liquids. Children in the formal operations stage are much more systematic, trying combinations with two bottles, then combinations with three. The key here is that the formal operations children approach this problem systematically; they have a set of patterned practices, which in itself is an abstraction. That is, these children realize that a system can achieve a desired goal. The concrete operations children do not appreciate the value of systematic thinking, mainly because they do not understand that the abstraction called systematic thinking can do powerful things.*

70%

Ask instructor for answers.

Exercise 12.3
Mapping a Longer
Lecture Excerpt

Your job is to read the following lecture excerpt on language learning, a continuation of the discussion of Piaget's four stages of intellectual development. As you read, take notes—condensing information and using the indenting format, laddering, and Cornell. Before you finish with your notes, write an appropriate title. Then, on a separate sheet of paper, create a study map that includes the important points made in your notes. Remember that mapping is individual, so your map may not look like the sample one in the Answer Key. Complete your study notes in the space provided.

We are going to continue our discussion of language today. I want to start out with some interesting facts. It has been shown through solid research that a child between the ages of one-and-a-half and six learns an average of nine words per day. With each new word the child is able to explain what she experiences in greater detail. The question today is: What is it that a child needs in order to begin to acquire language, and are there stages like Piaget's that describe language development? The first major step in learning language is the most difficult one for an infant. He must understand that a word represents a thing. A cake— what tastes so good—is represented by that strange sound. Once he makes that connection, words make sense and become an economical way of expressing his thinking.

---

*Adapted from Kalat, *Introduction to Psychology*, 3rd ed., pp. 229–233.

There are distinct stages in learning a language, what linguists call language acquisition. Infants up to six months begin by random sound-making called babbling. These sounds have no relationship to what they hear. Even deaf infants up to six months babble. By age one, infants begin to understand what they hear and can say a word or two. What do you think the first word is? It is something like "muh," or the word identifying the person closest to them—their mother. It is interesting to realize that most languages have a word similar to "muh" for Mother.

Let's now go to the child at age one-and-a-half. This little person can say about fifty words, yet she uses words in isolation. I mean to say that at this age the child cannot string words together. The baby can say "Hello" and "Mama" but usually not "Hello Mama." Most of these fifty words are nouns; some are verbs. There is some research, though, that shows children able to speak with many words at a time, but the parents often hear it as one word because it is so poorly said.

At two, the language magic begins, I would say. The toddler speaks in two- and three-word phrases. And these are not just phrases that the child has heard and is simply copying. I want to emphasize this point. For children, language is not simply copying what they hear. Language use is rather a creative process. Underline the word "creative." They make up their own phrases, their own sentences.

By age three, most children are making full sentences. But they are not usually adult sentences. The child is making up his own rules for certain language structures, especially with negatives. The child at three will often say, "I no want to go" for "I do not want to go." Here, it seems the child is making his own rule about negatives. What rule could this be? "No" before the verb makes the whole sentence negative. Parents often find these mistakes cute and do not correct them. But even if the parent did, the child would continue to make the mistake. It seems that the child needs to be ready to accept correction; and at this early age, the child cannot understand the concept of correcting his language.

By about age four, the child has mastered most of the rules of her language. Her vocabulary is still limited and develops as she gets older. And there are still a few errors in grammar and structure, but not the kinds that make understanding difficult. These young children often still cannot understand complex sentences from their parents.

I want to end with a very important concept. Language is maturational rather than experiential. Research shows that pumping lots of language into a child's head, or making the language experience rich, does not significantly improve a child's language abilities, except for maybe a slightly larger vocabulary. All children in all cultures—and this is the fascinating bit of research—mature at about the same rate and follow the same sequence I've outlined here. And there is also no research to suggest that the earlier a child talks, the smarter he is. Early talkers and late talkers all go through the same sequence outlined in my lecture today.*

80%

(Score = # of correct responses × 5)
Find answers on pp. 406–407.

---

*Adapted from Kalat, *Introduction to Psychology*, 3rd ed., pp. 235–238.

Place your lecture notes and your study map on a separate sheet of paper. Be sure to title your notes.

Exercise 12.4
Writing a Paragraph
from a Study Map

Your job is to write a paragraph from the information that you gathered in the previous lecture on language acquisition. Use only the information from your study map to answer the following question.

Essay question: In a well-organized paragraph, present the major stages in the development of a child's language. Identify the stages by age and discuss the important characteristics of each. Be sure your evidence is accurate.

70%
Ask instructor for answers.

Follow-up on the
Early Childhood
Development
Exercises

Now that you have completed these exercises, it may be helpful to see how your reading on this topic has changed some of your ideas about child psychology and development. You may want to go back and reread these exercises before you answer the following questions. Answer them either in small groups or individually.

1. How do you now think children are different from adults?

2. What are some of the more interesting bits of research regarding children acquiring language that you remember from the lecture on language? Do your childhood language memories support these findings?

3. What topics in child development would you now want to study further?

Study Skills Systems and Test-Taking Practices

Now that you have mastered reading and note-taking skills, you are ready to read textbook selections and be introduced to examination practices. In this part, you will learn about the SQ3R study system, which is an efficient way to read and remember textbook material. You will also learn how to take objective, essay, and math or science tests. Instructors rely on examinations to gauge how well you are doing.

13 The SQ3R Study System

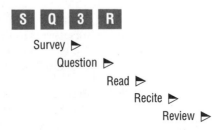

S Q 3 R

Survey ▷
    Question ▷
        Read ▷
          Recite ▷
            Review ▷

You have practiced locating main ideas and major details and have used several note-taking techniques. Now you are ready to combine these skills when you read your textbook. The SQ3R study system gives you both reading and note-taking practices to use as you read. The SQ3R system has been used successfully by students for a long time. Although many other study systems have emerged over the years, they all follow the essential pattern of SQ3R.

The letters in SQ3R stand for survey, question, read, recite, and review. Let's look at each of these steps.

Survey

In the survey step, you preview what you intend to read. Surveying is not word-for-word reading; rather, it is selective. Surveying is a central step in study reading; research has repeatedly shown that if you survey material before you read it, your comprehension significantly improves because you are able to predict more effectively when you read the material. In surveying, you should (1) read the titles and headings, (2) note graphics and aids, and (30 read the introduction or preface. Before you read, you should determine the length of the chapter, estimate the time it will take you to read it, determine which sections you are already familiar with, and predict whether the material will be difficult or easy for you to understand. By following these steps, you establish a reading focus.

Surveying an Entire Textbook   When you first get your textbook, you should briefly survey all of the chapters. Consider the following suggestions for doing this:

1. Read the preface, which contains introductory material written for the student. In the preface, the author gives reasons for writing the book, the topics covered, and suggestions for using the text.

2. Look carefully at the table of contents, which follows the preface. See how the book is organized. Is the organization simple or complicated? Are there a few divisions or several? If there are exercises, do the explanations precede the exercises, or are all the exercises at the end of the book? Since you will be using this text all semester, you need to know the answers to these questions.

   Some textbooks have two tables of contents—one short and the other detailed. Study both of them carefully.

3. See if there is an index, the alphabetical listing of topics found at the end of the textbook. Indexes are helpful when you want to find information fast. If your textbook has an index, familiarize yourself with it, so that you can use it as a study aid.

4. See if there is a glossary before the index. A glossary defines important terms that are used in the textbook. Instead of referring to a dictionary, you can use the glossary. Often, students do not even realize that their textbook has a glossary.

5. In some math and science textbooks, students will find an appendix, which comes before the index. In an appendix are charts, graphs, and tables that you need to use in solving problems found in the textbook.

6. In your survey, you may also discover an answer key, which is often located at the end of the textbook. Occasionally, you will find answer keys at the end of an exercise or at the end of a chapter. Some keys provide all of the answers, others just some of them. This text, for example, gives answers only to odd-numbered exercises. In some math texts, the author provides answers to the even- or odd-numbered problems within an exercise.

7. Now you are ready to get a sense of the entire textbook. Read through parts of the beginning, middle, and end. In this way, you can determine the author's style. Is it formal or conversational? It's helpful to have some sense of the author's style before you begin reading a specific chapter.

Surveying a Chapter of Text.   Consider the following suggestions in surveying a specific chapter.

1. Study the title of the chapter. Having read the title, do you think you know anything about the subject? Has your instructor covered this topic in lecture? Or is this an entirely new topic for you? By answering

these questions, you will give focus to your reading and improve your predicting skills.

2. At the beginning of many textbook chapters, you will find an outline or list of objectives the author intends to address. Since this is the significant information in the chapter, read it over carefully. Also, read the introductory paragraphs, which either summarize the chapter or introduce an interesting issue that the chapter will cover.

3. Most textbook writers divide their chapters into divisions and subdivisions. These headings are usually in boldface print or italics. Thumb through the chapter divisions. If there are no divisions, read through the first paragraph, the first sentence of the following paragraphs, and the last paragraph of the chapter. By doing this, you can determine the outline of the chapter.

4. If there are illustrations, graphs, or charts in the chapter, study them. See how this material relates to the chapter's divisions and subdivisions.

5. See if there are discussion or study questions at the end of the chapter. By reading these questions beforehand, you will know which topics the author considers most important. Also, see if a bibliography is included at the end. A bibliography lists additional books that you may wish to consult after you have read the chapter.

This chapter survey should take you no more than three or four minutes, but it is time well spent. Having surveyed, you now have a better idea of what to look for in the chapter.

Question

Questions help you identify important information. Sometimes you will make up a question before you read, then look for the answer. Other times you may have a study guide of questions provided by the teacher or printed at the end of the chapter so that you can think about the questions before you read or you can read a chapter part to find the answer. Since you have learned to read for main ideas and supporting details, you may wish to make up your own questions by turning various chapter headings into main-idea questions and then reading to determine the main idea and supporting details.

If you decide to make up your own questions, keep the following issues in mind: Ask yourself: (1) What is the chapter topic, and how does the author respond to this topic? (2) What are the major characteristics, steps, events, causes, or results that explain this topic? and (3) Are any terms defined?

Making up your own questions may be difficult at first, but it will give direction to your reading. The successful college student invariably knows the right kinds of questions to ask. Start looking at words in boldface print, italics, and the first sentences of paragraphs. From this information make up your own questions. For example, if your economics chapter prints **Deficit Spending** in boldface, you could write: "What is deficit spending?" Or, if your consumer behavior chapter begins its first paragraph with "Husbands and wives influence each other's buying preferences," you could turn this statement into a question: "How do husbands and wives influence each other's buying preferences?" By the time you finish reading a textbook chapter, you may have written ten to fifteen questions and answered them.

Read

Only after surveying and questioning are you ready to read—an active skill that calls on all of the critical reading skills you have learned. Along with your questions, you should have a pen or felt-tip marker (hi-liter). Whenever you come upon a main idea in a paragraph or a detail that supports the main idea, mark this information, either by underlining or highlighting the words. But remember: *Do not underline too much.* In most cases, all you need to mark is the part of the sentence where you read the important or core information—material that often answers the questions you have posed. If you overmark a page of text, you will become confused when you review for an exam. And not knowing what to review, you might read the entire page over. Study Figure 13-1, which is an example of an overly marked up textbook page.

Here are ten tips for marking your textbooks:

1. Mark main ideas with a double line, curved line, hi-liter, or the red end of a red and blue pencil. Mark only one main idea per paragraph, and mark only the key parts of this main idea. If the main ideas in a group of paragraphs are related, number them 1, 2, 3, and so on.

2. Mark major details with a single line, hi-liter, or the blue end of a red and blue pencil. Look for definitions, characteristics, examples, steps, causes, or effects. Try not to underline more than two details per paragraph, and mark only the key parts of these detail sentences. If you find that the details follow a pattern, number these details 1, 2, 3, and so on.

3. For very important statements, place an asterisk(*) in the margins next to them. These asterisks will become your signals to study this important information.

4. In some cases you may want to mark both the detail and its type. If you do so, use the following abbreviations in the margins: *ex, cause, eff, step,* or *char.*

5. Circle the key parts of a definition if the author has not already highlighted it in boldface or italics. Remember the importance of definitions in learning a subject. You should place the abbreviation "def" in the margins to direct you to the definition when you review your markings. You may also want to write the term on one side of a 3×5 card and its definition on the opposite side, so that at the end

What are the size and consequences of military spending?

The Size and Consequences of Military Spending

Study figures

Total world military spending in 1983 amounted to more than $811 billion, about 6.1 percent of total world production (world GNP) for that year. The U.S. Arms Control and Disarmament Agency estimates that military spending in 1985 was close to $1 trillion. A look back at Table 21.1 will show you that these levels of spending are more than the combined GNPs of the poorest sixty-seven countries of the world—an indication of what could be done for them if the resources were not used for military spending.

World military spending in real terms (constant dollars) is more than twelve times as great as it was fifty years ago, and the character of the spending is shifting in favor of sophisticated weaponry and away from personnel. This shift is not helping employment in the countries that produce the hardware (mainly the United States, the Soviet Union, France, the United Kingdom, and West Germany) because the hardware is produced by skilled personnel working in high-technology firms. The main effect of the spending is therefore to draw skilled people who are already employed in nondefense industries into industries that produce military hardware.

See how military spending affects the number of jobs

One study in the United States estimated that a billion dollars spent on defense in 1975 would have created 76,000 jobs in defense industries, compared with 184,000 jobs in the fields of health and education. The study concluded that defense spending creates less employment than other forms of spending.

The Military-Industrial Complex *What is the military-industrial complex?*

In his farewell address in 1961, President Dwight D. Eisenhower warned the country of the danger of a "military-industrial complex." By that phrase, the President meant that military spending could become so important in terms of employment, money, and votes that Congress would be obliged to vote for ever-increasing military budgets whether the nation needed them or not.

Study these figures as well

Despite Eisenhower's warning, U.S. defense spending accounted for one-third of estimated total tax receipts for 1987. The military-industrial complex employs 30 percent of the nation's mathematicians and one of every four scientists and engineers, a development that helps explain America's failure to compete with other industrial nations in civilian markets.

When 10 percent of all jobs in the country depend on defense spending, politicians are pressured to vote for weapons systems whether or not they are considered effective. One example is the B-1 bomber program that, despite misgivings even in the Pentagon about the need for the plane or its effectiveness, now involves contractors in seventeen states producing B-1s at a minimum price of $1.25 billion each.

Figure 13-1 *Textbook page overly marked up. (Source: Philip C. Starr,* Economics: Principles in Action, *5th ed. [Belmont, Calif.: Wadsworth, 1988], p. 394.)*

of the semester you will have collected all of the important definitions for your course on these cards. You may also want to include an example to help you remember the definition.

6. If a sentence is particularly difficult to understand even after rereading and attempting to paraphrase it, place a question mark in the margin. When you review, you will be alerted to what you did not understand.

7. Do not include too many written comments in the margins. You should reserve these comments for short summaries of important points, paraphrases of difficult sentences, and inferences that you make. For example, if you note that one main idea or supporting detail is more important than the others, you might want to write in the margin "Most important main idea" or "Most important supporting detail." Some students find that their marginal comments are more important than their underlinings.

8. Do not begin marking your chapter right away, because once you have marked something you will have a hard time erasing it. Read through several paragraphs first. Then go back and underline the main ideas and supporting details. Often in rereading you can more easily pick out the important parts of a paragraph. In fact, you may want to mark some of the most important points in pencil as you study and then mark in detail during the recite step (discussed below).

9. Be consistent with your markings. Use the system suggested above, or make up your own. Some students prefer to write comments and summaries in the margins, while others use their own personal symbols. Just be sure that you employ the same underlining symbols and abbreviations throughout the textbook. Otherwise, when you review, you will not be able to quickly separate main ideas from supporting details. Some students learn better from their underlinings, others from their comments. Try out all of these suggestions and any of your own techniques to determine which devices help you learn best.

10. Think of textbook marking as active reading. Your markings should be your signals that you understand the form and content of the chapter. If you mark passively, you will not retain the important points made in the chapter. Figure 13-2 is an example of a successfully marked up textbook page.

Even if you methodically follow the above ten steps, there will be times when you will not completely understand what you have read. Almost everyone has to reread all or part of a textbook chapter sometime during the semester. In fact, research shows that most students retain only about 50 percent of textbook material the first time they read it. If a chapter is difficult, you may want to put it aside after you have read it

What is the size of military spending?

The Size and Consequences of Military Spending

Total world military spending in 1983 amounted to more than $811 billion, about 6.1 percent of total world production (world GNP) for that year. The U.S. Arms Control and Disarmament Agency estimates that military spending in 1985 was close to $1 trillion. A look back at Table 21.1 will show you that these levels of spending are more than the combined GNPs of the poorest sixty-seven countries of the world—an indication of what could be done for them if the resources were not used for military spending.

Amazing figures

World military spending in real terms (constant dollars) is more than twelve times as great as it was fifty years ago, and the character of the spending is shifting in favor of sophisticated weaponry and away from personnel. This shift is not helping employment in the countries that produce the hardware (mainly the United States, the Soviet Union, France, the United Kingdom, and West Germany) because the hardware is produced by skilled personnel working in high-technology firms. The main effect of the spending is therefore to draw skilled people who are already employed in nondefense industries into industries that produce military hardware.

Cause/effect of Military Spending on Employment

One study in the United States estimated that a billion dollars spent on defense in 1975 would have created 76,000 jobs in defense industries, compared with 184,000 jobs in the fields of health and education. The study concluded that defense spending creates less employment than other forms of spending.

The Military-Industrial Complex *What is the military-industrial complex?*

In his farewell address in 1961, President Dwight D. Eisenhower warned the country of the danger of a "military-industrial complex." By that phrase, the President meant that military spending could become so important in terms of employment, money, and votes that Congress would be obliged to vote for ever-increasing military budgets whether the nation needed them or not.

Def: Military Industrial Complex

Despite Eisenhower's warning, U.S. defense spending accounted for one-third of estimated total tax receipts for 1987. The military-industrial complex employs 30 percent of the nation's mathematicians and one of every four scientists and engineers, a development that helps explain America's failure to compete with other industrial nations in civilian markets.

More amazing figures

When 10 percent of all jobs in the country depend on defense spending, politicians are pressured to vote for weapons systems whether or not they are considered effective. One example is the B-1 bomber program that, despite misgivings even in the Pentagon about the need for the plane or its effectiveness, now involves contractors in seventeen states producing B-1s at a minimum price of $1.25 billion each.

Military Spending by the LDCs *How do LDCs affect military spending?*

In rich and poor countries alike, the opportunity costs of military spending can be measured by the loss of public projects aimed at improving health, education, and welfare. But in many LDCs, these costs can worsen a poverty level that is already intolerable.

Figure 13-2 Textbook page appropriately marked up. (Source: Philip C. Starr, Economics: Principles in Action, 5th ed. [Belmont, Calif.: Wadsworth, 1988], p. 394.)

once, and reread it in a day or two. Often, if you reread difficult material after it has "settled" for awhile, you will find that the material is more understandable.

Recite

Having study read and marked the important parts of your chapter, you are now ready to write what you have learned. In the recite step of the SQ3R, you summarize what you have read. This step is critical because it lets you know how much of the material you have understood and remembered.

When you begin to recite, read for a short period of time—approximately ten minutes. During this time, mark the passage and make marginal comments. Some students have found that they can read and mark only one chapter subsection at a time, often just answering the question they have made up from the subtitle. No matter how small a part of the chapter you have read, close your textbook after you have reviewed your underlining and commentary in the margins. Then, in the section of your notebook designated for study reading notes, take notes on what you just read, using any note-taking format that you are comfortable with. Title and date each study-reading entry, as in the following example:

Less Developed Countries pp. 350–352   10/12/95

Some students have found that they can more successfully mark what they have read during this recite step. They often mark some material during the read step with pencil; then during their recite, they use a pen or highlighter to underscore main ideas and major details and make marginal comments.

You may want to use the Cornell Note-taking System when you recite. If you do, write the section title, pages, and date on the top line. To the right of the vertical line, summarize the main idea and supporting details of the section without looking back at the book. Leave spaces to make corrections and additions to your notes. Then look back at the chapter to see if you omitted anything important, and edit your notes. These notes will be useful study tools for exams. You can fold the notes on the vertical line, read the topic or question to the left of the line, and attempt to answer it from memory. Reread and recite until recall is accurate.

Look at how the Cornell System effectively summarizes and quizzes a student on material she has underlined regarding military spending. Note how this student has posed questions in the margins in anticipation of the exam she will take on this material.

	Military Spending, pp. 394–396 *11/12/95*
What was the military spend-ing in 1983 and 1985?	1983: $811 billion in federal money 1985: $1 trillion

What is the effect of military spending on employment?	Military spending produces more skilled workers in military and fewer jobs outside of military
Define <u>Military-Industrial Complex.</u>	Military and industrial leaders who work together to receive more money for military projects.
What were employment figures for mathematicians and scientists?	Military-industrial complex uses ⅓ of all mathematicians and ¼ of all scientists.
What is expense of B-1?	B-1 costs $1.25 <u>billion</u> each.

In the beginning, your reciting notes may not be very efficient. With the first few sets of notes, you may have to review your textbook to see if your notes are both accurate and thorough. As the semester progresses, extend your study reading sessions from ten to fifteen minutes, then from fifteen to twenty. By the end of the semester, you should be able to study read for fifty minutes and accurately recite what you have read. Even the best students can do only one hour of concentrated reading of textbook material at one sitting.

With particularly difficult chapters, you may want to break up your reading into shorter sessions. If you do this, you may even want to write out some short, specific goals to complete. Look at the following goals for reading an economics chapter:

1. Read for ten minutes, or complete one page of the chapter on military spending.
2. Summarize this page.
3. Break for five minutes.
4. Read for ten more minutes, recite, and take another five-minute break.

Once you have completed your reading notes, it is wise to review them. As you reread these notes and quiz yourself, you may also want to make study maps of the material. A carefully designed study map is a helpful study aid just before an exam.

Review

Review is the final step in the SQ3R system. You will study this step thoroughly in Chapters 15 and 16 on test-taking procedures. For now, just remember that reviewing is your insurance that you will remember what you worked hard to learn. When you review, you (1) study your lecture notes, (2) reread your text markings, (3) review your study reading notes, and (4) study your study maps or design study maps of what you have read so that you can tie the material together.

You should now be able to predict the sorts of questions you will be asked on exams. Write your predicted exam questions in your notebook. You should not review the night before the exam. You need to review throughout the semester. You will retain more of the reading material if you edit and review your notes after every study reading session. This will help you do a better job of taking class lecture notes and participating fruitfully in class discussions. Then review all your markings and your study reading notes one week before a major exam. Predict exam questions, and use mnemonic techniques, as explained in Chapter 14, when you need to memorize particularly difficult material. Cramming may help you pass the test, but it will not help you retain the material.

Some instructors have added an additional step to the SQ3R, changing it to SQ4R, or "review again." They believe that reviewing is very important and often not completed in one step, so many reviews are necessary. Research has shown that almost no one can retain all textbook information in one careful reading; so reviewing again is not a sign of a learning problem, but what most students need to do in order to retain most of the textbook material they study.

Summary

The SQ3R is a study system for you to use when you read your textbooks. The S stands for survey—taking a general look at your reading task. Q involves questioning—writing key questions whose answers will help you understand the reading. The first R is read, where you mark up key points and make accurate inferences. In the second R—recite—you summarize what you have read; this step is critical because it tells you what you have learned. The last R stands for review; here, you go over your markings and notes to retain what you have learned. Often it is necessary to review the material several times before you can be sure that you know it.

The SQ3R is a sensible study reading system. By using the SQ3R system, you approach your study reading in an orderly fashion—surveying, questioning, reading, reciting, and reviewing.

Summary Box   *The SQ3R Study System*

What is it?	*Why do you use it?*
A systematic approach to reading textbook material	To understand textbook material
	To retain textbook material
S = survey	To take better notes in lecture class
Q = question	To ask intelligent questions in class
R = read	To participate in class discussion
R = recite	To recall material for exams
R = review	

Skills Practice

In the following exercises, you will practice the SQ3R study system. Some of the exercises contain material that you are already familiar with from your work in Part 2.

Exercise 13.1
Underlining from
Textbook Excerpts

The following three excerpts are from textbooks in various fields. Your job is to read each excerpt, survey it, and write at least two questions in the margins. Then, in each paragraph, underline the main idea twice and one or two major details once. Be sure to mark only the important parts of the main ideas and major details.

1. Catching More Fish and Fish Farming

Fish are the major source of animal protein for more than one-half of the world's people, especially in Asia and Africa. Fish supply about 55 percent of the animal protein in Southeast Asia, 35 percent in Asia as a whole, 19 percent in Africa, about 25 percent worldwide—twice as much as eggs and three times as much as poultry—and 6 percent of all human protein consumption. Two-thirds of the annual fish catch is consumed by humans and one-third is processed into fish meal to be fed to livestock.

Between 1950 and 1970, the marine fish catch more than tripled—an increase greater than that occurring in any other human food source during the same period. To achieve large catches, modern fishing fleets use sonar, helicopters, aerial photography, and temperature measurement to locate schools of fish and lights and electrodes to attract them. Large, floating factory ships follow the fleets to process the catch.

Despite this technological sophistication, the steady rise in the marine fish catch halted abruptly in 1971. Between 1971 and 1976 the annual catch leveled off and rose only slightly between 1976 and 1983. A major factor in this leveling off was the sharp decline of the Peruvian anchovy catch, which once made up 20 percent of the global ocean harvest. A combination of overfishing and a shift in the cool, nutrient-rich currents off the coast of Peru were apparently the major factors causing this decline, which also threw tens of thousands of Peruvians out of work. Meanwhile, world population continued to grow, so between 1970 and 1983 the averge fish catch per person declined and is projected to decline even further back to the 1960 level by the year 2000.*

2. Soul

Soul or rhythm and blues is the popular music associated with America's black population. Its musical qualities reveal some aspects of African music, especially in the style of singing. It is emotional and forceful, with

---

*G. Tyler Miller, Jr., *Living in the Environment*, 4th ed. (Belmont, Calif.: Wadsworth, 1985), p. 153. Used by permission.

calls and exclaimed words. Open chords and parallel chord movement are characteristic of its harmony. The music is often loud.

Some writers include gospel music in the soul category, and the relationships are close between these styles. Prominent names in soul music include James Brown, The Jackson Five (one of whom was Michael Jackson), Patti LaBelle, Aretha Franklin, and the groups associated with the Motown sound.

Sometimes the same song will reach the top of popularity charts in the soul, country, and general popular music listings, but only occasionally. For example, the Beatles were never particularly popular with blacks. The ethnic associations of popular music influence its acceptance with various segments of the population. The preference is based on the style and timbre of the music rather than on the message of the words, although the background of the performer makes some difference. A few songs with a message about war, poverty, or ecology achieved limited popularity in the late 1960s and early 1970s, but the trend then returned to the overwhelmingly favorite topic of popular songs: love and its pains and joys.*

3. Matter: Types, States, Properties, and Changes

A lump of coal, an ice cube, a puddle of water, air—all are samples of matter. Matter is anything that occupies space and has mass. *Mass* is the quantity of matter in substance.

A substance or pure substance is one of millions of different types of matter found in the world. Any substance can be classified as either an element or a compound. An element is one of the 108 basic building blocks of all matter. Examples include iron, sodium, carbon, oxygen, and chlorine. Scientists have discovered 90 naturally occurring elements on Earth and have made small quantities of 18 others in the laboratory.

A compound is a form of matter in which two or more elements are held together in a fixed ratio by chemical bonds. Water, for example, is a combination of the elements hydrogen and oxygen, and sodium chloride (the major ingredient in table salt) is a combination of the elements sodium and chlorine. About 5 million compounds of the 108 known elements have been identified, and about 6,000 new compounds are added to the list each week. With proper guidance, you could make a new compound yourself. At least 63,000 compounds are combined in the food we eat, the air we breathe, the water we drink, and the countless products we use.†

Answers will vary. Find sample underlinings on pp. 408–409.

Exercise 13.2
More Underlining
from Textbook
Excerpts

The following are three more excerpts from textbooks in different fields. Again, survey each excerpt and write at least two questions in the margins. Then, underline main ideas twice and major details once, or use

---

*Charles R. Hoffer, *The Understanding of Music*, 6th ed. (Belmont, Calif.: Wadsworth, 1989), pp. 517–518.
†G. Tyler Miller, Jr., *Chemistry: A Basic Introduction*, 4th ed. (Belmont, Calif.: Wadsworth, 1987), p. 2. Used by permission.

any other marking system that is comfortable for you. Mark only the important parts.

1. Early Primate Evolution

The evolutionary history of the primates is not clear-cut, with one form gradually replacing another. Fossils have not yet been recovered for a few critical time periods. Moreover, there are periods in which closely related forms coexisted for some time, with some destined to leave descendant populations and others to become evolutionary dead-ends. What we will be describing, then, are some of the known branches on a very "bushy" evolutionary tree.

The oldest known primate fossils date from the Paleocene (65 million to 54 million years ago). Again, they were morphologically similar to existing tree shrews, with a relatively small brain and a long snout. Although many of those forms died out, some left descendants that evolved into the true prosimian forms of the Eocene (54 to 38 million years ago).

The Eocene climate was somewhat warmer than the Paleocene, and tropical rain forests flourished—as did the early prosimians. These primates were characterized by an increased brain size, an increased emphasis on vision over smell, and more refined grasping abilities. This was the time of divergences that led, eventually, to the modern-day lemurs, lorises, and tarsiers. It was also the time of divergences that led to the first anthropoids.*

2. Humans in Nature: Hunter-Gatherers

Early humans survived without claws, fangs, or great speed. That they did so, and multiplied, is due to three major cultural adaptations—all the product of intelligence: (1) the use of *tools* for hunting, collecting and preparing food, and making protective clothing, (2) learning to live in an often hostile environment through effective *social organization* and *cooperation* with other human beings, and (3) the use of *language* to increase the efficiency of cooperation and to pass on knowledge of previous survival experiences.

Our early hunter-gatherer ancestors cooperated by living in small bands or tribes, clusters of several families typically consisting of no more than 50 persons. The size of each band was limited by the availability of food. If a group got too large it split up. Sometimes these widely scattered bands had no permanent base, traveling around their territory to find the plants and animals they needed to exist. Hunter-gatherers' material possessions consisted mostly of simple tools such as sharpened sticks, scrapers, and crude hunting weapons. Much of their knowledge could be described as ecological—how to find water in a barren desert and how to locate plant and animal species useful as food. Studies of

---

*Cecie Starr and Ralph Taggart, *Biology: The Unity and Diversity of Life*, 4th ed. (Belmont, Calif.: Wadsworth, 1987), pp. 644–645. Used by permission.

Bushmen, Pygmies, and other hunter-gatherer cultures that exist today have shown the uncertainty of success in hunting wild game; thus often most of the food of primitive people was provided by women, who collected plants, fruits, eggs, mollusks, reptiles, and insects.

Many people tend to believe that hunter-gatherers spent most of their time in a "tooth and claw" struggle to stay alive. But research among hunter-gatherer societies in remote parts of the world cast doubt on this idea. These "primitive" people may hunt for a week and then spend a month on vacation. They have no bosses, suffer from less stress and anxiety than most "modern" people, and have a diet richer and more diverse than that of almost everyone else in the world today, rich and poor alike.*

3. Cultural Continuity and Discontinuity

Ruth Benedict (1938) characterized American culture as containing major discontinuities between what is expected of children and what is expected of adults. Children in our culture are not expected to be responsible; they are supposed to play, not work. Few children in America have the opportunity to contribute in any meaningful way to the basic tasks of society. Children take on responsibility only when they become adults. A second major discontinuity is that children are required to be submissive, but adults are expected to be dominant. This is especially true for males. Sons must obey their fathers, but as fathers they must dominate their sons. A third major discontinuity has to do with sex. As children, Americans are not allowed to engage in sexual behavior, and for many people, just the thought of childhood sexuality is repellent. As adults, however, especially as men and women marry, sex is considered to be a normal, even valued, activity.

In great contrast to the discontinuities experienced by the individual learning to participate in American culture is the continuity of socialization among many native American societies. The Cheyenne, a Plains Indian tribe, exhibit a great degree of continuity in their culture. Cheyenne children are not treated as a different order of people from adults. They are regarded as smaller and not yet fully competent adults, although by American standards the competence of Cheyenne children is quite astounding. The play of small children centers on imitation of, and real participation in, adult tasks. Both boys and girls learn to ride horses almost as soon as they can walk. This skill is related to the importance of the horse in traditional Cheyenne culture, in which buffalo were hunted on horseback. By the time they are six, little boys are riding bareback and using the lasso. By eight, boys are helping to herd the horses in the camp. As soon as they can use them, boys get small but good-quality bows and arrows. Little girls who are just toddlers help their mothers carry wood and water. Boys and girls learn these activities in play, in which the routine of family life is imitated. Girls play "mother" to the smallest children; boys imitate the male roles of hunter and war-

---

*Miller, *Living in the Environment*, p. E2. Used by permission.

rior and even the rituals of self-torture that are part of Cheyenne religious ceremonies.

Control of aggression is an important value among the Cheyenne, and aggression rarely occurs within the group of adults. A chief rules not by force and dominance but by intelligence, justice, and consideration for others. The needs of the group are more important than the needs of the individual. The Cheynne learn this lesson at an early age. Infants who cry are not physically punished, but they will be removed from the camp and their baskets hung in the bushes until they stop. This is an early lesson in learning that one cannot force one's will on others by self-display. Aggression and lack of control of one's emotions do not bring rewards for either children or adults; rather, they result in social isolation.*

> Answers will vary. Ask instructor for sample underlinings.

Exercise 13.3
Applying the SQ3R System to a Textbook Excerpt

In this exercise, you will be reading a longer textbook excerpt on poverty. You will be asked to survey, make up questions, read, recite, and review. When you have completed these five steps, you will be asked to answer some questions that show how well you understood the excerpt.

A. Survey. Give yourself one minute to survey the following excerpt, noting (1) the title and subtitles and (2) words in italics and boldface type. If you have extra time, begin reading the first paragraph or two. When your time is up, answer the questions that follow without looking back.

Poverty in the Developing Countries

(1) This section is about poverty among nations. Poverty is, of course, a relative matter. Whenever there is any inequality in the distribution of income, some people will always be poor relative to others. But much of the world is so abjectly poor that some observers speak of *absolute* poverty, a condition of life so destitute that its victims are chronically on the verge of death.

(2) Almost 1 billion people—one-quarter of the world's population—are in this category. A quarter of a million people in Calcutta are homeless. They eat, live, and die in the streets. Three million people in Bolivia (out of a total population of five million) have a life expectancy of thirty years. The average Bolivian eats less than half an ounce of meat per year; in effect, the peasant population is too poor to eat any meat at all.

What Is a "Less Developed" Country?

(3) Several phrases are used to describe countries that are poorer than others: underdeveloped countries, third world countries, sometimes even fourth or fifth world countries. Economists have no specific criteria or explicit definitions of such terms. A nation's position is usually

---

*Serena Nanda, *Cultural Anthropology,* 3rd ed. (Belmont, Calif.: Wadsworth, 1987), pp. 131, 134. Used by permission.

determined by dividing its GNP by population (per capita GNP) so that there is a ladder of countries from rich to poor—from $21,920 per person per year in the United Arab Emirates to $110 per person per year in Ethiopia in 1984.

(4) Usually, all countries are classified as either "more developed" or "less developed." The World Bank in its *Development Report for 1986* uses six subcategories of less developed countries, which we will overlook for the sake of brevity. Instead, we will use just the two categories "more developed" and "less developed" and set the dividing line at $1,000 per person per year, although such a division is arbitrary and often unrevealing. We know that GNP says little about the quality of life. Moreover, a per capita GNP figure conceals the distribution of income within a nation. For example, per capita GNP in Brazil was about $2,000 a year in 1984, but 30 million of Brazil's 133 million people had average annual incomes of $77. Because this section is about the less developed countries, we will use a common abbreviation, LDCs, to indicate that group of about 90 of the 170-odd countries of the world.

The Trouble with Comparing Per Capita GNPs

(5) When we use per capita GNPs to compare countries, we find ourselves trapped by numbers that offer little help in describing real differences in standards of living. Not only is GNP an imperfect measure of welfare or progress *within* a country, it has even less meaning when used for comparisons among countries. Two examples will clarify this point.

(6) In a poor, less developed country (LDC) like Tanzania, with a per capita GNP of $210 per year, the $210 figure is imperfect because it is based primarily on cash transactions. But much of Tanzania's production and consumption typically involves little or no cash. The people in Tanzania's villages feed themselves out of their own production. Therefore, in most cases, per capita GNP figures in poor countries understate their true incomes. Of course, that doesn't mean such people are rich. We could double the numbers, and these people would still be abjectly poor by any standard.

(7) In another example, let's look at the comparative lifestyles of Americans and New Zealanders. In the fall of 1978, New Zealand's per capita GNP was about half that of the United States. But it would be very foolish to conclude that New Zealanders' standard of living was half that of the average American. Fresh food prices were generally half of U.S. prices, so that with much lower wages, the New Zealanders ate just as well as or better than Americans. Housing costs (rents and home purchase prices) were also about half of ours. Education, medical care, and retirement pensions were all provided from a highly progressive schedule of income taxes. In one specific case, a highly skilled New Zealander construction worker retired from his job at age 60. At the time of retirement, he earned $3.80 per hour—by our standards an abysmally low wage after a lifetime of work. Nevertheless, he owned a home and automobile free and clear, had $50,000 in the bank, and began receiving a pension of 80 percent of his highest earnings. He and his wife were comfortable and content, traveled overseas occasionally, and had no

financial worries. However, New Zealanders also have to contend with the high prices of imported products like automobiles.

(8) So how does one evaluate these differences in lifestyles? Can one say that Americans are better off than New Zealanders or vice versa? The question is impossible to answer. Nevertheless, the GNP per capita method of comparison among different countries is the method most commonly used.

(9) In one attempt to improve on the GNP per capita measure, economists devised an index called the **Physical Quality of Life Index (PQLI)**. The PQLI is a composite of a nation's life expectancy, infant mortality, and literacy. The index is 97 for Sweden, 94 for the United States, 35 for Bangladesh. The index reveals the weaknesses of looking only at GNP per capita: GNP per capita in Saudi Arabia is a healthy $10,530 (1984), but its PQLI is only 28.

(10) In this section we review the plight of the LDCs, including the distribution of the world's income, the reasons why the more developed countries (particularly the United States) should be concerned about world poverty, the two major problems of population increase and lack of capital, and some conclusions.*

1. The chapter excerpt has no charts and graphs.

a. true
b. false

2. The excerpt does not use italics for emphasis.

a. true
b. false

3. The excerpt makes use of boldface print.

a. true
b. false

4. The subtopic "What Is a 'Less Developed' Country?" will probably

a. define this term
b. discuss poverty in the United States
c. discuss the average wages in Europe
d. discuss the quality of life in North America

5. The title suggests that this chapter will mainly concern itself with

a. the wealthy countries of the world
b. the industrialized countries of the world
c. the poorer countries of the world
d. overpopulation

1. _____

2. _____

3. _____

4. _____

5. _____

80%

(score = # correct × 20)
Find answers on p. 409.

---

*Philip C. Starr, *Economics: Principles in Action*, 5th ed. (Belmont, Calif.: Wadsworth, 1988), pp. 383–385.

B. Question.   Now go back to the excerpt, and from the title, subtitles, and terms in boldface print, write four questions that this excerpt appears to address. You will answer these questions as you read the chapter.

1. _____

2. _____

Answers will vary. Find
sample outline on
p. 409.

3. _____

4. _____

C. Read and Recite.   Begin study reading to the end of paragraph 4, underlining main ideas and major details and making marginal comments. Keep your four questions in mind. Then close the book and recite, using the indenting format. Finally, apply the Cornell note-taking system to your notes and study the material.

Answers will vary. Find
sample answers on
pp. 409–410.

Now study the rest of the excerpt, and follow the same procedures as those you used to read and recite the first half of the excerpt.

Now look back at your outlines. From them, make up a study map that ties all of the information together.

D. Review. Now study your underlinings, outline, and study map. When you think you have learned the most important points of the excerpt, answer the following questions without looking back.

Examination: Poverty in the Developing Countries

Directions: Choose the letter that correctly answers the following ten questions. Place all of your answers in the answer box.

1. How many people in the world are in absolute poverty?

   a. 4 billion
   b. 3 billion
   c. 2 billion
   d. 1 billion

2. Absolute poverty means that the people

   a. are often sick due to lack of food
   b. sometimes have no food to eat
   c. are on the verge of death from starvation
   d. die from starvation within a year

3. The poorest country in the world by economic standards is

   a. Ethiopia
   b. Bolivia
   c. India
   d. Iraq

4. Which term is *not* used to group countries according to poverty?

   a. more developed
   b. mildly developed
   c. less developed
   d. none of these

5. LDCs make up

   a. one-fourth of the world
   b. one-third of the world
   c. one-half of the world
   d. over half of the world

6. The excerpt suggests that "GNP" is an accurate and informative term.

   a. true
   b. false

7. The excerpt suggests that Americans are

   a. clearly better off economically than people in other countries

---

1. _____

2. _____

3. _____

4. _____

5. _____

6. _____

7. _____

8. _____

9. _____

10. _____

_____
80%

(score = # correct × 10)
Find answers on p. 410.

    b. not better off economically than people in other countries

    c. not easily described by the economic terms "GNP" and "per capita"

    d. as well off economically as the Japanese

8. "PQLI" stands for:

    a. Poor Quality of Life Index

    b. Physical Quality of Life Index

    c. Population Quality and Life's Illnesses

    d. none of these

9. The PQLI considers *all* of the following factors except

    a. life expectancy

    b. unemployment

    c. infant mortality

    d. literacy

10. The excerpt ends by suggesting that the United States should

    a. not be concerned about world poverty

    b. be concerned about world poverty

    c. give economic aid in the form of food to the ten poorest countries

    d. devise a new system for describing LDCs

Exercise 13.4
Writing a Paragraph
Using SQ3R

Once again review your textbook markings, study notes, and study map for the textbook excerpt in Exercise 13.3. When you can remember the important points in the excerpt, close your books and notes and answer the following essay question.

Essay question: In an organized paragraph, define "absolute poverty" and "LDCs." Then provide two examples of why it is hard to determine the poverty level of a particular country.

Use the following outline to list the important points that you want to make in your paragraph.

Definitions:

absolute poverty: _____

LDCs: _____

I. Examples of Difficulty in Determining Poverty Levels of a Country

    A. _____

    B. _____

80%
Ask instructor for answers.

14 Memory Aids

A good memory is a key to learning. Knowing how memory is stored in the brain will give you a better understanding of how to become a more successful student. Also, in understanding how memory works, you can see how memory aids, called *mnemonic practices*, help you learn.

How Does Memory Work?

The study of the brain and learning, called cognitive psychology, is relatively new. All that students in this field have to work with at this time are theories, at best.

Cognitive psychologists are now suggesting that there are two kinds of memory: short-term and long-term. Everything you learn begins in short-term memory; you read or listen to something, and it enters short-term memory. Almost everything that goes into short-term memory is quickly forgotten, because forgetting is much easier for the brain than remembering. When something stays with you, it has entered long-term memory.

The best way to put information into long-term memory is through *rehearsal*. Rehearsal involves practice; with study material, that would involve rereading, discussing, summarizing, or paraphrasing. When you rehearse information, the brain records it, somewhat as a computer records bits of information on tape or chips. When you learn, the brain records the information with a physical mark on the cerebrum (the learning part of the brain). These marks are called *neural traces*, or memory grooves. Well-rehearsed information creates well-defined neural traces. If you learn something improperly, the neural trace will not be

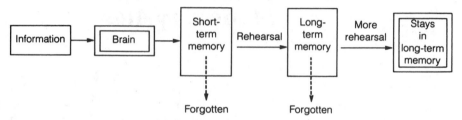

Figure 14-1   *How the brain remembers.*

well defined, and it will probably return to short-term memory and be forgotten. Study Figure 14-1 to see how the brain remembers.

How do you keep information in long-term memory? To remember, you should (1) study for short periods, (2) take short rest periods between study periods, (3) review what you have learned, and (4) study different subjects in succession.

Studying for short intervals (twenty-five to fifty minutes) has several advantages. First, realize that the brain forgets more than it remembers; so if you take in less information, you have a better chance of remembering it. Remember, though, that these study periods must be concentrated. You need to reread and recite what you have read. This concentrated reading is what you have learned to do in the SQ3R system.

Another characteristic of the brain is that it tends to rehearse what you have learned even after you have stopped studying. You are unaware of this rehearsal. When you read for a certain length of time, you need to take a relaxing break. Even if the break has nothing to do with what you have studied, your brain will still be rehearsing this new material. Like food being digested, new information needs to sit in the brain awhile before it can enter long-term memory. Remember, though, that you need to carefully schedule your study breaks. Reading for twenty minutes and then taking a three-hour break will not train your brain to remember. If you plan to study in three intervals at night, for example, your breaks should be no more than twenty minutes long.

A third fact to know about the brain is that it tends to forget more during the first twenty-four hours than at any other time. Since you tend to forget more at first, make a point of reviewing what you have learned soon after you have read your textbook or listened to a lecture. What you review today will have a better chance of staying in long-term memory.

A final characteristic of memory is that the brain tends to forget if it is processing similar bits of information. This mental process is known as *interference*. The brain seems to take in more if two chunks of information are different. So it is wiser to study for two dissimilar courses than two similar courses in succession. For example, you will remember more of your psychology chapter if you do some chemistry problems afterward than if you were to follow your psychology reading with reading a chapter of sociology.

Concentration Tips

Concentration can simply be defined as thinking with intensity. Of course, intense thinking is the best way to study. Apart from the optimal study area tips and goal-setting suggestions that were discussed in Chapter 2, there are several specific tips about concentrating that will improve your memory:

1. When you begin to study, don't look up or away from your study material. Each time you look out the window next to your desk or at your friends in the library, you break your intense thinking about the study material. The more you practice not being interrupted, the better your levels of concentration will be.

2. Walter Pauk, in his *How to Study in College*, offers an interesting technique to improve concentration. Each time your mind wanders, place a check on a blank sheet of paper next to your study materials. You may begin by making over twenty check marks during a study period; but if you keep up this practice, you will probably find that you will have fewer occasions to make a check mark, so your concentration will be improving.*

3. Be sure you are not hungry when you study. Hunger is a very powerful distraction. If you find that you are hungry as you are studying, take a snack break; then get back to work.

Memory Tips

From this very general introduction to learning theory, you can design certain successful learning practices. Consider the following learning hints:

1. Something learned well the first time is not easily forgotten. Study new information slowly and carefully, asking questions as you go along.

2. Relate new information to several contexts. Putting information into proper context is called *association*. The more contexts that you place information in, the more likely you are to remember this new material. If you are learning the meaning of "ostentatious," for example, it is best for you to learn both its dictionary meaning as well as its synonyms; its history, or etymology; and words related to it, such as "ostensibly," "ostentation," and "ostentatiousness." With each new context that you place the word in, you are creating more memory grooves, all of which are associated with "ostentatious."

   Similarly, the more you read in several fields, the more contexts you make, and the easier it will be for you to attach new information to them. Many composition theorists and language experts are now

*Walter Pauk, *How to Study in College*, 2nd ed. (Boston: Houghton Mifflin, 1974), p. 42.

saying that students learn to speak and write better if they read widely. Creating several contexts seems to be central to successful learning.

3. Organize any information that you read or study into patterns, often into main ideas and major details. Organizing information into recognizable patterns is known as *categorization*. When students categorize information, they have a better chance of keeping it in long-term memory. Even if information seems disorganized, try to find an order; most information is built upon patterns.

4. Reviewing is another important way to remember. Psychological studies have shown that if you have once learned something and have forgotten it, you will have an easier time relearning it. Spaced review helps keep information in long-term memory. Don't leave your reviewing of notes and textbook markings until the night before an exam.

5. On a few occasions, you will be asked to learn a particular sequence or list that has no pattern, such as the colors in the light spectrum or the planets in the solar system. When this happens, use one of the following five mnemonic practices: a mnemonic sentence, an acronym, an abbreviation, a visualization, or a gimmick.

Mnemonic Sentences.   Your biology instructor may want you to remember the order of classifications in the animal kingdom. There is no logic to this nomenclature, so you might want to create a *mnemonic* sentence that will help you recall each term. Your job is to remember the following divisions in the animal kingdom and their proper sequence: kingdom, phylum, class, order, family, genus, and species. You note that the beginning letters for the classifications are K, P, C, O, F, G, S. Thus, to remember each term, think of a seven-word sentence whose words begin with the seven letters in the biology classifications. You might think of something like: "King Paul called out for Gus and Sam." This sentence will probably stay with you during an exam, when you need to recall this classification sequence.

Acronyms.   You use an acronym to abbreviate a phrase. *Acronyms* are made up of the first letter of each word of the phrase; these letters make a word or a new word. NATO, for example, stands for North Atlantic Treaty Organization, and its initial letters can be pronounced as a word. You can make up your own acronyms when you cannot use categorization to remember a particular chunk of information. For example, if you cannot remember the parts of an atom, you can create the acronym PEN to stand for "proton," "electron," and "neutron."

Abbreviations.   You can use abbreviations in a similar fashion. *Abbreviations* are made up of the first letter of each word in a phrase. Unlike acronyms, these abbreviations do not spell out a word. MVM could be your abbreviation for remembering the three planets besides Earth that are closest to the Sun: Mercury, Venus, and Mars.

Visualizations.   Another successful memory aid is called a *visualization*. In a visualization, you attach what you need to learn to something visual. You have already learned something about visualizing when you studied the spatial-geographic pattern (see Chapter 6). Here, you learned that in biology and geography courses it is helpful to see how one part of an organism or location relates to another.

Visualizing can also prove helpful in learning unrelated pieces of information; you create a picture that incorporates the information into it. For example, if you cannot remember that lapis lazuli is a semiprecious stone, you may want to invent a scene in which a queen has a beautiful stone in her lap. Note the pun on the word "lap." This scene with the jewel on the queen's lap should help you recall the first part of the word and the fact that this stone is precious, worn by queens. You should use such an elaborate visual strategy, though, only when association and categorization have failed to make the proper learning connections for you.

Gimmicks.   Gimmicks can also be used to trigger your memory when the conventional learning strategies have failed. *Gimmicks* are simply word games or tricks to help you remember; they are often used in learning to spell difficult words. If you have difficulty spelling "conscience," for example, you might remember its spelling if you learned the slogan "There is a *science* to spelling the word *conscience*." Similarly, if you cannot remember that the noun "principal" refers to a person, you could think of your principal as your *pal*. By remembering "pal," you will no longer confuse *principal*, the person, with *principle*, the rule or belief. Instructors will often teach you these spelling gimmicks, but you may be imaginative enough to make up your own.

Summary

The brain has two storage capacities: short-term and long-term memory. As a student, it is your goal to transfer as much information as possible to long-term memory. You can place more information into long-term memory by studying in short, concentrated periods, by taking spaced study breaks, and by regularly reviewing what you have studied. You will also remember more if you relate what you have learned to several contexts (association). By studying the same material in lecture, in your textbook, and in your study notes, you begin to see it from several perspectives. Categorization is another key learning principle; whenever possible, try to divide information into general and specific categories.

When information has no particular pattern, you may want to use verbal and visual gimmicks to learn it. Generally, though, the most effective way to learn new material is to learn it right the first time—by putting it into logical categories and associating it with what you already know about it.

Summary Box   *Memory Aids*

What are they?	*Why do you use them?*
Study techniques that help place information into long-term memory Three basic learning principles: (1) rehearsal, (2) association, and (3) categorization Some of the more successful memory practices: (1) concentration techniques, (2) mnemonic sentences, (3) acronyms, (4) abbreviations, (5) visualizations, and (6) spelling gimmicks	To help you retain information and easily recall it for examinations

Skills Practice

Exercise 14.1 Applying Memory Aids to Study Material

Your job is to use a memory aid to learn the following ten pieces of information. Your answers, of course, will vary from those of other students.

1. Think of a gimmick to help you remember the difference in spelling and meaning between *stationery* (writing paper) and *stationary* (not moving).

2. Think of a gimmick that will help you remember the difference in spelling and meaning between *allusion* (reference) and *illusion* (unreal image).

3. Think of a gimmick that will help you remember the difference in meaning between *among* (used in comparing three or more) and *between* (used in comparing no more than two).

4. Think of a gimmick that will help you remember the difference in spelling and meaning between *capital* (meaning chief, or principal) and *capitol* (meaning a building that is the seat of government).

5. Think of a visualization that will help you remember that Nimrod was a mighty hunter referred to in the Bible. Describe the scene in a sentence or two.

6. Think of an acronym that will help you remember the colors of the light spectrum: red, orange, yellow, green, blue, indigo, and violet. Remember that an acronym is a word that is made up of the first letter of each word in the series you want to learn.

7. Think of a mnemonic sentence that will help you remember the first five presidents of the United States: Washington, Adams, Jefferson, Madison, and Monroe.

8. Think of an abbreviation that will help you recall the three most populous cities in the world: Tokyo, Mexico City, and Sao Paulo.

9. Imagine that you need to remember for your anthropology class the three different kinds of societies: egalitarian, rank, and stratified. Think of an abbreviation to help you recall these three types of societies.

Answers will vary. Find sample answers on p. 412.

10. Assume that you have to learn the meaning of *zealous* (eager or passionate). Use the learning theory of association to help you recall the meaning and uses of *zealous*. Add prefixes and suffixes to this word.

Exercise 14.2
Self-Evaluation:
Applying Memory
Tips and Theory to
Your Studies

The following ten questions will test the learning theories that you learned in the introduction. Answer these questions as they pertain to your studies. You may want to share your answers with other students and your instructor; there are no right or wrong answers.

1. To test the theory of interference, study back to back for courses that are similar in content. What problems do you find?

2. To test the theory of interference, study back to back for courses that are different in content. What happens? Do you learn more easily?

3. To test the theory of rehearsal, read for thirty to fifty minutes, but do nothing else. Do not take notes, do not discuss the material, and do not review. Then take a ten-minute break. After the break, recite what you remember. Is your summary complete? What information did you miss?

4. To again test the theory of rehearsal, read for thirty to fifty minutes, but this time take notes, discuss, and review. Then take a ten-minute break. Finally, recite what you remember. Is your summary complete? Is it better than the summary in question 3?

5. To test your rehearsing skills, go over your study notes, lecture notes, text markings, and study maps for one of your classes. See which rehearsal techniques you find most helpful. In a sentence or two, discuss how the following rehearsal techniques helped you remember the material:

   a. underlining: _____

   _____

   b. making marginal notes: _____

   _____

   c. summarizing: _____

   _____

   d. paraphrasing: _____

   _____

   e. making study maps: _____

   _____

   f. reviewing your textbook underlinings and notes: _____

   _____

   g. reviewing your study maps: _____

   _____

   h. other techniques: _____

   _____

6. In a difficult course requiring textbook reading, use the check-marking technique to improve your concentration. Try this technique for several days. In a sentence or two, discuss how or if your reading concentration improved.

7. Of the courses you are taking, choose one that requires you to memorize. Make up an acronym to help you remember a chunk of information.

8. Of the courses you are taking, choose one that requires you to memorize certain material. Make up an abbreviation or mnemonic sentence to help you learn this material.

9. Choose a course you are taking that has a difficult word you need to learn. Think of a gimmick that will help you remember either its spelling or its meaning.

10. Find another word for the course that you used for question 8. Create a visualization that will help you remember the meaning of that word.

Answers will vary. Ask instructor for sample answers.

15 Suggestions for Taking Objective Tests

Objective tests

◑ Multiple choice   ◑ True-false   ◑ Matching

So far you have learned to read your textbook critically, take notes from your textbook and from lectures, and use memory aids when you cannot remember information. You use all of these skills when you prepare for an exam. In most courses, how well you do on exams determines how well you do in the course.

You will be taking two kinds of exams: objective and essay. Each type of exam requires a different set of practices. This chapter looks at objective tests.

What Are Objective Tests?

For objective tests, you often need to have learned many details and understood the basic concepts. You will have little or no writing to do, because objective exams are often machine-scored. Thus you are usually required to mark the correct response from among two to five choices on the answer sheet. Objective tests usually follow three formats: multiple-choice, true-false, and matching. You will study each type later.

How to Prepare for Objective Tests

If your economics instructor announces that you will be taking a 100-question multiple-choice exam the following week, how should you study for it? Cramming the night before, of course, goes against the principle of learning effectively through spaced intervals. Preparing for a 100-question exam should take you three to five days.

In this period, you should first review your textbook markings. You should be looking for highlighted main ideas and supporting details. Then read your marginal comments, which often give insights not stated in the textbook. If you come upon any new insights or want to underline additional information, do so at this time.

Third, review your study reading notes. These notes will probably repeat much of what you studied in your textbook, but reading the same information from a new perspective will provide an additional context

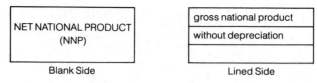

Figure 15-1 *Study card defining* net national product.

for you to remember the material. Fourth, review your lecture notes, underlining key points and making marginal comments as you did in your textbook. Study especially carefully those parts of your notes that are not mentioned in your textbook.

As you study your lecture and study notes, you will come across definitions that you need to remember. Put these terms on 4 × 6 cards, with the term on the blank side of the card and the definition on the lined side. The night before the exam, study these cards carefully. Divide your cards into two piles as you study—those terms that you know and those that you don't. By the end of the night, you want to have all of your cards in the "I know" pile. Your cards should look like the one shown in Figure 15-1, which defines "net national product."* Some students prefer to write these definitions on a sheet of paper, with the term on the left side of the page and the definition to the right, as in the following list of economic terms:

Term	*Explanation*
net national product (NNP)	gross national product without depreciation
gross national product (GNP)	sum of government purchases, consumption, investments, and exports
national income (NI)	net national product without indirect business taxes

The only problem with such a study sheet is that you cannot be sure that you have learned the term, as you can with the cards. On your sheet, you cannot separate the "I knows" from the "don't knows."

Along with note cards and study sheets, you should also design study maps. Look at how the study map in Figure 15-2 relates the same economic terms. The visual nature of study maps may help you remember these terms more easily.

Another very effective way to prepare for an examination is to devise organizational charts. Organizational charts can help you organize study

---

*Walter Pauk, *How to Study in College*, 2nd ed. (Boston: Houghton Mifflin, 1974), p. 172.

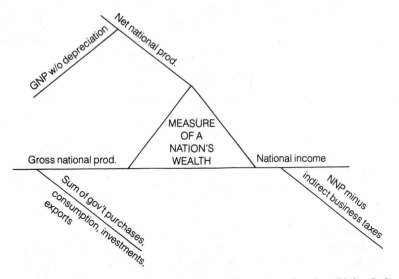

Figure 15-2   *Study map relating economic terms. (Source: Information taken from Philip C. Start, Economics: Principles in Action, 2nd ed. [Belmont, Calif.: Wadsworth, 1978], pp. 174–175.)*

material using few words and a small amount of space. In Chapter 6, you learned about the major organizational patterns that are used to categorize material that you read and study. Of these patterns, cause-effect, problem-solution, comparison-contrast, thesis-support, and description can be applied easily to organizational charts. Look at how the following organizational chart uses the descriptive pattern to characterize the various types of psychological approaches. See how the following chart* is clearly divided into psychological approaches and their descriptions:

Psychological Approach	*Description*
Quantitative	Measures individual differences
Biological	Studies nervous system, genetics, hormones
Cognitive	Studies thought and knowledge
Social	Examines behavior in social context
Clinical	Treats emotional trouble

Similar organizational charts can be created to condense information on the following psychological issues: contrasting behavioral psychology with cognitive psychology, listing the possible causes of schizophrenia,

---

*James W. Kalat, *Introduction to Psychology*, 3rd ed. (Belmont, Calif.: Wadsworth, 1993), p. 14.

proposed psychological solutions to teenage drug use, or evidence showing that psychotherapy is unsuccessful. Organizational charts are best used when you have finished studying your textbook material and your notes and you want to organize the material into small, easily learned units of information.

Finally, you should carefully read any instructor handouts. These handouts often present important material, and your instructor may even design questions from them. Also, if your instructor has provided you with a syllabus, you may want to review the titles of each class meeting to see how the topics relate to one another. If the syllabus does not have titles, review the titles that you have given each lecture.

On the night before the exam, concentrate on concepts; do not cram for details at that point.

How to Answer Multiple-Choice Questions

Multiple-choice questions are the most commonly used objective questions. In the multiple-choice format, a question or statement is posed; this section is called the *stem*. Three to five choices follow, which either answer the question or complete the statement. It is up to you to eliminate the incorrect choices and find the correct one. Look at the following multiple-choice example on Sigmund Freud:

stem   1. According to Freud, the three parts of human consciousness are

choices
      a. the ego, the id, and the libido
      b. the id, the alterego, and the ego
      c. the id, the ego, and the superego
      d. the child, the adult, and the parent

If you know something about Freudian psychology, you know that the correct answer is c. You either write c on your answer sheet or darken c on your answer grid.

Hints on Taking Multiple-Choice Exams

1. Read the stem and each choice as if it were a separate true-false statement. In the previous example, you would have read "According to Freud, the three parts of the human consciousness are the ego, the id, and the libido." Then determine whether this statement is true or false.

2. If you determine the statement to be false, draw a line through it (if your instructor allows you to mark on the exam), as in the following:

    1. According to Freud, the three parts of the human consciousness are
      a. the ego, the id, and the libido

By crossing out, you eliminate choices. You also save yourself time by preventing your eyes from returning to incorrect choices.

3. Continue to eliminate incorrect choices until you find the correct answer. In some difficult questions, two choices may appear correct to you. If this happens, reread the stem to pick up any shades of meaning in the words; then reconsider the two choices. Look at the following question on short-term memory, from which two choices have already been eliminated:

> 2. The best example of the use of short-term memory is
>
>   a. reciting key points in reading material
>   b. repeating a phone number just told to you
>   c. ~~understanding what categorization means and using this information on an essay exam~~
>   d. ~~remembering the name of a friend whom you have not seen for eight years~~

You can eliminate c and d, because both are examples of information that has been in long-term memory for a long time. Both a and b, however, refer to recently learned information. In rereading the stem, note that the question is asking for the *best* example of short-term memory. Reciting helps put information into long-term memory, so b is the best answer. You need to use your best skills in logic and critical reading when you come upon two choices that both seem correct.

4. Question choices that include absolute terms of qualification, such as "always," "never," and "only." Choices using these terms are frequently incorrect because they need to be true in every case, and few statements are always true. Look at the following question on categorization:

> 3. Which statement best describes categorization?
>
>   a. Categorization and association are never both used to learn new information.
>   b. Categorization is always used to learn disorganized information.
>   c. Categorization is an unsuccessful learning technique.
>   d. Categorization is an effective learning technique used by students in several disciplines to learn new material.

You would be correct in omitting both a and b as correct answers, because the qualifiers "never" and "always" insist that these statements be true in every case. If you can think of one exception for each choice, you can eliminate that choice. You are then left with c and d. Knowing that categorization is a basic learning principle, you would choose d as the correct answer.

5. Look for choices that give complete information. Although incomplete answers may not be false, they do not qualify as acceptable choices. Study this question on rehearsal:

4. Which statement gives the best definition of rehearsal?

   a. Rehearsal is a learning process involving rereading.
   b. Rehearsal is a learning process involving rewriting.
   c. Rehearsal is a learning process that helps put information into long-term memory.
   d. Rehearsal is a learning process that may use all of the senses to place information into long-term memory.

Although choices a, b, and c are all partially correct, choice d is like the main idea for the three preceding choices, so it is the best choice.

6. Read carefully for the terms "not," "except," and "but" in the stem. These words completely change the meaning of the question. If you skip over these terms, you may know the answer, yet still choose incorrectly. Consider the following question on rehearsal:

   5. As a learning process, rehearsal includes all of the following activities except

      a. rereading
      b. reciting
      c. discussing
      d. reading

Note how the word "except" reverses the question, asking you to choose the activity that does not involve rehearsal. Choice d is that activity. If you had overlooked "except," you could have chosen a, b, or c—all acceptable rehearsal activities.

7. Be careful to read all of the choices, especially those that say "all of these," "both a and b," or "none of these." Instructors who carefully design multiple-choice questions often make "all of these" or "both a and b" correct choices. "None of these" frequently serves as a filler choice, when the test maker has run out of interesting choices. Look at the following question on neural traces and see how the option "both a and b" is thoughtfully designed as the correct choice:

   6. A neural trace is

      a. a mark on the cerebrum
      b. also called a memory groove
      c. only induced by drugs
      d. both a and b

Had you not read all of the choices, you could have marked a as the correct choice.

8. With multiple-choice questions, make educated guesses. If you can eliminate two of the four choices, you have a 50 percent chance of

choosing the correct answer. Be sure that your instructor or the test does not penalize you for guessing. Some standardized tests do. Even if there is a guessing penalty, if you have narrowed your choices down to two, make an educated guess. If you cannot eliminate two or more of the choices, don't spend too much time on that particular question. If there is no guessing penalty, make your choice quickly and move on to the next question. If there is a guessing penalty and you cannot narrow your choices down to two, leave that answer blank.

Many instructors criticize multiple-choice exams, saying that the best indicator of what a student knows is an essay exam. Although this is a valid point, multiple-choice questions are the most frequently used type of objective question on standardized tests. You will be taking such tests in your college career, so you need to have an efficient set of practices for taking them.

| *How to Answer True–False Questions* | True–false questions are also popular on objective exams. Unlike multiple-choice questions, which may have up to five choices, true–false questions have only two. Your chance of being correct is always 50 percent. Instructors emphasize details when they design true–false questions; so when you study for a true–false test, you need to look carefully at the details. |

Hints on Taking True–False Exams

1. For a statement to be true, each part must be true. One detail in the statement can make the entire statement false. When you read a true–false statement, look for the following: the "who," the "what," the "why," the "when," the "where," and the "how much." The answer to each of these questions must be correct for you to mark the entire statement true. Look at the following true–false question on Jean Piaget, and see if it correctly answers the "who," the "what," and the "when":

   Jean Piaget made some revolutionary discoveries about child behavior during the nineteenth century.

   The "who" (Jean Piaget) and the "what" (child behavior) are correct, but the "when" is not. Piaget did his research during the twentieth century.

   Study the key parts of this statement on the Los Angeles School District:

   With 48 percent of its 490,000 students Spanish-speaking, the Los Angeles School District continued to search for competent bilingual teachers in 1987.

With this question, the "who," the "what," and the "when" are correct. The Los Angeles School District was concerned with hiring more bilingual teachers in 1987. But the "how many" is incorrect; the correct enrollment for this school district in 1987 was 590,000. Because this one bit of information is incorrect, you must mark the entire question incorrect.

2. Like multiple-choice questions, true–false questions also may use qualifiers such as "never," "always," and "only." These qualifiers frequently make the statements false. On the other hand, less definite qualifiers like "often," "may," "many," "most," "frequently," and "usually" tend to make the statement true. Read the following true–false statement on association:

> The memory technique of association is always used when you learn a new word.

Although association is successfully used in vocabulary learning, it is not always used. The word "always" makes this statement false. If you can think of one case in which the statement is untrue, then the statement is false. But see how a less inclusive qualifier can make the same statement true:

> The memory principle of association is often used when a student learns new words.

The word "often" allows for the statement to have some exceptions. Because of the flexibility that "often" gives this statement, you can mark this statement true.

3. In designing true–false questions, instructors frequently match terms with inappropriate definitions. So in preparing for a true–false test, be sure that you know your definitions and your people. Read this example on categorization:

> Categorization involves placing a word in several contexts in order to remember it. Association, not categorization, is the process of placing a word in several contexts.

The test maker consciously exchanged "association" with "categorization." If you did not know the meaning of both words, you may not have chosen the correct answer.

How to Answer Matching Questions

Of the three kinds of examination questions, matching questions are the hardest to answer correctly by guessing. In answering matching questions, you need to know the information very well. In the matching format, you are given a list of words in one column and a list of explanations of these words in a second column, often to the right of the first list. It is your job to match correctly the word with the explanation.

Hints on Taking Matching Exams

1. Look at both columns before you begin answering. Are there terms in one column and definitions in another? people in one column and descriptions of them in another? people in the left column and quotations in the right column? What pattern do you detect in the following example from learning theory?

   1. neural trace
   2. rehearsal
   3. association

   a. a process of placing information into several contexts to ensure retention
   b. a process of transferring information from short-term memory to long-term memory
   c. a physiological mark on the cerebrum storing a bit of information

   In this set, terms are on the left, definitions on the right.

2. With each correct match, cross out the term and the explanation of it (if your instructor does not plan to reuse the test). In this way, you save time by not rereading material that you have already covered. Look at how crossing out is used for the following matching questions.

   ____c____ 1. ~~neutal trace~~
   _____ 2. rehearsal
   _____ 3. association

   a. a process of placing information into several contexts to ensure retention
   b. a process of transferring information from short-term memory to long-term memory
   c. ~~a physiological mark on the cerebrum storing a bit of information~~

3. If the information in the right-hand column is lengthy, begin reading in this column first. Read the explanation; then match it with the appropriate term. You save time by not rereading the lengthy explanations.*

How to Take Objective Tests

Here are some suggestions to use when you are taking an objective test:

1. Read over all of the directions carefully. Know what you need to do.

2. Plan your time. If your test has three parts—true–false, multiple-choice, and matching—divide your exam hour into equal time

---

*James Shepherd, *College Study Skills* (Boston: Houghton Mifflin, 1990), p. 247.

allotments. Check your watch so that you do not stay on any one section of the exam for too long.

3. Read through the questions quickly to determine the difficulty level of the exam.

4. Answer the easiest sections first. Since you have a better chance of getting the easier questions right, do not wait until the end of the hour to answer them.

5. Do not spend too much time on any one question. If you are unsure about an answer, make an educated guess. Then place a mark to the left of the question so that if you have time, you can go back to it.

6. Check your numbering so that the number on your answer sheet corresponds to the number on your exam booklet. Students often place a correct answer on the wrong number of their answer grid and get the question wrong.

7. If possible, leave five to ten minutes at the end of the exam to review your answers. Check for carelessness. Change only those answers you are reasonably sure are incorrect. Do not change a guess; more often the guess is correct and the correction is not.

Summary

There are three major types of objective tests: multiple-choice, true–false, and matching. Each type of question requires a different set of practices. The multiple-choice question is the most commonly used objective question. With multiple-choice and true–false questions, you can make educated guesses; matching questions, on the other hand, leave little room for guesswork. With matching questions, you need to know names and definitions well.

Multiple-choice questions are frequently used on entrance and professional exams. Thus it is important to develop a successful set of practices for answering them.

Summary Box   *Objective Tests*

What are they?	*How do you take them?*
Examinations, frequently machine-scored, that test the breadth of your knowledge on a subject Three most common types: multiple-choice, true–false, and matching	Multiple-choice: learn to eliminate incorrect answers; cross them out and consider other choices True–false: look for statements that are absolute; they are frequently false Matching: see how the columns are organized; with each match that you make, cross out the statement in one column and the name or term in the other

Skills Practice

*Exercise 15.1
Answering Multiple-
Choice Questions*

Read the following textbook excerpt about incest taboos from an anthropology textbook. Underline important points and make marginal comments. After reading, recite either by taking notes or by making a study map. When you think you know the material, answer the five multiple-choice questions that follow. Before you answer these questions, you may want to refer to pp. 304–307, which deal with practices to use when answering multiple-choice questions.

Marriage Rules: Incest Taboos

Every society has rules about mating. In all societies, there are some prohibitions on mating between persons in certain relationships or from certain social groups. The most universal prohibition is that on mating among certain kinds of kin: mother-son, father-daughter, and sister-brother. The taboos on mating between kin always extend beyond this immediate family group, however. In our own society, the taboo extends to the children of our parents' siblings (in our kinship terminology called first cousins); in other societies, individuals are not permitted to mate with others who may be related up to the fifth generation. These prohibitions on mating (that is, sexual relations) between relatives or people classified as relatives are called *incest taboos.*

Because sexual access is one of the most important rights conferred by marriage, incest taboos effectively prohibit marriage as well as mating among certain kin. The outstanding exception to the almost universal taboo on mating and marriage among members of the nuclear family are those cases of brother-sister marriage among royalty in ancient Egypt, in traditional Hawaiian society, and among Inca royalty in Peru. Incest taboos have always been of interest to anthropologists, who have attempted to explain their origin and persistence in human society, particularly as they apply to primary (or nuclear) family relationships. Many theories have been advanced, and we will look here at four major ones.

Inbreeding Avoidance

The inbreeding avoidance theory holds that mating between close kin produces deficient, weak children and is genetically harmful to the species. The incest taboo is therefore adaptive because it limits inbreeding. This theory, proposed in the late nineteenth century, was later rejected for a number of decades on the ground that inbreeding could produce advantages as well as disadvantages for the group, by bringing out recessive genes of both a superior and an inferior character. Recent work in population genetics has given more weight to the older view that inbreeding *is* usually harmful to a human population. The proportion of negative recessive traits to adaptive recessive ones is very high, and in the human animal, inbreeding has definite disadvantages. Furthermore, these disadvantages are far more likely to appear as a result of the mating of primary relatives (mother-son, father-daughter, sister-brother) than of other relatives, even first cousins. It would seem, then, that the biological adaptiveness of the incest taboo as it applies to the nuclear family must be considered in explaining both its origins and its persistence.

The question raised here, of course, is how prescientific peoples could understand the connection between close inbreeding and the biological disadvantages that result. But the adaptive results of the incest taboo need not have been consciously recognized in order to persist; rather, groups that had such a taboo would have had more surviving children than groups without the taboo. This reproductive advantage would eventually account for its universality as groups without the taboo died out.*

Directions: Choose the correct letter to answer the following questions. Place all answers in the answer box.

1. Which of the following is not an example of the incest taboo?

   a. mother mating with son
   b. brother mating with sister
   c. close friends mating with each other
   d. father mating with daughter

2. Exceptions to the incest taboo have sometimes been allowed with

   a. the lower class
   b. royal families
   c. the middle class
   d. all of these

3. The inbreeding avoidance theory suggests that incest leads to

   a. miscarriages
   b. marital problems
   c. genetically weak children
   d. none of these

4. Recent research in genetics has

   a. rejected the inbreeding avoidance theory
   b. supported the inbreeding avoidance theory
   c. neither supported nor rejected the inbreeding avoidance theory
   d. questioned the need for the incest taboo

5. Anthropologists believe that the incest taboo evolved in prescientific cultures because

   a. of their strong religious beliefs

1. _____

2. _____

3. _____

4. _____

5. _____

_____
80%

(score = # correct × 20)
Find answers on p. 413.

---

*Serena Nanda, *Cultural Anthropology*, 3rd ed. (Belmont, Calif.: Wadsworth, 1987), pp. 205–206. Used by permission.

b. of their rigid family structure
c. ancient cultures passed on all of their traditions from one generation to the next
d. those who ignored it died out

Exercise 15.2
Answering True–
False Questions

Read the following textbook excerpt on the sun from an environmental studies textbook. Underline the important points and make marginal comments. After reading, recite either by outlining or by making a study map. When you think that you have learned the information, answer the five true–false questions that follow. You may want to refer to pp. 307–308, which present practices to use in answering true–false questions. Remember that true–false questions often test your knowledge of details.

The Sun: Source of Energy for Life on Earth

Just as an economy runs on money, the ecosphere runs on energy. *The source of the radiant energy that sustains all life on Earth is the sun.* It warms the Earth and provides energy for the photosynthesis in green plants. These plants, in turn, synthesize the carbon compounds that keep them alive and that serve as food for almost all other organisms. Solar energy also powers the water cycle, which purifies and removes salt from ocean water to provide the fresh water upon which land life depends.

The sun is a medium-sized star composed mostly of hydrogen. At its center, the sun is so hot that a pinhead of its material could kill a person over 161 kilometers (100 miles) away. Under the conditions of extremely high temperatures and pressures found in the interior of the sun, light nuclei of hydrogen atoms are fused together to form slightly heavier nuclei of helium atoms. In this process of *nuclear fusion* some of the mass of the hydrogen nuclei is converted into energy.

Thus, the sun is a giant *nuclear-fusion reactor* 150 million kilometers (93 million miles) away from the Earth. Every second, the sun converts about 3.7 billion kilograms (4.1 billion tons) of its total mass into energy. It has probably been in existence for 6 billion years, and estimates are that it has enough hydrogen left to keep going for at least another 8 billion years.*

Directions: Read the following statements. Write A for true and B for false. Place all answers in the answer box.

1. The major element that makes up the sun is nitrogen.
2. In the sun's middle, heat transforms lighter helium to heavier hydrogen.
3. The sun is 140 kilometers (92 million miles) away from the earth.

1. _____

2. _____

3. _____

4. _____

5. _____

80%

Ask instructor for answers.

---

*G. Tyler Miller, Jr., *Living in the Environment*, 4th ed. (Belmont, Calif.: Wadsworth, 1985), p. 32. Used by permission.

4. The sun has been called a giant nuclear-fission reactor.

5. The sun was created 8 billion years ago and will not die for another 6 billion years.

Exercise 15.3
Answering Matching
Questions

Read the following excerpt, which defines musical terms from a music history textbook. Underline important points and make marginal comments. After reading, recite either by outlining or by making a study map. When you think that you know the material, answer the five matching questions that follow. You may want to refer to p. 309, which presents practices to use in answering matching questions.

Musical Terminology

Certain musical terms are basic to an understanding of music literature. The first term to learn is *music,* which is defined as a combination of sounds that are organized and meaningful, occurring in a prescribed span of time and usually having pitch. In the definition of music is another term, *pitch,* which is defined as the degree of highness or lowness of a sound. Related to pitch is *interval.* Interval is defined as the distance between two pitches. The most fundamental interval is an *octave.* Finally, *melody* is defined as pitches sounded one after another, presented in a logical series that forms a satisfying musical unit.*

Directions: Match a letter from column B with the appropriate number in column A. Place all answers in the answer box.

Column A	Column B
1. octave	a. a combination of pitches forming a pleasing unit
2. pitch	b. a combination of organized sounds that happen in time and usually have pitch
3. melody	c. the distance between two pitches
4. interval	d. the highness or lowness of a sound
5. music	e. the most fundamental interval

1. _____

2. _____

3. _____

4. _____

5. _____

_____
80%
(score = # correct × 20)
Find answers on p. 413.

---

*Adapted from Charles Hoffer, *The Understanding of Music,* 5th ed. (Belmont, Calif.: Wadsworth, 1985), pp. 22–24. Used by permission.

16 Suggestions for Taking Essay Exams and Math or Science Tests

Essay types		
◖ Short answer	◖ Short essay	◖ Extended essay

Key words in essays		
◖ Significant	◖ Defend	◖ Analyze
◖ Summarize	◖ Trace	◖ Compare/contrast

Essay exams are different in many ways from objective tests. Unlike objective tests, which ask you to remember many details, essay exams make you choose main ideas and major details from a large body of material and then form an organized response. When you are writing an essay exam, you need to recall main ideas and major details quickly. Problem-solving questions in math and the sciences are similar to essay questions. The major difference is that instead of using words, you are using numbers and symbols. In both an essay exam and a math or science problem, you need to use skills in logic and organization. Unlike objective exams, the best essay and math or science exams ask you to generate important information yourself.

How to Prepare for an Essay Exam

When preparing for an essay exam, you again need to review your textbook underlinings, textbook comments, study reading notes, lecture notes, organizational charts, and study maps. (See the section in Chapter 15 titled "How to Prepare for Objective Tests.") Instead of trying to remember many details, as you would in preparing for an objective test, for an essay exam you need to concentrate on significant main ideas and details of support. Your job is to reduce a great deal of information into its significant points. This may not be easy for you at first.

If your instructor has provided you in advance with several possible essay topics, find information in your study material to answer them. If your instructor does not provide you with questions, check to see whether there are discussion questions at the end of your textbook chap-

> Question: Define the learning process of rehearsal, and
>   give specific examples of this learning technique.

Front Side

Figure 16-1   *Front of a study card, with an essay question.*

> Rehearsal
>
>   Def: the active use of the senses to place information
>   into long-term memory
>
>   Specific expls:
>
>   rereading—of sig info in your text (seeing)
>   writing—making study sheets or maps in the forms of
>   summaries (touching)
>   discussion—verbal exchange w yourself or in a disc
>   grp to put info into your own wds (hearing)

Back Side

Figure 16-2   *Back of a study card, answering the question.*

ters. Find the ones that you think are most important, then locate information that would best address each question. As you study, you should formulate your own essay questions from topics that you think are important. You can often design your own essay questions from the divisions and subdivisions of your textbook chapters or from the lecture titles in your syllabus or lecture notes.

After you have reviewed your notes and underlinings, write the three or four most likely essay topics on a separate sheet of paper or on the blank side of 5 × 8 note cards. These sheets and cards are similar to those mentioned in Chapter 15 for preparing for an objective exam. On the back side of the paper or the lined side of the card, answer the question, giving pertinent main ideas and major details. Use a numeral–

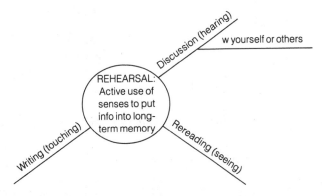

Figure 16-3 *Study map showing the answer to an essay question.*

letter or indenting format. Don't write this information in paragraph form at this time. Save your more thorough sentence writing for the essay exam itself. The cards or sheets of paper should look something like what is shown in Figures 16-1 and 16-2.

Once you have completed the study sheets or cards, turn each over to the question side to see if you can orally respond to the question. See if you can quickly remember the main idea and the necessary supporting details. If it is hard for you to remember the supporting details, use a memory aid. "RWD" is an abbreviation that you could design to remember "rereading, writing, and discussion"—the details for the essay question in Figure 16-1. Review these cards or sheets until you can respond promptly to each question. A key to doing well on an essay exam is being able to recall main ideas and accurate details with ease.

Study maps are also good tools to use when you study for essay tests. Figure 16-3 shows how the information on rehearsal can be neatly arranged into a study map. If you had several terms to learn associated with rehearsal, you could effectively learn them all in an organizational chart.

How to Read an Essay Question

Having studied well for your essay test, you are now ready for the questions. Understanding the intent of the question is as important as being prepared for the exam. Study the following key terms, which are commonly used in essay questions, and learn how they are used.

Words That Ask for Retelling of Material

summarize, survey, list, outline

If these words appear in your question, you are being asked to give only the important points. You should not concentrate on many details or on analyzing any one point in depth.

Sample question: List the major stages in the development of the human fetus.

To answer this question well, you should list each step in the fetal development of the child. You should then briefly comment on each stage, but you do not need to discuss the relationship of one stage to another or the importance of any of these stages.

Words That Ask You to Make Inferences

discuss, explain

These are two of the most frequently used words in essay questions. They ask you to give the "why" of an argument. You must carefully choose those details that clarify your main idea.

Sample question: Discuss four reasons for the entry of the United States into World War II.

In this question, you need to choose those examples that account for the United States's entry into World War II. These reasons are often your own, so be sure to include terms of qualification when you are presenting opinions—words like *may, might, likely, it is suggested,* and so on. See pp. 166–167 for a more thorough list of qualifiers.

A Word That Asks You to Define

define

Define usually asks you for a short answer, no more than three or four sentences. You are not asked to analyze, just to give the term's major characteristics. Just as a dictionary definition is concise, so should your response be concise.

Sample question: Define prejudice as used in sociology.

Here you are being asked to explain prejudice from a sociological perspective. You are not being asked to list its various meanings or to explain its history. Your focus should be on how prejudice relates to sociology.

Words Showing Similarities and Differences

compare, contrast

Compare means to show both similarities and differences. To avoid confusion, some instructors use the phrase "compare and contrast." *Contrast* used singly means to show differences. With contrast questions, you are treating opposite sets of information, so use transitions of contrast: *unlike, conversely,* and so on. With strict comparison questions, you are treating similar sets of information; here, use transitions of similarity, such as *likewise, similarly,* and so on. See p. 107 for a more thorough list of transitions of comparison and contrast.

Sample question: Compare and contrast the attitudes of Presidents Reagan and Carter regarding social welfare programs.

In this question, you need to cite programs and legislation from both administrations that show similarities and differences.

Words That Ask You to Critique

analyze, examine, evaluate

Questions using these words are asking you to express a point of view. When you evaluate, you must even judge the merit of your topic. The details you choose are important because they present the bulk of your argument. Critique words are often used in essay questions in the humanities—literature, art, music, film—where you are asked to judge the value of a poem, a painting, or a film. These questions can be difficult because you are being asked to do more than summarize.

Sample question: Analyze the major characters in Dickens's *Great Expectations.* Are these characters successful?

This question is asking you to choose characters in the novel whose actions and traits make them believable. Ultimately, you are judging the success of Dickens's characters. So you need to choose carefully those details that demonstrate Dickens's success or failure in rendering character.

A Word That Asks You to Take a Stand

defend

Defend is often used in speech topics or in essay questions in political science or history. With defend questions, you take a definite stand, presenting only evidence that supports this position. In this sense, defend questions ask you to ignore evidence that goes against your position.

> *Sample question:* Defend the premise that nuclear arms will one day lead to nuclear holocaust.

In answering this question, you should discuss only how nuclear arms are a threat to peace. If you suggested that nuclear arms are a deterrent to war, you would weaken your argument.

A Word That Shows Connections

trace

Trace is mainly used in history essay questions where you are asked to discuss a series of events and show their relationship to one other. Again, you need to be selective in choosing details that support the connections you see.

> *Sample question:* Trace the development of labor unions in the United States from 1900 to the present.

In this question, you need to choose the important figures and events that led to the formation of unions in the United States; you also need to show how events or individuals influenced other events or individuals.

Words That Ask for Important Information

significant, critical, key, important, major

In most subjects, instructors use these words to guide you in presenting only meaningful evidence. These terms subtly ask you to distinguish the significant from the insignificant. An instructor using these words will often criticize your essay if you fail to choose the important evidence.

> *Sample question:* Discuss three key factors that led to the Great Depression in the United States.

Your instructor may have discussed ten factors, but you are asked to discuss only three. Here, you need to review the ten factors to determine which three have priority. This is difficult to do because you are both summarizing and evaluating information.

Kinds of Essay Questions

Three basic types of essay questions are used on exams: those that ask for a short answer, the short essay, and the extended essay. Each type requires a different set of practices.

The Short-Answer Question.   In the short-answer question, you are asked to respond in a phrase, a sentence, or several sentences. In a one-hour exam, you can expect to answer up to twenty short-answer questions. The key to doing well is to be as concise and specific as you can. In biology and geology courses using short-answer questions, instructors are often looking for the breadth and accuracy of your knowledge, not your writing style. Ask your instructor whether you need to answer the short-answer questions in sentences. If the answer is no, answer in phrases; you will be able to write more during the hour. In contrast, in an English course your instructor will probably want you to answer the short-answer questions in complete sentences that are correctly punctuated.

Look at the following short-answer question and study the response that received full credit.

> *Question:* Name and identify the three branches of the federal government.
> *Answer:*
>
> 1. legislative: makes laws; made up of House and Senate
> 2. executive: sees that laws are carried out; President
> 3. judicial: sees that laws are enforced; Supreme Court and other federal courts

This student has presented accurate information in an organized way. Beside each government branch, the student describes the activity, then names the person or agency responsible.

Now see how this same question is answered poorly.

> *Question:* Name and identify the three branches of the federal government.
> *Answer:*
>
> 1. legislative: works on laws; made up of two houses
> 2. executive: the President
> 3. judicial: courts

This student has not presented the information in an organized way or with enough detail. Although the student names the legislative branch, "works on laws" is vague. With the executive branch, the student names the President but does not describe the function. With the judicial branch, the Supreme Court is not specifically named, nor does the student mention the Court's function.

The Short-Essay Question.   The short-essay question asks you to write an organized paragraph of several sentences. In an hour, you should be able to answer up to five such questions. Your goal when writing the short-essay answer is to present your main idea or thesis right away, then present accurate details of support. These details must follow logically from your main idea. If you have completed the writing assignments in this book, you are familiar with how a convincing paragraph is put together.

Read the following short-essay question and the response that received full credit.

Question: Discuss the three major characteristics of human language.
Answer:

Human language has three qualities that distinguish it from animal communication. First, human language uses a limited number of sounds that produce thousands of utterances. Second, human speech is not imitative. The human being can generate a sentence never heard before. Finally, human language can discuss what is not there. Human beings can discuss the past and future as well as the present.

Do you see how the student directly addresses the question? The main-idea sentence comes first, stating that there are three characteristics of human language. Then the sentences of support discuss these characteristics. The student has used the transitions "first, second, and finally" to direct the reader to these three characteristics.

Now consider this second response, which is both poorly organized and less detailed.

Question: Discuss the three major characteristics of human language.
Answer:

Human language has three qualities. Human language uses few sounds. Also, human language uses sentences. Humans can also discuss what is not there. Philosophers have spent centuries discussing what language is all about.

Note how the main-idea sentence is too general, so the student makes no attempt to distinguish human language from animal language. Note how the second detail sentence, "Also, human language uses sentences," does not discuss how the human being can generate sentences that have never before been uttered. This supporting detail does not directly address the uniqueness of human language. Note how the last sentence, "Philosophers have spent centuries discussing what language is all about," introduces an entirely new topic, so the paragraph loses its focus.

The Extended Essay Question.   You will often be asked to write on only one topic during a one-hour exam. Obviously, your instructor is expecting

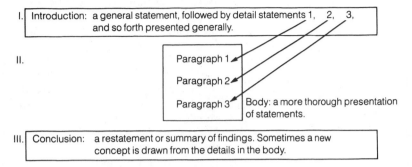

Figure 16-4   *Diagram of an extended essay.*

you to write more than one paragraph during this hour. In an hour, you should be able to write several organized paragraphs. This type of essay response is known as the extended essay.

In structure, the extended essay resembles the short essay. The main idea of the paragraph becomes the first paragraph, or introduction, of the extended essay. The detail sentences of the paragraph then each become separate paragraphs. Together, these paragraphs are referred to as the body. Unlike the short essay, the extended essay has a concluding paragraph, called the conclusion, which often summarizes the key points of the essay. Look at Figure 16-4, which shows the structure of the extended essay and states the purpose of its three parts.

The extended essay is difficult to write well at first because you must successfully use several organizational skills. Start by committing the information in Figure 16-4 to memory, so that each essay you write has a recognizable introduction, body, and conclusion. Also, begin using transitions to join sentences and to hook one paragraph to another. By using such transitions as *for example* or *to conclude,* you will give additional order to your essay. In Chapter 6, on organizational patterns, there are lists of several transitions that you may want to review and use in your extended essays.

Read the following extended essay question and response. See if you can locate the introduction, the body, and the conclusion, and note how transitions are used.

Question: Discuss the three major functions of religion.
Answer:

(1) Every society has a religion of some sort. Although the beliefs and expressions of religion vary from one culture to another, three basic functions emerge when you study all religions. For one, religion helps clarify the unexplained. Second, religion helps reduce anxiety among its followers. Third, religion helps give order to society.

(2) Every culture has tried through religion to answer such questions as where the universe came from and where we go after death.

Western religions explain their origin in the Book of Genesis. In this book, we learn that one God created parts of the universe and the world on separate days. Eastern religions see many gods as creating the universe. Western religions believe that human souls live after death, whereas Eastern religions such as Hinduism believe that human beings are reincarnated into other beings after death.

(3) Prayer seems to be part of all religions. In each culture, prayer seems to relieve anxiety. In many African cultures, tribesmen perform rituals to help crops grow or to cure the sick. Prayer in Western cultures works similarly. Western priests often ask their parishioners to pray for the health of their sick loved ones. In each case, prayer becomes an outlet to relieve anxiety.

(4) Finally, religion has an important ordering effect on society. Religious services almost always accompany births, baptisms, marriages, and deaths. And the faithful are invited to witness these events. Such group activities give to the members of the religion a sense of community. Just think of how many wars have been fought over religious beliefs, and you will realize how closely tied religion is to social structure.

(5) In conclusion, it is clear that religion still plays an important role in human life. Through the ages religion has helped explain the mysteries of the universe, comforted people in their grief, and given to each culture a set of social rules.

Note how paragraph 1 presents the three issues that the essay intends to discuss. Paragraphs 2, 3, and 4 give the necessary support for the main idea that religion is found in every society. Each paragraph in the body centers its discussion on a separate function of religion. Nowhere in these paragraphs does the discussion lose its focus.

Note also the transitions that signal different sections of the essay: "for one," "second," and "third" in paragraph 1, and "in conclusion" in paragraph 5. Finally, note that the conclusion summarizes the major points made in the essay.

If you want to study other acceptable models of the extended essay, read some of the longer passages that appear at the end of most exercise sections in this book. These longer passages are often modeled after the extended essay.

Now consider how this same question is answered in a disorganized way. Look at this essay to see what is lacking in the introduction, the body, and the conclusion.

Question: Discuss the three major functions of religion.
Answer:

(1) Religion has been used to explain the unexplainable. Each culture has certain creation myths and beliefs about an afterlife. There are many similar creation myths in Western and Eastern religions.

(2) All cultures seem to pray. Prayers help people's problems. People pray in various ways throughout the world. The end is always the same.

(3) Religion has a purpose in society. Many social functions are somehow related to religion. People get together and feel a bond. That is another important function of religion.

Did you note that this essay has no introduction? If you did not have the question before you, you would not know what question this essay was trying to answer. Furthermore, the evidence is vague. In the body, creation myths are mentioned, but no specific creation myths of East and West are discussed. Similarly, the relationship between social functions and religion is presented, but no rituals such as marriage and funerals are introduced. An instructor evaluating this essay would mark it down for its lack of direction and relevant details.

In the next section of this chapter, which analyzes math and science problems and tests, you will see parallels to what you have just learned about essay tests.

How to Prepare for a Math or Science Test

As in preparing for exams in other courses, for a math or science test you will be studying lecture notes, textbook underlinings and comments, and study notes. The study notes are usually solutions to problems. Before you begin studying for your math or science test, see if your instructor has provided you with some sample problems. Also, be sure you know whether you will be allowed to look at your textbook or notes during the test.

You should spend a week reviewing all important material. Because the last class session before an exam in math and science courses is usually a review, it would be helpful if you had done most of your studying before this session. In this review session, you will have the opportunity to ask questions that may have come up during your studying.

When you study, spend most of your time reviewing the problems and solutions shown in your textbook, completed in lecture and study notes, and done as homework. Trace the logic used to solve each problem. While you are reviewing, use note cards to write down important theorems, laws, formulas, and equations. Know these cards well, because you will probably need to recall this information quickly on the exam.

Look at the sample study card in Figure 16-5, from a chemistry study review. Note that the name of the formula is listed on the blank side, and

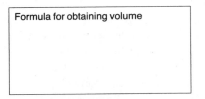

Blank Side   Lined Side

Figure 16-5 *Study card from a chemistry study review.*

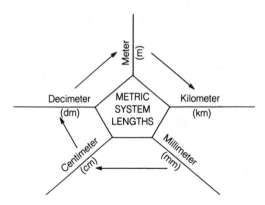

Figure 16-6   *Study map of the metric system.*

the formula itself and a sample solution using the formula are on the lined side. Using the blank side of the card, you can test yourself to see whether you can recall the variables of the formula.

When it is possible to design a study map of math and science information, do so. Since math and science courses build from one lecture to another, seeing connections among units is most helpful; study maps often help you see these connections more easily. Figure 16-6 shows how the metric system is presented via a study map. In this map, the units of measure become progressively larger as your eyes move clockwise.

You can also efficiently learn this material on the metric system by devising an organizational chart like the following:

Metric System Measures

Unit	Size
millimeter	.0001 meter
centimeter	.001 meter
decimeter	.1 meter
dekameter	10 meters
hektometer	100 meters
kilometer	1000 meters

Once you have made these study cards, study maps, and organizational charts, choose three to five problems that you have never done and that will probably be on your test. Complete each problem, and time yourself. If you have difficulty moving from one step to another, try to figure out your confusion. Go back to your notes and textbook.

If your instructor allows crib notes, or notes that list certain formulas and rules, write these out neatly. But do not use these notes as a crutch. Crib notes should be used when you need to use a formula or theorem that is hard to remember.

The night before the exam, do not cram. Just go over your study cards and maps.

How to Take a Math or Science Test

Instructors in math or science generally score an exam by looking at the steps that you used to arrive at a solution. They are often more interested in the way you solved the problem than in the correct answer.

Before you start solving a problem on your test, be sure you know what is being asked of you. The two most commonly used words on math and science tests are *solve* and *prove*. Both words ask you to present the logic of your solution, not just give an answer. Look at the following question on the metric system and its solution.

Question: How many kilograms are there in 2543 grams?

Detailed Solution	*Vague Solution*
1. $1 \text{ kg} = 1000 \text{ grams}$	$\dfrac{2543}{1000} = 2.543$
2. $\text{kg} = \dfrac{\text{g}}{1000}$	
3. $\text{kg} = \dfrac{2543}{1000}$	
4. $\text{kg} = 2.543$	
5. 2.543 kg	

Do you see how you can easily follow the pattern of thought in the first solution? Step 1 shows the conversion, step 2 the formula, and steps 3 and 4 the procedures used to solve the equation. The second answer does not present any of these steps and so does not explain why 1000 is to be divided into 2543.

Hints to Use in Solving Math or Science Problems

Use these steps to solve math or science problems on homework or on exams.

1. Read the question carefully. Determine the unknown. If you have to, write out the unknown in the margin. In the previous solution, kg is the unknown.

2. Reread the question to determine the known quantities. In the previous solution, 2543 grams is the known. You may want to write out the known in the margin as well.

3. Then figure out what the problem is asking you to do.

4. Write out the formulas or equations you need to solve the problem. In the example, the needed formula is $1000 \text{ g} = 1 \text{ kg}$. Then plug your knowns into the formula, and solve for the unknown.

5. When you arrive at an answer, check it by rereading the question. Is it reasonable? In the example, 254,300 kg would be illogical, because you know that kilograms are heavier than grams. You can often spot a simple computational error, such as multiplying when you should have divided, by rereading the question with your answer in mind.

6. If you cannot solve the problem, list the formulas that you know can be used to solve it. Most instructors give partial credit.

Hints for Taking Math, Science, or Essay Tests

Here are some tips for taking all the kinds of examinations discussed in this chapter:

1. Read the directions carefully. Know how many questions you have to answer and the point value assigned to each question.

2. Read through each question, underlining such key words as *analyze*, *solve*, or *major*.

3. Answer the easiest questions first.

4. Jot down a brief outline of what you intend to say for each question or a list of equations you need to use in solving each problem. With these phrases and formulas, you will be able to structure your answers. They will also help you if you draw a momentary blank during the exam.

5. Plan your time wisely. If you are to answer two essay questions or two problems during the hour, be sure to start the second question or problem halfway through the hour.

6. When writing the essay or solving the problem, use only one side of the paper and leave margins. If you want to add information, you can put it either in the margins or on the back side of the paper.

7. If you are pressed for time, list the equations that you intended to use or an outline of the rest of your answer. You will probably get partial credit by including these abbreviated responses.

8. Save at least five minutes at the end of the exam time to review for errors in computation or in spelling, punctuation, and diction.

9. With essay exams, do not expect to write the perfect essay. Your goal is to present accurate information in an organized way.

Summary

Unlike objective tests, which ask you to remember many details, essay tests ask you to present the important points of what you have studied in an organized way and to reduce what you have learned to its essentials. This process of evaluating all that you have studied to find the significant points may be difficult at first. The three most commonly used essay exams are the short-answer exam, the short-essay exam, and the extended essay exam.

Math and science questions are like essay questions; for both, you must present information in a logical way. In place of words, math and science tests use numbers and symbols. Instructors are often looking not just for the correct answer but for how you arrived at your answer.

Effective writing skills and the ability to solve math and science problems are skills that employers are coming to value more and more. Two of your more important goals in college should therefore be to develop efficient writing and problem-solving skills.

Summary Box   *Essay Exams and Math or Science Tests*

What are they?	*How do you do well on them?*
Essay exams: ask for organized responses on material that you have studied; can be short answer, short essay, or extended essay	By reducing information to its essentials By presenting accurate information in an organized way
Math or science tests: ask you to use numbers and symbols to solve a problem in a logical way	By determining known and unknown quantities By choosing correct formulas By showing the steps that you used to arrive at your answer

Skills Practice

**Exercise 16.1
Answering Short-
Essay Questions**

Read the following excerpt on Martin Luther King, Jr., from a sociology textbook. Underline the important points, and make marginal comments. After reading, recite what you have learned, either by taking notes or by creating a study map. When you think that you know the information well, answer the essay question that follows. You may want to reread p. 322, on the short essay.

Martin Luther King, Jr.: The Power of Protest

The civil rights movement invented new techniques for minorities to gain power and influence in American society. *Mass protest* is a technique by which groups seek to obtain a bargaining position for themselves that can induce desired concessions from established powerholders. It is a means of acquiring a bargaining leverage for those who would otherwise be powerless. The protest may challenge established groups by threatening their reputations (unfavorable publicity), their economic position (a boycott), their peace and quiet (disruption of daily activities), or their security (violence or the threat of violence). The protest technique appeals to powerless minorities who have little to bargain with except their promise *not* to protest.

The nation's leading exponent of *nonviolent* protest was Dr. Martin Luther King, Jr. Indeed, King's contributions to the development of a philosophy of nonviolent, direct-action protest on behalf of African Americans won him international acclaim and the Nobel Peace Prize in 1964. King first came to national prominence in 1955, when he was only twenty-five years old; he led a year-long bus boycott in Montgomery, Alabama, to protest discrimination in seating on public buses. In 1957 he formed the Southern Christian Leadership Conference (SCLC) to provide encouragement and leadership to the growing nonviolent protest movement in the South.

In 1963 a group of Alabama clergymen petitioned Martin Luther King, Jr., to call off mass demonstrations in Birmingham, Alabama. King, who had been arrested in the demonstrations, replied in his famous "Letter from Birmingham Jail":

> You may well ask, "Why direct action? Why sit-ins, marches, etc.? Isn't negotiation a better path?" You are exactly right in your call for negotiation. Indeed, this is the purpose of direct action. Nonviolent direct action seeks to create such a crisis and establish such creative tension that a community that has constantly refused to negotiate is forced to confront the issue. It seeks to so dramatize the issue that it can no longer be ignored. . . .
>
> One may well ask, "How can you advocate breaking some laws and obeying others?" The answer is found in the fact that there are *unjust* laws. I would be the first to advocate obeying just laws. One has not only a legal but a moral responsibility to obey just laws. Conversely, one has a moral responsibility to disobey unjust laws. . . .
>
> One who breaks an unjust law must do it *openly, lovingly* . . . and with a willingness to accept the penalty. I submit that an individual who breaks a law that conscience tells him is unjust, and willingly accepts the penalty by staying in jail to arouse the conscience of the community over its injustice, is in reality expressing the very highest respect for law.

Nonviolent direct action is a technique requiring direct mass action against laws regarded as unjust, rather than court litigation, political campaigning, voting, or other conventional forms of democratic political activity. Mass demonstrations, sit-ins, and other nonviolent direct-action tactics often result in violations of state and local laws. For example, persons remaining in offices, halls, or buildings after being asked by authorities to leave ("sit-ins") may be violating trespass laws. Marching in the street may entail the obstruction of traffic, "disorderly conduct," or "parading without a permit." Mass demonstrations often involve "disturbing the peace" or refusing to obey the lawful orders of a police officer. Even though these tactics are nonviolent, they do entail *disobedience to civil law.*

Civil disobedience is not new to American politics. Its practitioners have played an important role in American history, from the patriots who participated in the Boston Tea Party, to the abolitionists who hid runaway slaves, to the suffragists who paraded and demonstrated for women's rights, to the labor organizers who picketed to form the nation's major industrial unions, to the civil rights marchers of recent years. Civil disobedience is a political tactic of minorities. (Because majorities can more easily change laws through conventional political activity, they seldom have to disobey them.) It is also a tactic attractive to groups wishing to change the social status quo significantly and quickly.

The political purpose of nonviolent direct action and civil disobedience is to call attention or "to bear witness" to the existence of injustices. Only laws regarded as unjust are broken, and they are broken openly, without hatred or violence. Punishment is actively sought rather than avoided because punishment will further emphasize the injustices of the law. The object of nonviolent civil disobedience is to stir the conscience of an apathetic majority and to win support for measures that will eliminate the injustices. By accepting punishment for the violation of an unjust law, persons practicing civil disobedience demonstrate their sincerity. They hope to shame the majority and to make it ask itself how far it will go to protect the status quo.*

Essay question: In your own words, define nonviolent direct action. Then list three actions that would be considered examples of this nonviolent protest. Finally, explain Martin Luther King's understanding of nonviolent direct action.

80%

(score = # correct × 10)
Find answers on p. 413.

Exercise 16.2
Answering Problem-Solving Questions

Read the following excerpt on the metric system. Underline the important points, and make marginal comments. After reading, recite what you have learned either by taking notes or by creating a study map. When you think you know the information well, solve the following problem. You may want to refer to pp. 327–328, which discuss practices to use in solving math or science problems.

Metric (SI) Prefixes

Values of measurements can be expressed in the fundamental metric or SI units such as meters, kilograms, and seconds. They can also be expressed in larger or smaller units by multiplying the fundamental unit by 10 or some multiple of 10, such as 1,000 (or 10^3) or 0.001 (10^{-3}) (see Table 2-2). Note that any multiple of 10 can be expressed as a positive power of 10 such as 10^3 and 10^6 or a negative power of 10 such as 10^{-3} and 10^{-6}. The power to which 10 is raised is called an *exponent*, and numbers such as 10^3, 10^{-6}, and 8.2×10^4 are called *exponential numbers*.

In the metric or SI system, units are based on 10, and prefixes are used to indicate how many times a base unit is to be multiplied or divided by 10 to form larger or smaller units.

---

*Thomas R. Dye, *Power and Society*, 6th ed. (Pacific Grove, Calif.: Brooks/Cole, 1993), pp. 252–253.

Table 2-2   *Commonly Used Prefixes and Multiplier Factors for the Metric System*

Prefix	Abbreviation	Multiply Base Unit By
kilo	k	10^3 or 1,000
deci	d	10^{-1} or 0.1
centi	c	10^{-2} or 0.01
milli	m	10^{-3} or 0.001
micro	μ	10^{-6} or 0.000001

Table 2-3   *Metric Prefixes and Units for Length and Mass*

Length	Mass
1 km (kilometer) = 1,000 m (meters)	1 kg (kilogram) = 1,000 g (grams)
1 dm (decimeter) = 0.1 m (meter)	1 dg (decigram) = 0.1 g (gram)
1 cm (centimeter) = 0.01 m (meter)	1 cg (centigram) = 0.01 g (gram)
1 mm (millimeter) = 0.001 m (meter)	1 mg (milligram) = 0.001 g (gram)
1 μm (micrometer) = 0.000001 m (meter)	1 μg (microgram) = 0.000001 g (gram)

The SI prefixes most commonly used in introductory chemistry are given in Table 2-2.

Table 2-3 summarizes the use of these prefixes for units of length and mass. The values in metric units for some common objects are

Width of home movie film = 8 mm

Average ski length = 1.60 m to 1.80 m, or 160 cm to 180 cm

Mass of a new nickel = 5 g

Mass of a 150-lb human = 68.2 kg*

Problem: How many millimeters are there in 27.5 kilometers? In arriving at a solution, show all of your work. List the known quantity, the unknown quantity, and the conversion formulas.

75%

Ask instructor for sample answer.

---

*G. Tyler Miller, Jr., *Chemistry: A Basic Introduction,* 4th ed. (Belmont, Calif.: Wadsworth, 1987), pp. 35–36. Used by permission.

Applying SQ3R to Textbook Material

The four reading selections in Part Five are excerpts from college textbooks; the first two are excerpts from chapters, and the last two are entire chapters. In each selection, you will be applying all the skills you have studied in previous parts of this book. If you do well on the examinations on these four selections, you should be adequately prepared for the kinds of tests you will be taking in most of your college courses.

Study Reading 1

Climate

This excerpt from an environmental science textbook discusses weather and those variables in nature that influence it. This excerpt relies on three basic organizational patterns: definition, cause–effect, and spatial–geographic. Read over the following suggestions; they should help you learn this information more easily.

1. Read over the definitions carefully. Mark the key words and phrases that explain these terms. Since there are many definitions in this excerpt and since they are critical to understanding the physical laws related to weather and climate, concentrate on learning these words and how the various terms relate to one another.

2. Study the cause–effect statements carefully. Many of them relate to the effect of warm and cold winds or fronts on the weather. Be sure you can identify both cause and effect. If you do not remember the characteristics of the cause–effect pattern, refer to pp. 101–102.

3. Much of what is said in this excerpt can be visualized. Study the two illustrations carefully; also, when wind and precipitation movements are described, use your spatial–geographic abilities to visualize these processes. If you do not remember the spatial–geographic pattern, refer to p. 105.

4. Because of this excerpt's reliance on the cause–effect and spatial–geographic structures, you can best remember much of this information by designing study maps that illustrate various natural processes of weather and climate. When you are reviewing the material, you may want to design a few study maps.

5. Before you take the quiz on this excerpt, you should not only know the meanings of the key terms but also be able to explain the important cause–effect patterns that underlie the physical processes involved in weather and climate.

A. Survey

Take three minutes to survey this chapter excerpt. Read the title of the excerpt, the titles of the various sections, and any terms that are highlighted. Also, study the two illustrations to see how they relate to the excerpt. Finally, if time permits, read through the first and last paragraphs of the excerpt to get a sense of its style and level of difficulty.

Before you read, you should know the meaning of one word that is not defined in this excerpt: *Topography* refers to the surface features of a region, including the hills, valleys, lakes, rivers, canals, bridges, and roads.

When you have finished with your survey, answer the questions that follow without looking back at the excerpt. Place all of your answers in the answer box.

Global Patterns of Climate

G. Tyler Miller, Jr.

Weather and Climate

(1) **Weather** is the day-to-day variation in atmospheric conditions, such as temperature, moisture (including precipitation and humidity), sunshine (solar electromagnetic radiation), and wind. When the atmosphere thins to nothing, as on the moon or in space, there is no weather. **Climate** is the generalized weather at a given place on Earth over a fairly long period of time such as a season, 1 year, or 30 years. Climate involves seasonal and annual averages, totals, and occasional extremes of the day-to-day weather pattern for an area. Climate is the weather you expect to occur at a particular time of the year in your hometown, whereas weather is the actual atmospheric conditions in your hometown on a particular day.

Global Air Circulation Patterns

(2) Heat from the sun and evaporated moisture are distributed over the Earth as a result of global circulation patterns of atmospheric air masses. Three major factors affecting the pattern of this global air circulation are (1) the uneven heating of the equatorial and polar regions of the Earth, which creates the driving force for atmospheric circulation; (2) the rotation of the Earth around its axis, which causes deflection of air masses moving from the equator to the poles and from the poles back to the equator; and (3) unequal distribution of land masses, oceans, ocean currents, mountains, and other geological features over the Earth's surface.

(3) An *air mass* is a vast body of air in which the conditions of temperature and moisture are much the same at all points in a horizontal direction. A warm air mass tends to rise, and a cold air mass tends to sink. Air in the Earth's atmosphere is heated more at the equator, where the sun

G. Tyler Miller, Jr., Living in the Environment, *4th ed. (Belmont, Calif.: Wadsworth, 1985), pp. 41–43. Used by permission.*

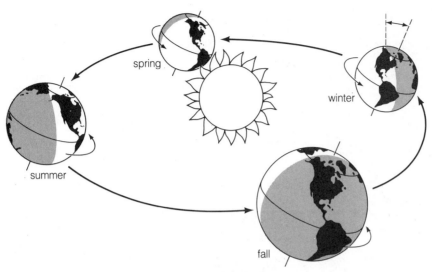

Figure 3-8 *The seasons in the northern hemisphere are caused by variations in the amount of incoming solar radiation as the Earth makes its annual rotation around the sun. Note that the northern end of the Earth's axis tilts toward the sun in summer, making the northern hemisphere warmer, and away from it in winter, making the northern hemisphere cooler.*

is almost directly overhead, than at the poles, where the sun is lower in the sky and strikes the Earth at an angle. Because of this unequal heating, warm equatorial air tends to rise and spread northward and southward toward the Earth's poles as more hot air rises underneath, carrying heat from the equator toward the poles. At the poles the warm air cools, sinks downward, and moves back toward the equator. In addition, because of the Earth's annual rotation around the sun, the sun is higher in the sky in summer (July for the northern hemisphere and January for the southern hemisphere) than in winter (January for the northern hemisphere and July for the southern hemisphere). Such annual variations in the duration and intensity of sunlight lead to seasonal variations in the different hemispheres and at the poles (Figure 3-8).

(4) The Earth's daily rotation on its axis (Figure 3-8) not only results in night and day; it also produces the major wind belts of the Earth. The general tendency for large air masses to move from the equator to the poles and back is modi-fied by the twisting force associated with the Earth's rotation on its axis. This force deflects air flow in the northern hemisphere to the right and in the southern hemisphere to the left (Figure 3-9). This distortion of the Earth's general air circulation causes the single air movement pattern that would exist in each hemisphere on a nonrotating Earth to break up into three separate belts of moving air or *prevailing ground winds:* the polar easterlies, the westerlies, and the trade-winds (Figure 3-9). The equatorial calm is known as the doldrums (Figure 3-9). These three major belts of prevailing winds in each hemisphere contribute to the distribution of heat and moisture around the planet that leads to differences in climate in different parts of the world.

(5) A *front* is the boundary between two colliding air masses. When a warm air mass and a cold air mass collide, the warm air flows up the front slope of the cold air as if it were a mountain slope, and the cold air forms a wedge near the ground. If prevailing winds cause the cold air mass to push the warm air mass back, we have an

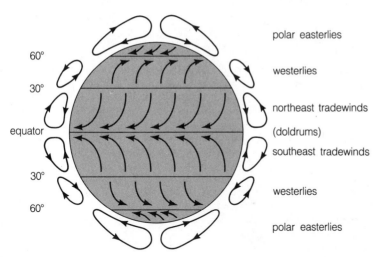

60°
30°
equator
30°
60°

polar easterlies

westerlies

northeast tradewinds

(doldrums)

southeast tradewinds

westerlies

polar easterlies

Figure 3-9 *The Earth's daily rotation on its axis deflects the general movement of warm air from the equator to the poles and back to the right in the northern hemisphere and to the left in the southern hemisphere. This twisting motion causes the air flow in each hemisphere to break up into three separate belts of prevailing winds.*

advancing *cold front.* If the reverse happens, we have an advancing *warm front,* and when no motion of the air masses takes place, we have a *stationary front.* An advancing cold or warm front usually brings bad weather because of the rain, snow, and strong winds that are found in the vicinity of its moving air masses.

(6) The boundary where the warm tropical air masses pushed from the south by the prevailing westerlies collide with the cold polar air masses pushed from the north by the polar easterlies (Figure 3-9) is known as the *polar front.* This front is of major importance in determining the weather and climate of the North American continent. Depending on the relative strength of the polar easterlies and the westerlies, the polar front swings northward and southward in a rather unpredictable way. In general, it moves toward the equator during the winter and recedes to the poles during the summer.

(7) The general global circulation pattern of air masses (Figure 3-9) also influences the distribution of precipitation over the Earth's surface. A great deal of the sun's heat goes not just into

warming the Earth's surface but also into evaporating water from the oceans and other bodies of water that cover about three-fourths of the Earth's surface. Evaporation of water from the land and transpiration of moisture from the leaves of plants also contribute water vapor to the atmosphere. A single apple tree, for example, may transpire 6,790 liters (1,800 gallons) of water vapor into the atmosphere during its six-month growing season. The amount of water vapor in the air is called its *humidity.* The amount of water vapor the air is holding at a particular temperature expressed as a percentage of the amount it could hold at that temperature is known as its *relative humidity.* When air with a given amount of water vapor cools, its relative humidity rises; when this same air is warmed, its relative humidity drops. Thus, warm air can hold more water vapor than cold air, explaining why the humidity tends to rise in warmer summer months.

(8) When an air mass rises it cools, which causes its relative humidity to increase. Once the relative humidity of the rising air mass reaches

100 percent, any further decrease in temperature causes tiny water droplets or ice crystals to condense on particles of dust in the atmosphere to form *clouds*. As these droplets and ice crystals in clouds are moved about in turbulent air, they collide and coalesce to form larger droplets and crystals. Eventually they can become big enough to be pulled downward by gravitational attraction toward the Earth's surface in the form of *precipitation* such as rain, sleet, snow, or hail. Thus, almost all clouds and forms of precipitation are caused by the cooling of an air mass as it rises. Conversely, when an air mass sinks, its temperature rises and its relative humidity can decrease to the point where it can't release its moisture as rain or snow.

(9) Air rising in the tropics is both hot and moist. As this air rises and cools, some of its water vapor is converted to water droplets, giving up some heat in the process. These droplets form the clouds from which tropical rains fall, helping explain why the tropics are wet and thus covered with lush vegetation. Conversely, areas north and south of the equator where the airflow is mainly downward—such as the deserts of the U.S. Southwest and the Sahara—tend to be dry because sinking air can hold more moisture.

(10) An air mass tends to take on the temperature and moisture characteristics of the surface over which it moves. Thus, the climate and weather of a particular area are also affected by the distribution of land and water over the Earth's surface because these surfaces react differently to the incoming rays of the sun. In general, land surfaces are heated rapidly by the sun. Because this heat does not penetrate deeply, land surfaces also cool rapidly. This means that interior land areas not near a large body of water usually have great differences between daily high and low temperatures. Water, however, warms up slowly, holds a much larger quantity of heat than the same volume of land surface, and cools slowly. As a result, the surface layer of air over the oceans is cooler in summer and warmer in winter than that over the continents. Because warm air rises, a net inflow of cool ocean air moves onto the continents in summer, and in winter there is a net outflow of cool air from the continents onto the oceans. Land and sea breezes result from the land being colder than the water at night and early morning but warmer later in the day.

(11) The Earth's rotation, prevailing winds, and variations in water temperature give rise to ocean currents such as the Gulf Stream, which carries warm waters from the Florida Straits northward along the Atlantic Coast and on to the British Isles. Such currents affect the climate of coastal areas near their flow. For example, air moving across the warm Gulf Stream acquires heat and moisture and influences the climate and weather along the East Coast. The climate of the East Coast is also affected by the cold Labrador Current, which flows southward as far as Norfolk, Virginia. The cool Japan Current has a major effect on the climate and weather of the West Coast of the United States.

Effects of Topography on Local Climate and Weather

(12) Topographical factors can often make local climatic conditions different from the general climate of a region. Such local climatic patterns are called *microclimates*. For example, forests have lower wind speeds and higher relative humidity than open land. Buildings in cities also disrupt wind-flow patterns and heat absorption patterns and cause cities to have different microclimates than surrounding nonurban areas.

(13) Climate is also modified locally by the presence of mountains. An increase in altitude results in a decrease in the density (mass per unit of volume) of the atmosphere, which in turn leads to a decrease in the temperature of the atmosphere. Thus, because of their higher altitudes, mountains tend to be cooler and windier than adjacent valleys. They also act as barriers to interrupt the flow of prevailing winds and the movement of storms. For example, because most U.S. mountain ranges run north and south, they disrupt the flow of the prevailing westerlies.

(14) Mountain ranges also affect precipitation patterns. When prevailing winds reach a

mountain range, the air rises and may decrease in temperature to the condensation level (100 percent humidity). When this occurs, precipitation may occur on the windward side of the range as the air flows upward. After flowing over the mountain crests, the air flows down the lee side of the range. As this happens, it becomes warmer and its relative humidity can decrease to the point where it can't release its moisture as air or snow. Thus, slopes on the lee side of the mountain range and the land beyond these slopes generally lack abundant precipitation. This *rain shadow effect* is the main reason that arid and semiarid deserts lie to the east of the Coast Ranges and the Cascade and Sierra Nevada ranges of California.

1. _____

2. _____

3. _____

4. _____

5. _____

_____
80%
(score = # correct × 20)
Ask instructor for answers.

1. This chapter excerpt makes use of

   a. boldface print
   b. italics
   c. underlining
   d. both a and b

2. The two illustrations relate weather to the Earth's

   a. annual rotation
   b. daily rotation
   c. annual and daily rotation
   d. mountain ranges

3. A topic that will not be covered in this excerpt is

   a. air circulation
   b. weather and climate
   c. topography and weather
   d. the greenhouse effect

4. This excerpt makes no use of mathematical equations.

   a. true
   b. false

5. The title of this excerpt suggests that climate will be analyzed in relation to

   a. all the continents of the Earth
   b. North America
   c. the North and South Poles
   d. the mountainous areas of the Earth

B. Question

Having surveyed this excerpt, make up five questions that you will answer as you study read. Use the chapter title, subdivision titles, and boldface and italicized terms to help you to make up these questions. Answer these questions as you read the chapter.

Ask instructor for sample questions.

1.

2.

3.

4.

5.

C. Read and Recite

1. After you have written these five questions, you can begin study reading. Underline important points and make marginal comments. Remember, do not underline too much. Read paragraphs 1–7. Afterward, on a separate sheet of paper, recite what you have read, using the Cornell note-taking system. When you have finished, go back to these seven paragraphs to see if your summary is complete and accurate.

2. Now read paragraphs 8–14. Follow the same procedures as you did for paragraphs 1–7: Recite on a separate sheet of paper, then return to these paragraphs to see if your summary is complete and accurate. Make any necessary additions to your summary.

D. Review

Now you are ready to review all of your material. Read over text underlinings, marginal comments, and your two summaries. You may also want to make study maps from some of this material. Finally, go back to your original five questions to see if you can answer them without any help.

Examination: Global Patterns of Climate

Directions: Give yourself fifty minutes to complete the following questions. Be sure to budget your time to answer all three parts: matching, multiple choice, and short essay.

I. Matching: Match up the following terms with the appropriate definitions. Each term should be matched up to only one definition. Place the letter of the correct definition in the answer box next to the appropriate number. (24 points)

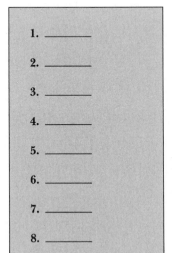

1. _____
2. _____
3. _____
4. _____
5. _____
6. _____
7. _____
8. _____

1. microclimate
2. climate
3. weather
4. front
5. air mass
6. precipitation
7. humidity
8. relative humidity

a. amount of water vapor in the air at a specific temperature in comparison to what it could be at that temperature
b. rain, sleet, snow, or hail
c. the boundary between two colliding air masses
d. general weather at a specific place on Earth over a long period of time
e. local patterns of climate
f. day-to-day change in atmospheric conditions
g. a body of air with similar temperature and moisture
h. amount of water vapor in the air

II. Multiple Choice: Choose the letter that correctly completes each question or statement. Place all answers in the answer box. (36 points)

9. Warm air masses are

    a. below cold air masses
    b. above cold air masses
    c. mixed in with cold air masses
    d. found only at the equator

10. The Earth's wind belts are caused by

    a. the Earth's annual rotation
    b. the Earth's daily rotation
    c. ocean currents
    d. land masses

11. The belt of moving air at the equator is known as the

    a. westerlies
    b. easterlies
    c. tradewinds
    d. doldrums

12. Bad weather is usually caused by the movement of a

    a. cold front
    b. warm front
    c. stationary front
    d. both a and b

13. An important force determining weather conditions in North America is the

    a. polar front
    b. westerlies
    c. doldrums
    d. tradewinds

14. Humidity in the air increases when

    a. an air mass heats up
    b. an air mass cools
    c. a cold front meets a stationary front
    d. it is midday

15. Land tends to be heated

    a. rapidly by the sun
    b. slowly by the sun
    c. as rapidly as water
    d. as slowly as water

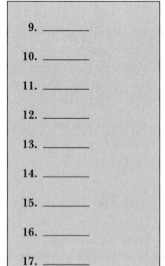

9. _____

10. _____

11. _____

12. _____

13. _____

14. _____

15. _____

16. _____

17. _____

16. An important factor affecting the weather of the British Isles is the

    a. Arctic snow
    b. doldrums
    c. westerlies
    d. Gulf Stream

17. Weather and climate seem to be influenced by

    a. unknown variables
    b. few variables
    c. several variables
    d. the Earth's rotation only

70%

Ask instructor for answers.

III. Short Essay: In a paragraph, discuss how mountains affect weather patterns. In your paragraph, mention (1) mountain altitude and air density, (2) how U.S. mountains affect the westerly winds, and (3) precipitation differences between windward and leeward sides of mountains. (40 points)

Study Reading 2

Physical Measurement

This excerpt is from a chapter in a college chemistry textbook. The style is straightforward, but this simplicity is deceiving. You may need to re-read many of the sections in order to master them and to use this knowledge in solving specific problems. Use the following suggestions to master the material in this excerpt:

1. Read the definitions carefully, underlining or circling important parts. You need to know what each term in this excerpt means, so read to understand every part of each definition.

2. Read for cause–effect patterns. You may want to reread the section on cause and effect on pp. 101–102. The cause–effect statements in this excerpt are direct, so don't look for terms of qualification.

3. Read the sample problems and solutions carefully. Follow the solution to each problem step by step. Be sure that you understand each step before you go on to the next.

4. Memorize the formulas regarding temperature conversion. Learn what each abbreviation means and how each term relates to the others.

5. After you finish reading the excerpt, complete the exercises. These problems will give you needed practice in converting the temperatures from one scale to another.

6. By the time you have finished the excerpt, you should be able to recall without help the meanings of the terms. You should also be able to write out the conversion formulas and correctly use each one.

A. Survey

Take three minutes to survey the chapter excerpt. Read the title, the titles of each section, the terms and statements that are highlighted, and the summary and exercises at the end of the excerpt. If time permits, begin reading the first several paragraphs.

Before you read, you should know the meaning of two terms that are not defined in this excerpt. *Kinetic energy* is the energy that matter possesses because of its motion; *SI* (for Système International) is an updated form of the metric system used in the sciences.

When you have finished, answer the questions that follow without looking back at the excerpt. Place all of your answers in the answer box.

Measurement and Units

G. Tyler Miller, Jr.

2.5 Heat and Temperature

Heat Units and Measurement

(1) The official SI unit for heat or any other form of energy is the **joule (J)** (pronounced jool). Many chemists, however, still use an older heat unit known as the calorie (cal). Although the calorie unit·is gradually being phased out, it is still widely used so that we need to be able to convert between joules and calories. A **calorie (cal)** is defined as the amount of heat energy required to raise the temperature of 1 g of water from 14.5° to 15.5°C. One calorie is equal to 4.184 joules.

$$1 \text{ cal} = 4.184 \text{ J} \quad \text{or} \quad \frac{4.184 \text{ J}}{1 \text{ cal}}$$

(2) Since both the joule and the calorie represent relatively small quantities of heat energy, the larger quantities of heat usually encountered in physical and chemical changes are often expressed in kilojoules (kJ) and kilocalories (kcal or Cal). Respectively, these units are equal to 1,000 J and 1,000 cal. Since 1 cal equals 4.184 J, 1 kcal (kilocalorie) equals 4.184 kJ (kilojoules).

(3) The kilocalorie (also abbreviated Cal with a capital *C*) is the unit used in dietary tables to show the energy content of various types of food. Thus, a piece of pie containing 500 Cal (or 500 kcal) contains 500,000 or 5×10^5 cal. Individual energy requirements for the human body depend on a number of factors, including body weight and the amount of physical activity. A person weighing 68.2 kg (150 lb) and carrying out moderate physical activity typically needs about 8.4×10^3 kJ or 2.0×10^3 kcal of food energy a day.

Heat and Temperature

(4) It is important to distinguish between heat and temperature. **Heat** or thermal energy can be roughly described as a measure of the total kinetic energy of all the particles in a sample of matter.[1] The relative "hotness" or "cold-

---

G. Tyler Miller, Jr., Chemistry: A Basic Introduction, 2nd ed. (Belmont, Calif.: Wadsworth, 1981), pp. 51–55; p. 59; p. 61. Used by permission.

[1]Heat or thermal energy also includes the rotational and vibrational energy of the particles along with the potential energy of attractions between particles. Since these energies are normally small (except at high temperatures), heat or thermal energy is primarily a measure of the total energy of motion (kinetic energy) of the particles.

ness" of a sample of matter is described by measuring its temperature. **Temperature** is a measure of the average (not the total) kinetic energy of the particles in a sample of matter.

(5) The heat (total kinetic energy) and temperature (average kinetic energy) of a given sample of matter are quite different quantities, just as the total mass of the members of a chemistry class is quite different from the average mass of the class. The heat in a given sample of matter depends on the amount of matter present in the sample. In contrast, the temperature of an object does not depend on the amount of matter in the sample. A cup of hot coffee contains a larger quantity of heat than a drop of the same coffee, but the temperatures of the liquid in the cup and the drop are the same.

(6) When one object has a higher temperature than another object, we know from experience that some of the energy from the hotter object will flow in the form of heat to the cooler object. You discovered this the first time you touched a hot stove or other hot object. In more formal language, then, temperature determines the direction in which heat energy flows when two samples of matter are brought into contact with one another.

Heat is a measure of the total kinetic energy of all the particles in a sample of matter.

Temperature is a measure of the average kinetic energy of the particles in a sample of matter.

Temperature Measurement

(7) A **thermometer** is a device used to measure the temperature of a sample of matter. The most commonly used thermometer is the mercury thermometer. To measure and compare temperatures throughout the world, scientists have established several standard temperature scales. The three major temperature scales are the *Fahrenheit (F) scale*, the *Celsius (C) scale* (formerly known as the centigrade scale), and the *Kelvin (K) scale* (Figure 2-7). A unit of temperature on each scale is called a **degree**. A super-

script, °, is used before the C abbreviation for Celsius and before the F abbreviation for Fahrenheit to indicate a degree. This superscript is not used for Kelvin temperature, since the Kelvin is defined as a unit of temperature. Thus, 100°C is read *100 degrees Celsius* and 273 K is read *273 Kelvin*. The term °*K* or *degrees Kelvin*, however, is still a widely used relic of an earlier version of the metric system. Most everyday measurements of temperature in the United States are reported in Fahrenheit temperature, although this scale is being phased out as the United States converts to the metric system. Scientists use both the Celsius and the Kelvin scales. The official SI temperature scale, however, is the Kelvin (K) scale.

(8) As shown in Figure 2-7, the **Fahrenheit temperature scale** is defined by assigning to the normal boiling point of water a temperature of 212°F and to the freezing point of water the temperature of 32°F. Since the difference between 212 and 32 is 180, the glass length between the two reference points is divided into 180 equal segments, each denoting a Fahrenheit degree. For the **Celsius temperature scale** the boiling point of water is assigned a value of 100°C and the freezing point of water is assigned the value of 0°C. This allows the distance between these two reference points to be divided into 100 equal units, each representing a Celsius degree. On the **Kelvin temperature scale**, the normal boiling point of water is 373.15 K (approximately 373 K) and the freezing point of water is 273.15 K (approximately 273 K). The value of 0 K is the absolute zero of temperature on the Kelvin scale. This value is equal to −273.15°C or −459.75°F (Figure 2-7).

Temperature Conversions

(9) Conversions between Fahrenheit and Celsius temperatures can be made using two simple formulas. Since 100 degrees on the Celsius scale is the same as 180 degrees on the Fahrenheit scale (Figure 2-7), then 1°C = 1.8°F. Thus, the unit conversion factor between Celsius and Fahrenheit is 1.8°F/1°C (or 9°F/5°C). The zero point on the Fahrenheit scale is 32°F compared

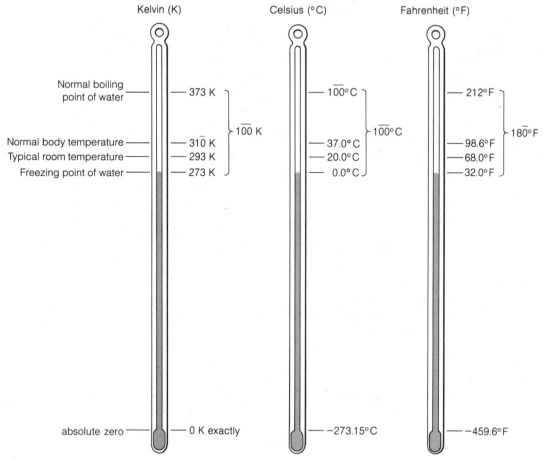

Kelvin (K) Celsius (°C) Fahrenheit (°F)

Normal boiling point of water — 373 K ⎫
⎬ 100 K
— 100°C ⎫
⎬ 100°C
— 212°F ⎫
⎬ 180°F

Normal body temperature — 310 K — 37.0°C — 98.6°F
Typical room temperature — 293 K — 20.0°C — 68.0°F
Freezing point of water — 273 K ⎭ — 0.0°C ⎭ — 32.0°F ⎭

absolute zero — 0 K exactly — −273.15°C — −459.6°F

Figure 2-7 *Comparison of the Kelvin (K), Celsius (°C), and Fahrenheit (°F) temperature scales.*

to 0°C for the Celsius scale. Thus, to convert any temperature on the Fahrenheit scale to the Celsius scale, we first subtract 32°F from the Fahrenheit temperature and then multiply by the appropriate conversion factor.

$$°C = \frac{1.0°C}{1.8°F} \times (°F - 32°F)$$

To convert from Celsius to Fahrenheit we multiply the Celsius temperature by the appropriate conversion factor and then add 32°F to the result.[2]

$$°F = \left(°C \times \frac{1.8°F}{1.0°C}\right) + 32°F$$

---

[2]Another set of formulas relating to Fahrenheit and Celsius scales is

$$°C = \frac{1.0°C}{1.8°F}(°F - 40°F) - 40°C$$

$$°F = \frac{1.8°F}{1.0°C}(°C + 40°C) - 40°F$$

The following examples illustrate the use of these conversions.

(10) *Example 2.12.* To help save energy, Americans have been asked to lower their thermostats to 65°F in cold weather. What is this temperature on the Celsius scale?

Solution

Unknown: °C

Known: 65°F

Plan: $°C = \dfrac{1.0°C}{1.8°F}(°F - 32°F)$

Result: $C = \dfrac{1.0°C}{1.8°F} \times (65°F - 32°F)$

$\qquad = \dfrac{1.0°C}{1.8°F}(33°F) = 18°C$

(11) *Example 2.13.* On a cold day in Alaska the temperature is −25°C. What is the equivalent Fahrenheit temperature?

Solution

Unknown: °F

Known: −25°C

Plan: $°F = \left(°C \times \dfrac{1.8°F}{1.0°C}\right) + 32°F$

Result: $°F = \left[(-25°C) \times \dfrac{1.8°F}{1.0°C}\right] + 32°F$

$\qquad = -45°F + 32°F = -13°F$

(12) Conversions between the Celsius and Kelvin scales are very easy. From Figure 2.7 we can see that 0 K = −273°C. Thus, °C = K − 273°

and K = °C + 273°. In other words, to convert °C to K we merely add 273 to the Celsius temperature. . . .

Accomplishments and Review

(13) After completing this chapter you should be able to do the following:

2.5   *Heat and Temperature:*

12. Distinguish between heat and temperature and give the units used for heat and temperature measurements.

13. Make conversions between the Fahrenheit (F), Celsius (C), and Kelvin (K) temperature scales.

Exercises

(14) *2.5   Heat and Temperature:*

26. Which of the following is the highest temperature: 250 K, 230°F, 120°C?

27. Make the following temperature conversions:
    a. Room temperature frequently averages 20.0°C. What is this on the Fahrenheit and Kelvin scales?
    b. Milk is pasteurized at 145°F. What is this on the Celsius and Kelvin scales?
    c. What is the normal body temperature of 98.6°F on the Celsius and Kelvin scales?
    d. The normal boiling point of ethyl alcohol is 79.0°C. What is its boiling point on the Kelvin scale?
    e. At normal atmospheric pressure the boiling point of liquid nitrogen is 77 K. What is the boiling point in degrees Celsius? Would nitrogen be a liquid or a gas at −100°C?

1. This excerpt makes use of

    a. boldface print
    b. italics
    c. illustrations
    d. all of these

2. The boldface statements on heat and temperature

a. define both terms
b. show the difference in the Fahrenheit, Celsius, and Kelvin temperature scales
c. show the difference between heat and temperature
d. both a and c

3. The problems that are presented in this excerpt are solved

a. step by step
b. by presenting the formulas
c. by presenting the known and unknown quantities
d. all of these

4. It appears that in this excerpt you will learn something about

a. the Fahrenheit scale
b. the Celsius scale
c. the Kelvin scale
d. all of these

5. Which topic will not be covered in this excerpt?

a. heat units
b. temperature measurement
c. temperature conversions
d. specific heat

1. _____

2. _____

3. _____

4. _____

5. _____

_____

80%

Ask instructor for answers.

B. Question

Having surveyed the chapter excerpt, write five questions that you intend to answer when you study read. Use the chapter title, section titles, and boldface print to formulate your questions. Answer these questions as you read the chapter.

1.

2.

3.

Ask instructor for sample questions.

4.

5.

C. Read and Recite

With these questions, you are ready to begin study reading. Use your best underlining and commenting skills, underlining sparingly and making marginal notes on important terms and formulas. Read the entire excerpt. Then, on a separate sheet of paper, use the Cornell note-taking system to recite what you have read. When you have completed your summary, go back to the excerpt to be sure that your summary is both accurate and complete. Make any additions to your summary at this time.

D. Review

Now you are ready to review your underlinings, your marginal comments, and your summary. Before you take the exam, you should solve Exercises 26 and 27 on p. 349. There will be a problem-solving section to the exam, and these problems will serve as review.

Examination: Measurement and Units

Directions: Give yourself fifty minutes to complete the following questions. Be sure to budget your time.

I. *Matching:*   Match up the following terms with the appropriate definitions. Each term should be matched up to only one definition. Place all answers in the answer box. (18 points)

1. joule
2. calorie
3. heat
4. temperature
5. Celsius temperature scale
6. Kelvin temperature scale

a. amount of heat required to raise the temperature of one gram of water from 14.5°C to 15.5°C
b. measure of the average kinetic energy in a sample of matter
c. official SI unit for heat or any other form of energy
d. boiling point of water about 373°; freezing point of water about 273°
e. boiling point of water 100°; freezing point of water 0°
f. measure of the total kinetic energy of all particles in a sample of matter

II. *Multiple Choice:*   Choose the letter that correctly completes each question or statement. Place all answers in the answer box. (27 points)

7. How many joules are in a calorie?

   a. 4184 J
   b. 418.4 J
   c. 41.84 J
   d. 4.184 J

8. The correct abbreviation for kilocalorie is

   a. cal
   b. Cal
   c. KC
   d. kc

9. The heat in a given sample of matter depends on the

   a. average energy of the particles in the sample
   b. amount of matter present in the sample
   c. average kinetic energy of the particles in the sample
   d. none of these

10. Heat tends to flow from a

    a. cooler object to a warmer object
    b. warmer object to a cooler object
    c. gas to a liquid
    d. liquid to a solid

11. On which temperature scale is the superscript ° not used?

    a. Fahrenheit
    b. Celsius
    c. Kelvin
    d. metric

12. On the Celsius scale, what is the boiling point of water?

    a. 0°
    b. 212°
    c. 373°
    d. 100°

13. On which scale is the difference between the boiling point of water and the freezing point of water 180?

    a. Fahrenheit
    b. Celsius
    c. Kelvin
    d. metric

14. In which scale is the difference between the boiling point of water and the freezing point of water 100?

    a. Fahrenheit
    b. Celsius
    c. Kelvin
    d. both b and c

15. 0 K is designated as

    a. absolute zero
    b. the freezing point of water
    c. the boiling point of water
    d. none of these

1. _____
2. _____
3. _____
4. _____
5. _____
6. _____
7. _____
8. _____
9. _____
10. _____
11. _____
12. _____
13. _____
14. _____
15. _____

III. *Problem Solving:* Complete the following two problems. You will get credit for determining the unknown quantity, the known quantity, the correct formula, and the correct answer. Show all your work.

1. In the desert areas of Southern California the temperature often goes as high as 44°C. What temperature is this on the Fahrenheit scale? (25 points)

    a. unknown: (5 points)

    b. known: (5 points)

    c. formula: (5 points)

    d. work: (5 points)

    e. answer: (5 points)

2. For experimental purposes Dr. Burns placed a virus at 120°F. What is the equivalent Kelvin temperature? (30 points)

    a. unknown: (5 points)

    b. known: (5 points)

    c. formulas: (10 points)

    d. work: (5 points)

    e. answer: (5 points)

70%

Ask instructor for answers.

Study Reading 3

Social Power

Unlike the previous two textbook excerpts that you have read, this one is an entire chapter, the first chapter in a sociology textbook. Study reading it will closely resemble the activities you will engage in when you read textbooks in college. Also, instead of answering objective questions about the chapter, you will be answering essay questions.

This selection introduces and defines the key concepts examined in the textbook. Thus it relies heavily on two organizational patterns: definition and comparison–contrast. You may want to reread the sections in Chapter 6 on these two organizational patterns (pp. 103–104 and 106–108) before you start your study reading of this chapter. And you may want to review how to answer extended essay and short-answer questions.

Use the following suggestions to master this chapter's material:

1. Read carefully for definitions. See how the definitions of terms interrelate. Identify and mark the key terms.

2. Look for comparisons and contrasts in the definitions and issues that the author presents. Make marginal comments about these comparisons.

3. Read the case study carefully, as well as the summary of the chapter and the discussion questions.

4. As you study read, see how your previous reading of sociology material in Chapter 6 and your reading of business material in Chapter 5 help you understand this chapter. You may want to review the exercises in Chapters 5 and 6 after you complete the study reading of this

chapter to clarify any questions about sociology or business that you may have had.

5. As you read the last section of the chapter—on ideology, race, and poverty—see whether you can apply any of your own experiences to the sociological issues that are explained.

A. *Survey*

Take four minutes to survey this chapter. Read the titles, subtitles, and terms in boldface and italics. Notice the chapter's special features: how the definitions are highlighted, the purpose of the case study, and the kinds of discussion questions at the end.

When you have finished, answer the questions that follow without looking back at the excerpt.

The Nature of Power

Thomas R. Dye

(1) Ordinary men and women are driven by forces in society that they neither understand nor control. These forces are embodied in governmental authorities, economic organizations and markets, social values and ideologies, accepted ways of life, and learned patterns of behavior. However diverse the nature of these forces, they have in common the ability to modify the conduct of individuals, to control their behavior, to shape their lives.

power   the capacity to affect the conduct of others through the real or threatened use of rewards and punishments

(2) *Power is the capacity to affect the conduct of individuals through the real or threatened use of rewards and punishments.* Power is exercised over individuals or groups by offering them some things they value or by threatening to deprive them of those things. These values are the *power base,* and they can include physical safety, health, and well-being; wealth and material possessions; jobs and means to a livelihood; knowledge and skills; social recognition, status, and prestige; love, affection, and acceptance by others; a satisfactory self-image and self-respect. To exercise power, then, control must be exercised over the things that are valued in society.

power   based on control of valued resources

unequally distributed

exercised in interpersonal relations

exercised through large institutions

(3) *Power is a special form of influence.* Broadly speaking, influence is the production of intended effects. People who can produce intended effects by any means are said to be influential. People who can produce intended effects by the real or threatened use of rewards and punishments are said to be powerful.

Power can rest on various resources. The exercise of power assumes many different forms—the giving or withholding of many different values. Yet power bases are usually *interdependent*—individuals who control

Thomas R. Dye, Power and Society, *6th ed. (Pacific Grove, Calif.: Brooks/Cole, 1993), pp. 4–14.*

certain resources are likely to control other resources as well. Wealth, economic power, prestige, recognition, political influence, education, respect, and so on, all tend to "go together" in society.

(4) *Power is never equally distributed.* "There is no power where power is equal." For power to be exercised, the "powerholder" must control some base values. By *control* we mean that the powerholder is in a position to offer these values as rewards to others or to threaten to deprive others of these values.

Power is a relationship among individuals, groups, and institutions in society. Power is not really a "thing" that an individual possesses. Instead, power is a relationship in which some individuals or groups have control over certain resources.

elite and masses the few who have power and the many who do not

(5) The *elite* are the few who have power; the *masses* are the many who do not. The elite are the few who control what is valued in society and use that control to shape the lives of all of us. The masses are the many whose lives are shaped by institutions, events, and leaders over which they have little control. Political scientist Harold Lasswell wrote, "The division of society into elites and masses is universal," and even in a democracy, "a few exercise a relatively great weight of power, and the many exercise comparatively little."[1]

(6) *Power is exercised in interpersonal relations.* Psychologist Rollo May wrote that "power means the ability to affect, to influence, and to change other persons."[2] He argued that power is essential to one's "sense of significance"—one's conviction that one counts for something in the world, that one has an effect on others, and that one can get recognition of one's existence from others. Power is essential to the development of personality. An infant who is denied the experience of influencing others or of drawing their attention to its existence withdraws to a corner of its bed, does not talk or develop in any way, and withers away physiologically and psychologically.

(7) *Power is exercised in large institutions*—governments, corporations, schools, the military, churches, newspapers, television networks, law firms, and so on. Power that stems from high positions in the social structures of society is stable and far-reaching. Sociologist C. Wright Mills observed: "No one can be truly powerful unless he has access to the command of major institutions, for it is over these institutional means of power that the truly powerful are, in the first instance, powerful."[3] Not all power, it is true, is anchored in or exercised through institutions. But institutional positions in society provide a continuous and important base of power. As Mills explained:

> If we took the one hundred most powerful men in America, the one hundred wealthiest, and the one hundred most celebrated away from the institutional positions they now occupy, away from their resources of men and women and money, away from the media of mass communication that are now focused upon them—then they would be powerless and poor and uncelebrated. For power is not of a man. Wealth does not

center in the person of the wealthy. . . . To have power requires access to major institutions, for the institutional positions men occupy determine in large part their chances to have and to hold these valued experiences.[4]

Power and the Social Sciences

social science the study of human behavior

(8) *Social science* is the study of human behavior. Actually, there are several social sciences, each specializing in a particular aspect of human behavior and each using different concepts, methods, and data in its studies. Anthropology, sociology, economics, psychology, political science, and history have developed into separate "disciplines," but all share an interest in human behavior.

(9) Power is *not* the central concern of the social sciences, yet all the social sciences deal with power in one form or another. Each of the social sciences contributes to an understanding of the forces that modify the conduct of individuals, control their behavior, and shape their lives. Thus, to fully understand power in society, we must approach this topic in an *interdisciplinary* fashion—using ideas, methods, data, and findings from all the social sciences.

Anthropology

anthropology the study of people and their ways of life

(10) *Anthropology* is the study of people and their ways of life. It is the most comprehensive of the social sciences. Some anthropologists are concerned primarily with people's biological and physical characteristics; this field is called *physical anthropology*. Other anthropologists are interested primarily in the ways of life of both ancient and modern peoples; this field is called *cultural anthropology*.

culture all the common patterns and ways of living that characterize society

(11) *Culture* is all the common patterns and ways of living that characterize society. The anthropologist tries to describe and explain a great many things: child rearing and education; family arrangements; language and communication; technology; ways of making a living; the distribution of work; religious beliefs and values; social life; leadership patterns; and power structures.

(12) Power is part of the culture or the way of life of a people. Power is exercised in all societies, because all societies have systems of rewards and sanctions designed to control the behavior of their members. Perhaps the most enduring structure of power in society is the family: power is exercised within the family when patterns of dominance and submission are established between male and female and between parents and children. Societies also develop structures of power outside the family to maintain peace and order among their members, to organize individuals to accomplish large-scale tasks, to defend themselves against attack, and even to wage war and exploit other peoples.

(13) In our study of power and culture, we shall examine how cultural patterns determine power relationships. We shall also examine patterns of authority in traditional and modern families and the changing power role of women in society. We shall examine the origins and devel-

opment of power relationships, illustrating them with examples of societies in which power is organized by family and kinship group (polar Eskimos), by tribe (Crow Indians), and by the state (the Aztec empire). Finally, as a case study, we shall look at the controversy over "sociobiology"—that is, the extent to which genetics or culture determines behaviors.

Sociology

sociology   the study of relationships among individuals and groups

(14) *Sociology* is the study of relationships among individuals and groups. Sociologists describe the structure of formal and informal groups, their functions and purposes, and how they change over time. They study social institutions (such as families, schools, churches), social processes (for example, conflict, competition, assimilation, change), and social problems (crime, race relations, poverty, and so forth). Sociologists also study social classes.

social stratification   the classification and ranking of members of a society

(15) All societies have some system of classifying and ranking their members—a system of *stratification*. In modern industrial societies, social status is associated with the various roles that individuals play in the economic system. Individuals are ranked according to how they make their living and the power they exercise over others. Stratification into social classes is determined largely on the basis of occupation and control of economic resources.

Power derives from social status, prestige, and respect, as well as from control of economic resources. Thus, the stratification system involves the unequal distribution of power.

(16) In our study of power and social class, we shall describe the stratification system in America and explore popular beliefs about "getting ahead." We shall discuss the differing lifestyles of upper, middle, and lower classes in America and the extent of class conflict. We shall examine the ideas of Karl Marx about the struggle for power among social classes. We shall describe the differential in political power among social classes in America. Finally, we shall explore the ideas of sociologist C. Wright Mills about a "power elite" in America that occupies powerful positions in the governmental, corporate, and military bureaucracies of the nation.

Psychology

psychology   the study of the behavior of people and animals

(17) *Psychology* may be defined as the study of the behavior of people and animals. Behavior, we know, is the product of both "nature and nurture"—that is, a product of both our biological makeup and our environmental conditioning. We shall examine the continuing controversy over *how much* of our behavior is a product of our genes versus our environment. There is great richness and diversity in psychological inquiry. For example, *behavioral psychologists* study the learning process—the way in which people and animals learn to respond to stimuli. Behavioral psychologists frequently study in experimental laboratory situations, with the hope that the knowledge gained can be useful in

understanding more complex human behavior outside the laboratory. *Social psychologists*, on the other hand, study interpersonal behavior—the ways in which social interactions shape an individual's beliefs, perceptions, motivations, attitudes, and behavior. Social psychologists generally study the whole person in relation to the total environment. *Freudian psychologists* study the impact of subconscious feelings and emotions and of early childhood experiences on the behavior of adults. *Humanistic psychologists* are concerned with the human being's innate potential for growth and development. Many other psychologists combine theories and methods in different ways in their attempts to achieve a better understanding of behavior.

personality all the enduring, organized ways of behavior that characterize an individual

(18) *Personality* is all the enduring, organized ways of behavior that characterize an individual. Psychologists differ over how personality characteristics are determined—whether they are learned habits acquired through the process of reinforcement and conditioning (behavioral psychology), products of the individual's interaction with the significant people and groups in his or her life (social psychology), manifestations of the continuous process of positive growth toward "self-actualization" (humanistic psychology), the results of subconscious drives and long-repressed emotions stemming from early childhood experiences (Freudian psychology), or some combination of all these.

(19) In our study of power and personality, we will examine various theories of personality determination in an effort to understand the forces shaping the individual's reaction to power. Using a Freudian perspective, we shall study the "authoritarian personality"—the individual who is habitually dominant and aggressive toward others over whom he or she exercises power but is submissive and weak toward others who have more power; the individual who is extremely prejudiced, rigid, intolerant, cynical, and power-oriented. We shall explore the power implications of B. F. Skinner's ideas of behavioral conditioning for the control of human behavior. To gain an understanding of humanistic psychology's approach to power relationships, we shall examine Rollo May's formulation of the functions of power for the individual and Abraham Maslow's theory of a "hierarchy of needs." Finally, in our case study, we shall describe the startling results of an experiment designed to test the relationship between authority and obedience.

Economics

economics the study of the production and distribution of scarce goods and services

(20) *Economics* is the study of the production and distribution of scarce goods and services. There are never enough goods and services to satisfy everyone's demands, and because of this, choices must be made. Economists study how individuals, firms, and nations make these choices about goods and services.

(21) Economic power is the power to decide what will be produced, how much it will cost, how many people will be employed, what their wages will be, what the price of goods and services will be, what profits will be made, how these profits will be distributed, and how fast the economy will grow.

(22) Capitalist societies rely heavily on the market mechanism to make these decisions. In our study of economic power, we shall explore both the strengths and weaknesses of this market system, as well as the ideas of economic philosophers Adam Smith and John Maynard Keynes. In addition, we shall consider the role of government in the economy, which has increased over the years. We shall then turn to an examination of America's vast wealth—how it is measured, where it comes from, and where it goes. We shall examine the relationship between wealth and the quality of life, which are not always equivalent things. We shall also examine the concentration of corporate power in America. Finally, in our case study, we shall discuss the power of the corporate managers, the "CEOs," and whether they use that power to benefit the stockholders or themselves.

Political Science

political science the study of government and politics
authority the legitimate use of physical force

(23) *Political science* is the study of government and politics. Governments possess *authority*, a particular form of power; that is, the legitimate use of physical force. By *legitimate*, we mean that people generally consent to the government's use of this power. Of course, other individuals and organizations in society—muggers, street gangs, the Mafia, violent revolutionaries—use force. But only government can legitimately threaten people with the loss of freedom and well-being to modify their behavior. Moreover, governments exercise power over all individuals and institutions in society—corporations, families, schools, and so forth. Obviously the power of government in modern society is very great, extending to nearly every aspect of modern life— "from womb to tomb."

(24) Political scientists from Aristotle to the present have been concerned with the dangers of unlimited and unchecked governmental power. We shall examine the American experience with limited, constitutional government and the meaning of democracy in modern society. We shall observe how the U.S. Constitution divides power, first between states and the national government, and second among the legislative, executive, and judicial branches of government. We shall examine the growth of power in Washington, D.C., and the struggle for power among the different branches. We shall also explore competition between political parties and interest groups and popular participation in decision making through elections. Finally, in our case study "Political Power and the Mass Media," we shall examine the growing power of television in American politics.

History

history the recording, narrating, and interpreting of human experience

(25) *History* is the recording, narrating, and interpreting of human experience. The historian recreates the past by collecting recorded facts, organizing them into a narrative, and interpreting their meaning. History is also concerned with change over time. It provides a perspective on the present by informing us of the way people lived in the past. History helps us understand how society developed into what it is today.

(26) The foundations of power vary from age to age. As power bases shift, new groups and individuals acquire control over them. Thus, power relationships are continuously developing and changing. An understanding of power in society requires an understanding of the historical development of power relationships.

(27) In our consideration of the historical development of power relationships, we shall look at the changing sources of power in American history and the characteristics of the individuals and groups who have acquired power. We shall describe the people of power in the early days of the republic and their shaping of the Constitution and the government it established. We shall discuss Charles Beard's interpretation of the Constitution as a document designed to protect the economic interests of those early powerholders. We shall also discuss historian Frederick Jackson Turner's ideas about how westward expansion and settlement created new bases of power and new powerholders. We shall explore the power struggle between northern commercial and industrial interests and southern planters and slave owners for control of western land, and the Civil War, which resulted from that struggle. In addition, we shall explore the development of an industrial elite in America after the Civil War, the impact of the depression on that elite, and the resulting growth of New Deal liberal reform. In a brief case study, "Reconstruction and Black History," we shall examine how history occasionally overlooks the experiences of powerless minorities and later reinterprets their contributions to society. Finally, we shall undertake a brief historical study, "Vietnam: A Political History," which argues that despite military victory, this war was "lost" through failures of America's political leadership.

Social Sciences and Social Problems

(28) Social problems—the major challenges confronting society— include ideological conflict, racism, sexism, poverty, crime, violence, urban decay, and international conflict. These problems do not confine themselves to one or another of the disciplines of social science. They spill over the boundaries of anthropology, economics, sociology, political science, psychology, and history—they are *interdisciplinary* in character. Each of these problems has its *historical* antecedents, its *social* and *psychological* roots, its *cultural* manifestations, its *economic* consequences, and its impact on *government* and public policy. The origins of these social problems, as well as the various solutions proposed, involve complex power relationships.

interdisciplinary study   the use of theory, methods, or findings from more than one social science

Ideological Conflict

(29) Ideas have power. Indeed, whole societies are shaped by systems of ideas that we call *ideologies*. The study of ideologies—liberalism, conservatism, socialism, communism, fascism, radicalism—is not a separate social science. Rather, the study of ideologies spans all the social sciences, and it is closely related to philosophy. Ideologies are integrated systems

ideology   an integrated system of ideas that rationalize and justify the exercise of power in society

of ideas that rationalize a way of life, establish standards of "rightness" and "wrongness," and provide emotional impulses to action. Ideologies usually include economic, political, social, psychological, and cultural ideas, as well as interpretations of history.

(30) Ideologies rationalize and justify power in society. By providing a justification for the exercise of power, the ideology itself becomes a base of power in society. Ideology "legitimizes" power, making the exercise of power acceptable to the masses and thereby adding to the power of the elite. However, ideologies also affect the behavior of the elite, because once an ideology is deeply rooted in society, powerholders themselves are bound by it.

(31) In our study of power and ideology, we shall first explore the ideology of *classical liberalism*—an ideology that attacked the established power of a hereditary aristocracy and asserted the dignity, worth, and freedom of the individual. Classical liberalism and capitalism justify the power of private enterprise and the market system. Whereas classical liberalism limits the powers of government, *modern liberalism* accepts governmental power as a positive force in freeing people from poverty, ignorance, discrimination, and ill health. It justifies the exercise of governmental power over private enterprise and the establishment of the welfare state. In contrast, *modern conservatism* doubts the ability of the governmental planners to solve society's problems; conservatism urges greater reliance on family, church, and individual initiative and effort.

(32) We shall then look at ideologies that have influenced other societies. *Fascism* is a power-oriented ideology that asserts the supremacy of a nation or race over the interests of individuals, groups, and other social institutions. *Marxism* attacks the market system, free enterprise, and individualism; it justifies revolutionary power in overthrowing liberal capitalist systems and the establishment of a "dictatorship of the proletariat." *Socialism* calls for the evolutionary democratic replacement of the private enterprise system with government ownership of industry.

We shall describe the current crisis of communism and the reasons for its collapse in eastern Europe and the former Soviet Union, and communism's unpopularity among the Chinese people. We shall also record the recent historic events of democratic movements in communist nations and shall provide a case study. "The Rise and Fall of Communism in the Former Soviet Union."

Racial and Sexual Inequality

(33) Historically, no social problem has challenged the United States more than racial inequality. It is the only issue over which Americans ever fought a civil war. We shall describe the American experience with racism and the civil rights movement, which brought about significant changes in American life. We want to understand the philosophy of that movement, particularly the "nonviolent direct action" philosophy of Nobel Peace Prize winner Dr. Martin Luther King, Jr. We shall describe the recent successes of blacks in acquiring political power. However, we

shall also examine continuing inequalities between blacks and whites in income, employment, and other conditions of life in the United States. Our case study describes the political rise of Douglas Wilder, the nation's first black governor. In addition, we confront sexism in American life, particularly in the economy. And we shall examine the arguments both for and against government efforts to assure "comparable worth" in the labor market. We shall describe the successes and failures of the women's movement in recent years and examine the constitutional status of abortion laws. Finally, we shall examine the controversy over "affirmative action" and "reverse discrimination" and its implication for how America is to achieve real equality.

Case Study

Bertrand Russell: Power Is to the Social Sciences What Energy Is to Physics

(34) Bertrand Russell (1872–1970), English philosopher and mathematician, is regarded as one of the twentieth century's greatest thinkers, mainly because of his contributions to mathematics and symbolic logic. However, Russell possessed a great breadth of interest that included history, economics, and political science, as well as education, morals, and social problems. He received the Nobel Prize in literature "in recognition of his many-sided and significant authorship, in which he has constantly figured as a defender of humanity and freedom of thought." He summarized his views about the importance of power in society in a book significantly entitled *Power: A New Social Analysis.**

(35) First of all, power is fundamental to the social sciences:

The fundamental concept in the social sciences is power, in the same sense in which energy is the fundamental concept in physics.

(36) Second, the desire for power as well as wealth motivates people:

When a moderate degree of comfort is assured, both individuals and communities will pursue power rather than wealth: they may seek wealth as a means to power, or they may forgo an increase of wealth in order to secure an increase of power, but in the former case as in the latter their fundamental motive is not economic. . . .

(37) Third, power takes many forms:

Like energy, power has many forms, such as wealth, armaments, civil authority, influence on opinion. No one of these can be regarded as subordinate to any other, and there is no one form from which the others are derivative. The attempt to treat one form of power, say wealth, in isolation can only be partially successful. . . . To revert to the analogy of physics: power, like energy, must be regarded as continually passing from any one of its forms into any other, and it should be the business of social science to seek the laws of such transformations.

(38) Finally, power produces social change:

Those whose love of power is not strong are unlikely to have much influence on the course of events. The men who cause social changes are, as a rule, men who strongly desire to do so. Love of power, therefore, is a characteristic of the men who are causally important. We should, of course, be mistaken if we regarded it as the sole human motive, but this mistake would not lead us so much astray as might be expected in the search for causal laws in social science, since love of power is the chief motive producing the changes which social science has to study.

Poverty and Powerlessness

powerlessness a social–psychological condition of hopelessness, indifference, distrust, and cynicism

(39) The American economy has produced the highest standard of living in the world, yet a significant number of Americans live in poverty. We shall observe that poverty can be defined as *economic hardship* or as *economic inequality* and that each definition implies a different governmental approach to the problem. Poverty can also be defined as *powerlessness*—a social-psychological condition of hopelessness, indifference, distrust, and cynicism. We shall then discuss whether or not there is a culture of poverty—a way of life of the poor that is passed on to future generations—and what its implications for government policy are. We shall describe government efforts to cope with poverty and discuss whether or not some government policies encourage poverty. We shall focus special attention on homelessness in America. Finally, we shall examine the future of the Social Security program in a look at "Senior Power."

Crime and Violence

a problem of democratic government to protect its citizens without violating individual liberty

(40) Governmental power must be balanced against *individual freedom.* A democratic society must exercise police powers to protect its citizens, yet it must not unduly restrict individual liberty. We shall explore the problem of crime in society, the constitutional rights of defendants, the role of the courts, and the relationship between drug use and crime. We shall also describe briefly the history of violence in American society and the continuous role that violence has played in American struggles for power. We shall summarize social-psychological explanations of violence, violence as a form of political activity, and violence as an aspect of lower-class culture. Finally, we shall examine the arguments for and against the death penalty as society's ultimate sanction.

Urban Life

(41) A variety of social problems affect the quality of life in the United States. The solution to these problems, if there is any solution, depends in great part on how government chooses to exercise its powers. We shall explore the growth of urban and suburban populations in the United States. We shall also explore the social patterns of urban life—the characteristic forms of social interaction and organization that typically emerge in a large metropolis—and the socioeconomic conflicts between cities and suburbs. We shall observe how our nation's communities are governed. We shall focus special attention on the social and economic problems of the inner city and how the concentration of social

problems can make them worse. Finally, we shall present a case study, "Community Power Structures," to compare power structures in different cities.

International Conflict

(42) The struggle for power is global. It involves all the nations and peoples of the world, whatever their goals or ideals. Nearly 200 nations in the world claim *sovereignty:* authority over their internal affairs, freedom from outside intervention, and political and legal recognition by other nations. But sovereignty is a legal fiction; it requires power to make sovereignty a reality. Over the years nations have struggled for power through wars and diplomacy. The struggle has led to attempts to maintain a fragile balance of power among large and small nations, as well as to attempts to achieve collective security through the United Nations and other alliances. Despite its internal problems, Russia remains a nuclear "superpower," together with the United States. In our discussion of the international system, we shall describe the nuclear "balance of terror" and the "triad" of weapons that maintains this balance. We shall describe the history of the Strategic Arms Limitations Talks (SALT) between the United States and the Soviet Union, the Intermediate-Range Nuclear Forces (INF) Treaty, and the major reductions in nuclear forces agreed to in the Strategic Arms Reduction Talks (START) Treaty. The collapse of communism in eastern Europe brought an end to the Soviet-dominated Warsaw Pact and changed the balance of power in Europe. We shall describe the NATO alliance and speculate on the future of the new Europe. The United States continues to face challenges around the world; we shall describe various regional mini-balances of power, notably in the Middle East. Finally, we shall observe the continuing need for U.S. military power in our case study. "American Military Power: Desert Storm."

sovereignty   authority over internal affairs, freedom from outside intervention, and recognition by other nations

Notes

1. Harold Lasswell and Abraham Kaplan, *Power and Society* (New Haven, Conn.: Yale University Press, 1950), p. 219.

2. Rollo May, *Power and Innocence* (New York: Norton, 1977), p. 20.

3. C. Wright Mills, *The Power Elite* (New York: Oxford University Press, 1956). p. 9.

4. Ibid., p. 10.

About This Chapter

Power in society is not just an abstract concept or a convenient focus for academic exercise. Nor is power something that is located exclusively in the nation's capitals. Power is very much a real factor that affects the lives of each of us. We experience it in some form in our families, in school, and at work; we feel its effects in the grocery store and on the highway. And we each react to it in characteristic ways. Our aim in this chapter was to understand just what power *is*. We also saw why it provides us with a useful perspective from which to gain a unified view of the social sciences and the social problems that concern us all.

Now that you have read this chapter, you should be able to

- define power in society and describe its characteristics;

- define the area of study of each of the social sciences, as well as their common focus, and discuss how each relates to power in society;

- identify the major social problems that the social sciences study and explain why they are interdisciplinary in nature and how they relate to power.

Discussion Questions

1. How would you define power? What characteristics of power deserve to be discussed in any definition of power?

2. Consider the power relationships that directly and indirectly affect your life. On the basis of your experiences and observations, assess the validity of these statements by Bertrand Russell: "The fundamental concept in the social sciences is power, in the same sense in which energy is the fundamental concept in physics. . . . When a moderate degree of comfort is assured, both individuals and communities will pursue power rather than wealth. . . . Love of power is the chief motive producing the changes which social science has to study."

3. Identify and briefly define the area of study of each of the social sciences. Discuss how you would study power from the perspective of each of these disciplines.

4. What is meant by the *interdisciplinary* study of social problems?

5. Choose two of the following social problems and briefly explain how they involve power: (a) racial and sexual inequality, (b) poverty, (c) crime and violence, (d) international conflict.

1. How are boldface print and italics used?

2. What is the case study generally about?

3. What types of questions are asked in the "Discussion Questions" section?

4. What are the three basic parts of this chapter?

5. Why do you think the various disciplines that you have studied in this textbook—business, sociology, anthropology—are introduced in this chapter?

80%

Ask instructor for answers.

B. Question

Having surveyed the chapter excerpt, write five questions that you intend to answer as you study read. Use the chapter title, section titles, italicized words and phrases, or any other feature of this chapter to formulate your questions. Answer these questions as you read the chapter.

1.

2.

3.

4.

Ask instructor for
sample questions.

5.

C. Read and Recite

With these questions, you are ready to begin study reading. Use your best underlining and commenting skills, making marginal notes on important terms and comparisons. Then on a separate sheet of paper, recite what you have read, and apply the Cornell note-taking system. When you have completed your summary, go back to the excerpt to be sure that your summary is both accurate and complete. Make changes to your summary and to the main points you highlighted by using the Cornell note-taking system.

Read and summarize paragraphs 1–27 first. Then read and summarize paragraphs 28–42.

D. Review

Now you are ready to review your underlinings, your marginal comments, and your summaries. You may want to make study maps that organize this material even more clearly.

Examination: Social Power

Directions: Give yourself two class sessions (100 minutes) to complete the following essay questions. Be sure to budget your time. Write all of your answers on separate sheets of paper or in a blue book.

I. Definitions: In a few sentences, define the following sociological terms. (25 points)

1. power

2. elite

3. social stratification

4. authority

5. sovereignty

II. *Short Essay:* Answer each question in an organized paragraph. (25 points)

6. Discuss the specific ways that the study of sociology differs from the study of psychology. (13 points)

7. Discuss the specific ways that the study of sociology differs from the study of political science. (12 points)

III. *Extended Essay:* In an essay of at least five paragraphs, define *ideology* and *ideological conflict.* Then explain two conflicts in ideology—for example, Marxism versus fascism and conservatism versus liberalism. Finally, choose *one* of the following three social issues and show how it has been treated differently by different ideologies: (1) women, (2) African Americans, or (3) the American poor. For example, discuss how the American poor are understood differently by a conservative ideology and by a liberal ideology. Your response may incorporate your own experiences or what you have previously studied about this issue. (50 points)

70%

Ask instructor for answers.

Study Reading 4

Methods and Concepts in Biology

Like Study Reading 3, this excerpt is a full chapter. It is the first chapter in an introductory biology textbook. As you study read this chapter, you will be mirroring what you do in your college courses when you study read the first chapter of a textbook for a particular course.

"Methods and Concepts in Biology" introduces key biological concepts and the scientific methodology that biologists use. As with most biology material, this chapter relies to a large degree on three organizational patterns: (1) definition, (2) cause–effect, and (3) sequence of events. You may want to review the key features of these organizational patterns on pp. 101–104 before you begin study reading this chapter.

Use the following study reading suggestions as you go through this chapter:

1. Read carefully for the definitions explaining key biological terms. Highlight these definitions and make appropriate marginal comments to remind you where these definitions are in the chapter.

2. Identify those biological activities that are described in terms of causes and effects; carefully separate out cause from effect. Note especially how the cause–effect pattern is used in the section on homeostasis (paragraphs 20–24).

3. Be alert to the sequence-of-events pattern, accurately listing the important steps. Note how the sequence-of-events structure explains the energy flow discussed in paragraphs 17–18 as well as the seven procedures that biologists use in the scientific method (paragraphs 53–59).

4. Note how this chapter is divided into two major sections: biological concepts and biological methods. Let these two topics be the umbrellas under which you begin to learn this material. As you recite and review, you may want to create study maps and organizational charts to learn the major concepts under each of these two topics.

5. Since there is a wealth of material in this chapter, determine how much material you can learn at one sitting. You may want to recite the material after you have read, marked, and commented on one or two subtopics. You may also want to break up this study material into two or more days of reading.

A. Survey

Take six minutes to survey this chapter. Read the title, subtitles, and terms in boldface print and italics. Note the special features of this chapter: figures, charts, short summaries in boldface, extended summary at the end, review questions, quizzes, and terms.

When you have finished, answer the questions that follow without looking back at the excerpt.

Methods and Concepts in Biology

Cecie Starr and Ralph Taggart

Key Concepts

(1) **1.** All organisms are alike in these respects: Their structure, organization, and interactions arise from the properties of matter and energy. They obtain and use energy and materials from their environment, and they make controlled responses to changing conditions. They grow and reproduce, and instructions for traits that they pass on from one generation to the next reside in their DNA.

(2) **2.** Organisms show great diversity in their structure, function, and behavior, largely as a result of evolution by means of natural selection.

(3) **3.** The theories of science are based on systematic observations, hypotheses, predictions,

Cecie Starr and Ralph Taggart, The Unity and Diversity of Life, *6th ed. (Belmont, Calif.: Wadsworth, 1992), pp. 3–16.*

and relentless testing. The external world, not internal conviction, is the testing ground for scientific theories.

Shared Characteristics of Life

DNA and Biological Organization

(4) Picture a frog on a rock, busily croaking. Without even thinking about it, you know that the frog is alive and the rock is not. At a much deeper level, however, the difference between them blurs. Frogs, rocks, and all other living or nonliving things are composed of the same particles (protons, electrons, and neutrons). The particles are organized into atoms, in every case according to the same physical laws. At the heart of those laws is something called **energy**—a capacity to make things happen, to do work. Energetic interactions bind atom to atom in predictable patterns, giving rise to the structured bits of matter we call molecules. Energetic inter-

actions among molecules hold a rock together—and they hold a frog together.

(5) It takes a special type of molecule called deoxyribonucleic acid, or **DNA**, to set living things apart from the nonliving world. No chunk of granite or quartz has it. DNA molecules contain the instructions for assembling each new organism from carbon, hydrogen, and a few other kinds of "lifeless" molecules. By analogy, think of what you can do with just two kinds of ceramic tiles in a crafts kit. With a little effort, you can glue the tiles together according to the kit's directions, so that you can produce many organized patterns of tiles (Figure 1.2). Similarly, the organization of life emerges from lifeless matter with DNA "directions," some raw materials, and energy.

(6) Look carefully at Figure 1.3, which outlines the levels of organization in nature. The quality of "life" actually emerges at the level of cells. A *cell* is the basic living unit. This means it has the capacity to maintain itself as an independent unit and to reproduce, given appropriate sources of energy and raw materials. Amoebas and many other single-celled organisms lead such independent lives.

(7) A *multicelled organism* is more complex, with specialized cells typically arranged into tissues, organs, and often organ systems. Its cells depend on the integrated activities of one another, but each generally retains the capacity for independent existence. How do we know this? Individual cells that have been removed from humans and other multicelled organisms can be kept alive under controlled laboratory conditions.

(8) The next, more inclusive level of organization is the *population*: a group of single-celled or multicelled organisms of the same kind occupying a given area. A congregation of penguins at a rookery in Antarctica is an example. Moving on, the populations of whales, seals, fishes, and all other organisms living in the same area as the penguins make up a *community*.

(9) The next level, the *ecosystem*, includes the community *and* its physical and chemical environment. The most inclusive level of organization is the *biosphere*. The biosphere includes all regions of the earth's waters, crust, and atmosphere in which organisms live.

(10) **The structure and organization of nonliving *and* living things arise from the fundamental properties of matter and energy.**

(11) **The structure and organization *unique* to living things starts with instructions contained in DNA molecules.**

Metabolism

(12) You never, ever will find a rock engaged in metabolic activities. Only living cells can do this. **Metabolism** refers to the cell's capacity to (1) *extract and transform energy* from its surroundings and (2) *use energy* and so maintain itself, grow, and reproduce. In essence, metabolism means "energy transfers" within the cell.

(13) A growing rice plant nicely illustrates this aspect of life. Like other plants, it has cells that engage in *photosynthesis*. The cells convert sunlight energy to chemical energy, which is then parceled out to the tasks of building sugars, starch, and other good things from simple raw materials in the environment. (Chemical energy is remarkable stuff. Cells use it to build large molecules out of smaller bits. They also use it to split molecules apart and liberate various bits.) In photosynthesis, energy from sunlight drives the attachment of a bit of phosphate to a certain molecule, which thereby becomes known as ATP. ATP is a generous molecule. It readily transfers chemical energy to other molecules that function as metabolic workers (enzymes), building blocks, or energy reserves.

(14) In rice plants, energy reserves are especially concentrated in starchy seeds—rice grains—from which more rice plants may grow. The energy reserves in countless trillions of rice grains also provide energy for billions of rice-eating humans around the world. How? In rice plants, humans, and most other organisms, stored chemical energy can be tapped for use by way of another metabolic process, called *aerobic*

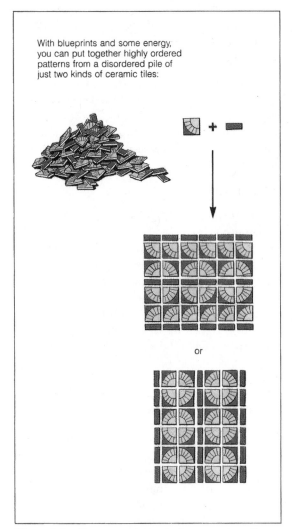

With blueprints and some energy, you can put together highly ordered patterns from a disordered pile of just two kinds of ceramic tiles:

or

Figure 1.2   *Emergence of organized patterns from disorganized beginnings. Two ceramic tile patterns are shown here. You probably can visualize other possible patterns using the same two kinds of tiles. Similarly, the organization characteristic of life emerges from pools of simple building blocks, given energy sources and specific DNA "blueprints."*

respiration. Later chapters will describe the splendid metabolic jugglings of photosynthesis and aerobic respiration. For now, the point to keep in mind is this:

(15) **Living things show metabolic activity: Their cells acquire and use energy to stockpile, tear down,**

Biosphere
Those regions of the earth's waters, crust, and atmosphere in which organisms can exist

⇧

Ecosystem
A community and its physical environment,

⇧

Community
The populations of *all* species occupying the same area

⇧

Population
Group of individuals of the same kind (that is, the same species) occupying a given area at the same time

⇧

Multicellular Organism
Individual composed of specialized, interdependent cells arrayed in tissues, organs, and often organ systems

⇧

Organ System
Two or more organs interacting chemically, physically, or both in ways that contribute to the survival of the whole organism

⇧

Organ
A structural unit in which tissues are combined in specific amounts and patterns that allow them to perform a common task

⇧

Tissue
A group of cells and intercellular substances functioning together in a specialized activity

⇧

Cell
Smallest *living* unit; may live independently or may be part of a multicellular organism

⇧

Organelle
Membranous sacs or other compartments that separate different metabolic reactions inside the cell

⇧

Molecule
A unit of two or more atoms of the same or different elements bonded together

⇧

Atom
Smallest unit of an element that still retains the properties of that element

⇧

Subatomic Particle
An electron, proton, or neutron; one of the three major particles of which atoms are composed

Figure 1.3   *Simplified picture of the levels of organization in nature, starting with the subatomic particles that serve as the fundamental building blocks of all organisms.*

build, and eliminate materials in ways that promote survival and reproduction.

Interdependency Among Organisms

(16) With few exceptions, a flow of energy from the sun maintains the great pattern of organization in nature. Plants and some other photosynthetic organisms are the entry point for this flow—the food "producers" for the world of life. Animals are "consumers." Directly or indirectly, they feed on the energy stored in plant parts. For example, zebras tap directly into the stored energy when they nibble on grass, and lions tap into it indirectly when they nibble on zebras. Certain bacteria and fungi are "decomposers." When they feed on the tissues or remains of other organisms, they break down complex molecules to simple raw materials—which can be recycled back to the producers.

(17) Figure 1.4 is a generalized picture of energy flow and the cycling of materials through the world of life.

(18) Energy flows to, within, and from single cells and multicelled organisms. It flows within and between populations, communities, and ecosystems. As you will see, interactions among organisms are part of the cycling of carbon and other substances on a global scale. They also have profound influence on the earth's energy "budget." Understand the extent of those interactions and you will gain insight into the greenhouse effect, acid rain, and many other modern-day problems.

(19) **All organisms are part of webs of organization in nature, in that they depend directly or indirectly on one another for energy and raw materials.**

Homeostasis

(20) It is often said that only living organisms "respond" to the environment. Yet a rock also responds to the environment, as when it yields to gravity and tumbles downhill or when it changes shape slowly under the battering of wind, rain, or tides. The real difference is this: *Organisms have the cellular means to sense environmental changes and make controlled responses to them.*

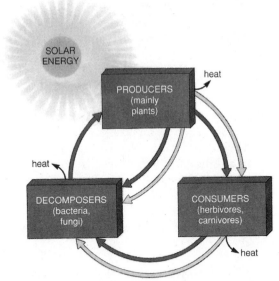

Figure 1.4   *Energy flow and the cycling of materials in the biosphere. Here, grasses of the African savanna are producers that provide energy directly for zebras (herbivores) and indirectly for lions and vultures (carnivores). The wastes and remains of all these organisms are energy sources for decomposers, which cycle nutrients back to the producers.*

They do so with the help of diverse **receptors**, which are molecules and structures that can detect specific information about the environment. When cells receive information from receptors, their activities become adjusted in ways that bring about an appropriate response.

(21) Your body, for example, can withstand only so much heat or cold. It must rid itself of harmful substances. Certain foods must be available to it, in certain amounts. Yet temperatures shift, harmful substances may be encountered, and food is sometimes plentiful and sometimes scarce.

(22) Even so, your body usually can adjust to the variations and so maintain internal operating conditions for its cells. **Homeostasis** refers to a state in which conditions in this "internal environment" are being maintained within a tolerable range. Homeostasis, too, is a common attribute of living things.

(23) Think about what happens after you eat and simple sugar molecules make their way into your bloodstream. Certain cells detect the rising level of sugar in your blood and cause molecules of insulin, a hormone, to be released. Most of your body's cells have receptors for insulin, which prods the cells into taking up sugar molecules. With this uptake, the blood sugar level returns to normal. Now suppose you can't eat when you should and your blood sugar level falls. Then, a different hormone prods cells in your liver and elsewhere to dig into their storehouses of energy-rich molecules. Those molecules are broken down into simple sugars, which are released into the bloodstream—and again the blood sugar level returns to normal.

(24) **All organisms respond to changing conditions through use of homeostatic controls, which help maintain their internal operating conditions.**

Reproduction

(25) We humans tend to think we enter the world rather abruptly and are destined to leave it the same way. Yet we and all other organisms are more than this. *We are part of an immense, ongoing journey that began billions of years ago.* Think about the first cell of a new human individual, which is produced when a sperm joins with an egg. The cell would not even exist if the sperm and egg had not been formed earlier, according to DNA instructions that were passed down through countless generations. With time-tested DNA instructions, a new human body develops in ways that will prepare it, ultimately, for *reproduction.* With reproduction, the journey of life continues.

(26) If someone asked you to think of a moth, would you simply picture a winged insect? What of the tiny fertilized egg deposited on a branch by a female moth? The egg contains all the instructions necessary to become an adult. By those instructions, the egg first develops into a caterpillar, a larval form adapted for rapid feeding and growth. The caterpillar eats and increases in size until an internal "alarm clock" goes off. Then its body enters a so-called pupal stage of development, which requires wholesale

remodeling. Some cells die, while other cells multiply and become organized in different patterns. Now the adult moth emerges. It is equipped with organs in which eggs or sperm develop. Its wings are brightly colored and flutter at a frequency that can attract a potential mate. In short, the adult stage is adapted for reproduction.

(27) None of these stages is "the insect." "The insect" is a series of organized stages from one fertilized egg to the next, each vital for the ultimate production of new moths. The instructions for each stage were written into moth DNA long before each moment of reproduction—and so the ancient moth story continues.

(28) **Each organism arises through *reproduction* (the production of offspring by one or more parents).**

(29) **Each organism is part of a reproductive continuum that extends back through countless generations.**

Mutation and Adapting to Change

(30) The word *inheritance* refers to the transmission, from parents to offspring, of structural and functional patterns characteristic of each kind of organism. In living cells, hereditary instructions are encoded in molecules of DNA. Those instructions have two striking qualities. They assure that offspring will resemble their parents—and they also permit *variations* in the details of their traits. By "trait" we mean some aspect of an organism's body, functioning, or behavior. For example, having five fingers on each hand is a human trait. Yet some humans are born with six fingers on each hand instead of five! Variations in traits arise through **mutations**, which are changes in the structure or number of DNA molecules.

(31) Many mutations are harmful, for the separate bits of information in DNA are part of a coordinated whole. A single mutation in a tiny segment of human DNA may lead to a genetic disorder such as hemophilia, in which blood cannot clot properly in response to a cut or bruise. Yet on rare occasions, a mutation may prove to be harmless, even beneficial, under prevail-

ing conditions. One type of mutation in light-colored moths leads to dark-colored offspring. What happens when a dark moth rests on a soot-covered tree? Bird predators simply do not see it. If most trees are soot-covered (as in industrial regions), light moths are more likely to be seen and eaten—so the dark form has a better chance of living long enough to reproduce. Under such conditions, the mutated form of the trait is more adaptive.

(32) An **adaptive trait** simply is one that helps an organism survive and reproduce under a given set of environmental conditions.

(33) **In all organisms, DNA is the molecule of inheritance: Its instructions for reproducing traits are passed on from parents to offspring.**

(34) **Mutations introduce variations in heritable traits.**

(35) **Although most mutations are harmful, some give rise to variations in form, function, or behavior that turn out to be adaptive under prevailing conditions.**

Life's Diversity

Five Kingdoms, Millions of Species

(36) Until now, we have focused on the unity of life—on characteristics shared by all organisms. Superimposed on this shared heritage is immense diversity. Many millions of different kinds of organisms, or **species**, inhabit the earth. And many millions more existed in the past and became extinct. Early attempts to make sense of life's diversity led to a classification scheme in which each species was assigned a two-part name. The first part designates the **genus** (plural, genera). It encompasses all the species having perceived similarities to one another. The second part designates a particular species within that genus.

(37) For instance, *Quercus alba* is the scientific name of the white oak. *Quercus rubra* is the name of the red oak. (Once the genus name has been spelled out, subsequent uses of it in the same document can be abbreviated—for example, to *Q. rubra.*)

(38) Life's diversity is classified further by using more inclusive groupings. For example, similar genera are placed in the same *family*, similar families into the same *order*, then similar orders into the same *class*. Similar classes are placed into a *division* or *phylum* (plural, phyla). In turn, phyla are assigned to a *kingdom*. Today, most biologists recognize the following five kingdoms:

Monera	*Bacteria. Single cells of relatively little internal complexity. Producers or decomposers.*
Protista	*Protistans. Single cells of considerable internal complexity. Producers or consumers.*
Fungi	*Fungi. Mostly multicelled. Decomposers.*
Plantae	*Plants. Mostly multicelled. Mostly producers.*
Animalia	*Animals. Multicelled. Consumers.*

Table 1.1 [p. 378] summarizes the main characteristics of life that have been described so far in this chapter. *Every living organism in all five kingdoms displays these characteristics.*

An Evolutionary View of Diversity

(39) If organisms are so much alike in so many ways, what could possibly account for their diversity? In biology, a key explanation is called evolution by means of natural selection.

(40) By way of example, suppose a DNA mutation gives rise to a different form of a trait in one member of a population—say, black moth wings instead of white. Suppose black wings prove to be adaptive in concealing the moth from predators. Because the black-winged moth has an advantage over a white moth right next to it on a soot-covered tree trunk, it lives to reproduce. So do its black-winged offspring—and so do *their* offspring.

(41) The variant form of this trait is now popping up with greater frequency. In time it may even become the more common form, so

Table 1.1 *Characteristics of Organisms in All Five Kingdoms*

1. Complex structural organization based on instructions contained in DNA molecules.

2. Directly or indirectly, dependence on other organisms for energy and material resources.

3. Metabolic activity by the single cell or multiple cells composing the body.

4. Use of homeostatic controls that maintain favorable operating conditions in the body despite changing conditions in the environment.

5. Reproductive capacity, by which the instructions for heritable traits are passed from parents to offspring.

6. Diversity in body form, in the functions of various body parts, and in behavior. Such traits are adaptations to changing conditions in the environment.

7. The capacity to evolve, based ultimately on variations in traits that arise through mutations in DNA.

that what was once a population of mostly white-winged moths now consists mostly of dark-winged moths. **Evolution** is taking place—the character of the population is changing through successive generations.

(42) Long ago, Charles Darwin used pigeons to explain how evolution might occur. Domesticated pigeons show great variation in their traits. Darwin pointed out that pigeon breeders who wish to promote certain traits, such as black tail feathers with curly edges, will "select" individual pigeons having the most black and the most curl in their tail feathers. By permitting only those birds to mate, they will foster the desired traits and eliminate others from their captive population.

(43) Thus Darwin used *artificial* selection as a model for natural selection.

(44) For now, these are the points to remember:

(45) **1.** Members of a population vary in form, function, and behavior, and much of this variation is heritable.

(46) **2.** Some forms of heritable traits are more adaptive than others; they improve chances of surviving and reproducing. Thus individuals

with adaptive traits tend to make up more of the reproductive base in each new generation.

(47) **3. Natural selection** is simply a measure of the difference in survival and reproduction that has occurred among individuals that differ from one another in one or more traits.

(48) **4.** Any population *evolves* when some forms of traits increase in frequency and others decrease or disappear over the generations. In this manner, variations have accumulated in different lines of organisms. Life's diversity is the sum total of those variations.

The Nature of Biological Inquiry

On Scientific Methods

(49) Species evolve in myriad directions, like branches growing in many directions on a single tree of life. Today we say this with confidence, but it was not always so. Awareness of evolution developed over centuries, as naturalists and travelers collected specimens of living and extinct organisms, then asked questions about the similarities and differences among them. Darwin and others proposed only tentative answers to those questions. Evidence supporting some of their an-

swers came much later, after generations of scientists devised a staggering number of ingenious ways to test them.

(50) If you have not had much exposure to the way scientists think and the methods they use to track down answers, you might believe that "doing science" is a mysterious ritual. There they are, exquisitely trained persons pondering terribly complex problems and doing experiments late into the night. Becoming a practicing scientist generally does require special training—but thinking scientifically does not.

(51) For example, any reasonably alert person might wonder about some of the organisms illustrated in this chapter. Why does the silkworm moth (*Hyalophora cecropia*) have such distinct, boldly patterned wings? Why don't all trees grow as tall as redwoods? Why do zebras have striped coats? Why don't dung beetles simply burrow under a dung pat instead of rolling a ball of the stuff great distances before putting it underground?

(52) There is no such thing as a single "scientific method" of investigating such questions. However, the following list is a good starting point for understanding how a scientist might proceed with such an investigation:

(53) **1.** Identify a problem or ask a question about some aspect of the natural world.

(54) **2.** Develop one or more **hypotheses**, or educated guesses, about what the solution or answer might be. This might involve sorting through what has been learned already about related phenomena.

(55) **3.** Think about what predictably will occur or will be observed if the hypothesis is correct. This is sometimes called the "if-then" process. (*If* gravity pulls objects toward the earth, *then* it should be possible to observe apples falling down, not up, from a tree.)

(56) **4.** Devise ways to *test* the accuracy of predictions drawn from the hypothesis. This typically involves making observations, developing models, and performing experiments.

(57) **5.** If the tests do not turn out as expected, check to see what might have gone wrong.

(Maybe a substance being tested was tainted, maybe a dial was set incorrectly or a relevant factor overlooked. Or maybe the hypothesis just isn't a good one.)

(58) **6.** Repeat or devise new tests—the more the better. Hypotheses that have been supported by many different tests are more likely to be correct.

(59) **7.** Objectively report the results from tests and the conclusions drawn from them.

(60) Using this list as a guide, let's return to the question posed earlier about the silkworm moth's wing pattern. Is it a mating "flag"? If so, it would help the male and female moths identify each other, rather than dallying with members of the wrong species and producing defective offspring. Or does the pattern camouflage the moths from bird predators? Maybe it blends with plants that the moths rest on during the day. (Moths fly at night, not during daylight hours.)

(61) These actually are two plausible explanations, based on what scientists have already learned about mate discrimination and camouflaging among insects in general. Returning to still another question, do dung beetles roll away their prize ball so other dung beetles won't get it? Or do they bury the ball in distant concealed places where predators are less likely to find the beetle larvae that will grow inside it?

(62) In nearly all cases, questions about what causes a natural phenomenon have more than one possible answer. In science, *alternative hypotheses are the rule, not the exception.*

Testing Alternative Hypotheses

(63) Identifying which of two or more hypotheses may be correct depends on tests. The trick here is to use each hypothesis as a guide for producing testable predictions. *If* the moth wing pattern functions in mate discrimination (the hypothesis), *then* it follows logically that mating should occur only at times of day when moths can see each other's wing patterns (the prediction).

(64) Scientists do not use "prediction" as fortunetellers do, to "look into the future." They

use it as a statement of what you should be able to observe in nature, if you were to go looking for it. Start from the observation that moths mate at night. If their wing pattern helps potential mates identify each other, then there won't be any moths mating on moonless nights. They won't be able to see the patterns.

(65) Suppose you test this prediction by stealthily watching moths on a moonless night. To your surprise, you see moths mating just as often in total darkness as in moonlight. Here is evidence of a mistaken prediction—and, by extension, a mistaken hypothesis.

(66) Whether test results support or undermine your hypothesis, you should repeat the test several times. Doing so will provide insight into the reliability of your findings. It's safe to say that most respectable conclusions in science rest on numerous studies, carried out by people who tried to test many alternative hypotheses.

(67) **By testing a prediction, you test the underlying hypothesis.**

The Role of Experiments

(68) The preceding example shows how you might test a prediction by simple observation. You also might be able to test it by **experiments**. These are tests in which nature is manipulated as a way to reveal its secrets. Generally, scientists try to design experiments in such a way that the results will clearly show that a hypothesis is mistaken. Why? It is often easy to *disprove* a hypothesis but almost impossible to *prove* one. (An infinite number of experiments would have to be performed to show that it holds true under all possible conditions.)

(69) Suppose you come up with another hypothesis about the wing pattern of *H. cecropia*. You propose that individuals with *altered* color patterns should have difficulty securing a mate. To test this, you sit out night after night, waiting for a peculiarly patterned moth to fly by. None does, so you decide to do an experiment. You *paint* the wings of a group of moths.

(70) In a fair test of your prediction, you do more than put the group of painted moths in a cage with unaltered ones to observe the outcome. You also have a **control group**, which is used to evaluate possible side effects of the manipulation of the experimental group. Ideally, members of a control group should be *identical* to those of an experimental group in every respect—*except* for the key factor, or **variable**, that is under study. The variable here is wing color pattern. You also make sure that the number of individuals in both groups is large enough to give you more confidence that the experimental outcome will not be due to chance alone. Two or three moths will tell you nothing.

(71) How can you be sure there are no other variables between the two groups that might influence the outcome of an experiment? After all, maybe paint fumes are as repulsive to a potential mate as the painted pattern. Maybe you rough up the moths when you handle them and somehow make them less desirable than those in the control group. Maybe the paint weighs enough to change the flutter frequency of the wings.

(72) And so you decide that the control group also must be painted, using the same kind of paint, the same kind of brushes, and the same amount of handling. But for this group, you *duplicate* the natural wing color pattern as you paint. Thus your experimental group and control group are identical except for the variable under study. If only those moths with altered wing patterns turn out to be unlucky in love, then your control group will help substantiate your hypothesis.

(73) **Experiments are tests in which nature is manipulated. They require careful design of a set of controls to evaluate possible side effects of the manipulation.**

About the Word "Theory"

(74) More than a century ago, Darwin unveiled his ideas about the evolution of species and ushered in one of the most dramatic of all scientific revolutions. The core of his thinking—that life's diversity is the outcome of evolution by natural selection—became popularly known as "the theory of evolution." We will be looking

closely at Darwin's scientific work in a later chapter, but here let's focus on the word *theory*.

(75) In science, a **theory** is a related set of hypotheses which, taken together, form a broad-ranging explanation about some fundamental aspect of the natural world. A scientific theory differs from a scientific hypothesis in its *breadth of application*. Darwin's theory fits this description—it is a big, encompassing "Aha!" explanation that, in a few intellectual strokes, makes sense of a huge number of observable phenomena. Think about it. His theory explains what has caused most of the diversity among many millions of different living things!

(76) There are many other major theories in biology. One explains what causes all offspring to resemble their parents, no matter what the species. Another explains what caused the mass extinction of the dinosaurs about 65 million years ago. We will be looking at these and other theories throughout the book. None is bigger in scope than Darwin's, but all do a good job of attempting to make sense of the natural world.

(77) Like hypotheses, theories are accepted or rejected on the basis of tests. For example, several competing theories about evolution were pushed vigorously in Darwin's time, but since then they have been tested and essentially rejected. After thousands of different tests, Darwin's theory still stands, with only some modification. Today, most biologists accept the modified theory as correct—but they still keep their eyes open for new evidence that might call it into question.

(78) Scientists admire tested theories for good reason. A tested theory serves as a general frame of reference for additional research, and research is what scientists do. If Darwin's theory is correct, then the diverse attributes of living things exist because, at least in the past, they helped individuals leave descendants. Therefore, when biologists look at a moth's wings, an immediate question comes to mind—"I wonder how that wing color helps that moth leave descendants." When using Darwin's theory as a guide to developing plausible hypotheses, they will probably focus on possible answers that

relate directly or indirectly to reproductive success—as we saw in our earlier example.

(79) **A scientific theory is an explanation about the cause or causes of a broad range of related phenomena. Like hypotheses, theories are open to tests, revision, and tentative acceptance or rejection.**

Uncertainty in Science

(80) Isn't anything ever "for sure" in science? Are there no comfortable, final conclusions? In an ultimate sense, no. Scientists must be content with *relative* certainty about whether an idea is correct or not. When a theory or hypothesis withstands exhaustive testing by many independent researchers, that "relative certainty" can be very great. Even so, there is always a chance that one of the tests has hidden flaws, which would invalidate the results. That is why scientific papers include a section on the methods employed for the tests they describe. This allows other scientists to check the procedures used, even to the point of duplicating the research. Knowing that others will scrutinize your ideas and the methods used to test them has a wonderful effect. It forces you to try to remain objective—even if you believe fiercely in what you propose.

(81) In short, individual scientists must keep asking themselves: "Are there tests or observations that will show my ideas to be incorrect?" They are expected to put aside pride or bias by testing their ideas, even in ways that might prove them wrong. Even if an individual scientist doesn't (or won't) do this, *others will*—for science proceeds as a community that is both cooperative and competitive. Ideas are shared, with the understanding that it is just as important to expose errors as it is to applaud insights.

(82) **The fact that scientists can and do change their mind when presented with new evidence is a *strength* of their profession, not a weakness.**

The Limits of Science

(83) The call for objectivity strengthens the theories that do emerge from scientific studies. Yet it also puts limits on the kinds of studies that

can be carried out. Beyond the realm of scientific analysis, certain events remain unexplained. Why do we exist, for what purpose? Why does any one of us have to die at a particular moment and not another?

(84) Answers to such questions are *subjective.* This means they come from within, as an outcome of all the experiences and mental connections that shape our consciousness. Because individuals differ so enormously in this regard, subjective answers do not readily lend themselves to scientific analysis.

(85) This is not to say that subjective answers are without value. No human society can function without a shared commitment to standards for making judgments, however subjective those judgments might be. Moral, aesthetic, economic, and philosophical standards vary from one society to the next. But all guide their members in deciding what is important and good, and what is not. All attempt to give meaning to what we do.

(86) Every so often, scientists stir up controversy when they explain part of the world that was previously considered beyond natural explanation—that is, belonging to the "supernatural." This is sometimes true when moral codes are interwoven with religious narratives, which grew out of observations by ancestors. Exploring some longstanding view of the world from a scientific perspective may be misinterpreted as questioning morality, even though the two are not remotely synonymous.

(87) For example, centuries ago Nicolaus Copernicus studied the movements of planets and stated that the earth circles the sun. Today the statement seems obvious. Back then, it was heresy. The prevailing belief was that the Creator had made the earth (and, by extension, humankind) the immovable center of the universe! Not long afterward a respected professor, Galileo Galilei, studied the Copernican model of the solar system. He thought it was a good one and said so. He was forced to retract his statement publicly, on his knees, and to put the earth back as the fixed center of things. (Word has it that when he stood up he muttered, "But it moves nevertheless.")

(88) Today, as then, society has its sets of standards. Today, as then, those standards may be called into question when a new, natural explanation runs counter to supernatural belief. When this happens it doesn't mean that scientists as a group are less moral, less lawful, less sensitive, or less caring than any other group. Their work, however, is guided by one additional standard: *The external world, not internal conviction, must be the testing ground for scientific beliefs.*

(89) **Systematic observations, hypotheses, predictions, tests—in all these ways, science differs from systems of belief that are based on faith, force, authority, or simple consensus.**

Summary

(90) **1.** All organisms are alike in the following characteristics:

a. Their structure, organization, and interactions arise from the basic properties of matter and energy.
b. They rely on metabolic and homeostatic processes.
c. They have the capacity for growth, development, and reproduction.
d. Their heritable instructions are encoded in DNA.

(91) **2.** There are many millions of different kinds of organisms. Each distinct kind of organism is called a species. Distinct species resembling one another more than they resemble other species are grouped into the same genus, and so on with increasingly inclusive groupings into family, order, class, phylum (or division), and kingdom.

(92) **3.** Diversity among organisms arises through mutations that introduce changes in the DNA. These changes lead to heritable variation in the form, functioning, or behavior of individual offspring.

(93) **4.** Individuals in a population vary in their heritable traits, and the variations influence their ability to survive and reproduce. Under prevailing conditions, certain varieties of a given trait may be more adaptive than others. They will be "selected" and others eliminated

through successive generations. The changing frequencies of different traits change the character of the population over time; it evolves. These points are central to the principle of evolution by natural selection.

(94) **5.** There are many scientific methods of gathering information. These are key terms associated with scientific inquiry:

(95) a. Theory: An explanation of a broad range of related phenomena. An example is the theory of how processes of natural selection bring about evolution.

(96) b. Hypothesis: A possible explanation of a specific phenomenon. Sometimes called an educated guess.

(97) c. Prediction: A claim about what an observer can expect to see in nature *if* a particular theory or hypothesis is correct.

(98) d. Test: The attempt to secure actual observations in order to determine whether they match the predicted or expected observations.

(99) e. Conclusion: A statement about whether and to what extent a particular theory or hypothesis can be accepted or rejected, based on the tests of predictions derived from it.

(100) **6.** The external world, not internal conviction, is the testing ground for scientific theories.

Review Questions

1. Why is it difficult to give a simple definition of life?

2. What does *adaptive* mean? Give some examples of environmental conditions to which plants and animals must be adapted.

3. Study Figure 1.3. Then, on your own, arrange and define the levels of biological organization. What concept ties this organization to the history of life, from the time of origin to the present?

4. In what fundamental ways are all organisms alike?

5. What is metabolic activity?

6. What are the "instructions" contained in DNA? What is a mutation? Why are most mutations likely to be harmful?

7. Outline the one-way flow of energy and the cycling of materials through the biosphere.

8. What does evolution mean?

9. Witnesses in a court of law are asked to "swear to tell the truth, the whole truth, and nothing but the truth." What are some of the problems inherent in the question? Can you think of a better alternative?

10. Design a test to support or refute the following hypothesis: The body fat in rabbits appears yellow in certain mutant individuals—but only when those mutants also eat leafy plants containing a yellow pigment molecule called xanthophyll.

Self-Quiz

1. The complex patterns of structural organization characteristic of life are based on instructions contained in _____ .

2. Directly or indirectly, all living organisms depend on one another for _____ .

3. _____ is the ability of organisms to extract and transform energy from the environment and use it during maintenance, growth, and reproduction.

4. _____ means maintaining the body's internal operating conditions within a tolerable range even when environmental conditions change.

5. Diverse structural, functional, and behavioral traits are considered to be _____ to changing conditions in the environment.

6. The capacity to evolve is based on variations in traits, which originally arise through _____ .

7. Organisms show _____ , the ability to transmit instructions for heritable traits from parents to offspring.

8. That each of us has great-great-great-great-grandmothers and grandfathers is an example of a unique property of life known as
_____ .

    a. metabolism   c. reproduction
    b. homeostasis   d. organization

9. A scientific approach to explaining various aspects of the natural world includes all of the following except _____ .
    a. hypothesis   c. faith and simple consensus
    b. testing   d. systematic observations

10. A related set of hypotheses that collectively explain some aspect of the natural world is a scientific _____ .
    a. prediction   d. authority
    b. test   e. observation
    c. theory

Selected Key Terms

adaptive trait	experiment	photosynthesis
aerobic respiration	Fungi	Plantae
Animalia	genus	population
biosphere	homeostasis	prediction
cell	hypothesis	Protista
community	inheritance	reproduction
control group	metabolism	species
DNA	Monera	test
ecosystem	multicelled	theory
energy	organism	variable
evolution	mutation	

1. The chapter begins with an introduction to:

    a. the central questions students ask about biology
    b. the key concepts presented in the chapter
    c. cellular biology
    d. the scientific method

2. Which subtopic is not part of this chapter?

    a. DNA and Biological Organization
    b. Metabolism
    c. Interdependency among Organisms
    d. Transfer of Viral Genes

3. There is one table in this chapter, and it deals with:

    a. DNA
    b. molecules
    c. the five animal kingdoms
    d. the scientific method

4. The subsection that seems to treat the scientific method is titled:

    a. The Nature of Biological Inquiry
    b. Shared Characteristics of Life
    c. Reproduction
    d. Mutation

5. What type(s) of questions make up the review and self-quiz?

    a. short answer
    b. fill-in
    c. multiple choice
    d. all of these

1. _____
2. _____
3. _____
4. _____
5. _____

_____
80%

Ask instructor for answers.

B. Question

Having surveyed the chapter, write ten questions that you intend to answer as you study read. Use the chapter title, section titles, italicized and boldface words and phrases, or any other visual features of this chapter to formulate your questions. Answer these questions as you read the chapter.

1. _____

2. _____

3. _____

4. _____

5. _____

6. _____

7. _____

8. _____

9. _____

10. _____

C. Read and Recite

With these questions in mind, you are ready to study read. Use all the study reading techniques you find helpful: underlining, highlighting, making marginal comments, and the Cornell note-taking system. When you have completed your recite, be sure that your summary is accurate, going back to sections of the chapter that you may not have thoroughly understood. Having studied your notes, write out questions in the left-hand margin that you think might be asked on the examination for this chapter.

Break this chapter into several read-and-recite sittings. You decide how many subsections you can study read in each sitting.

D. Review

Now you are ready to review all of your underlinings, marginal comments, and notes. You may want to create study maps and organizational charts to condense this material before taking the exam.

Examination: Methods and Concepts in Biology

Directions: Place your answers to Parts I–III in the answer box. Write answers to Parts IV and V on a separate sheet of paper.

I. True–False: Write T for true, F for false. (10 points)

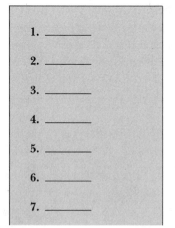

1. What seems to set living things apart from nonliving things is DNA.

2. An amoeba is a multi-celled organism.

3. All mutations are harmful.

4. The kingdom is the most specific category in the animal kingdom.

5. A protista is a single-celled organism that has little internal complexity.

6. In his study of pigeon breeders, Charles Darwin was relying on the concept of artificial selection.

7. The scientific method in biology must adhere to a single set of procedures.

8. Theories are more specific than hypotheses.

9. In most biological studies, there are two groups: the potential group and the control group.

10. An example of an objective question in biology is: Is it right to use rats in biological experiments?

II. Multiple Choice: Choose the letter that correctly completes each question or statement. (10 points)

11. A multi-celled organism is characterized as having:
   a. tissues
   b. organs
   c. organ systems
   d. all of these

12. Which is *not* an activity of metabolism?
   a. It extracts energy from its surroundings.
   b. It uses energy for an organism to grow.
   c. It transforms energy in an organism.
   d. It contains instructions for assembling new organisms.

13. Which is *not* an activity of photosynthesis?
   a. Sunlight energy is converted to chemical energy.
   b. It rids itself of harmful substances.
   c. It builds sugars and starches.
   d. It transfers chemical energy to other molecules.

14. A receptor in an organism is a:
   a. storage cell
   b. structure that detects changes in the environment
   c. reproductive cell
   d. structure that helps rebuild diseased cells

15. When sugar enters your body, what does *not* happen?
   a. Cells detect the entry of sugar molecules.
   b. Insulin is released.
   c. Some DNA is destroyed.
   d. Receptors for insulin are awakened.

16. What is the DNA molecule programmed to do?
   a. It allows the organism to resemble its parents.
   b. It permits variations in the traits the parents give to the organism.
   c. It prevents the organism from changing drastically from its parents.
   d. both a and b

8. _____
9. _____
10. _____
11. _____
12. _____
13. _____
14. _____
15. _____
16. _____
17. _____
18. _____
19. _____
20. _____
21. _____
22. _____
23. _____
24. _____
25. _____
26. _____
27. _____
28. _____
29. _____
30. _____

17. What does an an adaptive trait allow an organism to do?
   a. to survive
   b. to die
   c. to stop reproducing
   d. to make the most efficient use of energy

18. What group comes directly *after* phylum?
   a. kingdom
   b. class
   c. order
   d. family

19. What does a biologist normally do first in conducting research?
   a. develops a hypothesis
   b. tests accuracy of predictions
   c. identifies the problem
   d. predicts what will occur

29. A theory in biology is:
   a. more specific than a hypothesis
   b. a related set of hypotheses
   c. a series of biological facts
   d. not open to further experimentation

III. Matching: Match the following terms with the appropriate definition or description. Each term should be matched with only one definition. Place the letter of the correct definition in the answer box next to the appropriate number. (10 points)

21. energy	a. includes the variable under study
22. cell	b. grouped directly under genus
23. ATP	c. aspect of an organism's body, functioning, or behavior
24. aerobic respiration	d. metabolic process tapping stored energy
25. homeostasis	e. basic living unit
26. trait	f. It makes things happen.
27. adaptive trait	g. molecule transferring chemical energy to other molecules
28. species	h. state that maintains an organism in a tolerable range
29. control group	i. inherited characteristic, helping an organism survive
30. experimental group	j. does not include variable under study

IV. Short Essay: In two or three sentences each, answer the following questions on a separate sheet of paper. (10 points)

31. Discuss the biological cycle of producers, consumers, and decomposers, and provide an example of each.

32. Define natural selection and artificial selection, showing where these two terms differ. Provide an example of each.

V. Extended Essay: In a paragraph or two or in an organizational chart, answer the following question on a separate sheet of paper. (10 points)

33. List and define the levels of organization in nature after the cell. Then provide an example of an organism at each level.

70%

Ask instructor for answers.

Answer Key

Answers have been provided for most odd-numbered exercises. Ask your instructor for the answers to all even-numbered exercises, the essay questions and several short-answer questions, and the study reading selections in Part Five.

Chapter 4
Locating the Main Idea

Exercise 4.1
1. a **2.** d **3.** imp **4.** imp **5.** a **6.** a **7.** a **8.** a **9.** d **10.** imp

Exercise 4.3

Your wording may differ, but your answers should be essentially the same as these:

1. the Industrial Revolution
2. the effects of the Industrial Revolution on the farms
3. how the new inventions were run
4. the results of the new inventions on the farmer
5. machines in the early 1900s
6. how the machines of industrialization affected human life
7. industrialization's effect on the environment
8. the negative effect of industrialization on the environment
9. how industrialization affected society
10. the negative effects of industrialization on society
11. the city's effect on the environment
12. the city's negative effect on the environment
13. the Industrial Revolution's effect on the economy
14. the increased costs caused by the Industrial Revolution
15. the overall effects of the Industrial Revolution
16. the positive and negative effects of the Industrial Revolution
17. the Industrial Revolution and nature
18. the Industrial Revolution making human beings superior to nature
19. the superior attitude toward nature
20. questioning what this superior attitude means for human beings and nature

Exercise 4.5 **1.** d **2.** c **3.** b **4.** b **5.** a

Chapter 5
Locating Major and
Minor Details

Exercise 5.1

1. a, b, e		**5.** a, c, d		**8.** a, b, d	
2. a, b, d		**6.** a, b, c		**9.** a, c, d	
3. a, b, c		**7.** a, d, e		**10.** b, c, d	
4. a, c, e					

Exercise 5.3

1. MN	**11.** MA	**21.** MN	**31.** MA
2. MA	**12.** MI	**22.** MA	**32.** MA
3. MI	**13.** MN	**23.** MI	**33.** MN
4. MA	**14.** MA	**24.** MI	**34.** MA
5. MN	**15.** MA	**25.** MN	**35.** MI
6. MA	**16.** MI	**26.** MA	**36.** MA
7. MA	**17.** MA	**27.** MA	**37.** MN
8. MA	**18.** MA	**28.** MI	**38.** MA
9. MN	**19.** MA	**29.** MN	**39.** MA
10. MA	**20.** MN	**30.** MA	**40.** MI

Exercise 5.5

1. c **2.** a **3.** b **4.** d **5.** c

6. any of the following: American farmers and businessmen did much business in England, **or** Americans often exchanged precious metals and agricultural products with England for finished products, **or** Most of American business was structured on the cottage system, where goods were made at home.

7. The Industrial Revolution changed the way Americans produced goods.

8. any of the following: Large machines were used, and workers moved from their homes to their factories, **or** The reaper allowed for more grain to be planted or harvested, **or** The telegraph and railroad allowed material to be sold and moved more quickly.

9. American business must be sensitive to changes in the market and must change accordingly in order to be competitive.

10. minor detail, "that is"

Chapter 6
Identifying
Organizational
Patterns

Exercise 6.1

1. fact	**5.** fact	**9.** thesis	**13.** a
2. thesis	**6.** fact	**10.** fact	**14.** d
3. fact	**7.** thesis	**11.** a	**15.** d
4. thesis	**8.** fact	**12.** d	

Exercise 6.3

Your answers should be essentially the same as these, although your wording may differ. Each definition has two parts, each counting 5 points.

	Term	General Category	Examples
1.	conflict theory	studies why people disagree	crime
2.	deduction	logical process moving from general to specific	women's discrimination
3.	demography	study of population	movement of Mexicans to California in the 1990s
4.	empirical study	observer gathers data	how American men greet
5.	field research	observing in natural setting	political rallies
6.	hypothesis	conclusion drawn from intuition or observation	criminals as society's victims
7.	induction	conclusion reached by studying data	New Yorkers' attitudes toward taxes
8.	population	group meriting study	students in community colleges
9.	random selection	selecting data by chance	random numbering
10.	social interaction	how a person directs social responses	conversation

Exercise 6.5

1.	DEF or C-C	**6.**	DEF
2.	C-E	**7.**	C-E
3.	SEQ	**8.**	DEF
4.	C-C	**9.**	C-E
5.	SEQ	**10.**	C-C

Exercise 6.7

1. d
2. d
3. d
4. c
5. c

6. Factors other than money are involved in determining social status.

7. Some prestigious jobs are doctor, scientist, and Supreme Court justice—none of which makes a huge salary.

8. thesis–support

9. Spiritual and intellectual possessions are also valued by society.

10. thesis–support

Chapter 7
Summarizing and
Paraphrasing

Although your responses to the excerpt on p. 137 may differ, they should be similar to these:

(1) Who were the Nacirema? How did they live? What accounted for their extreme ideology of remaking the natural environment? Why did they disappear? What can we learn from a study of their culture?

(2) **Anthropology,** the comparative study of human societies and cultures, provides some answers to questions like these. The aim of anthropology is to describe, analyze, and explain the different ways of life, or cultures, through which human groups, or societies, have adapted to their environments. Anthropology is comparative in that it attempts to understand both similarities and differences among human societies, in both the past and the present. Only by the study of humanity in its total variety can we understand the origins and development of our species.

(3) Anthropologists study our species from its beginnings several million years ago right up to the present. We study human beings as they live in every corner of the earth, in all kinds of physical environments. Some anthropologists are now trying to project how human beings will live in outer space. It is this interest in humankind throughout time and in all parts of the world that distinguishes anthropology as a scientific and humanistic discipline. In other academic disciplines, human behavior is studied primarily from the point of view of Western society. "Human nature" is thought to be the same as the behavior of people as they exist in the modern industrial nations of Europe and the United States.

(4) Human beings everywhere consider their own behavior not only right, but natural. For example, both "common sense" and Western economic theory see human beings as "naturally" individualistic and competitive. But in some societies, human beings are not competitive, and the group is more important than the individual. Anthropologists see the Western idea of "economic man"—the individual motivated by profit and rational self-interest—as the result of the particular socioeconomic and political system we live in. It is not an explanation of the behavior of the Arapesh hunter in New Guinea, who makes sure he is not always the first to sight and claim the game, so that others will not leave him to hunt alone (Mead 1963:38). In anthropology, more than any other discipline, concepts of human nature and theories of human behavior are based on studies of human groups whose goals, values, views of reality, and environmental adaptations are very different from those of modern, industrial Western societies.

(5) In their attempts to explain human variation, anthropologists combine the study of both human biology and the learned and shared patterns of human behavior we call culture. Other academic disciplines focus on one factor—biology, psychology, physiology, or society—as the explanation of human behavior. Anthropology seeks to understand human beings as whole organisms who adapt to their environments through a complex interaction of biology and culture.*

I. Anthropology

  A. Definition: comparative study of human societies and cultures.
  B. Three basic aims: describe, analyze, and explain different cultures' adaptation to environment.

---

*Serena Nanda, *Cultural Anthropology,* 4th ed. (Belmont, Calif.: Wadsworth, 1991), p. 5.

C. How anthropology is different from other disciplines: interest in humankind throughout time and all over the world.

D. Two studies anthropology combines: human biology, culture

Exercise 7.1

Score your answers to the five questions, not the underlinings, which will probably differ from this sample underlining. Just check to see that the main ideas have been correctly underlined.

The Functions of Religion

The Search for Order and Meaning

(1) One of the most important functions of religion is to give meaning to and explain those aspects of the physical and social environment that are important in the lives of individuals and societies. Religion deals with the nature of life and death, the creation of the universe, the origin of society and groups within the society, the relationship of individuals and groups to one another, and the relation of humankind to nature. Anthropologists call this whole cognitive system a cosmology, or world view. Human societies create images of reality, often in symbolic ways, that serve as a framework for interpreting events and experiences, particularly those that are out of the ordinary. These "different realities" emerge as a way of imposing order and meaning on the world within which humans live and of giving humans the feeling that they have some measure of control over that world.

(2) Science and religion, which are often opposed in Western thought, are similar in that both involve "the quest for unity underlying apparent diversity; for simplicity underlying apparent complexity; for order underlying apparent disorder; for regularity underlying apparent anomaly" (Horton and Finnegan 1973). But where science provides explanations that are open to new data and explicitly acknowledges a possibility of various alternatives, religious systems tend not to be open to empirical testing.

(3) The separation between religion and science in our own society corresponds to our sharp separation of the supernatural and the natural. In other societies, these two concepts are less sharply separated. The supernatural can be seen as part of the natural and as intervening in all aspects of life. Thus, the kin group includes both living relatives and dead ancestors; power and leadership are often believed to have divine origins; rules of behavior are given divine sanction; and breaches are punished by the gods. The success of even ordinary undertakings in the physical world is ensured by enlisting the help of supernatural powers. Natural disasters, illness, and misfortune are believed to be caused by extrahuman or supernatural spirits. Natural and supernatural, human and natural, past, present, and future may be perceived as a unity in a way that violates the logic of Western thought. This makes it difficult for us to understand many non-Western religions and accounts for our eth-

nocentric labeling of them as "irrational," "contradictory," or the products of faulty thinking.

(4) **Reducing Anxiety and Increasing Control**   Many religious practices are aimed at ensuring success in carrying out a wide variety of human activities. Prayers and offerings are made to supernatural beings in the hope that they will aid a particular individual or community. Rituals are performed to call on supernatural beings and to control forces that appear to be unpredictable, such as those in the natural environment upon which humans depend for survival. One of the widespread practices used to control supernatural forces is magic. Although magical practices exist in many societies, magic seems to be more prominent in those in which there is less predictability in the outcome of events and thus less feeling of being in control of the social and physical environment. In the Trobriand Islands, for example, magic is not used for ordinary canoe trips within the lagoons, but only when the Islanders undertake the long-distance and dangerous canoe trips to other islands in their kula trade. Magic is also prevalent in sports and games of chance.

(5) Even if magic cannot "work" from the standpoint of Western science, it may be effective in achieving results indirectly, mainly by reducing the anxiety of the individuals and groups that practice it. This reduced anxiety allows them to proceed with more confidence, and the confidence may lead to greater success. Where technological advance and science are able to increase predictability and control over events and human relations, magic tends to become less important.

(6) **Maintaining the Social Order**   Religion has a number of important functions that either directly or indirectly help maintain the social order and the survival of a society. To begin with, religious beliefs about good and evil are reinforced by supernatural means of social control. Thus, religion is a powerful force for conformity in a society. Furthermore, through myth and ritual, social values are given sacred authority and provide a reason for the present social order. Religious ritual also intensifies solidarity by creating an atmosphere in which people experience their common identity in emotionally moving ways. Religion is also an important educational institution. Initiation rites, for example, almost always include the transmission of information about cultural practices and tradition.

(7) By supporting the present social order and defining the place of the individual in society and in the universe, religion also provides people with a sense of personal identity and belonging. When individuals have lost a positive identity, or when life has no meaning because of the disintegration of a traditional culture, religion can supply a new and more positive identity and become the basis for a new adaptation. Religion can also provide an escape from reality; in the religious beliefs of an afterlife or the coming of a Messiah, powerless people who live in harsh and deprived circumstances can create an illusion of power through the manipulation of religious symbols. Religion in these circumstances is an outlet for frustration, resentment, and anger and is a way of draining off energy that might otherwise be turned against the social system. In this way, religion indirectly contributes to maintaining the social order.

(8) In summary, <u>religion</u> has both <u>instrumental</u> and <u>expressive</u> functions. The <u>instrumental</u> aspect of <u>religion has to do with actions performed in the belief</u> that, if people do certain things, <u>they can influence the course of natural or social events</u> to their advantage. The <u>expressive aspect</u> of ritual refers to the <u>ways in which religious symbolism is used to express ideas about the relation of humans to nature, self to society, or group to group.</u> In its expressive aspect, religion is an important force for social integration.*

1. c   **2.** b   **3.** a   **4.** b   **5.** b

Exercise 7.3

Here is one correct way to underline this excerpt:

Kinds of Beliefs: Animism and Animatism

(1) A basic distinction in types of religious beliefs is that between animism and animatism. **Animism** is the belief that <u>not only living creatures but also inanimate objects have life and personality;</u> these supernatural persons are referred to as spirits, ghosts, or gods. Such beings are believed to <u>behave as people do</u>: They are <u>conscious</u>, they have <u>will</u>, and they feel the <u>same emotions as human beings</u> feel. Such spirits may reside in features of the physical environment, such as trees or stones, or they may reside in animals. In <u>hunting societies</u>—for example, the Lele of Africa and the Inuit—the <u>spirits</u> of <u>animals</u> are <u>worshipped because it is believed that a hunt will be successful only if an animal allows itself to be</u> killed. <u>Souls,</u> which may also reside in human bodies, are believed to be <u>able to leave the body at will,</u> temporarily during sleep or permanently as in death. Spirits or souls that leave the body at death turn into ghosts, which come in a variety of forms and relate in various ways to the living in different cultures.

(2) The distinction between a spirit and a god is mostly one of scale. A god is a supernatural being of great importance and power; a spirit is a lesser being. **Polytheism** <u>is the term used for a religion with many gods, and</u> **monotheism** <u>refers to a religion with only one god.</u> Whether a religion is polytheistic or monotheistic <u>is not so clear-cut</u> in real cultures, however. In so-called polytheistic religions, the many gods may be just so many aspects of the one god. <u>In India,</u> for example, it is said that there are <u>literally millions of gods;</u> yet even an uneducated Indian will understand that in some way (which does not confuse him or her, though it may confuse us), these are <u>all aspects of one divine essence.</u>

(3) The <u>Nuer are</u> another culture in which the <u>distinction between the Great Spirit and lesser spirits is fuzzy</u> to the outsider. The Nuer, of course, have no difficulty in understanding the different contexts in which different aspects of the Great Spirit are invoked. E. E. Evans-Pritchard (1968) describes a ceremony held to end a blood feud. All the

---

*Nanda, *Cultural Anthropology,* pp. 361–363.

speakers, representing both clans and including the Leopard Skin chief, addressed the various gods: Great Spirit, spirit of the sky, spirit of our community, spirit of the flesh (this refers to the divine power of the Leopard Skin chief), and spirit of our fathers. Each clan representative appealed to God not only as God but also as God in relation to the group he represented. The Leopard Skin chief referred to God in his special relation to his religious role as mediator, as well as to the priestly lineage he belonged to.

(4) Just as in polytheistic religions, in which all gods and spirits may be reflections of one god, so in monotheistic religions, the one god may have several aspects. In the Roman Catholic religion, for example, there is God the Father, the Son, and the Holy Ghost, in addition to a number of lesser supernatural spirits such as the saints, ghosts, the devil, and the souls of people in heaven, hell, and purgatory, as well as the souls of those living on earth.

(5) **Animatism** is the belief in an impersonal supernatural power. *Mana* is perhaps the most widely known term for this power. **Mana**, or supernatural power, may be inherent in the universe but may also be concentrated in individuals or in objects. We have seen earlier that Polynesian chiefs had a much higher degree of mana than ordinary people did. Mana is the key to success, but it can also be dangerous. That is why the belief in mana is so frequently associated with an elaborate system of taboos, or prohibitions. Mana is like electricity; it is a powerful force, but it can be dangerous when not approached with the proper caution.

(6) A cross-cultural approach seems to indicate that mana, or power, is often found in those areas (spatial, temporal, verbal, or physical) that are the boundaries between clear-cut categories. Hair, for example, is believed to contain supernatural power in many different cultures (remember the Old Testament story of Samson and Delilah). Hair is a symbol of the boundary between the self and the not-self. It is both part of a person and can be separated from the person. Hence its ambiguity and its power. Doorways and gates are also familiar symbols of supernatural power. They separate the inside from the outside and can thus serve as a symbol of moral categories such as good and evil, pure and impure. Because these symbols of boundaries contain supernatural power, they are frequently part of religious ritual and are surrounded by religious taboos.*

Although your wording will likely differ, most of the information in your outline should be essentially like this one:

I. Animism def: All objects, living and dead, are alive.

    A. Hunters worship animals because they believe animal soul must allow animal to be killed.

    B. Souls can leave body and turn into ghosts.

---

*Nanda, *Cultural Anthropology,* pp. 367–369.

II. Polytheism versus Monotheism

    A. Polytheists believe in many gods.

    B. Monotheists in one god.

    C. The distinction between monotheism and polytheism not clear in India and Nuer culture.

    D. The distinction between monotheism and polytheism not clear in Catholic religion.

III. Animatism def: Belief in power that is not in the form of a person.

IV. Mana—term for animatistic power.

    A. Both powerful and dangerous.

    B. Usually represented in objects that are on the boundary of the particular object, like hair on a human or the door of a temple.

    C. Characterized by many taboos and rituals.

    C. Allows you flexibility in dealing with life's uncertainties

    D. Gives you a value system in interpreting ethics, politics, and the arts

Exercise 7.5

Wording may vary, but paraphrases should be essentially the same as these. Take partial credit where you think it is appropriate.

15. The Aztecs were warlike mainly because war allowed commoners to improve their place in society and gave them rights in feasts where human flesh was eaten.

18. The Aztecs believed that eating human flesh was more a sacred than a physical act because it brought people closer to the gods.

21. By giving food to the gods and people in sacrifice, the Aztecs believed that everyone in their culture was reborn.

24. Sanday and Sahlins believe that politics, economics, and war relations encouraged the eating of human flesh; they do not agree with Harner that it was a purely physical act, considering his ideas too simple and too influenced by American economic thought.

31. What has been discussed does not prove that one belief is better than another, but it shows how anthropologists explain religion by studying the particular society's culture and religion.

Chapter 8
Reading and
Listening for
Inferences

Exercise 8.1

You may want to go back to the paragraphs marked *V* to see how they could be made more credible.

1. D **2.** V **3.** D **4.** V **5.** V **6.** D **7.** V **8.** D **9.** D **10.** V

Exercise 8.3

Wording may vary, but the information should be essentially the same as in the following answers. You may take partial credit where you think it is appropriate.

1. A "miracle" is an event that goes beyond human abilities. The author is suggesting that Mozart's accomplishments were almost unbelievable in their quality and genius.
2. To "astonish" is to shock. The author is expressing extreme surprise at Mozart's ability to compose at the age of five.
3. "Phenomenal" suggests exceptional abilities. Again, this word suggests that Mozart's musical abilities were superior.
4. "Impossible" suggests that something cannot be done. In regard to Mozart, this word again suggests his surprising greatness.
5. "Unfathomable" suggests that one cannot fully grasp something; in regard to Mozart, this word suggests the complexity of his musical abilities.
6. "Disastrous" suggests great hardship and suffering. This word shows how destructive Mozart's personal life was to his career.
7. A "giant" is someone who is extremely large; this word shows how important Mozart was perceived as a musician in relationship to others.
8. To "explore" is to travel and study carefully; this word suggests how carefully Mozart examined and used various types of classical music.
9. "Indelible" means that something cannot be erased or destroyed. It suggests that Mozart's music will endure.
10. A "genius" is one with exceptional talents, and the word aptly describes Mozart's musical abilities.

Answers to the question about the mood of this excerpt on Mozart will vary but should approximate this one:

All the words about Mozart's musical talent are strongly positive. The one word about his personal life, disastrous, is strongly negative, showing how different Mozart's life was from his musical contributions.

Chapter 9
Reading Graphs,
Charts and Tables

Exercise 9.1

1. d **2.** c **3.** b   **4.** b **5.** d **6.** b **7.** c **8.** b **9.** b **10.** c

Chapter 11
Commonly Used
Note-taking
Techniques: Numeral–
Letter, Indenting,
and Cornell

Exercise 11.1

Your wording may differ, but the condensed information should be essentially the same as shown here. You may take partial credit.

1. Def.: what people do when they buy, sell, or produce a product

2. Consumer behavior interdisciplinary, relying on sociology, anthropology, and psychology
3. Consumer behavior related to sociology in its focus on group behavior
4. Psychology shows how a person acts when purchasing a product—ex: motivation
5. Anthropology shows how culture determines buying—ex: ethnic preference
6. Def. consumer: anyone purchasing or using a product
7. Def. purchasing: getting an item from a seller
8. Later in course focus on where people buy and how they use products
9. Relationship between psychology and economics: how often people buy a product and why
10. Seeing yourself as consumer helps you understand yourself anthropologically, sociologically, and psychologically

Exercise 11.3

Your phrasing may differ from what is shown here, but the information should be essentially the same. Be sure that main ideas are separated from major details. Take 2 points for each correct entry and partial credit where you think it is appropriate. Do not include Cornell commentary in your scoring.

1. I. How American culture affects purchasing

What are basic American beliefs?

    A. Interest in buying material items
    B. Belief in self
    C. Optimism
    D. Order

2. I. Is there an American culture?

Comments on current American culture

    A. Movement away from material wealth
    B. Is it still optimistic?
    C. Self-reliance makes some afraid of being alone
    D. Is order valuable?

3. I. Ethnic groups questioning American culture

What is the influence of the ethnic market?

    A. African-Americans and Latinos huge marketing challenge
    B. Some fit into American mold
    C. Some of their buying interests different

4. I. How class influences purchasing

Key questions regarding class and purchasing

    A. How do lower, middle, and upper classes shape buying?
    B. Is class question difficult, like culture question?
    C. Does income influence buying?
    D. Does income influence beliefs?

5. I. Relationship of family and purchasing

How does family relate to purchasing?

    A. Family seems to have much to say
    B. Family gives certain values
    C. Which family member will product serve?
    D. Who is more powerful: father, mother, children?
    E. Purchasing decisions change as family gets older

6. Individual's influence on consumer behavior

Def. "brand loyalty"

    People learn—are not born to buy in certain way
    Consider past experience
    Def. brand loyalty: consistent buying of a product

7. How perception affects purchasing

How is perception related to buying?

    Each of us perceives products differently
    For some, price important
    For others, look or image important

8. Determining purchasing choice has no definite answers

No definite conclusions regarding buying

    Personality has effect on purchasing
    Ex: sports car versus station wagon buyer, shade of lipstick person buys

9. Attitude and buying

How sports stars and actors sell products

    Sports figures or actors help sell product
    Stars provide positive and negative images
    Attitudes help sell product

10. Attitudes difficult to change

Key challenge: changing purchasers' attitudes

    A marketing challenge
    Can marketing campaign change attitudes?
    Can changed attitudes change buying patterns?
    Researchers still unclear

Exercise 11.5

1.	=	**11.**	without
2.	>	**12.**	compare
3.	+ or &	**13.**	versus
4.	⊃	**14.**	incomplete
5.	re	**15.**	important
6.	nec	**16.**	principal
7.	pos	**17.**	continued
8.	incr	**18.**	number
9.	lg	**19.**	therefore
10.	max	**20.**	is both cause and effect

Exercise 11.7

You may take partial credit for your answers to 1–10. Answers will vary for 11–20.

1. Marketing is becoming an international activity.
2. It's easy to make large mistakes in this international market.
3. Many marketers do not understand cultural setting.
4. Anthropology helps consumer behavior to understand cultures.
5. Anthropologists use a study called cross-cultural research.
6. Cross-cultural research shows how cultures are the same and different.
7. Cross-cultural research studies attitudes regarding love in cultures.
8. Cross-cultural research also works with political power in each culture.
9. Cross-cultural research studies the cultural meaning of color.
10. In some cultures black and gray are good.
11. CCR resrch shows yllow, whte, gry, weak evrywhre
12. Red & blk strng clrs in ev country
13. Some mrktrs see ea cltr unque
14. ⊃ focus on local mrktng techs
15. othrs believe in stndrdzd mrktng plans
16. These mrktrs believe in cltrl uniformty in wrld
17. Sev cntrys as 1 mrkt
18. Toursm and mass media → sim mrktg needs
19. Mrktrs see Europe as 1 cntry
20. Answrs have pos or neg impct on ad campgn

Exercise 11.9

Below are sample responses. Your approach may differ.

Consumer Behavior and Ethics (Consumer Behavior = CB)

3 key ethical considerations

How is CB rel to ethics? Consider:
Trth in mrktng
Prdct quality
Prdct safety

What is role of FTC?

Mrktrs obliged to be hnst
Fdrl Trade Comms monitors ads (FTC = Federal Trade Commission)
Mny mail order frauds FTC has uncovrd
Pckgng and labeling impt concern
Ex: what is fat-free prdct?
FTC has made spec rqrmts

Consumers' role re product reliability

Prdct reliability
  What can consmr do if prdct a hazard?
    Read warranty (W = warranty)
      Exchange prdct or get rfnd
    W/expnsve prdct, see what W promises

What if W is bad?
  Consmr can go to court
    expensive and lngthy

Respndg to complaints in pos way
  Being honest, cmpnys incr profits
  Pays to be hnst
  Some compnys ask cstmrs to be frank re prdct

How can cmplnts be effctv?
  Provide useful info
  Cmpnys can rewrite Ws
  Fmlys and frnds oftn go to honest cmpny

How does ethics work 2 ways?

Ethics wrks 2 ways
  Both unethical cstmrs and unethical cmpnys
  Cstmrs and cmpnys need to wrk togethr
  Hnsty goes a long way
  Pays to be honest → profits for cmpny and satisfctn for cstmr

Chapter 12
Visual Note-taking Techniques: Laddering and Mapping

Exercise 12.1

Answers will vary. Take credit if you think your study maps clearly show the relationship between main idea and major details.

1.

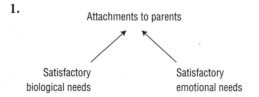

2.

Parallel Play		
At same time	At same place	Independently

3.

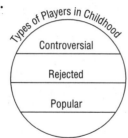

Types of Players in Childhood

- Controversial
- Rejected
- Popular

4.

Influence of older siblings on younger siblings

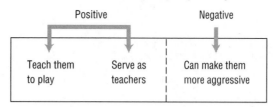

Positive		Negative
Teach them to play	Serve as teachers	Can make them more aggressive

5.

Birth order makes child

→ Have different prenatal care

→ Experience environment differently

6.

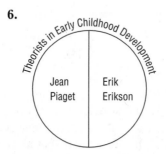

Theorists in Early Childhood Development

Jean Piaget | Erik Erikson

7.

Questions in Erikson's Stage:
Basic Trust versus Mistrust

1	2	3
Is my world predictable?	Do my parents care for my needs?	Do my parents love me?

8.

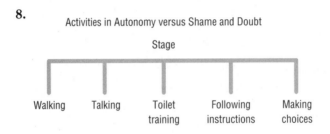

Activities in Autonomy versus Shame and Doubt

Stage

Walking   Talking   Toilet   Following   Making
training   instructions   choices

9.

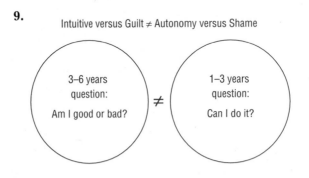

Intuitive versus Guilt ≠ Autonomy versus Shame

3–6 years
question:

Am I good or bad?

≠

1–3 years
question:

Can I do it?

10.

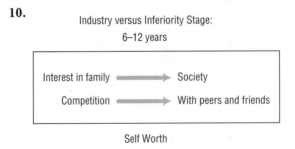

Industry versus Inferiority Stage:
6–12 years

Interest in family ⟶ Society

Competition ⟶ With peers and friends

Self Worth

Exercise 12.3

Your wording will vary from that shown here, but your answers should be essentially the same. Be sure that main ideas are clearly separated from major details. The study map that accompanies this outline is only an example. Score only your outline, not the study map.

Stages in Language Development

List major characteristics of each of the five stages.

Two key questions about language
How does a child learn language?
Are there stages?

From birth to 1 year
up to six months—babbling: "random sounds"
at one, understanding begins.
first word, "muh."

Age 1½
  50-word vocabulary
  Several words can be joined as one word.

What is meant by creative?

Age 2
  2–3 word phrases
  toddler not copying language
  important to note that language is a creative process—child
    creates entirely new sentences

Age 3
  full sentences
  Child makes up own language rules.
    Ex: "I no want to go."
  does not often understand parent correcting grammar errors

Age 4
  mastered most grammatical rules
  vocabulary still growing
  A few grammatical errors remain.

Important concept:
maturational

Key to remember that language is maturational
  All children follow the same stages in language learning.
  early talkers not necessarily smarter

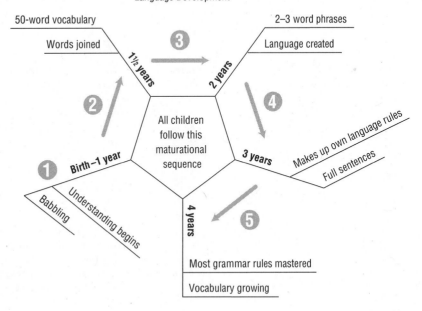

Maturational Stages in
Language Development

Chapter 13
The SQ3R Study
System

Exercise 13.1

The following are examples of correctly underlined and marked passages. Your underlinings may differ.

1. Catching More Fish and Fish Farming

How important is fish as a source of food?

Fish are the major source of animal protein for more than one-half of the world's people, especially in Asia and Africa. Fish supply about 55 percent of the animal protein in Southeast Asia, 35 percent in Asia as a whole, 19 percent in Africa, about 25 percent worldwide—twice as much as eggs and three times as much as poultry—and 6 percent of all human protein consumption. Two-thirds of the annual fish catch is consumed by humans and one-third is processed into fish meal to be fed to livestock.

Between 1950 and 1970, the marine fish catch more than tripled—an increase greater than that occurring in any other human food source during the same period. To achieve large catches, modern fishing fleets use sonar, helicopters, aerial photography, and temperature measurement to locate schools of fish and lights and electrodes to attract them. Large, floating factory ships follow the fleets to process the catch.

Why is fish catching declining?

Despite this technological sophistication, the steady rise in the marine fish catch halted abruptly in 1971. Between 1971 and 1976 the annual catch leveled off and rose only slightly between 1976 and 1983. A major factor in this leveling off was the sharp decline of the Peruvian anchovy catch, which once made up 20 percent of the global ocean harvest. A combination of overfishing and a shift in the cool, nutrient-rich currents off the coast of Peru were apparently the major factors causing this decline, which also threw tens of thousands of Peruvians out of work. Meanwhile, world population continued to grow, so between 1970 and 1983 the average fish catch per person declined and is projected to decline even further back to the 1960 level by the year 2000.

2. Soul

What are qualities of soul music?

Soul or rhythm and blues is the popular music associated with America's black population. Its musical qualities reveal some aspects of African music, especially in the style of singing. It is emotional and forceful, with calls and exclaimed words. Open chords and parallel chord movement are characteristic of its harmony. The music is often loud.

Who are prominent soul artists?

Some writers include gospel music in the soul category, and the relationships are close between these styles. Prominent names in soul music include James Brown, The Jackson Five (one of whom was Michael Jackson), Patti LaBelle, Aretha Franklin, and the groups associated with the Motown sound.

Sometimes the same song will reach the top of popularity charts in the soul, country, and general popular music listings, but only occasionally. For example, the Beatles were never particularly popular with blacks. The ethnic associations of popular music influence its acceptance with various segments of the population. The preference is based on the style and timbre of the music rather than on the message of the words, although the background of the performer makes some difference. A few songs with a message about war, poverty, or ecology achieved limited popularity in the late 1960s and early 1970s, but the trend then returned to the overwhelmingly favorite topic of popular songs: love and its pains and joys.*

3. Matter: Types, States, Properties, and Changes

What is matter? mass?

A lump of coal, an ice cube, a puddle of water, air—all are samples of matter. Matter is anything that occupies space and has mass. *Mass* is the quantity of matter in substance.

A substance or pure substance is one of millions of different types of matter found in the world. Any substance can be classified as either an element or a compound. An element is one of the 108 basic building blocks of all matter. Examples include iron, sodium, carbon, oxygen, and chlorine. Scientists have discovered 90 naturally occurring elements on Earth and have made small quantities of 18 others in the laboratory.

What is an element? compound?

A compound is a form of matter in which two or more elements are held together in a fixed ratio by chemical bonds. Water, for example, is a combination of the elements hydrogen and oxygen, and sodium chloride (the major ingredient in table salt) is a combination of the elements sodium and chlorine. About 5 million compounds of the 108 known elements have been identified, and about 6,000 new compounds are added to the list each week. With proper guidance, you could make a new compound yourself. At least 63,000 compounds are combined in the food we eat, the air we breathe, the water we drink, and the countless products we use.

Exercise 13.3

A. Survey

1. a **2.** b **3.** a **4.** b **5.** c

B. Question (answers will vary)

1. What is absolute poverty?
2. What is the definition of "less developed countries"?
3. How does GNP relate to understanding less developed countries?
4. What is the Physical Quality of Life Index?

C. Read and Recite (answers will vary)

	Poverty in the Developing Countries
def.: absolute poverty	Absolute poverty—people so poor their life is threatened
	1 billion people in absolute poverty
	Difficult to identify what a less developed country is

*Charles R. Hoffer, *The Understanding of Music*, 6th ed. (Belmont, Calif.: Wadsworth, 1989), pp. 517–518.

2 categories of countries	Two categories: less developed and more developed

why GNP inefficient	GNP imperfect measure
	    Often understates income of poor in LDCs
	    Ex: Tanzania people do not always use money in buying and selling

what PQLI measures	Physical Quality of Life Index (PQLI): considers infant mortality, life expectancy, and literacy abilities
	    Another way to study LDCs
	    Shows differences that GNP does not show
	    Ex: Saudi Arabia with low PQLI and high GNP

D. Review

1. d **2.** c **3.** a **4.** b **5.** d **6.** b **7.** c **8.** b **9.** b **10.** a

Compare the following sample study map and marked-up excerpt with yours.

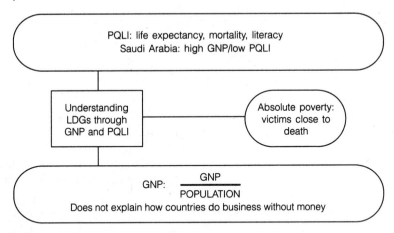

Poverty in the Developing Countries

(1) This section is about poverty among nations. Poverty is, of course, a relative matter. Whenever there is any inequality in the distribution of income, some people will always be poor relative to others. But much of the world is so abjectly poor that some observers speak of *absolute* poverty, a condition of life so destitute that its victims are chronically on the verge of death.

(2) Almost 1 billion people—one-quarter of the world's population—are in this category. A quarter of a million people in Calcutta are homeless. They eat, live, and die in the streets. Three million people in

def:
absolute
poverty

imp't
detail

Bolivia (out of a total population of five million) have a life expectancy of thirty years. The average Bolivian eats less than half an ounce of meat per year; in effect, the peasant population is too poor to eat any meat at all.

What Is a "Less Developed" Country?

*hard to
define LDCs*

(3) Several phrases are used to describe countries that are poorer than others: underdeveloped countries, third world countries, sometimes even fourth or fifth world countries. Economists have no specific criteria or explicit definitions of such terms. A nation's position is usually determined by dividing its GNP by population (per capita GNP) so that there is a ladder of countries from rich to poor—from $21,920 per person per year in the United Arab Emirates to $110 per person per year in Ethiopia in 1984.

(4) Usually, all countries are classified as either "more developed" or "less developed." The World Bank in its *Development Report for 1986* uses six subcategories of less developed countries, which we will overlook for the sake of brevity. Instead, we will use just the two categories "more developed" and "less developed" and set the dividing line at $1,000 per person per year, although such a division is arbitrary and often unrevealing. We know that GNP says little about the quality of life. Moreover, a per capita GNP figure conceals the distribution of income within a nation. For example, per capita GNP in Brazil was about $2,000 a year in 1984, but 30 million of Brazil's 133 million people had average annual incomes of only $77. Because this section is about the less developed countries, we will use a common abbreviation, LDCs, to indicate that group of about 90 of the 170-odd countries of the world.

The Trouble with Comparing Per Capita GNPs

(5) When we use per capita GNPs to compare countries, we find ourselves trapped by numbers that offer little help in describing real differences in standards of living. Not only is GNP an imperfect measure of welfare or progress *within* a country, it has even less meaning when used for comparisons among countries. Two examples will clarify this point.

ex #1

(6) In a poor, less developed country (LDC) like Tanzania, with a per capita GNP of $210 per year, the $210 figure is imperfect because it is based primarily on cash transactions. But much of Tanzania's production and consumption typically involves little or no cash. The people in Tanzania's villages feed themselves out of their own production. Therefore, in most cases, per capita GNP figures in poor countries understate their true incomes. Of course, that doesn't mean such people are rich. We could double the numbers, and these people would still be abjectly poor by any standard.

ex #2

(7) In another example, let's look at the comparative lifestyles of Americans and New Zealanders. In the fall of 1978, New Zealand's per capita GNP was about half that of the United States. But it would be very foolish to conclude that New Zealanders' standard of living was half that of the average American. Fresh food prices were generally half of U.S.

prices, so that with much lower wages, the New Zealanders ate just as well as or better than Americans. Housing costs (rents and home purchase prices) were also about half of ours. Education, medical care, and retirement pensions were all provided from a highly progressive schedule of income taxes. In one specific case, a highly skilled New Zealander construction worker retired from his job at age 60. At the time of retirement, he earned $3.80 per hour—by our standards an abysmally low wage after a lifetime of work. Nevertheless, he owned a home and automobile free and clear, had $50,000 in the bank, and began receiving a pension of 80 percent of his highest earnings. He and his wife were comfortable and content, traveled overseas occasionally, and had no financial worries. However, New Zealanders also have to contend with the high prices of imported products like automobiles.

key question

(8) So how does one evaluate these differences in lifestyles? Can one say that Americans are better off than New Zealanders or vice versa? The question is impossible to answer. Nevertheless, the GNP per capita method of comparison among different countries is the method most commonly used.

(9) In one attempt to improve on the GNP per capita measure, economists devised an index called the **Physical Quality of Life Index (PQLI)**. The PQLI is a composite of a nation's life expectancy, infant mortality, and literacy. The index is 97 for Sweden, 94 for the United States, 35 for Bangladesh. The index reveals the weaknesses of looking only at GNP per capita: GNP per capita in Saudi Arabia is a healthy $10,530 (1984), but its PQLI is only 28.

def.: PQLI

(10) In this section we review the plight of the LDCs, including the distribution of the world's income, the reasons why the more developed countries (particularly the United States) should be concerned about world poverty, the two major problems of population increase and lack of capital, and some conclusions.

Chapter 14
Memory Aids

Exercise 14.1

Here are possible answers:

1. Stationary refers to cold and warm air fronts. "Air" rhymes with "ary."
2. People who have illusions may be psychologically ill.
3. Between means that no more than two items are compared, and b is the second letter of the alphabet.
4. Capitol buildings are usually old.
5. Hunters carry spears and rods. I see a hunter with a rod in his hand chasing an animal.
6. Roy G. Biv (a name)
7. We Are Just Mighty Mice.
8. MTSP
9. ERS
10. zeal, zealously, zealot, zealousness

**Chapter 15
Suggestions for
Taking Objective
Tests**

**Chapter 16
Suggestions for
Taking Essay Exams
and Math or Science
Tests**

Exercise 15.1

1. c **2.** b **3.** c **4.** b **5.** d

Exercise 15.3

1. e **2.** d **3.** a **4.** c **5.** b

Exercise 16.1

Your wording will differ, but the information should be essentially the same as shown here. You may want to use the following method for calculating a score.

1. Take 4 points for defining nonviolent direct action as a peaceful action—through means other than legal action, political campaigns, and voting—by a large group to change a law seen as unjust by that group.

2. Take 3 points for mentioning these three activities: demonstrations, sit-ins, and boycotts.

3. Take 3 points for noting that Dr. King saw nonviolent direct action as a loving way of creating concern in a community for an unjust issue. King believed that all laws must be analyzed for their moral content, so that a law may be violated if the group considers it immoral.
Here is a sample paragraph receiving all 10 points:

> Nonviolent direct action is a peaceful activity by one or several people to change a law that is seen as unjust. This peaceful action does not rely on the courts, political campaigns, or voting to achieve its goal. Examples of nonviolent direct action include sit-ins, demonstrations, and boycotts. Dr. Martin Luther King, Jr., saw nonviolent direct action as the best way for a community to change an unjust law. King realized that some laws were considered constitutional but were, in fact, immoral. In these cases, King believed that an immoral law should be violated through nonviolent direct action.

Index

abbreviation
   as a memory device, 294–295
   in note taking, 230–234
adult learners, 7
advanced organizers, 256
association
   as a learning theory, 193

bar graph
   defined, 86
   how to read, 186–187

cards
   5 × 8, for study purposes, 316
   4 × 6, for study purposes, 12, 302
   3 × 5, in library, 37
catalog
   card, 37
   college, 3
   on-line, 37
categorization
   as a learning theory, 294
cause
   contributory, 102
   direct, 101
   indirect, 102
cause–effect
   as a major detail, 75–77
   as an organizational pattern, 101–102
CD-ROM, 38
chart
   defined, 189
   organizational, 302–304
circle graph
   defined, 185
   how to read, 185–186
cognitive psychology, 291
collaborative learning. *See* learning
college counselor, 4–5
comparison–contrast
   as an organizational pattern, 106–108
computer
   in library, 37–38
   network, 38
concentration, 293
condensing

in taking notes, 229–230
connotation, 167
context, 293
contrast. *See* comparison–contrast
Cornell Note-taking System, 225–226
counselor. *See* college counselor

definition
   as information in lecture, 229–230
   as information in a textbook, 274–276
   as an organizational pattern, 103–104
description
   as an organizational pattern, 108–109
details. *See* major details; minor details
Dewey decimal system, 35–36
dictionaries, 35
discussion
   as part of a lecture, 217–218
distractions
   when studying, 23
draft (of research paper), 41

encyclopedias, 34–35
essay test
   extended essay, 322–325
   how to prepare, 315–317
   short answer, 321
   short essay, 322
exam. *See* final and midterm.

fact
   defined, 106
flowchart, 190–192
final exam
   how to study for, 20

Gardner, Howard, 17
gimmicks
   as a memory technique, 295
goals
   long-term, 4
   short-term, 12
graphs. *See* bar, circle, *or* line

highlighting
   in textbook marking, 274

indenting note-taking format, 225
induction
   used in paragraphs, 49
inferences
   in details of support, 168–169
   in terms of qualification, 165–167
   in word choice, 167–168
interference, 292

laddering, 255
learners
   auditory, 18
   practical, 18
   quantitative, 17
   verbal, 17
   visual, 17
learning
   collaborative, 18
lecture
   defined, 215
   speaker, 215–216
   student obligations, 217–218
librarian
   reference, 39
library, 33–34
Library of Congress System, 36–37
locating sources, 39
line graph
   defined, 187
   how to read, 187–189

main ideas
   at the beginning of paragraph, 49
   at the end of paragraph, 49–50
   implied, 51
   in longer passages, 50–51
major details, 73–77
mapping
   defined, 255
   how to map, 255–256
   in studying for exams, 302, 317
marginal notes
   in lecture notes, 226
   in textbooks, 274–276
marking textbooks, 274–276
   highlighting, 274